# Essential Hindi Dictionary

Teach Yourself®

# Essential Hindi Dictionary

Hindi–English/English–Hindi

Rupert Snell

For UK order enquiries: please contact
Bookpoint Ltd, 130 Milton Park, Abingdon, Oxon OX14 4SB.
Telephone: +44 (0) 1235 827720. Fax: +44 (0) 1235 400454.

For USA order enquiries: please contact McGraw-Hill Customer Services, PO Box 545, Blacklick, OH 43004-0545, USA. Telephone: 1-800-722-4726. Fax: 1-614-755-5645.

For Canada order enquiries: please contact
McGraw-Hill Ryerson Ltd, 300 Water St, Whitby, Ontario L1N 9B6, Canada. Telephone: 905 430 5000. Fax: 905 430 5020.

*British Library Cataloguing in Publication Data:* a catalogue record for this title is available from the British Library.

*Library of Congress Catalog Card Number:* on file.

First published in UK 2004 as *Teach Yourself Hindi Dictionary* by Hodder Education, part of Hachette UK, 338 Euston Road, London NW1 3BH.

First published in US 2004 by The McGraw-Hill Companies, Inc.

This edition published 2011.



www.hoddereducation.co.uk

Typeset by Cenveo Publisher Services

Printed and bound by CPI Group (UK) Ltd, Croydon CR0 4YY

| | |
|---|---|
| Impression number | 10 9 8 7 6 5 4 3 2 1 |
| Year | 2014 2013 2012 2011 2011 |

# Contents


| | |
|---|---|
| *Meet the author* | vii |
| *Only got a minute?* | viii |
| *Only got five minutes?* | x |
| *Preface* | xiii |
| *The Devanagari script* | xiv |
| *The Hindi language* | xviii |
| *A concise grammar* | xxii |
| *Bibliography* | xxxv |
| *Abbreviations* | xxxvii |
| **Hindi–English dictionary** | 1 |
| **English–Hindi dictionary** | 93 |

# Meet the author

My contact with Indian culture began in about 1967, when I first heard Hindustani music – Ravi Shankar's recording of Raga Khamaj – in a booth in a provincial record shop in England. This musical encounter led me eventually to begin a BA in Hindi at the School of Oriental and African Studies, University of London, in 1970. From the outset, I forced myself to use my faltering Hindi whenever the chance came along, although not always with great success: one day in Anwar's Delicacies in London I asked for a पड़ोसी ('neighbour') when I actually wanted a समोसा ('samosa')! But Hindi speakers proved to be nothing if not neighbourly and as soon as I started valuing communication above grammar, my conversations in Hindi began to be more meaningful, and numerous trips to India helped build my confidence.

My interest in Hindi literature took me back in time to the old dialect of Braj Bhasha and eventually I wrote a PhD dissertation on a 16th-century text from the Braj devotional tradition. Teaching and researching both early and modern Hindi kept me gainfully employed at SOAS for more than three decades, after which I moved to the University of Texas at Austin, happily plying the same trade but now in the context of UT's Hindi–Urdu Flagship.

For me personally, Hindi has been the key to a rich and wonderful cultural world. Over the years I have learned to distinguish समोसा from पड़ोसी with much confidence; but thankfully not everything has changed, and Raga Khamaj sounds as good on my iPod now as it did on that vinyl LP more than 40 years ago.

*Rupert Snell*

# Only got a minute?

In deciding to learn Hindi, you are choosing a language that ranks in the top three or four languages of the world in terms of the number of people who speak it. This number is enlarged further if we consider the pairing of Hindi with Urdu, for the two languages are virtually identical in their everyday colloquial speech (although the scripts are different and their higher vocabulary comes from different sources — Sanskrit and Persian, respectively). Of course, English is also encountered alongside Hindi and Urdu, but although it is widely spoken in the big cities and in such domains as big business and international relations, English cannot compete with Hindi and the other Indian languages in their intimate connection with the culture of the Indian subcontinent.

Learning a new language is always a challenge, but Hindi presents no particular problems to the learner. It 'works' in ways that are familiar to speakers of European languages such as English, which is, after all, a distant cousin within the great overarching Indo-European family of languages. The Hindi script, called 'Devanagari', may look complicated at first sight, but, in fact, it is very easy to learn, being an extremely methodical and precise rendering of the phonetics of the language. 'What you see is what you get', so the learner can tell exactly how to pronounce a new word simply from its spelling (a benefit not to be found in English)!

A knowledge of Hindi is a pathway into the rich, complex and diverse worlds of Indian culture. The first step down that path is taken with learning the universal greeting word used by hundreds of millions of Hindi speakers every day: नमस्ते *namaste*! With this single word, deeply rooted in Indian civilization and yet fully a part of modern India, your journey begins…

# 5 Only got five minutes?

If English is your mother tongue and you are interested in India, you are starting your encounter with Hindi from the same perspective from which I, the author of this course, started mine. My motivation was to get as close as I could to the heart of the Indian cultural world that appealed to me so strongly. My initial point of contact had been Indian classical music, whose magic cast its spell on me in the late 1960s. Perhaps you have a similar motivation, or perhaps a very different one: maybe you are rediscovering Indian roots of your own, or are reaching out to someone close to you who comes from a Hindi-speaking background. In any case, I hope that this book is helpful to you and that it serves as a stepping stone to a familiarity with this rich and rewarding language.

I am often asked the question, 'How long did it take you to learn Hindi?', to which I have a standard answer: 'When I get there, I'll tell you.' Learning a language, especially if beginning in adulthood, is taking a walk down a long road, indeed – one that may be endless. But, having said that, it's also true that Hindi is a very learnable language. Its connections with English run deep and take many forms. To begin with, both languages are members of the great Indo-European family from which have sprung so many languages, from western Europe right across to Russia, South Asia and Iran. When we learners of Hindi encounter a word like दाँत *dā̃t* 'tooth' (think of a 'dentist') or a number like दस *das* 'ten' (think of a 'decimal') or any one of hundreds of words where Hindi–English parallels appear, we witness a connection that links Hindi to English through Sanskrit and Latin (their respective parent languages) all the way back to a common origin in Indo-European.

If all this seems a bit academic and obscure, there are other ways in which Hindi and English connect. The two languages have traded words with each other for centuries: words like 'cot' and 'shampoo' and 'bungalow' have come into English from Hindi, and words like स्टेशन *sṭeśan* and स्कूल *skūl* and डाक्टर *ḍākṭar* have made the opposite journey. One way and another, then, there are many ways in which the learner of Hindi finds connectivities with English. Most important of all, the entire grammatical system of nouns, verbs, adjectives and adverbs 'works' in ways that are closely parallel to the system we English speakers are familiar with, so there are no great conceptual challenges standing in our way.

Many introductions to Hindi begin with an array of statistics about its numbers of speakers, and it's true that, in this respect, Hindi is right up there with Chinese, English and Spanish as the languages with the most impressive statistics of all. In fact, the single north Indian state of Uttar Pradesh or 'UP', the heartland of the Hindi language and its associated culture, itself has a population of some 190 million – a population greater than any *country* in the world except for China, the United States, Indonesia... and the remainder of India! And UP is just *one* of the several states in which Hindi is spoken as a mother tongue. But numbers alone may not convince you of the need to add yet one more Hindi speaker by learning the language yourself and, naturally, there are other and better rewards awaiting you than membership of this enormous club. A knowledge of Hindi gives access to a treasure trove of culture and to perspectives on life that differ from and complement those of the English-speaking world. And because relatively few people from outside the Hindi-speaking community seek entry to it by learning the language, a person who makes this effort (that's you!) receives the warmest of welcomes, with everybody encouraging you in your efforts and congratulating you for what you have already achieved.

Looking back a few decades to when I started learning Hindi, I am a little envious of the resources now available to people starting out down that same road. Not only have many excellent primers and dictionaries come onto the market in recent years, there are also the huge resources of the internet to explore. Many learners of Hindi find that they can learn a lot through watching film clips and listening to film songs, all searchable through the web; and there are many guides to script, grammar, vocabulary and so on. Web searches using the Devanagari script will bring examples of real-life Hindi usage direct to your screen: for example, you could look up train times from Mathura Junction to Agra City, learning the usages for expressions like 'leaving at' and 'arriving at', warnings of possible cancellation and so on and, in so doing, you will discover things about the usage of the Hindi that even *this* book doesn't tell you! There are so many resources available now.

And yet all journeys begin with the first step – and that's where this book is going to help you. Whether or not you have some background in Hindi, steady progress in learning the language depends on a firm and solid understanding of the basics. For example, you need to know about gender (every noun is either masculine or feminine, and this will determine the form of associated adjectives and verbs), and you need to be able to express simple statements using the verb 'to be' before you can get into more complex and expressive statements with greater conversational potential! Think what a basic thing it is in English to be able to determine how to pluralize nouns: patterns such as *ship* > *ships*, *sheep* > *sheep*, *baby* > *babies* and *child* > *children* may seem second-nature to us as speakers of English, but newcomers to the language have to learn these things as grammatical rules. Similar rules apply with plurals in Hindi: मकान *makān* 'house' stays unchanged in the plural (like 'sheep'); but कमरा *kamrā* 'room' becomes कमरे *kamre* 'rooms', खिड़की *khiṛkī* 'window' becomes खिड़कियाँ *khiṛkiyā̃* 'windows', and छत *chat* 'roof' becomes छतें *chatẽ* 'roofs'! These are the essentials for building your language house. Start learning patiently at the ground floor and work steadily upwards.

Like all modern languages, Hindi looks both forwards and backwards. It looks forwards to ever changing contexts of language use that demand new words and new ways of saying things, and it looks backwards to a classical past in which the glories of Indian civilization lie recorded. To learn Hindi, then, is not only to approach modern India, but to have a view – eventually! – of the history and culture of the Indian subcontinent.

# Preface

This learner's dictionary aims to provide the essential vocabulary for a wide range of situations and has been designed as a practical accompaniment to the Hindi course books in the 'Teach Yourself' series. The English–Hindi section gives many examples of usage to help in the construction of phrases and sentences – which is why it fills more pages than the Hindi–English section. The conventions used in the dictionary (see Abbreviations), include the 'bomb' symbol (💣), which warns of usages that need particular care because their grammar differs from English equivalents: this special feature is designed to help learners keep their grammar on the straight and narrow.

A brief statement of the Hindi script (called देवनागरी *Devanāgarī*) shows the forms of the characters and the system of transliteration used here. In addition to this, all Hindi words are transliterated into the roman script throughout the dictionary.

An introduction to the Hindi language explains where the language gets its words from and how words from different sources can give very different stylistic effects; this section also explains that the aim of this dictionary is to supply words and phrases that will be suitable for everyday conversational and written usage. A concise grammar of Hindi sets out the main workings of the language, with examples.

I am very grateful to Marina Chellini, Lalita Du Perron, Amrik Kalsi, Aishwarj Kumar, Gyanam Mahajan, Rakesh Nautiyal, Vinita Ramani, Lucy Rosenstein, Nilanjan Sarkar and Aili Seghetti, whose suggestions about the content of this dictionary have been particularly useful.

# The Devanagari script

## Independent vowel forms ('vowel characters')

| | | | |
|---|---|---|---|
| अ *a* | आ *ā* | इ *i* | ई *ī* |
| उ *u* | ऊ *ū* | ऋ *ṛ* | |
| ए *e* | ऐ *ai* | ओ *o* | औ *au* |

## Consonants

| | | | | |
|---|---|---|---|---|
| क *ka** | ख *kha** | ग *ga** | घ *gha* | |
| च *ca* | छ *cha* | ज *ja** | झ *jha* | |
| ट *ṭa* | ठ *ṭha* | ड *ḍa** | ढ *ḍha** | ण *ṇa* |
| त *ta* | थ *tha* | द *da* | ध *dha* | न *na* |
| प *pa* | फ *pha** | ब *ba* | भ *bha* | म *ma* |
| य *ya* | र *ra* | ल *la* | व *va* | |
| श *śa* | ष *ṣa* | स *sa* | ह *ha* | |

## *Dotted consonants

These are identical in dictionary order to their undotted forms:

| | | | |
|---|---|---|---|
| क़ *qa* | ख़ *k͟ha* | ग़ *ġa* | ज़ *za* |
| ड़ *ṛa* | ढ़ *ṛha* | फ़ *fa* | |

## Dependent vowel forms ('vowel signs')

The characters shown above are actually entire *syllables*, each containing the 'inherent' vowel *a*. (This is silent at the end of a word unless following certain conjuncts.) The inherent vowel can be substituted by another vowel by the addition of a 'vowel sign':

| | | | |
|---|---|---|---|
| क *ka* | का *kā* | कि *ki* | की *kī* |
| कु *ku* | कू *kū* | कृ *kr̥* | |
| के *ke* | कै *kai* | को *ko* | कौ *kau* |

## Conjunct consonants

These indicate two adjacent consonant sounds forming one syllable. They usually consist of a truncated version of the first consonant joined to the full form of the second, as in these examples:

| | | | | | | |
|---|---|---|---|---|---|---|
| क | + | य | = | क्य | क्या *kyā* what? |
| च | + | छ | = | च्छ | अच्छा *acchā* good |
| ल | + | ल | = | ल्ल | दिल्ली *dillī* Delhi |
| स | + | त | = | स्त | हिन्दुस्तानी *hindustānī* Indian |

Some conjuncts are less easily recognizable from their components:

| | | | | | |
|---|---|---|---|---|---|
| क | + | त | = | क्त, क्त | शक्ति, शक्ति *śakti* power |
| क | + | ष | = | क्ष | क्षण *kṣaṇ* moment |
| ट | + | ट | = | ट्ट | छुट्टी *chuṭṭī* holiday |

| | | | | | |
|---|---|---|---|---|---|
| ट | + | र | = | ट्र | ट्रेन *ṭren* train |
| त | + | त | = | त्त | कुत्ता *kuttā* dog |
| त | + | र | = | त्र | पत्र *patra* letter |
| द | + | द | = | द्द | रद्द *radd* cancelled |
| द | + | भ | = | द्भ | अद्भुत *adbhut* wondrous |
| द | + | म | = | द्म | पद्म *padma* lotus |
| द | + | य | = | द्य | विद्या *vidyā* knowledge |
| द | + | व | = | द्व | द्वार *dvār* gateway |
| प | + | र | = | प्र | प्राण *prāṇ* breath |
| र | + | द | = | र्द | दर्द *dard* pain |
| र | + | मा | = | र्मा | शर्मा *śarmā* Sharma |
| श | + | र | = | श्र | श्री *śrī* Mr |
| ह | + | म | = | ह्म | ब्रह्मा *Brahmā* Brahma (a deity) |

The character ज्ञ *jña* is a conjunct of ज with ञ् *ña*, a nasal consonant (like the first 'n' in 'onion') that is not shown in our table because it never occurs alone; ज्ञ *jña* is usually pronounced 'gya'.

## Nasals

A nasalized vowel is produced by diverting part of the breath through the nose. Nasalized vowels are marked with a superscript sign called *candrabindu*, 'moon dot':

हाँ *hā̃* yes

कहाँ *kahā̃* where?

यहाँ *yahā̃* here

The 'moon' is optional and is always dropped wherever a vowel sign occupies the space above the line:

मैं *maĩ* I

नहीं *nahī̃* no

लोगों को *logõ ko* to people

The dot, here called *anusvār*, can also replace an 'n' or 'm' as the first element of a conjunct. That is, when writing a conjunct in which the first component is an 'n' or an 'm', there are two equally valid options:

अंडा = अण्डा *aṇḍā* egg

हिंदी = हिन्दी *hindī* Hindi

लंबा = लम्बा *lambā* long, tall

---

## Other signs

*Virām* is a small subscript sign that deletes the inherent 'a' vowel from a consonant: क *ka* becomes क् *k*. This provides a very useful alternative to writing awkward or complex conjuncts: अद्भुत *adbhut* can be written अद्‌भुत *adbhut*.

*Visarga* is a colon-like sign that represents a light aspiration; it is transliterated 'ḥ', and appears in a few Sanskrit loanwords such as अन्ततः *antataḥ* 'finally'.

The 'moon' used in *candrabindu* (see above) is used sporadically to mark an English 'o' vowel whose quality is not quite carried by its Hindi spelling with *ā* – thus चॉकलेट *cākleṭ* 'chocolate', जॉन *jān* 'John'. There is no transliteration equivalent.

Punctuation is the same as in English, except for the full stop, which is represented by a vertical line ( । ) called खड़ी पाई *khaṛī pāī*.

---

## Dictionary order

Vowels precede consonants, as in the sequence shown on p. xii.

Nasalized vowels precede un-nasalized ones: बसंत *basant* precedes बस *bas*.

Simple consonants precede conjunct ones: डिबिया *ḍibiyā* precedes डिब्बा *ḍibbā*.

# The Hindi language

## The Hindi language and its lexicon

Like its neighbouring languages in South Asia such as Bengali, Gujarati, Marathi, Nepali, Punjabi, Sinhala and Urdu, Hindi derives many of its structures and much of its vocabulary from Sanskrit, the classical language of ancient India. Sanskrit, in turn, shares a parentage with the classical languages of Europe: Latin, Greek and Sanskrit are all parallel members of the Indo-European language family, of which many South Asian languages form the Indo-Aryan subgroup. This makes modern South Asian languages distant relatives of European ones, as is apparent in the similarities between some Hindi words and their English equivalents: the Hindi for 'name' is नाम *nām*, the Hindi for 'father' is पिता *pitā* (compare Latin 'pater' and its English derivatives like 'paternal') and so on.

Though large numbers of Hindi words are derived from Sanskrit, many of them have undergone some morphological change during their long journey through time and therefore look different from their Sanskrit originals. For example, Hindi काम *kām* 'work' reflects Sanskrit कर्म *karma,* हाथी *hāthī* 'elephant' derives from Sanskrit हस्तिन *hastin* ('the one with a hand', i.e. 'a trunk') and the very useful number ढाई *ḍhāī* 'two-and-a-half' comes, rather more obscurely, from Sanskrit अर्धतृतीय *ardhatṛtīya* ('a half [less than] three'). Through scientific tabulations of these developments, philologists can track the process of linguistic change over the centuries. Words whose shapes have changed in the ways exemplified here are given the Sanskrit label तद्भव *tadbhava*, meaning 'derived-from-that'.

Sanskritic loanwords borrowed *directly* into Hindi in their Sanskrit form are called तत्सम *tatsama*, meaning 'same-as-that', i.e. unchanged, unmodified. These are of two main types: some, like संगीत *saṅgīt* 'music', are attested Sanskrit words, found in ancient literature. Others are neologisms based on Sanskrit elements, designed for new functions: thus 'television' is दूरदर्शन *dūrdarśan*, a loan translation in which *dūr* reflects the Greek *tele* 'distant' and *darśan* the Latinate 'vision'. A third category of Sanskritic words comprises those that do have an ancient pedigree but which have acquired new meanings in the modern context: in the Hindi expression शास्त्रीय संगीत *śāstrīy saṅgīt* 'classical music' the western concept of the 'classical' has been expressed through a Sanskrit loanword whose original sense related to scriptures and traditional learning.

Sanskrit is not the only source of words for Hindi and its neighbouring languages. Another major source is Persian, whose presence in India over many centuries greatly enriched the lexicon of north Indian tongues (rather as French enriched the Germanic language called English); an example is the word सितार *sitār* 'sitar', whose original Persian meaning is 'three-string'. The Persian lexicon, in turn, includes many words borrowed from Arabic and Turkish: the 'tabla' drum (तबला *tablā*) gets its name from the Arabic (and has the English 'tabor' as a distant relative), while the *-cī* suffix found in the word तबलची *tabalcī* 'tabla player, drummer' is a borrowing from Turkish.

Just to show how complex the situation can become, let's look at two more musical instruments from the Indian ensemble. The name of the drone instrument तानपूरा *tānpūrā* reflects another Persian original, *tambūra,* but has been 'Indianized' by assimilation to Sanskritic norms; and the wholly Indian name of the bowed lute सारंगी *sāraṅgī,* although often explained as meaning 'the voice of a hundred colours', actually has nothing at all to do with the number 'hundred' – the popular interpretation of the name merely shows how folk etymology romanticizes the linguistic picture.

The Perso-Arabic overlay on an Indian linguistic base not only enriched the lexicon of north India but also gave rise to Urdu, Hindi's sister language. At an elementary and colloquial level, Hindi and Urdu are virtually identical, but at a higher or more formal level the Sanskritic quality of Hindi and the Persianate quality of Urdu mark them as two distinct languages, each with its own literary and cultural conventions. Their separate orientations are shown most graphically in their writing systems: Urdu is written in the Persian script, which runs from right to left, and Hindi in the Devanagari script (inherited from Sanskrit) which, like India's other major writing systems, runs from left to right.

European languages have also contributed to the Hindi lexicon. Some common words like कमरा *kamrā* 'room' and बोतल *botal* 'bottle' come from Portuguese (Portugal had important trade links with late medieval India), while words like ट्रेन *ṭren* 'train' and स्टेशन *sṭeśan* 'station' are recognizably English. These last two examples show us, incidentally, how the English 't' sound is heard by the Indian ear: it is spelt with the hard retroflex ट *ṭa,* whereas the dental त *ta* in बोतल *botal* reflects the softer consonants of Portuguese.

These various elements from India and abroad combine to give Hindi a rich variety of words, styles and linguistic registers. The formal style, most often encountered in writing and in officialese, is called शुद्ध हिन्दी *śuddh hindī*, i.e. 'pure Hindi'; its so-called 'purity' does not reflect the genuinely vernacular quality that characterizes the true character and genius of Hindi, but rather a high proportion of loanwords from Sanskrit. This means that शुद्ध हिन्दी *śuddh hindī* can take on an archaic or formal tone, which can be a real hindrance in everyday contexts: if you want to say 'Excuse me, I need help with my car if you're free' you will sound pompous if you come out with the equivalent of 'Begging your indulgence, one requires assistance with one's vehicle should you perchance be at leisure'! Whereas many dictionaries favour an elaborately Sanskritized vocabulary, the one in your hand assumes that most users will generally prefer a natural, colloquial style of language; and colloquial Hindi makes full use of *all* its linguistic resources.

Thanks to the fact that Persian and Sanskrit have both contributed to the lexicon of modern Hindi, several different words may be available as the equivalents of a single word in English. Thus for the meaning 'year', Hindi has the Persian loanword साल *sāl* and the Sanskrit loanword वर्ष *varṣ*, alongside the colloquial Hindi word बरस *baras* which derives from the latter. (Compare English, whose word 'year' is Germanic, while the adjective 'annual' reflects a Latin root; 'annual' in Hindi is सालाना *sālānā* or वार्षिक *vārṣik*.) In the judgement of this dictionary, साल *sāl* and सालाना *sālānā* make the best all-purpose choice for everyday use, although many Hindi speakers might well prefer वर्ष *varṣ* and वार्षिक *vārṣik* in more formal contexts (बरस *baras* will also be heard quite often; it doesn't yield an adjective for 'annual'). As an *imperfect* guide to choosing between equivalents, then, Persian loans are more appropriate in colloquial speech than are Sanskrit ones.

Words of Persian origin can often be spotted by their inclusion of any of the characters क़ *qa,* ख़ *kha,* ग़ *ga,* ज़ *za, and* फ़ *fa*, while any word that includes the characters ऋ *ṛ,* ण *ṇa,* ष *ṣa* or क्ष *kṣa* is from Sanskrit; this information will help you choose between, say, लज़ीज़ *lazīz* and स्वादिष्ट *svādiṣṭ* – two very expressive words both meaning 'delicious' – according to the cultural context you find yourself in. The acceptance of Perso-Arabic vocabulary within Hindi is resisted by the purists, who wish to Sanskritize Hindi to the greatest degree possible; but even they cannot achieve a full linguistic cleansing, as the name 'Hindi' is itself of Persian origin.

The extent to which English loanwords should be admitted to Hindi is another contentious issue. These days, when the media deliver English to every corner of the globe with ruthless efficiency, many speakers of Hindi mix the two languages very freely, letting English expressions oust many a fine Hindi word with centuries of tradition behind it; even the syntax and idiom of Hindi are beginning to show the impact of English, whose high status in India reflects both a colonized past and a globalized present. Many would say that English erodes and usurps the true character of Hindi, while others would point out that all languages are subject to perpetual change. Looking at the situation positively, it can be seen as a gift to the English-speaking learner of Hindi, who can turn to an English word like कार *kār* 'car' if the Hindi गाड़ी *gāṛī* happens to slip the memory. Only a few such English-origin words find a place in this dictionary, however, since their usage is mostly straightforward and our main concern is with 'real' Hindi words!

Hindi numbers its speakers in the hundreds of millions. In fact, the term 'Hindi' covers a number of different regional dialects, and many people in northern India have such a dialect as the mother tongue that they use in everyday domestic contexts. But one particular dialect, called खड़ी बोली *Khaṛī Bolī* or 'upright speech' and deriving from the environs of Delhi, has become established as the 'modern standard' form of Hindi throughout the Hindi-speaking area; it is used widely in public contexts, as the medium of education, the language of the media, the vehicle of most Hindi literature and the link between speakers of the various dialects. By the name 'Hindi', therefore, books like this one refer to the modern standard version of the language.

# A concise grammar

## The main features of Hindi grammar

Hindi grammar can be categorized in ways similar to European languages and although it has many characteristics of its own, it is quite accessible to the learner. Here are a few of its characteristic features:

Hindi is a 'subject-object-verb' language – the verb usually comes at the end of the sentence.

Gender is distinguished in many verb forms and adjectives, but not in pronouns (whereas in English, 'He runs' shows gender in the pronoun and not in the verb).

Two main grammatical cases are distinguished – 'direct' and 'oblique'; *very* broadly, the distinction is similar to that between 'he' and 'him'.

Hindi makes frequent use of postpositions (whose function is that of prepositions in English): as the name implies, they *follow* the word they govern, as in दिल्ली में *dillī mẽ* 'in Delhi' – and they require that word to be in the oblique case – though many words such as दिल्ली *dillī* do not themselves show this change.

The pronoun and verb systems distinguish three different 'honorific' levels, to express varying degrees of formality in relation to a person; it is like the French 'vous/tu' distinction, but is more pervasive and includes third-person references.

Relative words beginning *j-* are distinguished from interrogative words beginning *k-*, as in जब *jab* 'when' and जहाँ *jahā̃* 'where' versus कब *kab* 'when?' and कहाँ *kahā̃* 'where?'.

Hindi makes a clear distinction between transitive and intransitive verbs: whereas English will use the same verb 'wash' in both 'I wash my clothes' and 'These clothes wash easily', Hindi has separate verbs for the two functions (the first, धोना *dhonā*, is transitive, describing an action done to an object; the second, धुलना *dhulnā* is intransitive, describing an action being done, and cannot take an object).

A process of verb pairing, called 'compounding', allows subtle shades of meaning to be brought to the description of an action; the effect is similar to the distinction in English between 'to write down' and 'to write out'.

Family connections are defined precisely, with a superbly full set of relationship terms: instead of just saying 'grandmother', Hindi distinguishes नानी *nānī* (maternal) from दादी *dādī* (paternal), and so on with even greater specific detail through all the many varieties of uncles, aunts etc.

The following paragraphs map out the main features of the grammar.

### 1 NOUNS

Every Hindi noun is either masculine or feminine. A typical contrast is between masculine nouns ending *-ā* (लड़का *laṛkā* 'boy') and feminine nouns ending in *-ī* (लड़की *laṛkī* 'girl'); but this accounts for only one type, and there is no simple way of knowing that मेज़ *mez* 'table' is feminine and मकान *makān* 'house' masculine; and furthermore, many nouns ending in *-ā* are feminine loanwords from Sanskrit. Gender distinctions are important in the various ways that nouns are pluralized:

| | SINGULAR | PLURAL |
|---|---|---|
| MASCULINE TYPE 1 | लड़का *laṛkā* | लड़के *laṛke* |
| MASCULINE TYPE 2 | मकान *makān* | मकान *makān* |
| FEMININE TYPE 1 | लड़की *laṛkī* | लड़कियाँ *laṛkiyā̃* |
| FEMININE TYPE 2 | मेज़ *mez* | मेज़ें *mezẽ* |

This simple paradigm accounts for most nouns in Hindi. Notice that all feminine nouns (and almost *no* masculine ones) have a nasalized final syllable in the plural. Thus masculine nouns with endings other than *-ā* all belong to type 2 (आदमी *ādmī* means both 'man' and 'men' and कवि *kavi* means both 'poet' and 'poets'). There is a small group of masculine *-ā* nouns that, despite appearances, belong to type 2: राजा *rājā* 'king',

पिता *pitā* 'father', चाचा *cācā* 'uncle' and a handful more. Feminine nouns with endings other than *-ī* belong to type 2 (thus कविता *kavitā* 'poem', कविताएँ *kavitāẽ* 'poems').

Hindi has no definite or indefinite article ('the' and 'a', respectively), although the numeral एक *ek* 'one' sometimes stands for 'a'.

## 2 ADJECTIVES

Adjectives agree in gender, number and case (see 3 'case and "postpositions"') with the nouns they qualify. Those ending in *-ā* mostly change to *-ī* in the feminine and to *-e* in the masculine plural: बड़ा लड़का *baṛā laṛkā* 'big boy', बड़ी लड़की *baṛī laṛkī* 'big girl', बड़े लड़के *baṛe laṛke* 'big boys'. No other adjectives change their endings.

छोटा *choṭā* 'little' with a MASCULINE TYPE 1 noun:

| | | |
|---|---|---|
| छोटा कमरा | *choṭā kamrā* | small room |
| छोटे कमरे | *choṭe kamre* | small rooms |

बड़ा *baṛa* 'big' with a MASCULINE TYPE 2 noun:

| | | |
|---|---|---|
| बड़ा आदमी | *baṛā ādmī* | big man |
| बड़े आदमी | *baṛe ādmī* | big men |

काला *kālā* 'black' with a FEMININE TYPE 1 noun:

| | | |
|---|---|---|
| काली कुरसी | *kālī kursī* | black chair |
| काली कुरसियाँ | *kālī kursiyā̃* | black chairs |

सफ़ेद *safed* 'white' with a FEMININE TYPE 2 noun:

| | | |
|---|---|---|
| सफ़ेद मेज़ | *sāfed mez* | white table |
| सफ़ेद मेज़ें | *sāfed mezẽ* | white tables |

सुंदर *sundar* 'beautiful' with a MASCULINE TYPE 2 noun:

| | | |
|---|---|---|
| सुंदर मकान | *sundar makān* | beautiful house |
| सुंदर मकान | *sundar makān* | beautiful houses |

## 3 CASE AND 'POSTPOSITIONS'

The work of English prepositions such as 'in', 'on', 'to' etc. is done in Hindi by *post*positions (में *mẽ* 'in', पर *par* 'on', को *ko* 'to'), so called because they come *after* the word they govern:

| | | |
|---|---|---|
| मकान में | *makān mẽ* | in the house |
| मेज़ पर | *mez par* | on the table |
| राम को | *rām ko* | to Ram |

Words governed by postpositions take a special case called the 'oblique'. In the singular, this change of a noun's case from direct to oblique is only visible in MASCULINE TYPE 1 nouns, whose direct *-ā* ending changes to *-e* in the oblique: कमरे में *kamre mẽ* 'in the room'.

Adjectives that qualify oblique nouns also become oblique:

| | | |
|---|---|---|
| छोटा कमरा (direct case) | *choṭā kamrā* | small room |
| छोटे कमरे में (oblique case before में *mẽ*). | *choṭe kamre mẽ* | in the small room |

This change from direct to oblique is not apparent in invariable adjectives like सुंदर *sundar*:

| | | |
|---|---|---|
| सुंदर कमरा (direct case) | *sundar kamrā* | beautiful room |
| सुंदर कमरे में (oblique case before में *mẽ*) | *sundar kamre mẽ* | in the beautiful room |

Feminine nouns and adjectives don't change in the oblique (singular):

| | | |
|---|---|---|
| छोटी मेज़ (direct case) | *choṭī mez* | small table |
| छोटी मेज़ पर (oblique case before पर *par*) | *choṭī mez par* | on the small table |

In the plural, oblique masculine adjectives retain their *-e* ending, feminine adjectives remain unchanged, but all nouns of both genders end *-õ*:

| | |
|---|---|
| छोटे कमरों में *choṭe kamrõ mẽ* | in small rooms |
| सफ़ेद मेज़ों पर *safed mezõ par* | on white tables |

बड़ी मेज़ों पर *baṛī mezõ par* on big tables

बड़े मकानों में *baṛe makānõ mẽ* in big houses

## 4 PRONOUNS

The personal pronouns show how Hindi distinguishes various different 'honorific' levels, as in its three distinct words for 'you': तू *tū* (intimate), तुम *tum* (familiar), and आप *āp* (formal). Here's a paradigm showing the pronouns with the verb 'to be':

| SINGULAR | PLURAL |
| --- | --- |
| मैं हूँ *maĩ hũ* I am | हम हैं *ham haĩ* we are |
| तू है *tū hai* you are (intimate) | तुम हो *tum ho* you are (familiar) |
| | आप हैं *āp haĩ* you are (formal) |
| यह है *yah hai* he, she, it, this is | ये हैं *ye haĩ* they/these are; he/she (formal) is |
| वह है *vah hai* he, she, it, that is | वे हैं *ve haĩ* they/those are; he/she (formal) is |

The difference between यह *yah* and वह *vah* is one of proximity: 'he/she/it' is normally वह *vah,* but यह *yah* is used for a subject that's near at hand; similarly ये *ye* (nearby) and वे *ve* (remote). The words यह *yah* and वह *vah* are often pronounced 'ye' and 'vo', respectively.

Honorific plurals are used not only in the second person, but also in the third person: the Hindi for 'they are' can mean 'he/she is' when speaking formally or respectfully of an individual. Thus वे बहुत बड़े आदमी हैं *ve bahut baṛe ādmī haĩ* could mean either 'They are very big men', or 'He is a very big man', depending on context. Feminine nouns, however, change their form only in numerical plurals, not in honorific plurals: लंबी औरतें *lambī auratẽ* can only mean 'tall women', it can't be an honorific version of 'tall woman'.

Pronouns have oblique forms as follows (some don't change):

| | DIRECT | OBLIQUE |
|---|---|---|
| I | मैं *maĩ* | मुझ *mujh* |
| you (intimate) | तू *tū* | तुझ *tujh* |
| he, she, it, this | यह *yah* | इस *is* |
| he, she, it, that | वह *vah* | उस *us* |
| we | हम *ham* | हम *ham* |
| you (familiar) | तुम *tum* | तुम *tum* |
| you (formal) | आप *āp* | आप *āp* |
| they etc. | ये *ye* | इन *in* |
| they etc. | वे *ve* | उन *un* |

## 5 POSSESSION

The postposition का *kā* is equivalent to the English apostrophe 's', so that राम का भाई *rām kā bhāī* means 'Ram's brother'. The word का *kā*, though a postposition, behaves like an adjective in agreeing with the following word, as in राम की बहिन *rām kī bahin* 'Ram's sister'.

Here are the possessive pronouns, which decline like adjectives:

| | |
|---|---|
| my, mine | मेरा *merā* |
| your/yours (intimate) | तेरा *terā* |
| his, her/hers, its | इसका *iskā,* उसका *uskā* |
| our/ours | हमारा *hamārā* |
| your/yours (familiar) | तुम्हारा *tumhārā* |
| your/yours (formal) | आपका *āpkā* |
| their/theirs | इनका *inkā,* उनका *unkā* |

Hindi has no verb for 'to have', so possession is indicated in other ways. With family and real estate, का *kā* or a possessive pronoun is used:

मेरे दो भाई/मकान हैं। *mere do bhāī/makān haĩ.*
I have two brothers/houses.

Other kinds of possession use the postposition के पास *ke pās*:

राम के पास बहुत पैसा है । *rām ke pās bahut paisā hai.*
Ram has a lot of money.

### 6 VERBS

(a) We've already seen the present tense of 'to be'. Its past tense is:

|  | SINGULAR | PLURAL |
|---|---|---|
| MASCULINE | था *thā* | थे *the* |
| FEMININE | थी *thī* | थीं *thī̃* |

(b) The infinitive verb consists of stem + -*nā* ending: as in लिखना *likhnā* 'to write'. The main forms of the verb are shown below; notice that some tenses use the verb 'to be' as an auxiliary. The first-person subject here is masculine; for the feminine, change each final -*ā* to -*ī* (मैं लिख रही थी *maĩ likh rahī thī* etc.) – but not in the perfective मैं ने लिखा *maĩ ne likhā*, for reasons explained in (d) below.

PRESENT IMPERFECTIVE
मैं लिखता हूँ *maĩ likhtā hū̃*  I write [habitually]

PAST IMPERFECTIVE
मैं लिखता था *maĩ likhtā thā*  I used to write

PRESENT CONTINUOUS
मैं लिख रहा हूँ *maĩ likh rahā hū̃*  I am writing

PAST CONTINUOUS
मैं लिख रहा था *maĩ likh rahā thā*  I was writing

PERFECTIVE
मैं ने लिखा *maĩ ne likhā*  I wrote

FUTURE
मैं लिखूँगा *maĩ likhū̃gā*  I shall write

SUBJUNCTIVE
मैं लिखूँ *maĩ likhū̃*  I may write/should I write?

(c) Here's the paradigm for the future tense (simply change each final vowel to *-ī* for the feminine):

मैं लिखूँगा *maĩ likhū̃gā* I shall write

तू लिखेगा *tū likhegā* you will write

यह/वह लिखेगा *yah/vah likhegā* he will write

हम लिखेंगे *ham likhẽge* we shall write

तुम लिखोगे *tum likhoge* you will write

आप लिखेंगे *āp likhẽge* you will write

ये/वे लिखेंगे *ye/ve likhẽge* they will write

(d) In the perfective (tenses that describe a one-off action in the past), transitive verbs use a special 'ergative' construction in which the logical subject takes the untranslatable postposition ने *ne* and the verb agrees with the logical object. Here are some sentences using the feminine noun किताब *kitāb* 'book' as object:

राम ने एक किताब पढ़ी । *rām ne ek kitāb paṛhī.*
Rām read a/one book.

राम ने दो किताबें पढ़ीं । *rām ne do kitābẽ paṛhī̃.*
Rām read two books.

The verb agrees with 'book(s)', not with 'Ram'. This does not happen with intransitive verbs – their verb agrees with the subject in the usual way. For example, the verb पड़ना *paṛnā* 'to fall' is intransitive and is used here with the masculine noun पानी *pāni* 'water, rain' and then with the feminine noun बर्फ़ *barf* 'snow':

पानी पड़ा *pānī paṛā* rain fell

बर्फ़ पड़ी *barf paṛī* snow fell

(e) Further perfective tenses are formed by adding an auxiliary borrowed from 'to be'. The system is closely to parallel to the English use of auxiliaries in 'has written', 'had written', etc.

राम ने दो किताबें लिखीं । *rām ne do kitābẽ likhī̃.*
Ram wrote two books.

राम ने दो किताबें लिखी हैं । *rām ne do kitābẽ likhī haĩ.*
Ram has written two books.

राम ने दो किताबें लिखी थीं। *rām ne do kitābẽ likhī thī̃.*
Ram had written two books.

राम ने दो किताबें लिखी होंगी। *rām ne do kitābẽ likhī hõgī.*
Ram will have written two books.

राम ने दो किताबें लिखी हों। *rām ne do kitābẽ likhī hõ.*
Ram may have written two books.

(f) Imperative (command) endings change with honorific level:

(तू) लिख *(tū) likh* write
[a very abrupt, potentially impolite command]

(तुम) लिखो *(tum) likho* write
[an informal, fairly casual command or request]

(आप) लिखिए *(āp) likhie* write
[a polite, fairly formal command or request]

The infinitive form (लिखना *likhnā*) can also be used as an imperative, especially referring to future contexts not expecting immediate compliance.

(g) Absolutives of the verb (meaning 'having written', 'having gone' etc.) are formed by adding *-kar* to the verb stem: लिखकर *likhkar*, जाकर *jākar*. The verb करना *karnā* 'to do' has the absolutive ending *-ke* (giving करके *karke*); this ending can also be used as a colloquial alternative to *-kar* in any verb (लिखके *likhke* 'having written' etc.)

(h) Compound verbs lie at the heart of Hindi's expressive powers, the basic meaning of one verb is given a particular shade of meaning by a second that hitches up to it. Used in this way, the verb लेना *lenā* 'to take' suggests that the 'doer' of the action takes benefit from it, whereas the verb देना *denā* 'to give' suggests that the action gives benefit to someone else.

लिखना *likhnā* to write

लिख लेना *likh lenā* to write down [for one's own use]

लिख देना *likh denā* to write out [for someone else's use]

Other verbs bring other kinds of emphasis, making this a superbly subtle way of colouring the meaning of a basic verb.

(i) Passive verbs in English are made using the verb 'to be' (active 'to write' becomes passive 'to be written'). Similarly, Hindi uses जाना *jānā*, literally meaning 'to go'.

ACTIVE

लिखना *likhnā* to write

मैं चिट्ठी लिखूँगा । *maĩ ciṭṭhī likhū̃gā.* I will write a letter.

PASSIVE

लिखा जाना *likhā jānā* to be written

चिट्ठी लिखी जाएगी । *ciṭṭhī likhī jāegī.* A letter will be written.

## 7 QUESTIONS

Statements are made into questions by adding the question word क्या *kyā* at the beginning (क्या चिट्ठी लिखी जाएगी? *kyā ciṭṭhī likhī jāegī?* 'will a letter be written?'). Other kinds of question involve one of a set of interrogatives beginning *k-*, as in कब *kab* 'when?' कितना *kitnā* 'how much?', कौन *kaun* 'who?' etc. Questions can also be conveyed by tone of voice alone: चिट्ठी लिखी जाएगी? *ciṭṭhī likhī jāegī?* 'The letter will be written?'.

## 8 WHICH NOUN IS THE SUBJECT?

Hindi has many constructions that put the experience (rather than the experiencer) at the centre of things: whereas English will say 'I like old films', Hindi will say 'old films are pleasing to me'. It's as if the world impinges on the individual, rather than the other way round. Constructions of this kind are very common, and in this dictionary they are highlighted with the 'bomb' symbol 💣 to show that the Hindi grammar works differently from the English.

A so-called 'को *ko* construction' is found in expressions for various types of need or compulsion. Several of these use the word चाहिए *cāhie* – literally 'is wanted/needed':

मुझ को वह किताब चाहिए । *mujh ko vah kitāb cāhie.*
I need/want that book.

राम को दो किताबें चाहिए । *rām ko do kitābẽ cāhie.*
Ram needs two books.

मुझ को यह किताब पढ़नी चाहिए । *mujh ko yah kitāb paṛhnī cāhie.*
I should read this book.

In the third sentence, the infinitive verb पढ़नी *paṛhnī* is feminine to agree with किताब *kitāb*.

### 9 ADVERBS

Hindi has many kinds of adverb (words that describe an action or verb, just as adjectives describe a thing or noun). Many are made up like the English adverb 'with difficulty', being based on a noun (you can't say 'difficultly'), using the postposition से *se* 'with':

मुश्किल से *muśkil se* with difficulty

आसानी से *āsānī se* with ease, easily

Another formula uses the noun रूप *rūp* 'form' to describe 'manner':

स्थायी रूप से *sthāyī rūp se* permanently

व्यक्तिगत रूप से *vyaktigat rūp se* personally

### 10 RELATIVE–CORRELATIVES

A relative clause will often pair up with a correlative clause. In the following examples, look out for a relative word (starting *j-*) at the beginning of the relative clause and its look-alike correlative at the beginning of the correlative clause. The translations here are literal, to show the construction of the Hindi.

जब बर्फ़ पड़ती है, तब मैं कमरे में रहता हूँ ।
*jab barf paṛtī hai, tab maĩ kamre mẽ rahtā hū̃.*
When snow falls, then I stay in the room.

जहाँ बर्फ़ पड़ती है, वहाँ बच्चे खेलते हैं ।
*jahā̃ barf paṛtī hai, vahā̃ bacce khelte haĩ.*
Where the snow falls, there the children play.

जो लड़का खेल रहा है वह बर्फ़ में गिरेगा ।
*jo laṛkā khel rahā hai vah barf mẽ giregā.*
The boy who is playing, (he) will fall in the snow.

जितनी बर्फ़ आज गिरी उतनी कल नहीं गिरेगी ।
*jitnī barf āj girī utnī kal nahī̃ giregī.*
How much snow fell today, that much won't fall tomorrow (i.e. not as much snow will fall tomorrow as fell today).

## 11 NUMBERS

० शून्य *śūnya*

| | | | | |
|---|---|---|---|---|
| १ एक | ११ ग्यारह | २१ इक्कीस | ३१ इकत्तीस | ४१ इकतालीस |
| *1 ek* | *11 gyārah* | *21 ikkīs* | *31 ikattīs* | *41 iktālīs* |
| २ दो | १२ बारह | २२ बाईस | ३२ बत्तीस | ४२ बयालीस |
| *2 do* | *12 bārah* | *22 bāīs* | *32 battīs* | *42 bayālīs* |
| ३ तीन | १३ तेरह | २३ तेईस | ३३ तैंतीस | ४३ तैंतालीस |
| *3 tīn* | *13 terah* | *23 teīs* | *33 taĩtīs* | *43 taĩtālīs* |
| ४ चार | १४ चौदह | २४ चौबीस | ३४ चौंतीस | ४४ चवालीस |
| *4 cār* | *14 caudah* | *24 caubīs* | *34 caũtīs* | *44 cavālīs* |
| ५ पाँच | १५ पंद्रह | २५ पच्चीस | ३५ पैंतीस | ४५ पैंतालीस |
| *5 pā̃c* | *15 pandrah* | *25 paccīs* | *35 paĩtīs* | *45 paĩtālīs* |
| ६ छह | १६ सोलह | २६ छब्बीस | ३६ छत्तीस | ४६ छियालीस |
| *6 chah* | *16 solah* | *26 chabbīs* | *36 chattīs* | *46 chiyālīs* |
| ७ सात | १७ सत्रह | २७ सत्ताईस | ३७ सैंतीस | ४७ सैंतालीस |
| *7 sāt* | *17 satrah* | *27 sattāīs* | *37 saĩtīs* | *47 saĩtālīs* |
| ८ आठ | १८ अठारह | २८ अट्ठाईस | ३८ अड़तीस | ४८ अड़तालीस |
| *8 āṭh* | *18 aṭhārah* | *28 aṭṭhāīs* | *38 aṛtīs* | *48 aṛtālīs* |
| ९ नौ | १९ उन्नीस | २९ उनतीस | ३९ उनतालीस | ४९ उनचास |
| *9 nau* | *19 unnīs* | *29 untīs* | *39 untālīs* | *49 uncās* |
| १० दस | २० बीस | ३० तीस | ४० चालीस | ५० पचास |
| *10 das* | *20 bīs* | *30 tīs* | *40 cālīs* | *50 pacās* |

| | | | | |
|---|---|---|---|---|
| ५१ इक्यावन | ६१ इकसठ | ७१ इकहत्तर | ८१ इक्यासी | ९१ इक्यानवे |
| 51 *ikyāvan* | 61 *iksaṭh* | 71 *ik'hattar* | 81 *ikyāsī* | 91 *ikyānve* |
| ५२ बावन | ६२ बासठ | ७२ बहत्तर | ८२ बयासी | ९२ बानवे |
| 52 *bāvan* | 62 *bāsaṭh* | 72 *bahattar* | 82 *bayāsī* | 92 *bānve* |
| ५३ तिरपन | ६३ तिरसठ | ७३ तिहत्तर | ८३ तिरासी | ९३ तिरानवे |
| 53 *tirpan* | 63 *tirsaṭh* | 73 *tihattar* | 83 *tirāsī* | 93 *tirānve* |
| ५४ चौवन | ६४ चौंसठ | ७४ चौहत्तर | ८४ चौरासी | ९४ चौरानवे |
| 54 *cauvan* | 64 *caũsaṭh* | 74 *cauhattar* | 84 *caurāsī* | 94 *caurānve* |
| ५५ पचपन | ६५ पैंसठ | ७५ पचहत्तर | ८५ पचासी | ९५ पचानवे |
| 55 *pacpan* | 65 *paĩsaṭh* | 75 *pac'hattar* | 85 *pacāsī* | 95 *pacānve* |
| ५६ छप्पन | ६६ छियासठ | ७६ छिहत्तर | ८६ छियासी | ९६ छियानवे |
| 56 *chappan* | 66 *chiyāsaṭh* | 76 *chihattar* | 86 *chiyāsī* | 96 *chiyānve* |
| ५७ सत्तावन | ६७ सरसठ | ७७ सतहत्तर | ८७ सत्तासी | ९७ सत्तानवे |
| 57 *sattāvan* | 67 *sarsaṭh* | 77 *sat'hattar* | 87 *sattāsī* | 97 *sattānve* |
| ५८ अट्ठावन | ६८ अड़सठ | ७८ अठहत्तर | ८८ अट्ठासी | ९८ अट्ठानवे |
| 58 *aṭṭhāvan* | 68 *aṛsaṭh* | 78 *aṭhhattar* | 88 *aṭṭhāsī* | 98 *aṭṭhānve* |
| ५९ उनसठ | ६९ उनहत्तर | ७९ उन्यासी | ८९ नवासी | ९९ निन्यानवे |
| 59 *unsaṭh* | 69 *unhattar* | 79 *unyāsī* | 89 *navāsī* | 99 *ninyānve* |
| ६० साठ | ७० सत्तर | ८० अस्सी | ९० नब्बे | १०० सौ |
| 60 *sāṭh* | 70 *sattar* | 80 *assī* | 90 *nabbe* | 100 *sau* |

| | |
|---|---|
| 1.5 | डेढ़ *ḍeṛh* |
| 2.5 | ढाई *ḍhāī* |
| 1,000 | हज़ार *hazār* |
| 100,000 | लाख *lākh* |
| 10,000,000 | करोड़ *karoṛ* (100 lakh, written 100,00,000) |
| 100,000,000 | अरब *arab* (10 *karoṛ*, written 10,00,00,000) |

The terms 'lakh' and 'crore' (Hindi करोड़ *karoṛ*) are in common use in English in the subcontinent.

# Bibliography

Editions and dates of publication may vary from those given here. Websites and their contents may change; their addresses were correct and their content appropriate at the time of writing.

## Hindi language courses and grammars

Bhatia, Tej, *Colloquial Hindi*. London, Routledge, 1996. [A highly readable coursebook; with recordings.]

Delacy, Richard and Sudha Joshi, *Elementary Hindi: an introduction to the language*. North Clarendon, Tuttle Publishing, 2009. [An excellent coursebook; with CDs.]

McGregor, R.S. *An Outline of Hindi Grammar*. 3rd edition. London, Oxford University Press, 1995. [Ideal for those wanting a formal grammar rather than a coursebook; with recordings.]

Snell, Rupert, with Simon Weightman, *Complete Hindi*. London, Hodder & Stoughton, 2010. [A coursebook that aims to cover all the major elements of the grammar; with CDs.]

Snell, Rupert, *Get Started in Hindi*. London, Hodder & Stoughton, 2010. [An untechnical introduction to the language; with CDs.]

Snell, Rupert, *Read and Write Hindi Script*. London, Hodder & Stoughton, 2010. [A detailed introduction to the script with examples of handwriting, signwriting and other stylized forms.]

Snell, Rupert, *Speak Hindi with Confidence*. London, Hodder & Stoughton, 2010. [A course in spoken Hindi on CD.]

## Dictionaries

Bahri, Hardev, *Advanced Learner's English–Hindi Dictionary*. Delhi, Rajpal, 1999. [A huge tome, with many examples of usage.]

Bahri, Hardev, *Learners' Hindi–English Dictionary*. 2nd edition. Delhi, Rajpal, 1983. [An excellent book for learners at all levels.]

Chaturvedi, Mahendra, and Bhola Nath Tiwari, *A Practical Hindi–English Dictionary*. 3rd edition. Delhi, National, 1996. [An ideal accompaniment to reading texts.]

McGregor, R.S., *The Oxford Hindi–English Dictionary*. Oxford, Oxford University Press, 1993. [The only Hindi–English dictionary to give etymologies; a major achievement of scholarship.]

NB: most of the handy pocket-size English–Hindi dictionaries currently available are designed for Hindi-speaking users and do not address the needs of learners of Hindi (for example, they do not show noun genders); so they are not listed here.

---

## Online resources

Many aids to the study of Hindi are now available through the internet. Here are some sites that may help you:

http://www.hindiurduflagship.org/. See the 'Resources' section in particular.

http://www.avashy.com/hindiscripttutor.htm. A convenient and interactive guide to Devanagari.

http://taj.chass.ncsu.edu/. 'A Door into Hindi' — the title says it all!

http://www.columbia.edu/itc/mealac/pritchett/00urduhindilinks/.
A cornucopia of Hindi and Urdu materials.

http://dsal.uchicago.edu/dictionaries/. Invaluable online versions of dictionaries in south Asian languages.

# Abbreviations

| | |
|---|---|
| F | feminine noun |
| M | masculine noun |
| N | a verb that regularly uses the ने *ne* construction in perfective tenses |
| n | a verb that sometimes uses the ने *ne* construction in perfective tenses |
| PL | plural |
| [...] | exemplifies how the meaning of a verb can be 'coloured' by extension into a compound verb |
| 💣 | (in English–Hindi section) indicates that the following Hindi clause has a different grammatical subject from its English equivalent; (*not* used with ने *ne* constructions) |
| — | (in English–Hindi section) introduces an example illustrating the meaning just given |
| adj. | adjective |
| adv. | adverb |
| gramm. | grammatically |
| intr. | intransitive verb (describes an action that happens to the subject: 'the chair broke', 'she arrived'); this and next are marked only when necessary to resolve ambiguity |
| tr. | transitive verb (describes an action done *to* a thing or person: 'he broke the chair', 'she ate an apple') |

# Hindi–English Dictionary

# अ *a*

अंक *aṅk*[M] number, figure, issue (of journal), mark

अंग *aṅg*[M] limb

अँगूठा *ãgūṭhā*[M] thumb

अँगूठी *ãgūṭhī*[F] ring (for finger)

अंधापन *andhāpan*[M] blindness

अँधेरा *ãdherā* dark;[M] darkness

अकेला *akelā* alone

अकेलापन *akelāpan*[M] loneliness

अकेले *akele* (adverb) alone

अक्तूबर *aktūbar*[M] October

**Insight**

अक्तूबर *aktūbar* — the dental 't' reflects an origin in, or the influence of, Portuguese 'outubro'. English loanwords usually show retroflex rather than dental consonants, as in डाक्टर *ḍākṭar*.

अंगूर *aṅgūr*[M] grape

अँग्रेज़ *ãgrez*[M] English person

अँग्रेज़ी *ãgrezī* (adj. & noun) English;[F] the English language

अंडा *aṇḍā*[M] egg

अंत *ant*[M] end

अंतर *antar*[M] difference

अंतर्राष्ट्रीय *antarrāṣṭrīy* international

अंतिम *antim* final

अंत्येष्टि *antyeṣṭi*[F] funeral

अंदर *andar* inside

अंदाज़ा *andāzā*[M] guess, estimate

अंधविश्वास *andhviśvās*[M] superstition

अंधा *andhā* (adj. & noun) blind;[M] blind man

अक्षर *akṣar*[M] syllable, letter

अक्सर *aksar* usually, often

अख़बार *akhbār*[M] newspaper; अख़बार-वाला *akhbār-vālā*[M] newspaper seller

अगर *agar* if

अगरबत्ती *agarbattī*[F] incense stick

अगला *aglā* next

अगस्त *agast*[M] August

अचानक *acānak* suddenly

अचार *acār*[M] pickle

अच्छा *acchā* good, nice

अच्छाई *acchāī*[F] good, merit

अजनबी *ajnabī*[M] stranger

अजीब *ajīb* strange, peculiar

अट्ठानवे *aṭhānve* ninety-eight

अट्ठावन *aṭṭhāvan* fifty-eight

अट्ठासी *aṭṭhāsī* eighty-eight

अठहत्तर *aṭh'hattar* seventy-eight

अठाईस *aṭhāīs* twenty-eight

अठारह *aṭhārah* eighteen

अड़तालीस *aṛtālīs* forty-eight

अड़तीस *aṛtīs* thirty-eight

अड़सठ *aṛsaṭh* sixty-eight

अड्डा *āḍḍā*[M] stand, base, haunt

अतिथि *atithi*[M] guest

अतिरिक्त *atirikt* extra, additional

अतिवाद *ativād*[M] extremism

अतिवादी *ativādī* (adj. & noun)[M] extremist

अतिशयोक्ति *atiśayokti*[F] exaggeration

अत्यंत *atyant* extremely, exceedingly

अथवा *athvā* or

अदरक *adrak*[F] ginger

अदालत *adālat*[F] court of law

अदा *adā*[F] grace, charm; flirtatious gesture; अदा करना *adā karnā*[N] to fulfil, perform, pay

अदृश्य *adṛśya* invisible, unseen

अद्भुत *adbhut* remarkable, astonishing, wonderful

अधिक *adhik* much, more; अधिक से अधिक *adhik se adhik* at the most, the maximum possible

अधिकार *adhikār*[M] right, authority

अधिकारी *adhikārī*[M] officer, official

अधेड़ *adheṛ* middle aged

अध्यक्ष *adhyakṣ*[M] head, chairman

अध्यक्षता *adhyakṣtā*[F] chairmanship, chairing

अध्ययन *adhyayan*[M] study, reading

अध्यापक *adhyāpak*[M] teacher

अध्यापिका *adhyāpikā*[F] teacher

अध्याय *adhyāy*[M] chapter

अनदेखा करना *andekhā karnā*[N] to ignore

अनपढ़ *anpaṛh* illiterate

अनबन *anban*[F] discord, dispute

अनमना *anmanā* out of sorts

अनाथ *anāth*[M] orphan, helpless person

अनाथालय *anāthālay*[M] orphanage

अनादर *anādar*[M] disrespect

अनिवार्य *anivārya* obligatory, essential, unavoidable, indispensable

अनिश्चित *aniścit* undecided, indefinite

अनुनासिक *anunāsik* (adj. & noun) nasal (in phonetics);[M] the sign ँ that indicates a nasalized vowel

अनुभव *anubhav*[M] experience

अनुभवी *anubhavī* experienced

अनुमति *anumati*^F permission

अनुमान *anumān*^M estimate, guess, conjecture

अनुयायी *anuyāyī*^M follower

अनुरोध *anurodh*^M entreaty, request

अनुवाद *anuvād*^M translation

अनुशासन *anuśāsan*^M discipline, control

अनुस्वार *anusvār*^M the dot that indicates a nasalized vowel in words like हैं *haĩ*, and which stands for a nasal consonant in conjunct characters, e.g. in हिंदी (= हिन्दी) *hindī*.

अनेक *anek* many

अनौपचारिक *anaupcārik* informal

अन्य *anya* other

अपना *apnā* one's own (i.e. 'my', 'your', 'her', 'their', etc., where such words refer to the subject of a clause: अमित अपनी पत्नी को तोहफ़े देता है *amit apnī patnī ko tohfe detā hai* 'Amit gives presents to his wife' – to his *own* wife, not to someone else's)

अपनाना *apnānā*^N to adopt, make one's own

अपमान *apmān*^M disrespect

अपमानित करना *apmānit karnā*^N to disrespect, show disrespect

अपराध *aprādh*^M offence, crime

अपराधी *aprādhī* (adj. & noun) guilty;^M criminal

अपवाद *apvād*^M exception

अपार *apār* boundless

अप्रैल *aprail*^M April

अफ़वाह *afvāh*^F rumour

अफ़सर *afsar*^M officer, official

अफ़्सोस *afsos*^M regret, pity

अब *ab* now; अब की बार *ab kī bār* this time

अभिनेता *abhinetā*^M actor

अभिनेत्री *abhinetrī*^F actress

अभिलाषा *abhilāṣā*^F desire

अभी *abhī* (emphatic form of अब *ab*) right now; अभी तक *abhī tak* yet, up to now

अभ्यास *abhyās*^M practice

अमरीकन *amrīkan* (adj. & noun)^M American

अमरीका *amrīkā*^M America

अमीर *amīr* rich, wealthy

अमरूद *amrūd*^M guava

अरब[1] *arab*^M an Arab; Arabia

अरब[2] *arab*^M a thousand million, a billion

अरबी *arabī* (adj. & noun) Arabian;^F the Arabic language

अरे *are* hey!; oh!

अर्ज़ी *arzī*^F application; अर्ज़ी देना *arzī denā*^N to apply

अर्थ *arth*^M meaning

अर्थशास्त्र *arthśāstra*^M economics

अलग *alag* separate, different

अलमारी *almārī*^F cupboard

अवतार *avtār*^M incarnation

अवधि *avadhi*^F set period of time, a while; limit of time

अवधी *avdhī*^F a dialect of Hindi: the language of Awadh (formerly 'Oudh') in Uttar Pradesh

अवश्य *avaśya* certainly, of course

अवसर *avsar*^M occasion, time, opportunity, chance

अविवाहित *avivāhit* unmarried

अवैध *avaidh* illegal

अश्लील *aślīl* obscene, vulgar

असंतुष्ट *asantuṣṭ* dissatisfied

असंभव *asambhav* impossible

असफल *asaphal* unsuccessful

असर *asar*^M effect, impact; असर पड़ना *asar parṇā* to have an effect

असल में *asal mē* in fact, really

असली *āslī* real, genuine

असहमति *asahmati*^F disagreement, difference of opinion

असहयोग *asahyog*^M non-cooperation

असुविधा *asuvidhā*^F inconvenience

अस्थायी *asthāyī* impermanent, temporary

अस्पताल *aspatāl*^M hospital

अहंकार *ahamkār*^M pride, egotism

अहम *aham* important

अहमियत *ahmiyat*^F importance

## आ *ā*

आँख *ā̃kh*^F eye; आँखें चार होना *ā̃khē cār honā* two people's gaze to meet

आँगन *ā̃gan*^M courtyard

आंदोलन *āndolan*^M movement (social or political)

आँसू *ā̃sū*^M tear

आइंदा *āindā* (adverb & noun) in future;^M the future

आईना *āīnā*^M mirror

आकर्षण *ākarṣaṇ*^M attraction

आकर्षित *ākarṣit* attracted

आकाश *ākāś*^M sky

आकाशवाणी *ākāśvāṇī*^F radio; the name of Indian state radio

आक्रमण *ākramaṇ*^M attack

आख़िर *ākhir* (adverb & noun) after all;^M end

आख़िरी *ākhirī* last, final

आग *āg*$^{F}$ fire

आगरा *āgrā*$^{M}$ Agra

---

**Insight**

आगरा *āgrā* — should such place names inflect in the oblique case? Some speakers say आगरे में *āgre mẽ*, some say आगरा में *āgrā mẽ*, so it's up to you!

---

आगे *āge* forward, further, ahead; आगे चलकर *āge calkar* in future, from now on; आगे निकलना *āge nikalnā* to overtake, pass

आग्रह *āgrah*$^{M}$ insistence

आज *āj* today; आज रात को *āj rāt ko* tonight; आज शाम को *āj śām ko* this evening

आजकल *ājkal* nowadays, these days

आज़ाद *āzād* free, independent

आज़ादी *āzādī*$^{F}$ freedom, independence

आज्ञा *ājñā*$^{F}$ (pronounced '*āgyā*') permission; आज्ञा देना *ājñā denā*$^{N}$ to give permission, to allow (to go)

आटा *āṭā*$^{M}$ fine flour

आठ *āṭh* eight; आठों पहर *āṭhõ pahar* all day long

आडंबर *āḍambar*$^{M}$ ostentation

आतंक *ātaṅk*$^{M}$ terror

आतंकवाद *ātaṅkvād*$^{M}$ terrorism

आतंकवादी *ātaṅkvādī* (adj. & noun)$^{M}$ terrorist

आतंकित *ātaṅkit* terror stricken

आत्मकथा *ātmakathā*$^{F}$ autobiography

आत्महत्या *ātmahatyā*$^{F}$ suicide

आत्मा *ātmā*$^{F}$ soul, the self

आत्मीय *ātmīy* (adj. & noun)$^{M}$ intimate

आत्मीयता *ātmīyatā*$^{F}$ intimacy

आदत *ādat*$^{F}$ habit

आदतन *ādatan* habitually

आदमी *ādmī*$^{M}$ man

आदर *ādar*$^{M}$ respect; (का) आदर करना *(kā) ādar karnā*$^{N}$ to respect

आदरणीय *ādarṇīy* respected (form of address used in formal correspondence)

आदर्श *ādarś* (adj. & noun)$^{M}$ ideal

आदान-प्रदान *ādān-pradān*$^{M}$ exchange

आदि *ādi* etc., and so on; [F]beginning

आदी *ādī* accustomed, habituated, used to

आदेश *ādeś*[M] order, command

आधा *ādhā* (adj. & noun)[M] half

आधार *ādhār*[M] basis

आधारित *ādhārit* based

आधी रात *ādhī rāt*[F] midnight

आध्यात्मिक *ādhyātmik* spiritual

आध्यात्मिकता *ādhyātmiktā*[F] spirituality

आनंद *ānand*[M] joy, pleasure, bliss

आना *ānā* to come; to have knowledge of a language (मुझको हिंदी आती है *mujhko hindī ātī hai* I know Hindi); to have a skill (मुझको खाना बनाना आता है *mujhko khānā banānā ātā hai* I know how to cook)

आप *āp* you

आपका *āpkā* your, yours

आपत्ति *āpatti*[F] objection

आपत्तिजनक *āpattijanak* objectionable

आपस में *āpas mẽ* among (a group)

आबादी *ābādī* [F]population

आभार *ābhār*[M] obligation, debt (of gratitude)

आभारी *ābhārī* indebted, grateful

आम[1] *ām*[M] mango

आम[2] *ām* ordinary; आम तौर पर *ām taur par* usually

आमदनी *āmdanī*[F] income

आय *āy*[F] income

आयु *āyu*[F] age (of a person)

आरंभ *ārambh*[M] beginning, commencement

आराम *ārām*[M] rest; आराम-कुरसी *ārām-kursī*[F] armchair; आराम से *ārām se* comfortably, easily; आराम करना *ārām karnā* [N] to rest

आरामदेह *ārāmdeh* comfortable (of a chair etc.)

आरी *ārī*[F] hand saw

आर्थिक *ārthik* financial, economic

आलसी *ālsī* lazy

आलू *ālū*[M] potato

आवश्यक *āvaśyak* necessary

आवश्यकता *āvaśyaktā*[F] necessity

आवाज़ *āvāz*[F] voice; sound

आविष्कार *āviṣkār*[M] discovery, invention

आशा *āśā*[F] hope

आशीर्वाद *āśīrvād*[M] blessing

आश्चर्य *āścarya*[M] surprise

आश्रम *āśram*[M] hermitage, home or refuge for people on a

spiritual path; one of the four stages of life in Hinduism

आसन *āsan*ᴹ seat, sitting; yoga posture

आस-पास *ās-pās* nearabout

आसमान *āsmān*ᴹ sky

आसान *āsān* easy

आसानी *āsānī*ᶠ ease; आसानी से *āsānī se* easily

आह *āh*ᶠ sigh; आह भरना *āh bharnā*ᴺ to sigh

आहट *āhaṭ*ᶠ footfall, sound of footsteps

आहिस्ता *āhistā* slowly

## इ *i*

इंग्लैंड *iṅglaiṇḍ*ᴹ England

इंतज़ाम *intazām*ᴹ arrangement; (का) इंतज़ाम करना *(kā) intazām karnā*ᴺ to arrange

इंतज़ार *intazār*ᴹ waiting; (का) इंतज़ार करना *(kā) intazār karnā*ᴺ to wait (for)

इंद्रिय *indriy*ᴹ sense organ; the senses

इकट्ठा *ikaṭṭhā* gathered, assembled, together

इकतालीस *iktālīs* forty-one

इकत्तीस *ikattīs* thirty-one

इकसठ *iksaṭh* sixty-one

इकहत्तर *ik'hattar* seventy-one

इक्कीस *ikkīs* twenty-one

इक्यानवे *ikyānve* ninety-one

इक्यावन *ikyāvan* fifty-one

इक्यासी *ikyāsī* eighty-one

इच्छा *icchā*ᶠ wish; इच्छा करना *icchā karnā*ᴺ to wish

इज़हार *izhār*ᴹ statement; इज़हार करना *izhār karnā*ᴺ to declare, make known

इजाज़त *ijāzat* permissionᶠ; इजाज़त देना *ijāzat denā*ᴺ to give leave, to allow (to go)

इतना *itnā* so much, so

इतने में *itne mẽ* then, at that time, meanwhile

इतवार *itvār*ᴹ Sunday

इतिहास *itihās*ᴹ history

इत्तिफ़ाक़ से *ittifāq se* by chance

इत्यादि *ityādi* etc., and so on

इधर *idhar* here, over here; recently, latterly; in my/our case; इधर-उधर *idhar-udhar* here and there, hither and thither

इनकार *inkār*ᴹ refusal

इनकार करना *inkār karnā*ᴺ to refuse (to, से *se*)

इनसान *insān*ᴹ person, human being

इनसानियत *insāniyat*ᶠ humanity, decency

इबादत *ibādat*ᶠ worship

इमारत *imārat*ᶠ building

इस *is* oblique of यह *yah;* इस लिए *is lie* so, because of this; इसी लिए *isī lie that's* why

इस्तरी *istrī*ᶠ iron (for ironing)

**Insight**

इस्तरी *istrī* — not to be confused with स्त्री *strī* 'woman', which many Hindi speakers pronounce (adding a prosthetic *i-*) as *istrī*. Many bad jokes result!

इम्तहान *imtahān*ᴹ exam; इम्तहान देना *imtahān denā* ᴺ to take an exam

इन *in* oblique of ये *ye*

इनाम *inām*ᴹ prize, reward, gift

इरादा *irādā*ᴹ intention

इलाक़ा *ilāqā*ᴹ area, district

इलाज *ilāj*ᴹ cure, remedy; का इलाज करना *kā ilāj karnā* ᴺ to cure, treat

इलायची *ilāycī*ᶠ cardamom

इशारा *iśārā*ᴹ sign, signal, hint, indication

इश्क़ *iśq*ᴹ love, passion

इश्तहार *iśtahār*ᴹ advertisement, poster

इस्तेमाल *istemāl*ᴹ use; इस्तेमाल करना *istemāl karnā* ᴺ to use

इस्पात *ispāt*ᴹ steel

## ई *ī*

ईंट *ĩṭ*ᶠ brick

ईंधन *ĩdhan*ᴹ fuel

ईद *īd*ᶠ the festival of Eid; ईद का चाँद *īd kā cā̃d*ᴹ a rare sight, someone seen 'once in a blue moon'

ईमानदार *īmāndār* honest, trust worthy

ईमानदारी *īmāndārī*ᶠ honesty

ईर्ष्या *īrṣyā*ᶠ jealousy

ईश्वर *īśvar*ᴹ God

ईसाई *īsāī* (adj. & noun)ᴹ Christian

**Insight**

ईस्वी *īsvī* – this adjective derives from ईसा *īsā* 'Jesus', also seen in the extended name ईसा मसीह *īsā masīh* 'Jesus the Messiah'.

## उ *u*

उँगली *ũglī*^F finger

उगना *ugnā* to grow (of plants etc.)

उगाना *ugānā*^N to grow, cultivate

उग्र *ugra* fierce, radical

उचित *ucit* appropriate, proper, right

उच्चारण *uccāraṇ*^M pronunciation

उछलना *uchalnā* to leap, fly up, spring up

उछालना *uchālnā*^N to throw, toss

उठना *uṭhnā* to get up, rise

उठाना *uṭhānā*^N to pick up, lift up, remove; to bear (expense)

उड़ना *uṛnā* to fly

उड़ान *uṛān*^F flight, a flight

उड़ाना *uṛānā*^N to fly, make fly; to squander (money)

उतना *utnā* that much

उतरना *utarnā* to get down, alight; to fall (of facial expression)

उतारना *utārnā*^N to take down, take off

उत्तर[1] *uttar* (adj. & noun)^M north

उत्तर[2] *uttar*^M reply

उत्तरदायित्व *uttardāyitva*^M responsibility

उत्तरदायी *uttardāyī* responsible

उत्सव *utsav*^M festival, celebration

उत्साह *utsāh*^M enthusiasm, zeal

उत्सुक *utsuk* keen, eager

उत्सुकता *utsuktā*^F keenness, eagerness

उदार *udār* liberal, generous

उदारता *udārtā*^F generosity

उदास *udās* sad, gloomy

उदाहरण *udāharaṇ*^M example

उद्देश्य *uddeśya*^M purpose, intention

उद्यान *udyān*^M garden

उधर *udhar* there, over there

उधार *udhār*^M loan; उधार देना *udhār denā*^N to lend; उधार लेना *udhār lenā*^N to borrow

उन *un* oblique of वे *ve*

उनचास *uncās* forty-nine

उनतालीस *untālīs* thirty-nine

उनतीस *untīs* twenty-nine

उनसठ *unsaṭh* fifty-nine

उनहत्तर *unhattar* sixty-nine

उन्नति *unnati*^F progress

उन्नीस *unnīs* nineteen

उन्यासी *unyāsī* seventy-nine

उपजाऊ *upjāū* fertile, productive

उपदेश *updeś*^M lesson, sermon

उपन्यास *upanyās*^M novel

उपन्यासकार *upanyāskār*ᴹ novelist

उपमहाद्वीप *upmahādvīp*ᴹ subcontinent

उपयुक्त *upyukt* appropriate

उपयोग *upyog*ᴹ use

उपयोगी *upyogī* useful

उपलब्ध *uplabdh* available

उपवास *upvās*ᴹ fast, fasting

उपस्थित *upasthit* present (not absent)

उपस्थिति *upasthiti*ᶠ presence, attendance

उपाधि *upādhi*ᶠ title; degree

उपाय *upāy*ᴹ way, means, scheme

उपासक *upāsak*ᴹ worshipper

उपेक्षा *upekṣā*ᶠ indifference, contempt

उम्मीद *ummīd*ᶠ hope

उम्मीदवार *ummīdvār*ᴹ candidate

उम्र *umra*ᶠ age

उर्दू *urdū*ᶠ Urdu

उलझन *uljhan*ᶠ entanglement, complication

उलझना *ulajhnā* to be caught up, entangled, ensnared

उलझाना *uljhānā* ᴺ to entangle, ensnare

उलटना *ulaṭnā* to overturn

उलटा *ulṭā* inverted, upside down, inside out; उलटे हाथ *ulṭe hāth* to the left (hand)

उलटी *ulṭī*ᶠ vomiting; उलटी करना *ulṭī karnā* ᴺ to vomit

उल्लू *ullū*ᴹ owl; fool

**Insight**

उल्लू *ullū* – despite being the vehicle of the goddess Lakshmi, the owl is an image of stupidity in India: hence उल्लू का पट्ठा *ullū kā paṭṭhā* 'owl's bairn' – a complete idiot. This contrasts with the owl's western association with wisdom (through a connection with Athena?).

उबलना *ubalnā* (intr.) to boil; उबला हुआ *ublā huā* boiled

उबालना ᴺ *ubālnā* (tr.) to boil

उभरना *ubharnā* to emerge, rise, well up

उमस *umas*ᶠ humidity, humid heat

उस *us* oblique of वह *vah*

उसका *uskā* his, her/hers, its

उस्ताद *ustād* (adj. & noun) skilled, skilful; ᴹ master, teacher; maestro (used as a title for Muslim musicians and artists)

## ऊ *ū*

ऊँचा *ũcā* high, tall; (of voice etc.) loud

ऊँट *ũṭ*^M camel

ऊन *ūn*^F wool

ऊनी *ūnī* woollen

ऊपर *ūpar* up, upstairs, above; ऊपरवाला *ūparvālā*^M 'the one above', God

ऊब *ūb*^F boredom

ऊबना *ūbnā* to be bored

एकता *ektā*^F unity

एकदम *ek dam* completely, utterly

एकवचन *ekvacan* singular (in grammar)

एकाएक *ekāek* suddenly

एकाध *ekādh* a few, one or two

एड़ी *eṛī*^F heel

एड्स *eḍs*^M AIDS

एतराज़ *etrāz*^M objection

**Insight**

ऊबना *ūbnā* in the sense of 'to be bored' is less common than the English loan बोर होना *bor honā*, which is well assimilated into Hindi.

ऊबड़-खाबड़ *ūbaṛ-khābaṛ* rough, bumpy

## ऋ *ṛ*

ऋण *ṛṇ*^M debt

ऋतु *ṛtu*^F season

ऋषि *ṛṣi*^M sage, seer

## ए *e*

एक *ek* one; a; एक एक करके *ek ek karke* one by one; एक साथ *ek sāth* together; -एक *-ek* (suffixed to number) about (e.g. दस-एक *das-ek* about ten, दो-एक *do-ek* one or two)

## ऐ *ai*

ऐतिहासिक *aitihāsik* historical

ऐनक *ainak*^F (pair of) glasses, spectacles

ऐश *aiś*^F pleasure, luxury

ऐसा *aisā* of this kind; ऐसा-वैसा *āisā-vaisā* so-so, mediocre

ऐसे *aise* in this way, thus; ऐसे ही *aise hī* for no particular reason, just casually

## ओ *o*

ओंठ[M] lip

ओढ़ना[N] *oṛhnā* to wrap, put on

ओझल *ojhal* out of sight, disappeared

ओर *or*[F] side, direction (see तरफ़ *taraf* for usages)

ओला *olā*[M] hail, hailstone

ओस *os*[F] dew

## औ *au*

औज़ार *auzār*[M] tool, implement

औपचारिक *aupcārik* formal; औपचारिक रूप से *aupcārik rūp se* formally

औपचारिकता *aupcāriktā*[F] formality

और *aur* and; more; और कुछ *aur kuch* something else; और कोई *aur koī* someone else; और तो और *aur to aur* other things apart; और भी *aur bhī* even more

औरत *aurat*[F] woman

औसत *ausat* (adj. & noun)[M] average

## क *ka*, क़ *qa*

कंकड़ *kaṅkaṛ*[M] a stone, pebble

कंजूस *kanjūs* (adj. & noun) mean;[M] miser

कंधा *kandhā*[M] shoulder

कंपनी *kampanī*[F] company, commercial firm

कंबल *kambal*[M] blanket

कई *kaī* several

कक्षा *kakṣā*[F] class (in school etc.)

कचहरी *kacahrī*[F] law court

कच्चा *kaccā* raw, half-baked/cooked, unripe; immature, untrained; unmetalled (of road)

कटना *kaṭnā* to be cut; to pass (of time)

कटोरी *kaṭorī*[F] small bowl

कट्टर *kaṭṭar* strict, fanatical

कट्टरपंथी *kaṭṭarpanthī* (adj. & noun) fanatical;[M] fanatic

कठिन *kaṭhin* hard, difficult

कठिनाई *kaṭhināī*[F] difficulty

कठोर *kaṭhor* hard, harsh

कड़वा *kaṛvā* bitter

कड़ा *kaṛā* hard, tough, strict, stern, rigid

कड़ाही *kaṛāhī*[F] frying pan

कतार *katār*[F] line

कथक *kathak*[M] name of a north Indian dance style

कथा *kathā*[F] story, tale

कथानक *kathānak*[M] narrative, plot

क़द *qad*[M] height, size, stature

क़दम *qadam*ᴹ step, pace

कन्या *kanyā*ᶠ girl, daughter

कपट *kapaṭ*ᴹ fraud, deceit

कपड़ा *kapṛā*ᴹ cloth; garment

कब *kab* when (interrogative)

कबूतर *kabūtar*ᴹ pigeon

कब्ज़ *kabz*ᶠ constipation

क़ब्र *qabra*ᶠ grave

कभी *kabhī* ever; कभी कभी *kabhī kabhī* कभी कभार *kabhī kabhār* sometimes; कभी नहीं *kabhī nahī̃* never

कम *kam* few, less; कम करना *kam karnā* ᴺ to reduce; कम से कम *kam se kam* at least; the smallest amount possible

कमज़ोर *kamzor* weak

कमज़ोरी *kamzorī*ᶠ weakness

कमर *kamar*ᶠ waist; कमर कसना/बाँधना *kamar kasnā*ᴺ / *bā̃dhnā*ᴺ to gird up the loins, prepare for action

कमरा *kamrā*ᴹ room

कमाई *kamāī*ᶠ earnings, income

कमाना *kamānā*ᴺ to earn

कमाल *kamāl*ᴹ wonder, miracle, astonishing feat

कमी *kamī*ᶠ lack, shortage

क़मीज़ *qamīz*ᶠ shirt

कम्प्यूटर *kampyūṭar*ᴹ computer

कर *kar*ᴹ tax

करना *karnā* ᴺ to do

करवाना *karvānā* ᴺ to cause to be done, to get done

क़रीब *qarīb* close, near

करोड़ *karoṛ*ᴹ a crore (ten million, i.e. a hundred lakhs: written 100,00,000)

क़र्ज़ *qarz*ᴹ debt, loan

कर्तव्य *kartavya*ᴹ duty

कर्म *karm*ᴹ action, deed, karma (fate determined by past deeds)

कर्मचारी *karmcārī*ᴹ employee, worker

कल *kal* yesterday; tomorrow

क़लम *qalam*ᴹ ⁽ᶠ⁾ pen

कला *kalā*ᶠ art

कलाई *kalāī* ᶠ wrist

कलाकार *kalākār*ᴹ artist

कलात्मक *kalātmak* artistic

कल्पना *kalpanā*ᶠ imagination

कल्पित *kalpit* imaginary

कवयित्री *kavayitrī* ᶠ poetess

कवि *kavi*ᴹ poet

कविता *kavitā*ᶠ poetry; poem

कष्ट *kaṣṭ*ᴹ trouble, inconvenience

कसना *kasnā* to tighten, be pulled tight; कसके *kaske* tightly, strongly

क़सम *qasam*^F oath; क़सम खाना *qasam khānā*^N to take an oath

कसरत *kasrat*^F exercise, training

क़साई *qasāī*^M butcher

कसूर *kasūr*^M fault, offence, guilt

कहना *kahnā*^N to say (to, से *se*); to call (इसको कुआँ कहते हैं *isko kuā̃ kahte haĩ* this is called a well, lit. 'they call this a well')

कहलाना *kahlānā* to be called

कहाँ *kahā̃* where?

कहानी *kahānī*^F story; short story (literary genre)

कहानीकार *kahānīkār*^M short story writer

कहावत *kahāvat*^F proverb, saying

कहीं *kahī̃* somewhere; somewhat; lest; कहीं और *kahī̃ aur* somewhere else; rather more; कहीं न कहीं *kahī̃ na kahī̃* somewhere or other; कहीं नहीं *kahī̃ nahī̃* nowhere; कहीं भी *kahī̃ bhī* anywhere

काँच *kā̃c*^M glass (the substance)

काँटा *kā̃ṭā*^M thorn; fork

काँपना *kā̃pnā* to tremble, shiver

का-की-के *kā–kī–ke* (postposition that shows possession, like English 'apostrophe s', e.g. मोहन की बहिन *mohan kī bahin*^F Mohan's sister)

काका *kākā*^M uncle (father's younger brother)

काकी *kākī*^F aunt (wife of father's younger brother)

काग़ज़ *kāgaz*^M paper; sheet of paper

काजू *kājū*^M cashew

काटना *kāṭnā*^N to cut

कान *kān*^M ear

काना *kānā* (adj. & noun) one eyed;^M one-eyed person

क़ानून *qānūn*^M law

कॉपी *kāpī*^F copy book, exercise-book

काफ़ी *kāfī* quite, very; enough

कॉफ़ी *kāfī*^F coffee

क़ाबू *qābū*^M power, control, hold

काम *kām*^M work; job of work, task; काम करना *kām karnā*^N to work; काम का होना *kām kā honā* to be of use

काम-चलाऊ *kām-calāū* make do

कामचोर *kāmcor* workshy, lazy

कामना *kāmnā*^F desire; lust

कामयाब *kāmyāb* successful

कामयाबी *kāmyābī*^F success

कार *kār*^F car

कारख़ाना *kār<u>kh</u>ānā*^M factory, workshop

कारण *kāraṇ*^M reason, cause

कार्य *kārya*[M] work, action, task

कार्यक्रम *kāryakram*[M] schedule, programme, plan of action

कार्यालय *kāryālay*[M] office

काल *kāl*[M] time, age, period; grammatical tense

काला *kālā* black

कालेज *kālej*[M] college

काश *kāś* would that, if only, how I would like…

किंतु *kintu* but

कि *ki* that (as conjunction); or; whether; when suddenly

कितना *kitnā* how much/many?

किताब *kitāb*[F] book

किधर *kidhar* where? which way?

किन *kin* plural of किस *kis*

किनारा *kinārā*[M] bank, edge

किफ़ायत *kifāyat*[F] economy, saving

किरण *kiraṇ*[F (M)] ray, beam

किराया *kirāyā*[M] rent, fare

किरायेदार *kirāyedār*[M] tenant

क़िला *qilā*[M] fort

किलो *kilo*[M] kilo

किलोमीटर *kilomīṭar*[M] kilometre

किस *kis* oblique of क्या *kyā*, and of कौन *kaun*; किस तरह *kis tarah* how?; किस लिए *kis lie* for what (reason)?, why?; किस समय *kis samay* at what time?

किसका *kiskā* whose?

किसान *kisān*[M] farmer, peasant

किसी *kisī* oblique of कोई *koī*

क़िस्त *qist*[F] instalment (partial payment); episode (in serial)

क़िस्म *qism*[F] sort, kind, manner

क़िस्मत *qismat*[F] fate

क़िस्सा *qissā*[M] story, tale

की ओर *kī or* towards

की ख़ातिर *kī khātir* out of consideration for, for the sake of

की तरफ़ *kī taraf* towards

की तरह *kī tarah* like, in the manner of

की तुलना में *kī tulnā mẽ* in comparison with

की बग़ल में *kī bagal mẽ* next to

की वजह से *kī vajah se* because of

की हैसियत से *kī haisiyat se* in the capacity of

कीचड़ *kīcaṛ*[F] mud, mire

कीड़ा *kīṛā*[M] insect, bug; rot, decomposition

क़ीमत *qīmat*[F] price, cost, value

क़ीमती *qīmtī* costly, valuable

कील *kīl*[M] nail, peg

कुआँ *kuā̃* (oblique कुएँ *kuẽ*)[M] well

कुछ *kuch* some; something; somewhat, rather; कुछ और *kuch aur* some more; कुछ नहीं *kuch nahī̃* nothing; कुछ भी नहीं *kuch bhī nahī̃* nothing at all

कुत्ता *kuttā*[M] dog

कुरता *kurtā*[M] kurta, loose shirt

कुरसी *kursī*[F] chair

कुल *kul*[M] total amount; कुल मिलाकर *kul milākar* all together, in total

कुली *kulī*[M] porter

कूदना *kūdna* to jump, leap

कृतज्ञ *kṛtajña* (pronounced 'kṛtagya') grateful

कृतज्ञता *kṛtajñatā* (pronounced 'kṛtagyatā')[F] gratitude

कृपया *kṛpayā* please

कृपा *kṛpā*[F] kindness, grace; कृपा करके *kṛpā karke* please; आपकी कृपा है *āpkī kṛpā hai* it's kind of you, thank you

केंद्र *kendra*[M] centre

के अंदर *ke andar* inside

**Insight**

के अंदर *ke andar* – not to be confused with के अंडर *ke aṇḍar*, a loan from English 'under', as in वह डाक्टर वर्मा के अंडर पी. एच. डी. कर रही है *vah ḍākṭar Varmā ke aṇḍar PhD kar rahī hai*, 'she is doing a PhD under Dr Varma'.

कुशल *kuśal* (adj. & noun) skilful; happy, blessed by good fortune;[M] well being

कुशलपूर्वक *kuśalpūrvak* safely

कुहनी *kuhnī*[F] elbow

कुहरा *kuhrā*[M] fog

कूटनीति *kūṭnīti*[F] diplomacy

कूटनीतिज्ञ *kūṭnītijña*[M] (pronounced 'kūṭnītigya') diplomat

कूड़ा *kūṛā*[M] rubbish, trash

कूड़ेदान *kūṛedān*[M] rubbish bin, trashcan

के अनुसार *ke anusār* according to

के अलावा *ke alāvā* as well as

के आगे *ke āge* ahead of, in front of

के आस-पास *ke ās-pās* in the vicinity of

के ऊपर *ke ūpar* above, on top of

के कारण *ke kāraṇ* because of

के ख़िलाफ़ *ke khilāf* against

के चारों ओर/तरफ़ *ke cārõ or/taraf* all around

के ज़रिये *ke zariye* through, by means of

के तहत *ke tahat* under, subject to

के दौरान *ke daurān* during

के द्वारा *ke dvārā* by

के नज़दीक *ke nazdīk* near

के नीचे *ke nīce* below, under

के पहले *ke pahle* before

के पार *ke pār* across

के पास *ke pās* near; in the possession of; to (e.g. किसी के पास जाना *kisī ke pās jānā* to go *to* a person)

के पूर्व *ke pūrv* before

के बजाय *ke bajāy* instead of, in place of

के बदले में *ke badle mẽ* instead of, in place of, in exchange for

के बाद *ke bād* after

के बारे में *ke bāre mẽ* about, concerning

के बावजूद *ke bāvjūd* in spite of

के बाहर *ke bāhar* outside

के बिना *ke binā* without

के बीच में *ke bīc mẽ* in the middle of, between, among

के माध्यम से *ke mādhyam se* through, by means of

के मारे *ke māre* stricken by; डर के मारे *ḍar ke māre* out of/ because of fear

के मुक़ाबले में *ke muqāble mẽ* in comparison with

के यहाँ *ke yahā̃* at the place of

के लिए *ke lie* for

के विरुद्ध *ke viruddh* against

के समान *ke samān* like, equal to

के साथ *ke sāth* with, in company of

के सामने *ke sāmne* opposite

के सिवा *ke sivā,* के सिवाय *ke sivāy* except for, but for

केतली *ketlī*^F kettle

केला *kelā*^M banana

केवल *keval* only

कैंची *kaĩcī*^F scissors

कैमरा *kaimrā*^M camera

कैसा *kaisā* how? (in health); what like? of what kind?

कैसे *kaise* how? in what manner?

को *ko* to; on (a date etc.); (also can mark an indirect or direct object)

कोई *koī* any, some; somebody; (with number) about; कोई न कोई *koī na koī* someone or other; कोई नहीं *koī nahī̃* nobody; कोई बात नहीं *koī bāt nahī̃* never mind; it doesn't matter; don't mention it

कोठा *koṭhā*ᴹ large (upstairs) room; warehouse; brothel

कोठी *koṭhī*ᶠ large house; bungalow

कोना *konā*ᴹ corner

कोमल *komal* soft, delicate; flat (of musical note)

कोयला *koylā*ᴹ coal

कोरा *korā* blank

कोशिश *kośiś*ᶠ attempt; (की) कोशिश करना (*kī*) *kośiś karnā*ᴺ to try

कोसना *kosnā* ᴺ to curse

कोहनी *kohnī*ᶠ elbow

कौन *kaun* who?

कौनसा *kaunsā* which?

क्या *kyā* what? (also converts a following statement into a 'yes/no' question, as in क्या तुम ठीक हो? *kyā tum ṭhīk ho?* 'are you OK?'); क्या बात है! *kyā bāt hai!* brilliant! wonderful! (lit. 'what a [fine] thing it is!'); क्या हुआ *kyā huā* what happened?; so what?

क्यों *kyõ* why

क्योंकि *kyõki* because

क्रम *kram*ᴹ order, sequence

क्रमश: *kramśaḥ* gradually, in proper sequence, respectively

क्रांति *krānti*ᶠ revolution

क्रांतिकारी *krāntikārī* (adj. & noun)ᴹ revolutionary

क्रिकेट *kriketַ*ᴹ cricket

क्रिया *kriyā*ᶠ action; verb

क्रिया-विशेषण *kriyā-viśeṣaṇ*ᴹ adverb

क्लास *klās*ᶠ class (in college etc.)

क्षण *kṣaṇ*ᴹ moment

क्षमता *kṣamtā*ᶠ capacity; ability

क्षमा *kṣamā*ᶠ pardon, forgiveness

क्षेत्र *kṣetra*ᴹ area, zone; sphere of action

## ख *kha*, ख़ *kha*

खंडहर *khaṇḍ'har*ᴹ ruin, ruined building, ruins

खच्चर *khaccar*ᴹ mule

खट्टा *khaṭṭā* sour

खड़ा *khaṛā* standing, upright; (of vehicles) parked; खड़ा करना *khaṛā karnā* ᴺ to park; खड़ा होना *khaṛā honā* to stand

खड़ी बोली *khaṛī bolī*ᶠ Khari Boli, the dialect on which modern standard Hindi and Urdu are based

ख़त *khat*ᴹ letter (correspondence)

ख़तरनाक *khatarnāk* dangerous

ख़तरा *khatrā*ᴹ danger; ख़तरे से ख़ाली *khatre se khālī* free from danger, safe

ख़त्म *khatm* finished; ख़त्म करना *khatm karnā* [N] to finish

ख़बर *khabar*[F] news, news item, information

ख़बरदार *khabardār* beware! watch out!

ख़याल *khayāl*[M] opinion, thought, idea

ख़रगोश *khargoś*[M] rabbit, hare

ख़राब *kharāb* bad, faulty

ख़राबी *kharābī*[F] fault, defect

ख़राश *kharāś*[F] hoarseness, irritation (of the throat)

ख़रीदना *kharīdnā*[N] to buy, purchase

ख़रोंच *kharõc*[F] scratch

ख़र्च *kharc*[M] expenditure; ख़र्च करना *kharc karnā* [N] to spend

ख़र्चा *kharcā*[M] expense, outlay

खलनायक *khalnāyak*[M] villain (in drama)

खाँसना *khā̃snā* to cough

खाँसी *khāsī*[F] cough

खाट *khāṭ*[F] bedstead, 'cot'

खाता *khātā*[M] ledger, account book

खादी *khādī*[F] homespun cloth

खान *khān*[F] mine, quarry

ख़ानदान *khāndān*[M] family, lineage

ख़ानदानी *khāndānī* ancestral, hereditary

खाना[1] *khānā*[M] food

खाना[2] *khānā*[N] to eat; to take, be the target for (a bullet, an insult)

ख़ाना *khānā*[M] place of work or activity (e.g. डाकख़ाना *ḍākkhānā*[M] post office); chamber of a gun; square on a chessboard; compartment

ख़ामोश *khāmoś* silent, quiet

ख़ामोशी *khāmośī*[F] silence, quietness

ख़ाली *khālī* empty, free, vacant; ख़ाली-हाथ *khālī-hāth* empty-handed

ख़ास *khās* special, particular; ख़ास तौर पर *khās taur par* specially, particularly

ख़ासियत *khāsiyat*[F] special feature, characteristic

खिड़की *khiṛkī*[F] window

खिलाना *khilānā*[N] to feed, give to eat

खिलौना *khilaunā*[M] toy

खिसकना *khisaknā* to slip away

खींचना *khī̃cnā*[N] to drag, pull; to draw, to take (photograph)

खीर *khīr*[F] a milky 'rice pudding' flavoured with cardamom

खीरा *khīrā*ᴹ cucumber

खुजली *khujlī*ᶠ itch, itchiness

ख़ुद *<u>kh</u>ud* oneself ('myself', 'yourself' etc.)

खुलकर *khulkar* openly

खुलना *khulnā* to open, be opened

खुला *khulā* open; खुले आम *khule ām* openly, in the open

ख़ुश *<u>kh</u>uś* pleased, happy

ख़ून *<u>kh</u>ūn*ᴹ blood; murder; ख़ून करना *<u>kh</u>ūn karnā* ᴺ to murder

ख़ूब *<u>kh</u>ūb* (adj. & adverb) good, nice; very well, brilliantly, proficiently, fully

ख़ूबसूरत *<u>kh</u>ūbsūrat* beautiful

ख़ूबसूरती *<u>kh</u>ūbsūrtī*ᶠ beauty

ख़ूबी *<u>kh</u>ūbī*ᶠ quality, point of excellence

**Insight**

ख़ुश *khuś* has the antonym बद *bad*, as in बदक़िस्मत *badqismat* 'unfortunate' and बदबू *badbū*ᶠ 'unpleasant smell, stink'.

ख़ुशक़िस्मत *<u>kh</u>uśqismat* fortunate

ख़ुशक़िस्मती *<u>kh</u>uśqismatī*ᶠ good luck, good fortune

ख़ुशख़बरी *<u>kh</u>uś<u>kh</u>abarī*ᶠ good news, glad tidings

ख़ुशबू *<u>kh</u>uśbū*ᶠ fragrance, pleasant smell; ख़ुशबूदार *<u>kh</u>uśbūdār* fragrant

ख़ुशहाल *<u>kh</u>uśhāl* well-to-do, prosperous

ख़ुशहाली *<u>kh</u>uśhālī*ᶠ prosperity

ख़ुशी *<u>kh</u>uśī*ᶠ pleasure, happiness; ख़ुशी से *<u>kh</u>uśī se* with pleasure, happily; ख़ुशियाँ मनाना ᴺ *<u>kh</u>uśiyā̃ manānā* to celebrate

खूँटी *khū̃ṭī*ᶠ peg

खेत *khet*ᴹ field, farming land

खेती-बाड़ी *khetī-bāṛī*ᶠ farming, agriculture

खेद *khed*ᴹ regret

खेल *khel*ᴹ game; खेल-कूद *khel-kūd*ᴹ sports

खेलना *khelnā* ᴺ to play (game)

ख़ैर *<u>kh</u>air* anyway, well, so much for that (draws a line under a topic)

खोट *khoṭ*ᴹ fault, defect

खोटा *khoṭā* fake, counterfeit, defective

खोदना *khodnā* ᴺ to dig

खोना *khonā* (intr.) to be lost; (tr.)ᴺ to lose

खोपड़ी *khoprī*^F shell (of coconut etc.); skull; head

खोया *khoyā*^M reduced milk (used in making sweets etc.)

खोलना^N *kholnā* to open, loosen, untie

ख़्याल *khyāl*: see ख़याल *khyāl*

ख़्वाब *khvāb*^M dream; ख़्वाब देखना *khvāb dekhnā*^N to dream, to have a dream

## ग *ga*, ग़ *ga*

गंगा *gaṅgā*^F Ganges

गढ़ *gaṛh*^M fort

गढ़ना *gaṛhnā*^N to mould, form, create

गणित *gaṇit*^M mathematics

गति *gati*^F speed, motion, gait; state

गद्दा *gaddā*^M mattress

गद्दी *gaddī*^M cushion; cushioned seat, throne

गद्य *gadya*^M prose

गधा *gadhā*^M donkey, ass; fool

गप *gap*^F chat; गप मारना *gap mārnā*^N to chat

**Insight**

गंगा *gangā* is the most sacred of India's rivers and is worshipped as a goddess (all rivers are female and their names are feminine nouns).

गंजा *ganjā* bald

गंदा *gandā* dirty; vile, horrible

गंभीर *gambhīr* serious, profound

गँवाना *gãvānā*^N to waste, squander

गज़ *gaz*^M yard (measure of length); bow (for a fiddle)

ग़ज़ब का *gazab kā* stupendous, amazing, wonderful

गड़बड़ *gaṛbaṛ* (adj. & noun) confused, muddled;^M (F) confusion, muddle, agitation

गड्ढा *gaḍḍhā*^M pit, ditch, hole

गपशप *gapśap*^F gossip

ग़म *gam*^M sorrow, care; ग़म खाना *gam khānā*^N to endure sorrow, to swallow grief

गमला *gamlā*^M flowerpot

गरज *garaj*^F thunder, roar

गरदन *gardan*^F neck

गरम *garam* hot, warm

गरमी *garmī*^F heat; गरमियाँ *garmiyā̃*^FPL summer

ग़रीब *garīb* poor

ग़रीबी *garībī*^F poverty

गर्भ *garbh*ᴹ womb; गर्भ से होना *garbh se honā* to be pregnant

गर्भवती *garbhvatī* pregnant

गर्व *garv*ᴹ pride

ग़लत *galat* wrong, incorrect

ग़लती *galtī*ᶠ error, mistake

गला *galā*ᴹ throat; voice; गला बैठना *galā baiṭhnā* to go hoarse; गले लगाना *gale lagānā* to hug, embrace

गली *galī*ᶠ lane, alley, narrow street

गवाह *gavāh*ᴹ witness

गवाही *gavāhī*ᶠ evidence, testimony

गहरा *gahrā* deep

गहराई *gahrāī*ᶠ depth; deep place, profundity

गाँठ *gā̃ṭh*ᶠ knot

गाँव *gā̃v*ᴹ village

गाजर *gājar*ᶠ carrot

गाड़ना *gāṛnā*ᴺ to sink, drive, bury, stick in

गाड़ी *gāṛī*ᶠ car; train; vehicle

गाढ़ा *gāṛhā* thick, dense, viscous; deep (in colour) strong (of tea etc.)

गाना[1] *gānā*ᴹ song, singing

गाना[2] *gānā*ᴺ to sing

गाय *gāy*ᶠ cow

गायक *gāyak*ᴹ singer

ग़ायब *gāyab* missing, absent, disappeared

गाल *gāl*ᶠ cheek

गाली *gālī*ᶠ abusive language, swear word; गाली देना *gālī denā*ᴺ to abuse, swear at

गिनना *ginnā*ᴺ to count

गिरजाघर *girjāghar*ᴹ church

गिरना *girnā* to fall, drop

गिरफ़्तार करना *giraftār karnā*ᴺ to arrest

गिराना *girānā*ᴺ to make/ let fall, drop

गिलहरी *gilahrī*ᶠ squirrel

गिलास *gilās*ᴹ tumbler, 'glass' (made of glass or metal)

गीत *gīt*ᴹ song

गीला *gīlā* wet, damp

गुंजाइश *gunjāiś*ᶠ scope, room

गुंडा *gunḍā*ᴹ lout, yob, thug, hooligan

गुंडागर्दी *gunḍāgardī*ᶠ thuggish behaviour

गुज़रना *guzarnā* to pass through/ by; to pass (of time); गुज़र जाना *guzar jānā* to pass away

गुजरात *gujarāt*ᴹ Gujarat

गुज़ारना *guzārnā*ᴺ to pass, spend (time)

गुज़ारा *guzārā*ᴹ livelihood, subsistence

गुठली *guṭhlī*ᶠ pit, stone (of fruit)

गुण *guṇ*ᴹ quality, virtue

गुप्त *gupt* secret, hidden

गुफा *guphā*ᶠ cave

गुब्बारा *gubbārā*ᴹ balloon

गुरु *guru*ᴹ guru, teacher

गुरुवार *guruvār*ᴹ Thursday

गुलाब *gulāb*ᴹ rose

गुलाबी *gulābī* pink

गुलाम *gulām*ᴹ slave

गुलामी *gulāmī*ᶠ slavery

गुसलख़ाना *gusal<u>kh</u>ānā*ᴹ bathroom

गुस्ताख़ *gustā<u>kh</u>* rude

गुस्ताख़ी *gustā<u>kh</u>ī*ᶠ rudeness, impertinence

गुस्सा *gussā* (adj. & noun) angry;ᴹ anger

गूंगा *gū̃gā* dumb

गूँज *gū̃j*ᶠ echo, hum

गूँजना *gū̃jnā* to echo, hum, reverberate

गूढ़ *gūṛh* hidden, mysterious

गेंद *gẽd*ᶠ ball

गेहूँ *gehū̃*ᴹ wheat

ग़ैरक़ानूनी *gairqānūnī* illegal

ग़ैरहाज़िर *gairhāzir* absent

ग़ैरहाज़िरी *gairhāzirī*ᶠ absence

ग़ोता *gotā*ᴹ dive, diving; गोता लगाना ᴺ *gotā lagānā* to dive

ग़ोताख़ोर *gotā<u>kh</u>or*ᴹ diver

गोद *god*ᶠ lap, embrace (as a babe in arms)

गोबर *gobar*ᴹ cow dung

गोभी *gobhī*ᶠ cabbage

गोरा *gorā* fair skinned; (adj. & noun)ᴹ 'white' person (unflattering usage!)

गोल *gol* (adj. & noun) round;ᴹ a sphere

गोल-चक्कर *gol-cakkar*ᴹ roundabout (on road)

गोली *golī*ᶠ tablet, pill; bullet; गोली मारना *golī mārnā*ᴺ to shoot

गोश्त *gośt*ᴹ meat

गोष्ठी *goṣṭhī*ᶠ seminar, meeting

ग़ौर *gaur*ᴹ attention; ग़ौर से *gaur se* attentively, closely

गौरव *gaurav*ᴹ pride

ग्यारह *gyārah* eleven

ग्राम *grām*ᴹ village (mostly used in compounds such as ग्राम-विकास *grām-vikās*ᴹ village/rural development)

ग्रामीण *grāmīṇ* (adj. & noun) rural;ᴹ villager

ग्राहक *grāhak*ᴹ customer

## घ *gha*

घंटा *ghaṇṭā*M hour

घंटी *ghaṇṭī*F bell

घसीटना *ghasīṭnā* N to drag

घाट *ghāṭ*M river steps, bank, landing place

घायल *ghāyal* wounded

**Insight**

घंटा *ghaṇṭā* — the original sense is 'bell, large bell' (one that chimes the hours). PairedM and F versions of a word often indicate large/small pairs: घंटा/घंटी *ghaṇṭā/ghaṇṭī*, गद्दा/ गद्दी *gaddā/gaddī*, etc.

घटना[1] *ghaṭnā*F event

घटना[2] *ghaṭnā* to lessen, decrease

घटाना *ghaṭānā* N to decrease, reduce, make less

घटिया *ghaṭiyā* (-*ā* invariable) of poor quality, cheap, inferior

घड़ी *ghaṛī*F clock, watch

घना *ghanā* thick, dense

घनिष्ठ *ghaniṣṭh* intimate, close

घनिष्ठता *ghaniṣṭhtā*F intimacy

घबराना *ghabrānā* to worry, be anxious

घमंड *ghamaṇḍ*M pride, conceit, arrogance

घर *ghar*M house, home; घर पर *ghar par* at home; घर की मुर्ग़ी साग बराबर *ghar kī murgī sāg barābar* 'chicken (cooked) at home counts as greens', i.e. familiarity breeds contempt

घरेलू *gharelū* domestic, to do with home

घास *ghās*F grass

घिरना *ghirnā* to be surrounded, encircled

घिसा-पिटा *ghisā-piṭā* worn out, overworked, hackneyed

घी *ghī*M ghee

घुटना *ghuṭnā*M knee

घुमाना *ghumānā* N to turn, revolve; to take on a tour, show around

घुसना *ghusnā* to enter (illicitly), to sneak into

घूँघट *ghũghaṭ*F veil, sari end

घूँट *ghũṭ*M gulp, draught, mouthful (of liquid), sip

घूँस *ghũs*F bribe; घूँस खाना N *ghũs khānā* to take a bribe

घूमना *ghūmnā* to turn; to tour, wander about

घृणा *ghṛṇā*F hatred

घेरना *ghernā* N to surround, encircle

घेरा *gherā*ᴹ siege; ring; enclosure

घोंटना *ghõṭnā*ᴺ to squeeze, strangle

घोंसला *ghõslā*ᴹ nest

घोड़ा *ghoṛā*ᴹ horse

## च *ca*

चंद *cand* a few

चंदा *candā*ᴹ subscription

चंद्र *candra*ᴹ moon

चंद्रबिंदु *candrabindu*ᴹ 'moon dot', the Devanagari sign ँ that indicates a nasalized vowel (as in हाँ *hã* 'yes')

चखना *cakhnā*ᴺ to taste

चचेरा भाई *cacerā bhāī*ᴹ cousin (son of father's brother)

चचेरी बहिन *cacerī bahin*ᶠ cousin (daughter of father's brother)

चटनी *caṭnī*ᶠ chutney

चढ़ना *caṛhnā* to climb, mount, ascend; to get into vehicle

चढ़ाव *caṛhāv*ᴹ rise, incline

चना *canā*ᴹ chickpea

चपाती *capātī*ᶠ chapati

चप्पल *cappal*ᶠ sandal

चबाना *cabānā*ᴺ to chew

चमकना *camaknā* to shine

चमचा *camcā*ᴹ spoon; a sycophant, flatterer

चमड़ा *camṛā*ᴹ leather

चमड़ी *camṛī*ᶠ skin

चम्मच *cammac*ᴹ spoon

चरना *carnā*ᴺ to graze

चरबी *carbī*ᶠ fat (part of meat), grease

चलना *calnā* to move, blow, flow; चल पड़ना *cal paṛnā* to set out; चल बसना *cal basnā* to die

चला आना *calā ānā* to come away; चला जाना *calā jānā* to go away

चलाना *calānā*ᴺ to drive; to run (a business etc.)

चवालीस *cavālīs* forty-four

चश्मा *caśmā*ᴹ (pair of) glasses, spectacles

चहकना *cahaknā* to sing, tweet (of birds)

चाँद *cā̃d*ᴹ moon

चाँदनी *cā̃dnī*ᶠ moonlight; चाँदनी रात *cā̃dnī rāt*ᶠ moonlit night

चाँदी *cā̃dī*ᶠ silver

चाक़ू *cāqū*ᴹ knife, penknife

चाचा *cācā*ᴹ uncle (father's younger brother)

चाची *cācī*ᶠ aunt (wife of father's younger brother)

चादर *cādar*$^{F}$ sheet, bedsheet

चाबी *cābī*$^{F}$ key

चाबुक *cābuk*$^{M}$ whip

चाय *cāy*$^{F}$ tea

चार *cār* four; (के) चारों ओर/तरफ़ *(ke) cārõ or/taraf* all around, surrounding

चाल *cāl*$^{F}$ gait, pace, movement

चालक *cālak*$^{M}$ driver

चालाक *cālāk* clever, cunning

चालान *cālān*$^{F}$ booking, committal (of a miscreant)

चालाकी *cālākī*$^{F}$ cunning

चालू *cālū* current, active; cunning, devious, slick

चावल *cāval*$^{M}$ rice

चाहना *cāhnā*$^{N}$ to want, wish; to like, love; (in perfective tense with ने *ne*) to try

चाहिए *cāhie* (is) wanted, needed

चिकना *ciknā* oily, sleek, smooth

चिट्ठी *ciṭṭhī*$^{F}$ letter, note

चिड़िया *ciṛiyā*$^{F}$ bird

चिड़ियाघर *ciṛiyāghar*$^{M}$ zoo

चिढ़ना *ciṛhnā* to be irritated

चिढ़ाना *ciṛhānā*$^{N}$ to irritate, annoy

चित्र *citra*$^{M}$ picture

चित्रकार *citrakār*$^{M}$ artist

चिथड़ा *cithṛā* (adj. & noun) tattered;$^{M}$ rag

चिन्ह *cinh*: see चिह्न *cihn*

चिमटा *cimṭā*$^{M}$ tongs

चिल्लाना *cillānā* to call, call out

चिह्न *cihn*$^{M}$ sign, mark, emblem

चींटी *cı̃ṭī*$^{F}$ ant

चीख़ना *cīkhnā*$^{M}$ to scream

चीज़ *cīz*$^{F}$ thing

चीता *cītā*$^{M}$ leopard, cheetah

**Insight**

चाहिए *cāhie* – as its meaning 'is wanted/needed' indicates, this form is an old passive (of the verb चाहना *cāhnā*) – an archaic form surviving in the modern language.

चाहे...चाहे *cāhe...cāhe* whether...or

चिंतन *cintan*$^{M}$ thought, reflection

चिंता *cintā*$^{F}$ anxiety, worry, concern

चीन *cīn*$^{M}$ China

चीनी[1] *cīnī*$^{F}$ sugar

चीनी[2] *cīnī* Chinese

चुंबन *cumban*$^{M}$ kiss, kissing

चुकना *cuknā* to have already done, finished doing (with verb stem: वह जा चुका है *vah jā cukā hai* 'he's already gone')

चुनना *cunnā*ᴺ to choose, select

चुनाव *cunāv*ᴹ election, selection, choice

चुनौती *cunautī*ᶠ challenge

चुप *cup* quiet, silent (not speaking)

चुपके से *cupke se* quietly

चुस्ती *custī*ᶠ smartness, agility

चूँकि *cū̃ki* since, because

चूड़ी *cūṛī*ᶠ bangle

चूतड़ *cūtaṛ*ᴹ bottom, buttocks

चूमना *cūmnā*ᴺ to kiss

चूर्ण *cūrṇ* (adj. & noun) crushed;ᴹ powder; digestive powder

चूसना *cūsnā*ᴺ to suck

चूहा *cūhā*ᴹ mouse, rat

चेचक *cecak*ᶠ smallpox

चेतावनी *cetāvanī*ᶠ warning

चेहरा *cehrā*ᴹ face

चोट *coṭ*ᶠ blow, injury, hurt; चोट लगना *coṭ lagnā* to get hurt

चोर *cor*ᴹ thief

चोरी *corī*ᶠ theft; चोरी होना *corī honā* theft to occur; to be stolen

चौंकना *caũknā* to be startled

चौंतीस *caũtīs* thirty-four

चौंसठ *caũsaṭh* sixty-four

चौक *cauk*ᴹ town square, marketplace

चौका *caukā*ᴹ eating/cooking space

चौकीदार *caukīdār*ᴹ watchman

चौकोन *caukon* (adj. & noun)ᴹ square

चौड़ा *cauṛā* wide, broad

चौड़ाई *cauṛāī*ᶠ width, breadth

चौथा *cauthā* fourth

चौथाई *cauthāī*ᶠ a quarter

चौदह *caudah* fourteen

चौबीस *caubīs* twenty-four

चौरानवे *caurānve* ninety-four

चौरासी *caurāsī* eighty-four

चौराहा *caurāhā*ᴹ crossroads

चौवन *cauvan* fifty-four

चौहत्तर *cauhattar* seventy-four

## छ *cha*

छँटना *chā̃ṭnā* to be pruned, trimmed, sorted; छँटा हुआ चोर *chā̃ṭā huā cor* a select thief, a fine example of a thief

छंद *chand*ᴹ poetic metre

छठा *chaṭhā* sixth

छत *chat*ᶠ roof

छत्तीस *chattīs* thirty-six

छपना *chapnā* to be printed

छप्पन *chappan* fifty-six

छब्बीस *chabbīs* twenty-six

छलकना *chalaknā* to splash, spill

छलकाना *chalkānā*^N to spill

छलाँग *chalā̃g*^F leap; छलाँग मारना *chalā̃g mārnā*^N to leap

छह *chah* six

छाता *chātā*^M umbrella

छाती *chātī*^F chest

छात्र *chātr*^M student

छात्रवृत्ति *chātravṛtti*^F scholarship, grant

छात्रा *chātrā*^F student

छियानवे *chiyānve* ninety-six

छियालीस *chiyālīs* forty-six

छियासठ *chiyāsaṭh* sixty-six

छियासी *chiyāsī* eighty-six

छिलका *chilkā*^M skin, peel, shell

छिहत्तर *chihattar* seventy-six

छींकना *chī̃knā* to sneeze

छीनना *chīnnā*^N to snatch

छीलना *chīlnā*^N to peel, pare

छुटकारा *chuṭkārā*^M release, freedom

छुट्टी *chuṭṭī*^F holiday; free time, time off

छुरी *churī*^F knife

**Insight**

छात्र *chātra*^M student, छात्रा *chātrā*^F student. Sanskrit loanwords ending in-*ā* are feminine (unlike vernacular Hindi nouns such as कमरा *kamrā* or लड़का *laṛkā*).

छाप *chāp*^F mark, stamp, brand

छापना *chāpnā*^N to print

छापा *chāpā*^M raid; छापा मारना *chāpā mārnā*^N to raid

छाया *chāyā*^F shadow, shade, reflection

छिड़ना *chiṛnā* to start up, a tune to sound (on an instrument); to break out (war)

छिपना *chipnā* to be hidden, to hide

छिपाना *chipānā*^N to hide, conceal

छूटना *chūṭnā* to leave (of a train etc.); to be left behind

छूना *chūnā*^N to touch

छेड़ना *cheṛnā*^N to stir up, instigate, irritate

छेद *ched*^M hole, crack, cut

छोटा *choṭā* small; छोटा-मोटा *choṭā-moṭā* minor, various, insignificant

छोड़ना *choṛnā*^N to leave, abandon, give up; को छोड़कर *ko choṛkar* apart from

## ज *ja*, ज़ *za*

जंगल *jaṅgal*ᴹ jungle, forest, the wilds

जंगला *jaṅglā*ᴹ grille, grating, lattice

जंगली *jaṅglī* wild

ज़ंजीर *zanjīr*ᶠ chain

जँभाई *jãbhāī*ᶠ yawn; जँभाई लेना *jãbhāī lenā*ᴺ to yawn

ज़ख़म *zakhm*ᴹ wound; ज़ख़म खाना *zakhm khānā*ᴺ to receive a wound, be wounded

ज़ख़मी *zakhmī* wounded

जगत् *jagat*ᶠ the world, universe

जगह *jagah*ᶠ place

जगाना *jagānā*ᴺ to awaken, arouse from sleep

जटिल *jaṭil* complex, complicated, involved

जड़ना *jaṛnā*ᴺ (intr. & tr.) to fix, stick on; to set, inlay

जड़ी *jaṛī*ᶠ medicinal herb

जड़ी-बूटी *jaṛī-būṭī*ᶠ medicinal herbs and roots

जन *jan*ᴹ person; people

जनता *jantā*ᶠ the people, the public (singular usage)

जनवरी *janvarī*ᶠ January

जना *janā*ᴹ person

जनाब *janāb* 'sir'

जन्म *janma*ᴹ birth; life in a sequence of lives (through rebirth)

जन्मदिन *janmadin*ᴹ birthday

जप *jap*ᴹ repeating (the name of God), telling (the rosary)

जपना *japnā*ᴺ to repeat (the name of God), to tell (the rosary), to chant

जब *jab* when; जब कि *jab ki* while, while on the other hand; जब तक *jab tak* until; जब भी *jab bhī* whenever; जब से *jab se* since the time when

जबड़ा *jabṛā*ᴹ jaw

ज़ंग *zaṅg*ᴹ rust

ज़बरदस्त *zabardast* powerful, vigorous, high-handed

ज़बरदस्ती *zabardastī*ᶠ high-handedness; ज़बरदस्ती से *zabardastī se* high-handedly, unjustly, unfairly

ज़बान *zabān*ᶠ tongue, language

जमा *jamā* (-*ā* invariable) collected, gathered, deposited, submitted

ज़माना *zamānā*ᴹ period, time

ज़मींदार *zamī̃dār*ᴹ landowner

ज़मीन *zamīn*ᶠ land

जय *jay*ᶠ victory; गांधीजी की जय! *gāndhījī kī jay!* victory to Gandhiji! (long live Gandhiji!)

ज़रा *zarā* a little, somewhat (ज़रा गरम *zarā garam* a little hot); just (ज़रा यह पकड़ो *zarā yah pakṛo* just hold this)

ज़रूर *zarūr* of course

ज़रूरत *zarūrat*[F] need

ज़रूरी *zarūrī* necessary, urgent

जल *jal*[M] water

जलना *jalnā* to burn; to feel jealous (of, *se*)

जलवायु *jalvāyu*[F] climate

जलाना *jalānā*[N] to light, to burn

जल्दबाज़ी *jaldbāzī*[F] haste, impetuousness

जल्दी *jaldī* (adverb & noun) quickly, early;[F] hurry

जवान *javān* (adj. & noun) young;[M] young man; soldier

जवानी *javānī*[F] youth, period of young adulthood

जाँचना *jā̃cnā*[F] to test, examine, assess

जागना *jāgnā* to be awake

जाड़ा *jāṛā*[M] cold; cold season

जाति *jāti*[F] caste, type, species, race

जातीय *jātīy* racial

जादू *jādū*[M] magic

जादूगर *jādūgar*[M] magician

जादूगरी *jādūgarī*[F] magic, magical arts

जान *jān*[F] life, soul, spirit; dear one, beloved; जान निकलना *jān nikalnā* life to leave, to be in great agony; जान बची तो लाखों पाए *jān bacī to lākhõ pāe* 'to survive is to acquire lakhs', i.e. just to survive is an accomplishment in itself

**Insight**

जान *jān* — the noun is feminine even when referring to a male. A wife may call her husband मेरी जान *merī jān* (or may not!).

जवाब *javāb*[M] answer, reply; जवाब देना *javāb denā*[N] to reply

ज़हर *zahar*[M] poison

जहाँ *jahā̃* where

जाँघ *jā̃gh*[F] thigh

जाँच *jā̃c*[F] inspection, test, check

जानकारी *jānkārī*[F] knowledge, information

जानना[N] *jānnā* to know; जान पड़ना *jān paṛnā* to seem, appear to be

जान-बूझकर *jān-būjhkar* deliberately, knowingly

जानवर *jānvar*ᴹ animal

जाना *jānā* to go

जाना-पहचाना *jānā-pahcānā* well known

जारी *jārī* ongoing, continuing, current

जाल *jāl*ᴹ net, mesh; web

जाली[1] *jālī* false, counterfeit

जाली[2] *jālī*ᶠ net, netting, lattice

जासूस *jāsūs*ᴹ spy

जासूसी *jāsūsī*ᶠ spying, espionage

ज़ाहिर *zāhir* clear, apparent

ज़िंदगी *zindagī*ᶠ life

ज़िंदा *zindā* (-*ā* invariable) alive

ज़िक्र *zikra*ᴹ mention

जिज्ञासा *jijñāsā* (pronounced 'jigyāsā')ᶠ curiosity

जितना *jitnā* as much/many as

ज़िद *zid*ᶠ obstinacy

ज़िद्दी *ziddī* obstinate, stubborn

ज़िम्मेदार *zimmedār* responsible

ज़िम्मेदारी *zimmedārī*ᶠ responsibility

ज़िल्लत *zillat*ᶠ humiliation

जी *jī* word of respect used after names and relationship terms; also used alone like 'sir', 'madam', and as a short form of जी हाँ *jī hā̃* 'yes'

जी नहीं *jī nahī̃* no

जी हाँ *jī hā̃* yes

जी-हुज़ूरी *jī-huzūrī*ᶠ sycophancy

जीतना *jītnā*ᴺ to win, conquer

जीना *jīnā* to live, be alive

जीभ *jībh*ᶠ tongue

जीवन *jīvan*ᴹ life

जीवित *jīvit* alive

जुआ *juā*ᴹ gambling; जुआ खेलना *juā khelnā*ᴺ to gamble

ज़ुकाम *zukām*ᴹ cold, head cold

जुटना *juṭnā* to join, gather; to be engaged in

जुदा *judā* (-*ā* invariable) separate, different

जुदाई *judāī*ᶠ separation, parting

जुरमाना *jurmānā*ᴹ fine, penalty

जुलना *julnā*: see मिलना-जुलना *milnā-julnā*

जुलाई *julāī*ᶠ July

जुलूस *julūs*ᴹ procession, demonstration; जुलूस निकालना *julūs nikālnā*ᴺ to lead a procession

जूझना *jūjhnā* to fight, contend

जूता *jūtā*ᴹ shoe; pair of shoes

जून *jūn*ᴹ June

जेठ *jeṭh*ᴹ brother-in-law (husband's elder brother)

जेब *jeb*ᶠ pocket

जेबकतरा *jebkatrā*ᴹ pickpocket

ज़ेवर *zevar*ᴹ (item of) jewellery

ज़ेवरात *zevarāt* plural of ज़ेवर *zevar*

जैसा *jaisā* of such a kind, like; जैसा... वैसा *jaisā... vaisā* as [one thing], so [another]

जैसे *jaise* like, as if; जैसे ही *jaise hī* as soon as, just as

जो *jo* (the one) who, which; जो कुछ *jo kuch* whatever; जो कोई *jo koī* whoever; जो भी *jo bhī* whoever, whatever

जोकर *jokar*ᴹ circus clown

जोड़ *joṛ*ᶠ joint (of the body)

जोड़नाᴺ *joṛnā* to add; to join, fix

जोड़ा *joṛā*ᴹ pair, couple; suit

ज़ोर *zor*ᴹ force, strength; ज़ोर से *zor se* with force, loudly; ज़ोर देना *zor denā*ᴺ to emphasize, stress

ज़ोरदार *zordār* forceful, powerful, strong

जोश *jos*ᴹ excitement, passion

जौ *jau*ᴹ barley

जौहरी *jauharī*ᴹ jeweller

ज्ञान *jñān*ᴹ (pronounced 'gyān') knowledge

ज़्यादा *zyādā* more; very; ज़्यादा से ज़्यादा *zyādā se zyādā* at the most; to the greatest extent

ज़्यादातर *zyādātar* (adj. & adverb) most, mostly

ज्योंही... त्योंही *jyõhī... tyõhī* as soon as... then

ज्वाला *jvālā*ᶠ flame, blaze

ज्वालामुखी *jvālāmukhī*ᴹ volcano

## झ *jha*

झंडा *jhaṇḍā*ᴹ flag

झकझक *jhakjhak* wrangling, arguing

झगड़ा *jhagṛā*ᴹ quarrel, row

झगड़ालू *jhagṛālū* quarrelsome

झट (से) *jhaṭ (se)* instantly

झटका *jhaṭkā*ᴹ jolt, jerk, shock

झाँकना *jhā̃knā*ᴺ to peep, peer, glance

झाड़ी *jhāṛī*ᶠ bush, shrub

झाड़ू *jhāṛū*ᴹ brush, broom; झाड़ू लगाना *jhāṛū lagānā*ᴺ to sweep

झींगुर *jhī̃gur*ᴹ cricket (insect)

झील *jhīl*ᶠ lake

झुकना *jhuknā* to bend, bow

झूठ *jhūṭh*ᴹ lie

झूठा *jhūṭhā* false

झूमना *jhūmnā* to sway

झूलना *jhūlnā* to swing

झूला *jhūlā*ᴹ swing

झेंप *jhẽp*ᶠ embarrassment

झेंपना *jhẽpnā* to be embarrassed

झोंपड़ी *jhõprī*^F hut

झोला *jholā*^M cloth shoulder bag

## ट *ṭa*

टंकी *ṭaṅkī*^F tank

टँगना *ṭãgnā* to hang, be hung, be suspended

टकराना *ṭakrānā* to collide

टकराव *ṭakrāv*^M clash

टक्कर *ṭakkar*^F collision; टक्कर लगना *ṭakkar lagnā* to collide

टखना *ṭakhnā*^M ankle

टट्टी *ṭaṭṭī*^F faeces, stool; टट्टी करना *ṭaṭṭī karnā*^N to pass faeces, to shit

टपकना *ṭapaknā* to drip; to drop in (unexpectedly)

टिकना *ṭiknā* to stop, stay, rest, be supported, be fixed

टिकाऊ *ṭikāū* stable, durable

टीला *ṭīlā*^M hillock, mound

टुकड़ा *ṭukrā*^M piece, bit

टूटना *ṭūṭnā* to break

टेकना *ṭeknā* to lean, prop, support

टेढ़ा *ṭeṛhā* crooked, twisted, complex, tricky; टेढ़ी खीर *ṭeṛhī khīr*^F a tricky task

टैक्सी *ṭaiksī*^F taxi

टोकरी *ṭokrī*^F basket

टोपी *ṭopī*^F hat

ट्रेन *ṭren*^F train

## ठ *ṭha*

ठंड *ṭhaṇḍ*^F cold; ठंड लगना *ṭhaṇḍ lagnā* to feel cold

**Insight**

टपकना *ṭapaknā* — a beautifully onomatopoeic word. Repeat the verb stem — टपक-टपक *ṭapak-ṭapak* — and you can hear the 'drip drip' of water.

टहलना *ṭahalnā* to stroll

टाँग *ṭãg*^F leg

टाँगना *ṭãgnā*^N to hang, suspend

टापू *ṭāpū*^M island

टालना *ṭālnā*^N to avoid, evade, put off

टिकट *ṭikaṭ*^F(M) ticket; stamp

ठंडा *ṭhaṇḍā* cold

ठप *ṭhap*, ठप्प *ṭhapp* stopped dead, paralysed, 'kaput' (of work, power supply etc.)

ठहरना *ṭhaharnā* to stop, stay, wait

ठाट *ṭhāṭ*, ठाठ *ṭhāṭh*^M grand style, magnificence

ठीक *ṭhīk* (adj. & adverb) OK, all right; exactly; ठीक करना *ṭhīk karnā*[N] to fix, put right; ठीक से *ṭhīk se* properly

ठुड्डी *ṭhuḍḍī*[F] chin

डकार *ḍakār*[F] belch, burp

डटना *ḍaṭnā* to be firm, stand firm; to be determined; डटकर *ḍaṭkar* stubbornly, resolutely

**Insight**

ठुड्डी पकड़ना *ṭhuḍḍī pakaṛnā* — to 'hold (someone's) chin' is to coax or entreat them, to talk them round with affectionate flattery.

ठेका *ṭhekā*[M] contract

ठेकेदार *ṭhekedār*[M] contractor

ठेठ *ṭheṭh* genuine, pure, unalloyed (e.g. of language free of loanwords)

ठेला *ṭhelā*[M] cart, handcart

ठेस *ṭhes*[F] hurt, shock; ठेस पहुँचाना *ṭhes pahũcānā*[N] to hurt, cause hurt

ठोस *ṭhos* solid, substantial

## ड *ḍa*

डंक *ḍaṅk*[M] sting; डंक मारना *ḍaṅk mārnā*[N] to sting

डंड *ḍaṇḍ*[M] stick, rod; punishment

डबल रोटी *ḍabal roṭī*[F] western-style bread, loaf

डर *ḍar*[M] fear

डरना *ḍarnā* to fear, be afraid (of, से *se*)

डरपोक *ḍarpok* (adj. & noun) timid; [M] timid person

डराना *ḍarānā*[N] to frighten, terrify

डाँटना *ḍā̃ṭnā*[N] to scold

डाक *ḍāk*[F] post; डाक-घर *ḍāk-ghar*[M] post office; डाक (की) टिकट *ḍāk (kī) ṭikaṭ*[F] postage stamp

डाकू *ḍākū*[M] dacoit (bandit)

डाक्टर *ḍākṭar*[M] doctor

**Insight**

डाक्टर *ḍākṭar* — this English loan has long since made itself at home in Hindi; Sanskritic synonyms such as चिकित्सक *cikitsak*[M] are used in formal contexts only.

डंडा *ḍaṇḍā*[M] stick, pole, staff

डाल *ḍāl*[F] branch (of a tree)

डालना *ḍālnā*[N] to put, pour, cast, throw

डिबिया *ḍibiyā*[F] small box

डिब्बा *ḍibbā*[M] box; railway compartment

डूबना *ḍūbnā* to sink, drown

डेढ़ *ḍeṛh* one and a half (grammatically singular)

ड्राइवर *ḍrāivar*[M] driver

## ढ *ḍha*

ढंग *ḍhaṅg*[M] way, manner, type, kind

ढकना *ḍhaknā* (intr. & tr.) to be covered; [N] to cover

ढकेलना *ḍhakelnā*[N] to shove, push

ढक्कन *ḍhakkan*[M] cover, lid

ढलना *ḍhalnā* to decline, wane

ढलान *ḍhalān*[M] slope, incline

ढाँचा *ḍhā̃cā*[M] framework, structure

ढाई *ḍhāī* two and a half

## त *ta*

तंग *taṅg* narrow; तंग आना[N] *taṅg ānā* get fed up, annoyed (with, से *se*); तंग करना *taṅg karnā*[N] to annoy, harass

तंदुरुस्त *tandurust* healthy, fit

तंदुरुस्ती *tandurustī*[F] health

तंदूर *tandūr*[M] clay oven

तंबाकू *tambākū*[M] tobacco

तक *tak* up to, until, as far as; even; for, up to (in time, e.g. दस दिन तक *das din tak* for ten days, up to ten days)

तकनीकी *taknīkī* technical

तकलीफ़ *taklīf*[F] suffering, pain, discomfort, inconvenience, trouble; तकलीफ़ देना *taklīf denā*[N] to inconvenience, to put (someone) to some trouble

तकिया *takiyā*[M] pillow

**Insight**

ढाई — a word meaning 'two and a half' has many uses: ढाई सौ *ḍhāī sau* '250', ढाई हजार *ḍhāī hazār* '2500', ढाई बजे *ḍhāī baje* 'half-past two', etc.!

ढाबा *ḍhābā*[M] roadside café

ढूँढ़ना *ḍhū̃ṛhnā*[N] to look for, search

ढेर *ḍher*[M] pile, heap, large amount

ढोना[N] *ḍhonā* to carry, lug

तख़्त *ta<u>kh</u>t*[M] sitting platform, throne

तजुर्बा *tajurbā*[M] experience

तट *taṭ*[M] bank (of river)

तत्त्व *tattva*[M] element

तथा *tathā* and

तथाकथित *tathākathit* so-called

तन *tan*ᴹ the body

तनख़ाह *tan<u>kh</u>āh,* तनख़्वाह *tan<u>kh</u>vāh*ᶠ pay, wages

तनना *tannā* to be stretched, to be made tight

तना *tanā*ᴹ trunk (of tree)

तनाव *tanāv*ᴹ tension

तब *tab* then

तबदीली *tabdīlī*ᶠ change; transfer

तबलची *tabalcī*ᴹ a tabla player

तबला *tablā*ᴹ tabla drum; the right-hand member of this pair (the left is बायाँ *bāyā̃*)

तबादला *tabādlā*ᴹ transfer

तबाह *tabāh* ruined

तबियत *tabiyat*ᶠ health

तभी *tabhī* only then; just then, at that very moment

तमाम *tamām* whole, entire

तमाशा *tamāśā*ᴹ show, spectacle, amusing sight

तमीज़ *tamīz*ᶠ etiquette, manners

तय *tay* decided, fixed; तय करना *tay karnā*ᴺ to decide; तय होना *tay honā* to be decided

तरफ़ *taraf*ᶠ side, direction; की तरफ़ *kī taraf* towards; किस तरफ़? *kis taraf?* which way?; इस/उस तरफ़ *is/us taraf* this/that way; (के) चारों तरफ़ *(ke) cārõ taraf* on all sides (of), all around

तरबूज़ *tarbūz*ᴹ water melon

तरह *tarah*ᶠ way, kind, type; तरह तरह का *tarah tarah kā* of various kinds

तरीक़ा *tarīqā*ᴹ way, method

तर्क *tark*ᴹ reasoning, logic; तर्क-वितर्क *tark-vitark*ᴹ debate, argument

तर्कसंगत *tarksaṅgat* logical

तलना *talnā*ᴺ to fry

तलवार *talvār*ᶠ sword

तलाक़ *talāq*ᴹ divorce

तलाक़-शुदा *talāq-śudā* (*-ā* invariable) divorced

तलाश *talāś*ᶠ search; (की) तलाश करना *(kī) talāś karnā*ᴺ to search (for)

तलाशना *talāśnā*ᴺ to search for

तवा *tavā*ᴹ griddle (for making roti)

तशरीफ़ *taśrīf*ᶠ honourable self (in the formal expression तशरीफ़ रखिए *taśrīf rakhie* please sit down, have a seat)

तसल्ली *tasallī*ᶠ consolation

तस्वीर *tasvīr*ᶠ picture; तस्वीर उतारना *tasvīr utārnā*ᴺ to take or draw a picture

तह *tah*$^{F}$ fold; तह करना *tah karnā*$^{N}$ to fold

तहज़ीब *tahzīb*$^{F}$ culture, refinement

ताई *tāī*$^{F}$ aunt (wife of father's elder brother)

ताऊ *tāū*$^{M}$ uncle (father's elder brother)

ताकि *tāki* so that, in order that

ताज महल *tāj mahal*$^{M}$ Taj Mahal

ताज़ा *tāzā* fresh

ताज्जुब *tājjub*$^{M}$ surprise, astonishment

ताड़ *tāṛ*$^{M}$ palm tree

तादाद *tādād*$^{F}$ numbers, quantity; भारी तादाद में *bhārī tādād mẽ* in large numbers

तानना *tānnā*$^{N}$ to stretch, tighten

तानाशाह *tānāśāh*$^{M}$ dictator

तानाशाही *tānāśāhī*$^{F}$ dictatorship

तापमान *tāpmān*$^{M}$ temperature

तार *tār*$^{M}$ wire

तारा *tārā*$^{M}$ star; pupil of eye

तारीख़ *tārīkh*$^{F}$ date

तारीफ़ *tārīf*$^{F}$ praise; (की) तारीफ़ करना *(kī) tārīf karnā*$^{N}$ to praise

ताला *tālā*$^{M}$ lock

तालाब *tālāb*$^{M}$ pond

ताली *tālī*$^{F}$ clap, clapping; तालियाँ बजाना *tāliyā̃ bajānā*$^{N}$ to clap

तालीम *tālīm*$^{F}$ training, education

ताश *tāś*$^{M}$ playing card(s)

तितली *titlī*$^{F}$ butterfly

तिरपन *tirpan* fifty-three

तिरसठ *tirsaṭh* sixty-three

तिरानवे *tirānve* ninety-three

तिरासी *tirāsī* eighty-three

तिहत्तर *tihattar* seventy-three

तीन *tīn* three

तीर्थ *tīrth*$^{M}$ place of pilgrimage

तीर्थ-यात्रा *tīrth-yātrā*$^{F}$ pilgrimage

तीव्र *tīvra* sharp, intense, fast; sharp (of musical note)

तीस *tīs* thirty

तीसरा *tīsrā* third; तीसरे पहर *tīsre pahar* in the afternoon

**Insight**

तारीख़ *tārīkh*$^{F}$— the feminine gender of this word becomes apparent in expressions such as *pahlī jūn* 'June 1st'. In Urdu, तारीख़ *tārīkh* has the additional sense of 'history' (which is इतिहास *itihās*$^{M}$ in Hindi).

तुझ *tujh* oblique of तू *tū*

तुतलाना *tutlānā* to lisp, to speak like a child

तुम *tum* you (familiar)

तुम्हारा *tumhārā* your, yours

तुरंत *turant* immediately

तुलना[1] *tulnā*[F] comparison; (की) तुलना करना *kī tulnā karnā*[N] to compare (with, से *se*)

तुलना[2] *tulnā* to be determined (on, पर *par*)

तू *tū* you (intimate); तू-तू मैं-मैं *tū-tū maĩ-maĩ*[F] trading insults, calling names, wrangling

तूफ़ान *tūfān*[M] storm

तेईस *teīs* twenty-three

तेज़ *tez* sharp, bright, strong, acute, quick

तेज़ी *tezī*[F] sharpness, speed

तेरह *terah* thirteen

तेरा *terā* your, yours (intimate)

तेल *tel*[M] oil

तैंतालीस *taĩtālīs* forty-three

तैंतीस *taĩtīs* thirty-three

तैनात *tainát* appointed, posted

तैयार *taiyār* ready, prepared; तैयार करना *taiyār karnā*[N] to make ready, prepare

तैयारी *taiyārī*[F] preparation

तैरना *tairnā* to swim

तो *to* so, then, as for...

तोता *totā*[M] parrot

तोड़ना[N] *toṛnā* to break, smash

तोप *top*[F] gun, cannon; 'big shot'

तोलना *tolnā*: see तौलना *taulnā*

तोहफ़ा *tohfā*[M] gift, present

तौर *taur*[N] way, manner

तौलना *taulnā*[N] to weigh

तौलिया *tauliyā*[M] towel

त्याग *tyāg*[M] renouncing, resignation

त्यागपत्र *tyāgpatra*[M] letter of resignation

त्यौहार *tyauhār*[M] festival

त्रुटि *truṭi*[F] error, defect

## थ *tha*

थकना *thaknā* to become tired

थका *thakā* tired

थकान *thakān*[F] tiredness

थकाना *thakānā*[N] to make tired, to exhaust

थपथपाना *thapthapānā*[N] to pat

थमाना *thamānā*[N] to hand over, pass

थाना *thānā*[M] police station

थामना *thāmnā*[N] to hold, take hold of; to check, restrain

थाली *thālī*[F] platter; tray of food including many small dishes

थूकना[n] *thūknā* to spit

थैला *thailā*[M] bag

थोड़ा *thoṛā* a little; थोड़ा-थोड़ा करके *thoṛā-thoṛā karke* a little at a time, bit by bit, gradually; थोड़ा-बहुत *thoṛā-bahut* a certain amount

## द *da*

दंगा *daṅgā*[M] riot

दंड *daṇḍ*[M] punishment

दंत-कथा *dant-kathā*[F] legend

दंपति *dampati* (adj. & noun)[M] married couple

दक्षिण *dakṣiṇ* (adj. & noun)[M] south

दख़ल *da<u>kh</u>al*[M] access, possession; grasp (of a subject); दख़ल देना *da<u>kh</u>al denā*[N] to interfere

दफ़ा *dafā*[F] time, occasion; clause in legal statute

दफ़्तर *daftar*[M] office

दबना *dabnā* to be pressed, to be oppressed, squashed; to yield

दबाना *dabānā*[N] to press; to oppress

दबाव *dabāv*[M] pressure

दबे पाँव *dabe pā̃v* stealthily

दम[1] *dam*[M] breath, life; दम लेना *dam lenā*[N] to take a breath, rest; दम मारना *dam mārnā*[N] to take a drag

दम[2] *dam*[M] moment

दया *dayā*[F] pity, compassion

दयालु *dayālu* compassionate, kind-hearted

दर *dar*[F] rate

दरअसल *dar'asal* in fact, actually

दरख़ास्त *dar<u>kh</u>āst*, दरख़्वास्त *dar<u>kh</u>vāst*[F] application, request

दरज़ी *darzī*[M] tailor

दरबार *darbār*[M] (royal) court

दरवाज़ा *darvāzā*[M] door

दरवान *darvān*[M] gatekeeper

दराज़ *darāz*[F] drawer

दरार *darār*[F] crack

दरिया *dariyā*[M] river

दरियादिल *dariyādil* generous

दरी *darī*[F] durrie, rug, mat

दर्जन *darjan*[F] dozen

दर्जा *darjā*[M] grade, type, level, class

दर्द *dard*[M] pain; दर्द करना *dard karnā*[N] to hurt

दर्शन *darśan*[M] sight, view, vision; (के) दर्शन करना *(ke) darśan karna*[N] to have an audience (of), be in the august presence (of); दर्शन देना *darśan denā*[N] to grant an audience, to allow a meeting

दल *dal*[M] party, faction

दलित *dalit* (adj. & noun) downtrodden, oppressed;[M] (member of) one of the 'oppressed' castes or classes

दवा *davā*[F] medicine

दवाई *davāī*[F] medicine

दवाख़ाना *davākhānā*[M] pharmacy

दशक *daśak*[M] decade

दस *das* ten

दस्त *dast*[M] diarrhoea; दस्त आना/लगना *dast ānā/lagnā* to have diarrhoea

दस्तावेज़ *dastāvez*[F] document, certificate

दस्तूर *dastūr*[M] custom, practice

दही *dahī*[M] yoghurt

दहेज *dahej*[M] dowry

दाँत *dā̃t*[M] tooth

दाख़िल *dākhil* admitted, registered

दाख़िला *dākhilā*[M] admittance

दाढ़ी *dāṛhī*[F] beard; दाढ़ी बनाना *dāṛhī banānā*[N] to shave

दादा *dādā*[M] grandfather (father's father)

दादी *dādī*[F] grandmother (father's mother)

दान *dān*[M] gift, donation, charity

दाम *dām*[M] price

दामाद *dāmād*[M] son-in-law

दायाँ *dāyā̃* right (opposite of left)

दाल *dāl*[F] daal, lentil; दाल-भात *dāl-bhāt*[M] rice-and-lentils, everyday fare

दावत *dāvat*[F] dinner, invitation to a dinner

दावा *dāvā*[M] claim; confidence; दावा करना *dāvā karnā*[N] to claim; दावे के साथ कहना *dāve ke sāth kahnā*[N] to say confidently

दाहिना *dāhinā* right (opposite of left); दाहिने *dāhine* on/to the right; दाहिनी तरफ़ *dāhinī taraf* on/to the right

दिक़्क़त *diqqat*[F] difficulty, inconvenience, problem

दिखना *dikhnā* to appear, be seen; to seem

दिखाई देना/पड़ना *dikhāī denā/paṛnā* to appear, be seen

दिखाना *dikhānā*[N] to show

दिन *din*[M] day; दिन भर *din bhar* all day

दिमाग़ *dimāg*[M] brain, mind

दिल *dil*[M] heart; दिल लगना *dil lagnā* (one's heart) to feel at home, to be at ease

दिलचस्प *dilcasp* interesting

दिलचस्पी *dilcaspī*[F] interest

दिलाना *dilānā*ᴺ to cause to be given

दिलासा *dilāsā*ᴹ consolation, solace

दिल्ली *dillī*ᶠ Delhi

दिवस *divas*ᴹ day

दिशा *diśā*ᶠ direction, point of the compass

दिसंबर *disambar*ᴹ December

दीखना *dīkhnā* to be seen, appear, be visible

दीन *dīn* wretched, humble

दीया *dīyā*ᴹ lamp

दीयासलाई *dīyāsalāī*ᶠ match

दीवार *dīvār*ᶠ wall

दुआ *duā*ᶠ prayer, blessing; आपकी दुआ है *āpkī duā hai* through your blessing all is well (a formulaic response to an enquiry after one's health)

दुःख *duḥkh*ᴹ sorrow, pain, distress

दुखी *dukhī* sad, distressed

दुगुना *dugunā* (adj. & noun)ᴹ double; twice the amount

दुनिया *duniyā*ᶠ world; the world

दुपट्टा *dupaṭṭā*ᴹ scarf

दुबला *dublā* thin; दुबला-पतला *dublā-patlā* slight of build, 'lean and thin'

दुबारा *dubārā* again, a second time

दुर्घटना *durghaṭnā*ᶠ accident

दुर्लभ *durlabh* rare, hard to find

दुश्मन *duśman*ᴹ enemy

दुश्मनी *duśmanī*ᶠ enmity

दूध *dūdh*ᴹ milk

दूधवाला *dūdhvālā*ᴹ milkman

दूर *dūr* far, distant; दूर करना *dūr karnā*ᴺ to remove, get rid of

दूरदर्शन *dūrdarśan*ᴹ television; 'Doordarshan' ('DD'), Indian national television network

**Insight**

दुःख *duḥkh* – the colon-like sign is called विसर्ग *visarg* and is pronounced as a light '*h*', although many speakers ignore it in pronunciation. The verb दुखना *dukhnā*, further from its Sanskrit origin, has no *visarg*.

दुकान *dukān*ᶠ shop

दुकानदार *dukāndār*ᴹ shopkeeper

दुखना *dukhnā* to hurt, ache

दूरबीन *dūrbīn*ᶠ telescope

दूरी *dūrī*ᶠ distance

दूसरा *dūsrā* second; other

दृढ़ *dṛṛh* firm, resolute

दृश्य *dṛśya*ᴹ sight, scene

दृष्टि *dṛṣṭi*ᶠ sight, view, point of view

देखना *dekhnā*ᴺ to look, to see

देखभाल *dekhbhāl*ᶠ care, supervision; (की) देखभाल करना *kī dekhbhāl karnā*ᴺ to look after

देन *den*ᶠ contribution, gift, legacy

देना *denā*ᴺ to give; to allow to, let (with oblique infinitive: हमको जाने दो *hamko jāne do* 'let us go')

देर *der*ᶠ a while, length of time; delay; देर से *der se* late

देवता *devtā*ᴹ a god

देवनागरी *devnāgarī*ᶠ Devanagari, the script used for Hindi (and Sanskrit, Marathi, Nepali and many dialects)

देवर *devar*ᴹ brother-in-law (husband's younger brother)

देवी *devī*ᶠ goddess; lady

देश *deś*ᴹ country

देश-भक्त (adj. & noun) *deś-bhakt* patriotic,ᴹ patriot

देश-भक्ति *deś-bhakti*ᶠ patriotism

देह *deh*ᶠ body

देहांत *dehānt*ᴹ death, bodily demise; (का) देहान्त होना *(kā) dehānt honā* to die, pass away

देहात *dehāt*ᴹ rural area, countryside

देहाती *dehātī* (adj. & noun) rural, rustic;ᴹ a villager, a rustic

दैनिक *dainik* daily

दो *do* two

दोनों *donõ* both, the two

दोपहर *dopahar*ᴹ noon, early afternoon

दोबारा *dobārā* again, a second time

दोष *doṣ*ᴹ fault, offence; दोष लगाना *doṣ lagānā*ᴺ to accuse

दोषी *doṣī* (adj. & noun) at fault, guilty;ᴹ guilty person; दोषी ठहराना *doṣī ṭhahrānā*ᴺ to prove guilty

दोस्त *dost*ᴹ'ᶠ friend

दोस्ती *dostī*ᶠ friendship

दोहराना *dohrānā*ᴺ to repeat

दौड़ *dauṛ*ᶠ race, run

दौड़ना *dauṛnā* to run

दौरा *daurā*ᴹ tour, circuit; attack, fit, seizure

द्रव *drav* (adj. & noun)ᴹ liquid

द्रव्य *dravya*ᴹ substance, wealth

द्वारा *dvārā* by, by means of, through

द्वीप *dvīp*ᴹ island

## ध *dha*

धंधा *dhandhā*ᴹ profession, occupation, trade (can bear a derogatory undertone)

धक्का *dhakkā*ᴹ push, shove

धड़ *dhaṛ*ᴹ trunk, body

धड़कन *dhaṛkan*ᶠ throbbing, beating, heartbeat, palpitation

धड़कना *dhaṛaknā* to throb, beat, palpitate

धन *dhan*ᴹ wealth

धनी *dhanī* wealthy

धन्य *dhanya* blessed, fortunate

धन्यवाद *dhanyavād* thank you

धब्बा *dhabbā*ᴹ stain, blot

धमकी *dhamkī*ᶠ threat

धमाका *dhamākā*ᴹ explosion, loud noise, crash

धर्म *dharm*ᴹ religion; dharma

धागा *dhāgā*ᴹ thread

धातु *dhātu*ᶠ metal; element

धार *dhār*ᶠ edge (of blade)

धारा *dhārā*ᶠ flow, current

धारावाहिक *dhārāvāhik*ᴹ serial (in newspaper/on television)

धार्मिक *dhārmik* religious

धीमा *dhīmā* low, faint (of sound)

धीरज *dhīraj*ᴹ courage, patience, fortitude

धीरे धीरे *dhīre dhīre* slowly

धुंध *dhundh*ᴹ mist, fog, haze

धुँधला *dhũdhlā* dim, faint, hazy, vague

धुआँ *dhuā̃*ᴹ smoke (oblique धुएँ *dhuē̃*)

धुन *dhun*ᶠ tune, folk tune

धुलना *dhulnā* to be washed

धुलवाना *dhulvānā*ᴺ to cause to be washed, to get washed

धुलाई *dhulāī*ᶠ (act of) washing

धूप *dhūp*ᶠ sunshine; धूप खाना *dhūp khānā*ᴺ to bask in the sun

धूमधाम *dhūmdhām*ᴹ pomp and show

धूम्रपान *dhūmrapān*ᴹ smoking

धूल *dhūl*ᶠ dust

धैर्य *dhairya*ᴹ patience, fortitude

धोखा *dhokhā*ᴹ trick, deceit; धोखा देना *dhokhā denā*ᴺ to trick, hoodwink

धोखेबाज़ *dhokhebāz* (adj. & noun) fraudulent;ᴹ fraudulent person, trickster

धोखेबाज़ी *dhokhebāzī*ᶠ deceitful practice

धोना *dhonā*ᴺ to wash

धोबी *dhobī*ᴹ washerman

ध्यान *dhyān*ᴹ attention; meditation; (पर) ध्यान देना

*(par) dhyān denā*^N to pay attention (to); ध्यान से *dhyān se* attentively, carefully; (का) ध्यान रखना *dhyān rakhnā*^N to take care (of)

नखरा *nakhara*^M affectation, flirtatious mannerism

नगर *nagar*^M town, city

नज़दीक *nazdīk* close, near; nearby

**Insight**

ध्यान *dhyān* — this Sanskrit loanword, so common in Hindi, is also the ultimate source for the Japanese word 'zen'.

## न *na*

नंगा *naṅgā* naked

नंगापन *naṅgāpan*^M nakedness

नंदोई *nandoī*^M brother-in-law (husband of husband's sister)

नंबर *nambar*^M number; turn, chance

न *na* not (used especially with subjunctive verbs or uncertain statements); don't (in commands); is it not so? (rhetorically, after a statement); न कि *na ki* and not, rather than (हिन्दी बोलो, न कि अँग्रेज़ी *hindī bolo, na ki ãgrezī* speak Hindi, not English); न ... न *na ... na* neither ... nor; न जाने *na jāne* God knows

नई *naī*, नए *nae*: see नया *nayā*

नक़ल *naqal*^F copy, copying

नक़ली *naqalī* imitation, fake

नक़्शा *naqśā*^M map, plan

नज़र *nazar*^F glance, sight; the 'evil eye' of jealousy; नज़र डालना^N to glance, throw a glance; नज़र लगना *nazar lagnā* to be caught by the evil eye

नटखट *naṭkhaṭ* naughty, mischievous

नतीजा *natījā*^M result

नदी *nadī*^F river

ननद *nanad*^F sister-in-law (husband's sister)

नन्हा *nanhā* tiny

नफ़रत *nafrat*^F dislike, hatred; (से) नफ़रत करना (se) *nafrat karnā*^N to dislike, hate

नब्बे *nabbe* ninety

नम *nam* damp, moist, humid

नमक *namak*^M salt

नमकीन *namkīn* salty, savoury; ^M savoury snack

नमस्कार *namaskār* hello, goodbye

नमस्ते *namaste* hello, goodbye

नमी *namī*ᶠ dampness, humidity

नमूना *namūna*ᴹ sample, example, specimen

नया *nayā* (ᶠ नई *naī*, ᴹᴾᴸ नए *nae*) new

नयापन *nayāpan*ᴹ newness

नरक *narak*ᴹ hell

नरसों *narsõ* three days ago/hence

नर्स *nars*ᶠ nurse

नल *nal*ᴹ tap, pipe

नवंबर *navambar*ᴹ November

नवाँ *navā̃* ninth

नवासी *navāsī* eighty-nine

नशा *naśā*ᴹ intoxication

नशीला *naśīlā* intoxicating

नष्ट *naṣṭ* destroyed

नस *nas*ᶠ vein; nerve; sinew

नसल *nasal*ᶠ breed, race

नसलवाद *nasalvād*ᴹ racialism

नसलवादी *nasalvādī* (adj. & noun)ᴹ racialist

नहाना *nahānā* to bathe

नहीं *nahī̃* not, no; नहीं तो *nahī̃ to* otherwise; of course not!

नाई *nāī*ᴹ barber

नाक *nāk*ᶠ nose

नाख़ून *nākhūn*ᴹ nail (of finger, toe)

नागरिक *nāgarik*ᴹ citizen

नाच *nāc*ᴹ dance, dancing

नाचना *nācnā* to dance

नाटक *nāṭak*ᴹ drama, play

नाड़ा *nāṛā*ᴹ trouser string

नाड़ी *nāṛī*ᶠ artery; pulse

नाता *nātā*ᴹ relationship, connection

नातिन *nātin*ᶠ granddaughter (daughter's daughter)

नाती *nātī*ᴹ grandson (daughter's son)

नादान *nādān* innocent, ignorant, foolish

नाना *nānā*ᴹ grandfather (mother's father)

नानी *nānī*ᶠ grandmother (mother's mother)

नापना *nāpnā*ᴺ to measure

नापसंद करना *nāpasand karnā*ᴺ to dislike

नाम *nām*ᴹ name; (का) नाम लेना *kā nām lenā*ᴺ to take the name (of), to mention; (का) नाम न लेना *(kā) nām na lenā*ᴺ to be far from doing (something)

नामुमकिन *nāmumkin* impossible

नारा *nārā*ᴹ slogan

नाराज़ *nārāz* displeased, angry

**Insight**

ना- *nā-* is a Persian prefix with the negative sense of 'un-', 'dis-' etc. Thus नामुमकिन *nāmumkin* 'impossible'. नाराज *nāraz* 'displeased', नासमझ *nāsamajh* 'unwise'.

नारियल *nāriyal*[M] coconut

नाला *nālā*[M] nullah, seasonal stream; drain

नाली *nālī*[F] tube, pipe; drain, channel

नारी *nārī*[F] woman

नाव *nāv*[F] boat, ship

नाश्ता *nāśtā*[M] breakfast, snack; नाश्ता करना *nāśtā karnā*[N] to have breakfast

नासमझ *nāsamajh* unwise, foolish

नास्तिक *nāstik* (adj. & noun)[M] atheist

निंदा *nindā*[F] blame, censure; (की) निंदा करना *(kī) nindā karnā*[N] to blame, speak ill of

निकलना *nikalnā* to emerge, come/go out

निकालना *nikālnā*[N] to extract, bring/take out

निगम *nigam*[M] corporation

निगरानी *nigrānī*[F] watch, surveillance

निगलना *nigalnā*[N] to swallow

निचला *niclā* lower

निचोड़ *nicoṛ*[M] extract, essence

निचोड़ना *nicoṛnā*[N] to squeeze; to wring out

निजी *nijī* private, personal

निदेशक *nideśak*[M] director, guide, supervisor

निन्यानवे *ninyānve* ninety-nine

निपटना *nipaṭnā* to be completed, finished; to be dealt with, be done and finished

निपटाना *nipṭānā*[N] to complete, to get done with, to settle

निपुण *nipuṇ* skilful, expert

निपुणता *nipuṇtā*[F] skilfulness

निबंध *nibandh*[M] essay

निबटना *nibaṭnā* etc.: see निपटना *nipaṭnā*

निभाना *nibhānā* [N] to fulfil, carry out, maintain, fulfil (a role)

निमंत्रण *nimantraṇ*[M] invitation

नियति *niyati*[F] fate, destiny

नियम *niyam*[M] rule, law

नियमित रूप से *niyamit rūp se* regularly

नियुक्त *niyukt* appointed; नियुक्त करना *niyukt karnā*ᴺ to appoint

नियुक्ति *niyukti*ᶠ appointment (in a job)

निरर्थक *nirarthak* meaningless

निराला *nirālā* strange, distinctive

निराश *nirāś* disappointed, despondent

निराशा *nirāśā*ᶠ disappointment; despair

निरीक्षण *nirīkṣaṇ*ᴹ inspection

निरोध *nirodh*ᴹ prevention; condom (trade name)

निर्णय *nirṇay*ᴹ decision, judgement

निर्देशक *nirdeśak*ᴹ director, guide, supervisor

निर्दोष *nirdoṣ* innocent, blameless

निर्भर *nirbhar* dependent

निवास *nivās*ᴹ residence

निवासी *nivāsī*ᴹ resident

निवेदन *nivedan*ᴹ formal request

निशान *niśān*ᴹ mark, target

निश्चय *niścay*ᴹ decision; (का) निश्चय करना *(kā) niścay karnā*ᴺ to decide (to)

निश्चित *niścit* decided, definite

निष्पक्ष *niṣpakṣ* objective, impartial

निहायत *nihāyat* extremely

नींद *nī̃d*ᶠ sleep; नींद आना *nī̃d ānā* sleep to come, to get to sleep; नींद खुलना/टूटना *nī̃d khulnā/ṭūṭnā* sleep to end, to wake up

नीच *nīc* low, mean

नीचा *nīcā* low; नीचा दिखाना *nīcā dikhānā*ᴺ to humiliate, to do down

नीचे *nīce* below, down; downstairs

नीति *nīti*ᶠ polity, moral conduct, policy

नीयत *nīyat*ᶠ intention

नीला *nīlā* blue

नुक़ता *nuqtā*ᶠ

नुक़सान *nuqsān*ᴹ loss, damage, harm

नृत्य *nṛtya*ᴹ dance

नेक *nek* good, decent

नेता *netā*ᴹ leader, politician

नेपाल *nepāl*ᴹ Nepal

नेपाली *nepālī* (adj. & noun) Nepali;ᴹ a Nepali;ᶠ the Nepali language

नैतिक *naitik* moral, ethical

नोक *nok*ᶠ point, tip

नौ *nau* nine

नौकर *naukar*ᴹ servant, employee

नौकरशाही *naukarśāhī*ᶠ bureaucracy

नौकरी *naukarī*ᶠ job, employment

नौजवान *naujavān*ᴹ a youth, young man

नौसेना *nausenā*ᶠ navy

## प *pa*

पंखा *paṅkhā*ᴹ fan

पंडित *paṇḍit*ᴹ pandit, learned man, (Brahmin) scholar

पंद्रह *pandrah* fifteen

पकड़ना *pakaṛnā*ᴺ to catch

पकना *paknā* to be cooked; to ripen; hair to turn grey

पकाना *pakānā*ᴺ to cook

पक्का *pakkā* ripe; fully made; certain, definite (of plans etc.); out-and-out

पक्ष *pakṣ*ᴹ side (in argument), wing

पक्षी *pakṣī*ᴹ bird

पखवारा *pakhvārā*ᴹ fortnight

पगड़ी *pagṛī*ᶠ turban

पचना *pacnā* to be digested

पचपन *pacpan* fifty-five

पचहत्तर *pachattar* seventy-five

पचानवे *pacānve* ninety-five

पचाना *pacānā*ᴺ to digest

पचास *pacās* fifty

पचासी *pacāsī* eighty-five

पच्चीस *paccīs* twenty-five

पछताना *pachtānā* to regret, feel remorse

पटाका *paṭākā,* पटाखा *paṭākhā*ᴹ firework

पट्टी *paṭṭī*ᶠ bandage

पड़ना *paṛnā* to fall; to be, prove to be (e.g. यह चादर छोटी पड़ेगी *yah cādar choṭī paṛegī* this sheet will be (too) small; to have to (here पड़ना *paṛnā* follows the infinitive: मुझे जाना पड़ेगा *mujhe jānā paṛegā* I'll have to go); पड़ा (हुआ) *paṛā (huā)* lying

पड़ाव *paṛāv*ᴹ halting place; leg or stage of journey

पड़ोस *paṛos*ᴹ neighbourhood

पड़ोसिन *paṛosin*ᶠ neighbour

पड़ोसी *paṛosī*ᴹ neighbour

पढ़ना *paṛhnā* to study; ᴺ to read

पढ़ा-लिखा *paṛhā-likhā* educated, literate

पढ़ाई *paṛhāī*ᶠ studies, studying

पढ़ाना *paṛhānā*ᴺ to teach

पतंग *pataṅg*ᴹ kite (flying toy)

पतंगा *pataṅgā*ᴹ moth

पतला *patlā* thin

पता *patā*ᴹ address; awareness (मुझको पता है *mujhko patā hai* I know; मुझको पता नहीं *mujhko patā nahī̃* I don't know); पता चलना *patā calnā* to become aware, come to know (मुझको पता चला कि… *mujhko patā calā ki…* I came to know that…)

पति *pati*ᴹ husband
पत्ता *pattā*ᴹ leaf
पत्थर *patthar*ᴹ stone; a stone
पत्नी *patnī*ᶠ wife
पत्र *patra*ᴹ letter (correspondence)
पत्रकार *patrakār*ᴹ journalist
पत्रकारिता *patrakāritā*ᶠ journalism
पत्रिका *patrikā*ᶠ journal, magazine
पद *pad*ᴹ position (in employment); hymn
पदार्थ *padārth*ᴹ substance, material, object
पधारना *padhārnā* to come, to take a seat (in formal usage)
पनीर *panīr*ᴹ cheese
पन्ना *pannā*ᴹ page
परंतु *parantu* but
परंपरा *paramparā*ᶠ tradition
परंपरागत *paramparāgat* traditional
पर[1] *par* on; at; पर से *par se* from on
पर[2] *par* but
पर[3] *par*ᴹ wing, feather
परत *parat*ᶠ layer
परदा *pardā*ᴹ curtain; veil; purdah
परवाह *parvāh*ᶠ care, concern, heed; परवाह करना *parvāh karnā*ᴺ to care, to mind, to take notice
परसों *parsõ* the day after tomorrow; the day before yesterday
परस्पर *paraspar* mutual
परहेज़ करना *parhez karnā*ᴺ to abstain (from, से *se*)
परिचय *paricay*ᴹ introduction, acquaintance
परिचित *paricit* acquainted; परिचित कराना *paricit karānā*ᴺ to introduce
परिणाम *pariṇām*ᴹ result, consequence
परिवर्तन *parivartan*ᴹ change, alteration
परिवार *parivār*ᴹ family
परिश्रम *pariśram*ᴹ hard work, labour, toil
परिश्रमी *pariśramī* hard working
परिस्थिति *paristhiti*ᶠ circumstance
परी *parī*ᶠ fairy
परीक्षा *parīkṣā*ᶠ examination; परीक्षा देनाᴺ *parīkṣā denā* to take an exam
परे *pare,* से परे *se pare* beyond, above
परेशान *pareśān* anxious, worried
परेशानी *pareśānī*ᶠ anxiety, concern
परोसना *parosnā*ᴺ to serve (food), to dish out

पर्यटक *paryaṭak*ᴹ tourist

पर्यटन *paryaṭan*ᴹ tourism

पर्याप्त *paryāpt* sufficient

पर्यावरण *paryāvaraṇ*ᴹ environment

पलंग *palang*ᴹ bed

पल *pal*ᴹ moment; पल भर *pal bhar* for a single moment

पलटना *palaṭnā* to overturn; to turn back

पलटाना *palṭānā*ᴺ to turn (something) over

पवित्र *pavitra* pure, sacred

पशु *paśu*ᴹ beast, animal

पश्चिम *paścim*ᴹ west

पश्चिमी *paścimī* western

पसंद *pasand* pleasing (यह मुझ को पसंद है *yah mujh ko pasand hai* I like this); पसंद करना *pasand karnā*ᴺ to prefer, choose

पसंदीदा *pasandīdā* (-*ā* invariable) chosen, favourite, liked

पसली *paslī*ᶠ rib

पसीना *pasīnā*ᴹ sweat

पहचान *pahacān*ᶠ recognition; characteristic feature

पहचानना *pahacānnā*ᴺ to recognize

पहनना *pahannā*ᴺ to put on, wear

पहनाना *pahnānā*ᴺ to cause to wear, to dress (someone)

पहर *pahar*ᴹ 'watch', three-hour segment of the day

पहरा *paharā*ᴹ watch, guard

पहला *pahlā* first

पहले *pahle* firstly; previously

पहलू *pahlū*ᴹ aspect, side

पहाड़ *pahāṛ*ᴹ hill, mountain

पहाड़ी[1] *pahāṛī* mountainous; from the hills or mountains

पहाड़ी[2] *pahāṛī*ᶠ hill, hillock

पहिया *pahiyā*ᴹ wheel

पहुँचना *pahũcnā* to reach, arrive

पहुँचानाᴺ *pahũcānā* to deliver, convey

पाँच *pā̃c* five; पाँचवाँ *pā̃cvā̃* fifth

पाँव *pā̃v*ᴹ foot, leg

पाकिस्तान *pākistān*ᴹ Pakistan

पागल *pāgal* mad, crazy

पागलख़ाना *pāgal<u>kh</u>ānā*ᴹ lunatic asylum, madhouse

पाठ *pāṭh*ᴹ reading, lesson, chapter

पाठक *pāṭhak*ᴹ reader

पात्र *pātra*ᴹ container; character (in drama etc.)

पाद *pād*ᴹ fart; पाद मारना/छोड़ना *pād mārnā*ᴺ/*choṛnā*ᴺ to fart

पान *pān*[M] paan, betel leaf (with additives) for chewing as a digestive and stimulant

पाना *pānā*[N] to find, obtain; to be able, to manage to (with verb stem: राम नहीं जा पाया *rām nahī̃ jā pāyā* 'Ram didn't manage to go')

पानी *pānī*[M] water; rain

पाप *pāp*[M] sin

पापा *pāpā*[M] father, papa

पापी *pāpī* (adj. & noun) sinful;[M] sinner

पाबंदी *pābandī*[F] proper observance (of time etc.); restriction, rule

पार *pār* across

पार करना *pār karnā*[N] to cross (road etc.)

पालथी *pālthī*[F] cross-legged posture; पालथी मारकर बैठना *pālthī mārkar baiṭhnā* to sit cross-legged

पास *pās* (adverb) nearby

पास करना *pās karnā*[N] to pass (an exam)

पिंजरा *pĩjrā*[M] cage

पिछड़ा *pichṛā* lagging, backward, left behind

पिछला *pichlā* previous, last

पिछवाड़ा *pichvāṛā*[M] rear (of building)

पिता *pitā*[M] father

पिलाना *pilānā*[N] to give to drink, to serve a drink

पीछा *pīchā*[M] rear; (का) पीछा करना *(kā) pīchā karnā*[N] to follow, pursue

पीछे *pīche* behind, later, afterwards

पीटना *pīṭnā*[N] to beat, thrash

पीठ *pīṭh*[F] back

पीड़ा *pīṛā*[F] pain

पीड़ित *pīṛit* pained, suffering, afflicted

पीढ़ी *pīṛhī*[F] generation

पीतल *pītal*[M] brass

पीना *pīnā*[N] to drink; to smoke

पीला *pīlā* yellow

पीसना *pīsnā*[N] to grind

पुकारना[N] *pukārnā* to call out

पुण्य *puṇya* (adj. & noun) virtuous, sacred;[M] merit (earned by good actions)

पुरज़ा *purzā*[M] part, component (of a machine); scrap, piece (of paper)

पुरस्कार *puraskār*[M] prize, award

पुराना *purānā* old (of things only; for people, see बूढ़ा *būṛhā)*

पुल *pul*[M] bridge

पुलिंदा *pulindā*[M] packet, bundle

पुलिस *pulis*[F] police

पुलिसवाला *pulisvālā*[M] policeman

पुल्लिंग *pulliṅg* masculine (in grammatical gender)

पृथ्वी *pṛthvī*[F] earth, planet

पृष्ठ *pṛṣṭh*[F] page (of book)

पृष्ठभूमि *pṛṣṭhbhūmi*[F] background

पेंसिल *pensil*[F] pencil

पे *pe* = पर *par* on (etc.)

**Insight**

पे *pe* (for its synonym पर *par* 'on') is often heard in speech but rarely used in writing, which tends towards the more formally 'correct' forms.

पुस्तक *pustak*[F] book

पूँछ *pũ̄ch*[F] tail

पूछताछ *pūchtāch*[F] enquiry

पूछना *pūchnā*[N] to ask (with से *se* – राम से पूछो *rām se pūcho* ask Ram)

पूजा *pūjā*[F] worship, adoration

पूड़ी *pūṛī*[F] poori, a deep-fried roti

पूरा *pūrā* full, complete; पूरा करना *pūrā karnā*[N] to complete; पूरा पड़ना *pūrā paṛnā* to be enough, to suffice

पूर्ण *pūrṇ* full, complete

पूर्व[1] *pūrv* east

पूर्व[2] *pūrv* former

पूर्वज *pūrvaj*[M] ancestor, forebear

पूर्वाग्रह *pūrvāgrah*[M] prejudice

पूर्वी *pūrvī* eastern

पेचीदा *pecīdā* twisted, complicated

पेच *pec*, पेंच *pẽc*,[M] screw

पेचकश *peckaś*[M] screwdriver

पेट *peṭ*[M] stomach, belly

पेटी[1] *peṭī*[F] belt

पेटी[2] *peṭī*[F] box, chest

पेड़ *peṛ*[M] tree

पेश *peś* presented; पेश आना *peś ānā* to come across as, to behave (towards, से *se*); पेश करना *peś karnā*[N] to present

पेशा *peśā*[M] profession

पेशाब *peśāb*[M] urine; पेशाब करना[N] *peśāb karnā* to urinate, pee

पेशेवर *peśevar* professional

पैंट *paiṇṭ*[M] trousers

पैंतालीस *paĩtālīs* forty-five

पैंतीस *paĩtīs* thirty-five

पैंसठ *paĩsaṭh* sixty-five

पैतृक *paitṛk* paternal, ancestral

पैदल *paidal* on foot

पैदा *paidā* (-*ā* invariable) born, produced; पैदा होना *paidā honā* to be born; पैदा करना *paidā karnā*ᴺ to produce

पैदाइश *paidāiś*ᶠ birth

पैदाइशी *paidāiśī* inborn, innate

पैदावार *paidāvār*ᴹ produce

पैर *pair*ᴹ foot; पैर की उँगली *pair kī ũglī*ᶠ toe

पैसा *paisā*ᴹ money; paisa, 100th of a rupee

पोंछना *põchnā*ᴺ to wipe, mop

पोतना *potnā*ᴺ to smear, daub

पोता *potā*ᴹ grandson (son's son)

पोती *potī*ᶠ granddaughter (son's daughter)

पोशाक *pośāk*ᶠ dress, clothing

पौधा *paudhā*ᴹ plant

पौन *paun* three-quarters; पौने *paune* a quarter less than the full unit (e.g. पौने चार किलो *paune cār kilo* 3.75 kilos, पौने चार बजे *paune cār baje* a quarter to four)

प्याज़ *pyāz*ᴹ⁽ᶠ⁾ onion

प्यार *pyār*ᴹ love, affection

प्यारा *pyārā* beloved, dear, sweet, lovely

प्याला *pyālā*ᴹ cup

प्यास *pyās*ᶠ thirst; प्यास लगना *pyās lagnā* thirst to strike — to feel thirsty

प्रकार *prakār*ᴹ type, kind, way

प्रकाश *prakāś*ᴹ light

प्रकृति *prakṛti*ᶠ nature

प्रगति *pragati*ᶠ progress

प्रगतिवादी *pragativādī* progressive

प्रचलित *pracalit* current, widespread

प्रति *prati*ᶠ copy (of book)

प्रतिध्वनि *pratidhvani*ᶠ echo

प्रतिबिंब *pratibimb*ᴹ reflection

प्रतिभा *pratibhā*ᶠ genius, talent, brilliance

प्रतिशत *pratiśat* per cent

प्रतिष्ठा *pratiṣṭhā*ᶠ reputation, prestige

प्रतिष्ठित *pratiṣṭhit* esteemed, established

प्रतिस्पर्धा *pratispardhā*ᶠ rivalry

प्रतीक *pratīk*ᴹ symbol

प्रथम *pratham* first

प्रथा *prathā*ᶠ custom, practice

प्रदर्शन *pradarśan*ᴹ show, demonstration

प्रदर्शनी *pradarśanī*F exhibition

प्रदूषण *pradūṣaṇ*M pollution

प्रदेश *pradeś*M state, region

प्रधान मंत्री *pradhān mantrī*M prime minister

प्रभाव *prabhāv*M influence, effect

प्रभावशाली *prabhāvśālī* influential

प्रभावित करना *prabhāvit karnā*N to influence, impress

प्रमाण *pramāṇ*M evidence

प्रयास *prayās*M effort, attempt, endeavour

प्रयोग *prayog*M use, usage; (का) प्रयोग करना *(kā) prayog karnā*N to use; to experiment

प्रयोजन *prayojan*M purpose, objective

प्रवेश *praveś*M entry; entrance

प्रवृत्ति *pravṛtti*F tendency, inclination

प्रशंसा *praśansā*F praise; (की) प्रशंसा करना *(kī) praśansā karnā*N to praise

प्रशिक्षण *praśikṣaṇ*M training

प्रश्न *praśn*M question

प्रसन्न *prasann* pleased, happy, glad

प्रसन्नता *prasanntā*F gladness, satisfaction

प्रसिद्ध *prasiddh* famous

प्राकृतिक *prākṛtik* natural, concerning nature

प्राचीन *prācīn* ancient

प्राध्यापक *prādhyāpak*M lecturer

प्राप्त करना *prāpt karnā*N to obtain, attain

प्रार्थना *prārthanā*F prayer, entreaty

प्रिय *priy* dear, favourite

प्रेम *prem*M love

प्रेमी *premī*M lover

प्रोग्राम *progrām*M programme, schedule, routine

प्रोत्साहन *protsāhan*M encouragement

प्रोत्साहित करना *protsāhit karnā*N to encourage

## फ ***pha***, फ़ ***fa***

फंदा *phandā*M trap, snare

फँसना *phãsnā* to be trapped, stuck, ensnared

फँसाना*N* *phãsānā* to trap, to ensnare

फटना *phaṭnā* to be torn, to tear, to burst

फफोला *phapholā*M blister

फ़रमाइश *farmāiś*F request, order

फ़रवरी *farvarī*F February

फ़रिश्ता *fariśtā*M angel

फ़र्क़ *farq*ᴹ difference; फ़र्क़ पड़ना *farq paṛnā* a difference to be felt (कोई फ़र्क़ नहीं पड़ता *koī farq nahī̃ paṛtā* it makes no difference)

फ़र्ज़ *farz*ᴹ duty, obligation

फ़र्श *farś*ᴹ ⁽ᶠ⁾ floor

फल *phal*ᴹ fruit

फ़िकर *fikar*, फ़िक्र *fikra*ᶠ anxiety, worry, concern

फिर *phir* then; again; फिर भी *phir bhī* even so; फिर से *phir se* again

फिरना *phirnā* to turn, turn back

फ़िलहाल *filhāl* in the meantime

फ़िल्म *film*ᶠ film

**Insight**

फल *phal* 'fruit' has the same metaphorical sense as the English — as in 'the fruits of action' etc. See also सफल *saphal* 'fruitful, successful' and असफल *asaphal* 'fruitless, unsuccessful'.

फलना *phalnā* to bear fruit, to thrive

फलवाला *phalvālā*ᴹ fruitseller

फ़लाना *falānā* so-and-so, such-and-such

फ़सल *fasal*ᶠ crop

फाँसी *phā̃sī*ᶠ noose; hanging; फाँसी देना *phā̃sī denā*ᴺ to hang, to sentence to death

फाटक *phāṭak*ᴹ gate

फाड़ना *phāṛnā*ᴺ to tear, split

फ़ायदा *fāydā*ᴹ profit, advantage, gain; फ़ायदा उठाना *fāydā uṭhānā*ᴺ to exploit, benefit from, make good use of

फ़ालतू *fāltū* spare, extra, surplus

फावड़ा *phāvṛā*ᴹ spade

फ़िल्मी *filmī* to do with films or film culture; melodramatic

फिसलना *phisalnā* to slip

फीका *phīkā* bland, dull, insipid

फ़ीता *fītā*ᴹ tape, ribbon, shoelace

फ़ीस *fīs*ᶠ fee, fees

फुफेरा भाई *phupherā bhāī*ᴹ cousin, son of father's sister

फुफेरी बहिन *phupherī bahin*ᶠ cousin, daughter of father's sister

फ़ुरसत *fursat*ᶠ leisure, free time

फुलका *phulkā*ᴹ chapati

फुसफुसाना *phusphusānā* to whisper

फूँकना *phū̃knā*ᴺ to blow, puff

फूटना *phūṭnā* to burst, break, crack

फूफा *phūphā*$^{M}$ uncle, father's sister's husband

फूफी *phūphī*$^{F}$ aunt, father's sister

फूल *phūl*$^{M}$ flower

फूलगोभी *phūlgobhī*$^{F}$ cauliflower

फूलना *phūlnā* to flower; to swell

फेंकना *phẽknā*$^{N}$ to throw, chuck

फेफड़ा *phephṛā*$^{M}$ lungs

फ़ेल होना *fel honā* to fail (exam etc.)

फैलना *phailnā* to spread

फैलाना *phailānā*$^{N}$ to spread

फ़ैसला *faislā*$^{M}$ decision, judgement

फोटो *foṭo*$^{M}$ photograph; फ़ोटो खींचना *foṭo khĩcnā*$^{N}$ to take a photo

फोड़ना *phoṛnā*$^{N}$ to burst, break, crack

फ़ोन *fon*$^{M}$ telephone; phone call; फ़ोन करना *fon karnā*$^{N}$ to telephone

फ़ौज *fauj*$^{F}$ army

फ़्रांसीसी *frānsīsī* (adj. & noun) French;$^{M}$ Frenchman; $^{F}$ French language

फ़्लैट *flaiṭ*$^{M}$ flat, apartment

## ब *ba*

बंद *band* closed, shut; बंद करना *band karnā*$^{N}$ to close, shut, turn off

बंदर *bandar*$^{M}$ monkey

बंदी *bandī*$^{M}$ prisoner

बंदूक़ *bandūq*$^{F}$ rifle, gun

बँधना *bā̃dhnā* to be tied, bound

बकबक *bakbak*$^{F}$ gabbling

बकरा *bakrā*$^{M}$ billygoat

बकरी *bakrī*$^{F}$ goat; she-goat

बकवास *bakvās*$^{F}$ nonsense, chatter

बक्सा *baksā*$^{M}$ box

बग़ल *bagal*$^{F}$ armpit; side की बग़ल में *kī bagal mẽ* by the side of, next to, near

बग़ीचा *bagīcā*$^{M}$ garden

बग़ैर ... के *bagair ... ke*, के बग़ैर *ke bagair* without

बचना *bacnā* to be saved, to survive, escape

बचपन *bacpan*$^{M}$ childhood

बचा *bacā* left, remaining, saved

बचाना$^{N}$ *bacānā* to save, rescue; बचाओ! *bacāo!* Help!

बच्चा *baccā*$^{M}$ child

बजना *bajnā* to chime, sound

बजाना *bajānā*$^{N}$ to play (music)

बजे *baje* (expresses time): दो बजे *do baje* two o'clock

बटुआ *baṭuā*$^{M}$ purse, wallet

बटोरना *baṭornā*$^{N}$ to gather, store up

बड़ा *baṛā* big, senior, important

बढ़ई *baṛhaī*[M] carpenter

बढ़कर *baṛhkar* better, greater

बढ़ना *baṛhnā* to increase, advance, grow

बढ़ाना *baṛhānā*[N] to extend, to make increase, advance, grow

बढ़िया *baṛhiyā* (-*ā* invariable) fine, choice, superior

बनना *bannā* to become; to be; to be made; to pretend to be

बनाना *banānā*[N] to make

बना-बनाया *banā-banāyā* ready-made

बनावटी *banāvaṭī* artificial

बनियान *baniyān*[F] vest

बयान *bayān*[M] statement, account, description

**Insight**

बढ़िया *baṛhiyā* 'superior' has the antonym घटिया *ghaṭiyā* 'inferior'; they derive from बढ़ना *baṛhnā* 'to increase' and घटना *ghaṭnā* 'to decrease' respectively; both adjectives are invariable, as in बढ़िया चाय *baṛhiyā cāy*[F].

बतलाना *batlānā*[N] to tell

बताना *batānā*[N] to tell

बत्ती *battī*[F] light, lamp

बत्तीस *battīs* thirty-two

बदतमीज़ *badtamīz* rude, discourteous

बदतमीज़ी *badtamīzī*[F] rudeness, discourtesy

बदतर *badtar* worse

बदमाश *badmāś* (adj. & noun) villainous, wicked;[M] villain

बदला *badlā*[M] exchange, revenge

बदसूरत *badsūrat* ugly

बधाई *badhāī*[F] congratulation

बयालीस *bayālīs* forty-two

बयासी *bayāsī* eighty-two

बरगद *bargad*[M] banyan (tree)

बरतन *bartan*[M] utensil, dish

बरताव *bartāv*[M] behaviour, treatment (of someone)

बरदाश्त करना *bardāśt karnā*[N] to tolerate, put up with

बरबरता *barbartā*[F] barbarity

बरबाद *barbād* destroyed, ruined; बरबाद करना *barbād karnā*[N] to ruin, waste

बरस *baras*[M] year

बरसात *barsāt*[F] rainy season, rains

बरसाती *barsātī*^F rooftop room

बरसाना *barsānā*^N to rain, to pour down

बरात *barāt*^F bridegroom's party in a wedding; procession of this party to bride's house

बराबर *barābar* equal, level, constant

बर्फ़ *barf*^F (M) ice; snow

बल[1] *bal*^M strength

बल[2] *bal*^M twist, bend, wrinkle; बल खाना *bal khānā*^N to be twisted, to wind

बलात्कार *balātkār*^M rape

बलिदान *balidān*^M sacrifice

बल्कि *balki* but, rather

बवासीर *bavāsīr*^F piles, haemorrhoids

बसंत *basant*^M spring (season)

बस[1] *bas* enough!, no more!

बस[2] *bas*^M power, control

बस[3] *bas*^F bus

बसना *basnā* to settle, dwell

बसाना *basānā*^N to inhabit, to establish a home

बसेरा *baserā*^M abode

बस्ती *bastī*^F settlement; slum

बहत्तर *bahattar* seventy-two

बहन *bahan*^F sister

बहना *bahnā* to flow; (of wind) to blow

बहनोई *bahanoī*^M brother-in-law (sister's husband)

बहरा *bahrā* deaf

बहस *bahas*^F argument, dispute, controversy

बहादुर *bahādur* brave

बहादुरी *bahādurī*^F bravery

बहाना[1] *bahānā*^M pretext, excuse

बहाना[2] *bahānā*^N to make flow, to set adrift, to wash away; to squander

बहाव *bahāv*^M flow, current

बहिन *bahin*^F sister

बहुत *bahut* very; much, many

बहुवचन *bahuvacan*^M plural

बहू *bahū*^F daughter-in-law; bride

बाँका *bā̃kā* crooked, bent; foppish

बाँग *bā̃g*^F crowing

बाँटना *bā̃ṭnā*^N to distribute, share, divide

बाँध *bā̃dh*^M dam

बाँधना *bā̃dhnā*^N to tie

बाँस *bā̃s*^M bamboo

बाँसुरी *bā̃surī*^F flute

बाँह *bā̃h*^F arm, upper arm

बाईस *bāīs* twenty-two

बाक़ायदा *bāqāydā* proper, regular

बाक़ी *bāqī* remaining, left

बाग़ *bāg*[M] garden, park

बाघ *bāgh*[M] tiger

-बाज़ *-bāz*[M] -player, doer of (e.g. पतंगबाज़[M] *pataṅgbāz* kite flyer, रंडीबाज़ *raṇḍībāz* whore monger)

बाज़ार *bāzār*[M] market

बाढ़ *bāṛh*[F] flood

बात[F] matter, idea, thing said; बात करना *bāt karnā*[N] to talk, converse (to/with, से *se*); कोई बात नहीं *koī bāt nahī̃* it doesn't matter, never mind, don't mention it; बात बनना *bāt bannā* to go well, an aim to be achieved (बात नहीं बनी *bāt nahī̃ banī* it didn't work out)

बातचीत *bātcīt*[F] conversation

बातूनी *bātūnī* talkative

बाद *bād* later (चार साल बाद *cār sāl bād* four years later); बाद में *bād mẽ* later, later on

बादल *bādal*[M] cloud

बादशाह *bādśāh*[M] emperor

बादाम *bādām*[M] almond

बानवे *bānve* ninety-two

बाप *bāp*[M] dad

बाबा *bābā*[M] grandfather; father; old man; term of endearment for a child

बाबू *bābū*[M] title of address for a respected man; clerk

बायाँ *bāyā̃* left; बाएँ *bāẽ* on/to the left; बाईं तरफ़ *bāī̃ taraf* on/to the left;[M] the 'left-hand' tabla drum

बार *bār*[F] time, occasion; इस बार *is bār* this time; कितनी बार *kitnī bār* how many times; कई बार *kaī bār* several times

बारह *bārah* twelve

बारात *bārāt*: see बरात *barāt*

बारिश *bāriś*[F] rain; बारिश होना *bāriś honā* to rain

बारी *bārī*[F] turn (in game etc.)

बारीक *bārīk* fine, slender, delicate

बारीकी *bārīkī*[F] fineness, subtlety, minute detail

बाल[1] *bāl*[M] hair

बाल[2] *bāl*[M] child, infant

बाल-बच्चे *bāl-bacce*[MPL] children

बालक *bālak*[M] child

बालटी *bālṭī*[F] bucket

बालू *bālū*[F] sand

बावन *bāvan* fifty-two

बासठ *bāsaṭh* sixty-two

बासी *bāsī* stale

बाहर *bāhar* out; outside, away (from home)

बिंदी *bindī*F dot, mark; forehead mark

बिंदु *bindu*MF dot, drop, point

बिकना *biknā* to be sold

बिगड़ना *bigaṛnā* to malfunction, go wrong; to lose temper

बिगाड़ना *bigāṛnā*N to spoil, ruin, harm

बिछाना *bichānā*N to spread out, lay out (bed etc.)

बिछौना *bichaunā*M bedding

बिजली *bijlī*F electricity; lightning

बिठाना *biṭhānā*N to make sit

बिताना *bitānā*N to pass (time)

बिल *bil*M hole (lived in by rodent or snake)

बिलकुल *bilkul* absolutely

बिल्ली *billī*F cat

बिस्तर *bistar*M bedding, bed

बीच *bīc*M middle; बीच में *bīc mẽ* in the middle; इस बीच *is bīc* meanwhile

बीज *bīj*M seed

बीड़ी *bīṛī*F beedie, small cigarette

बीतना *bītnā* to pass, be spent (time)

बीमार *bīmār* ill, sick

बीमारी *bīmārī*F sickness

बीवी *bīvī*F wife

बीस *bīs* twenty

बुआ *buā*F aunt (father's sister)

बुख़ार *bukhār*M fever

बुढ़िया *buṛhiyā*F old woman

बुज़ुर्ग *buzurg* (adj. & noun) elderly; M old person

बुझना *bujhnā* to be extinguished, to go out

बुझाना *bujhānā*N to extinguish, to put out

बुढ़ापा *buṛhāpā*M old age

बुद्ध *buddh* (adj. & noun) enlightened; M the Buddha

बुद्धि *buddhi*F intelligence, wisdom

बुद्धिजीवी *buddhijīvī* (adj. & noun)M intellectual

बुद्धिमान *buddhimān* intelligent, wise

बुद्धू *buddhū*M fool, dumbo

बुधवार *budhvār*M Wednesday

बुनियाद *buniyād*F basis, foundation

बुनियादी *buniyādī* basic

बुरा *burā* bad; बुरा मानना *burā mānnā* to take offence; बुरी तरह (से) *burī tarah (se)* badly

बुलबुला *bulbulā*M bubble

बुलाना *bulānā*N to call; to invite

बुहारना *buhārnā*N to sweep

बू *bū*F smell, scent, odour

बूआ *būā: see* बुआ *buā*

बूढ़ा *būṛhā* elderly

बृहस्पतिवार *bṛhaspativār*$^{M}$ Thursday

बेईमान *beīmān* dishonest

बेईमानी *beīmānī*$^{F}$ dishonesty

बेकार *bekār* useless; out of work

बेकारी *bekārī*$^{F}$ unemployment

बेचना *becnā*$^{N}$ to sell

बेचारा *becārā* helpless, wretched, poor

बेचैन *becain* restless, ill at ease

बेचैनी *becainī*$^{F}$ restlessness

बेटा *beṭā*$^{M}$ son

बेटी *beṭī*$^{F}$ daughter

बेबस *bebas* helpless, powerless

बेरोज़गार *berozgār* unemployed

बेरोज़गारी *berozgārī*$^{F}$ unemployment

बेवक़ूफ़ *bevaqūf* (adj. & noun) stupid; $^{M}$ fool

बेवक़ूफ़ी *bevaqūfī*$^{F}$ stupidity

बेवफ़ा *bevafā* faithless

बेवफ़ाई *bevafāī*$^{F}$ faithlessness

बेशक *beśak* without doubt, of course

बेहतर *behtar* better

बेहोश *behoś* unconscious

बैंक *baink*$^{M}$ bank (financial)

बैंगन *baĩgan*$^{M}$ aubergine

बैठक *baiṭhak*$^{F}$ sitting room

बैठना *baiṭhnā* to sit

बैठा *baiṭhā* seated, sitting

बैल *bail*$^{M}$ bullock, ox

बैलगाड़ी *bailgāṛī*$^{F}$ bullock cart

बोतल *botal*$^{F}$ bottle

बोर *bor* bored

बोरा *borā*$^{M}$ sack

बोरियत *boriyat*$^{F}$ boredom

बोलना *bolnā*$^{n}$ to speak

बोली *bolī*$^{F}$ speech, dialect

बौछाड़ *bauchāṛ*$^{F}$ shower (of rain)

बौद्ध *bauddh* (adj. & noun) Buddhist; $^{M}$ a Buddhist

बौद्धिक *bauddhik* intellectual, mental

ब्याह *byāh*$^{M}$ marriage, wedding

ब्योरा *byorā*$^{M}$ details, detailed statement

ब्रज भाषा *braj bhāṣā*$^{F}$ Braj Bhasha, a dialect of Hindi from the Braj district in western Uttar Pradesh

ब्राह्मण *brāhmaṇ*$^{M}$ Brahmin, member of priestly caste

## भ ***bha***

भक्ति *bhakti*$^{F}$ loving devotion

भगवान *bhagvān*$^{M}$ God, the supreme being

भजन *bhajan*$^{M}$ devotional song, hymn

भटकना *bhaṭaknā* to roam, stray

भतीजा *bhatījā*ᴹ nephew

भतीजी *bhatījī*ᶠ niece

भद्दा *bhaddā* ugly, awkward

भयंकर *bhayaṅkar* fearful

भय *bhay*ᴹ fear, dread

भयानक *bhayānak* fearsome

भर *bhar* the whole of, full: दिन भर *din bhar* all day long; भर पेट खाना *bhar peṭ khānā*ᴺ to eat one's fill

भरती *bhartī*ᶠ filling; admission, enrolment; भरती होना *bhartī honā* to be admitted, enrolled

भरना *bharnā* (intr. & tr.) to be filled;ᴺ to fill

भरोसा *bharosā*ᴹ trust, reliance

भला *bhalā* good, decent, kind

भलाई *bhalāī*ᶠ goodness, decency, kindness

भले ही *bhale hī* though it may well be that...

भवदीय *bhavdīy* yours sincerely (ending a letter)

भविष्य *bhaviṣya*ᴹ future

भव्य *bhavya* grand, splendid, magnificent

भाई *bhāī*ᴹ brother

भाग *bhāg*ᴹ part, share

भागना *bhāgnā* to run away, flee

भाग्य *bhāgya*ᴹ fortune, fate

भाग्यवान *bhāgyavān* fortunate

भाजी *bhājī*ᶠ cooked vegetables, vegetable curry

भात *bhāt*ᴹ boiled rice

भानजा *bhānjā*ᴹ nephew, sister's son

भानजी *bhānjī*ᶠ niece, sister's daughter

भाना *bhānā* to be liked, be pleasing, to appeal

भाप *bhāp*ᴹ steam

भाभी *bhābhī*ᶠ sister-in-law, elder brother's wife

भार *bhār*ᴹ weight, burden

भारत *bhārat*ᴹ; भारत सरकार *bhārat sarkār*ᶠ the Government of India

भारतवर्ष *bhāratvarṣ*ᴹ India

भारतीय *bhāratīy* (adj. & noun)ᴹ Indian

भारी *bhārī* heavy; भारी-भरकम *bhārī-bharkam* bulky

भारीपन *bhārīpan*ᴹ heaviness

भाव *bhāv*ᴹ state of being; emotion, sentiment; rate, price

भावना *bhāvnā*ᶠ feeling, emotion

भावात्मक *bhāvātmak* emotional

भावुक *bhāvuk* sentimental

भालू *bhālū*^M bear

भाषण *bhāṣaṇ*^M speech, lecture

भाषा *bhāṣā*^F language

-भाषी *-bhāṣī*-speaking (e.g. हिन्दी-भाषी *hindī-bhāṣī* Hindi-speaking)

भिंडी *bhiṇḍī*^F lady's fingers, okra

भिखारी *bhikhārī*^M beggar

भिजवाना *bhijvānā* to have sent (by someone), to cause to be sent

भिन्न *bhinn* different

भी *bhī* also; even (follows emphasized word); भी ... भी *bhī ... bhī* both ... and

भीख *bhīkh*^F alms; भीख माँगना *bhīkh mā̃gnā*^N to beg

भीगना *bhīgnā* to get soaked

भीड़ *bhīṛ*^F crowd; भीड-भाड़ *bhīṛ-bhāṛ*^F crowd, crush, throng

भीतर *bhītar* inside

भुनभुनाना *bhunbhunānā* to grumble, fume, rage

भू *bhū*^F earth, world, land

भूकंप *bhūkamp*^M earthquake

भूख *bhūkh*^F hunger; भूख लगना *bhūkh lagnā* hunger to strike, to feel hungry

भूखा *bhūkhā* hungry

भूगोल *bhūgol*^M geography

भूत *bhūt*^M ghost; the past

भूतपूर्व *bhūtpūrv* former, previous

भूनना *bhūnnā*^N to roast

भूमंडल *bhūmaṇḍal*^M the earth, the globe

भूमंडलीकरण *bhūmaṇḍalīkaraṇ*^M globalization

भूमि *bhūmi*^F land

भूमिका *bhūmikā*^F role, part; introduction (to a book)

भूमिगत *bhūmigat* underground

भूरा *bhūrā* brown

भूल *bhūl*^F mistake, error; भूल-सुधार *bhūl-sudhār*^M correction of mistakes

भूलना *bhūlnā* to forget; to err, stray; भूलकर भी *bhūlkar bhī* even by mistake; भूल जाना *bhūl jānā* to forget

भेंट *bhẽṭ*^F meeting; formal gift

भेड़ *bheṛ*^F sheep

भेजना *bhejnā*^N to send

भेद *bhed*^M difference; secret, mystery

भेदभाव *bhedbhāv*^M discrimination

भैया *bhaiyā*^M brother

भोगना *bhognā*^N to enjoy, suffer, undergo, reap fruits of past actions

भोजन *bhojan*^M food; भोजन करना *bhojan karnā*^N to eat, dine (formal)

भोला *bholā* simple, innocent

भौंकना *bhaũknā* to bark

भ्रष्ट *bhrașṭ* corrupt

भ्रष्टाचार *bhrașṭācār*ᴹ corruption

भ्रांति *bhrānti*ᶠ error, delusion, misconception

## म *ma*

मंगल *maṅgal* (adj. & noun) auspicious, happy;ᴹ good fortune, well being, state of grace

मंगलवार *maṅgalvār*ᴹ Tuesday

मँगवाना *mãgvānā*ᴺ to order (especially through someone else)

मँगाना *mãgānā*ᴺ to order, ask for

मंच *manc*ᴹ stage, platform

मंज़िल *manzil*ᶠ storey; stage of journey, day's travel

मँडराना *mãḍrānā* to hover around, float about

मंत्री *mantrī*ᴹ minister (political)

मंदिर *mandir*ᴹ temple (shrine)

मई *maī*ᶠ May

मकड़ी *makṛī*ᶠ spider

मकान *makān*ᴹ house; मकान-मालिक *makān-mālik*ᴹ landlord

मक्खन *makkhan*ᴹ butter

मक्खी *makkhī*ᶠ fly; मक्खियाँ मारना *makkhiyā̃ mārnā*ᴺ to 'kill flies', i.e. to laze about

मगर *magar* but

मगरमच्छ *magarmacch*ᴹ crocodile

मचना *macnā* to be created (of noise etc.)

मच्छर *macchar*ᴹ mosquito

मच्छरदानी *macchardānī*ᶠ mosquito net

मछली *machlī*ᶠ fish

मज़दूर *mazdūr*ᴹ labourer

मज़बूत *mazbūt* robust, strong

मजबूर *majbūr* compelled

मजबूरी *majbūrī*ᶠ compulsion

मज़ा *mazā*ᴹ fun, excitement, pleasure, enjoyment; मज़ा आना *mazā ānā* to feel enjoyment, have fun

मज़ाक़ *mazāq*ᴹ joke

मज़ाक़िया *mazāqiyā* humorous

मत *mat* don't (in commands: मत जाओ *mat jāo* don't go)

मतलब *matlab*ᴹ meaning; self-interest

मदद *madad*ᶠ help; (की) मदद करना *(kī) madad karnā*ᴺ to help

मन *man*ᴹ mind, heart; मन करना *man karnā*ᴺ, मन होना *man honā* to feel like (doing something); मन लगना *man lagnā* to feel at home

मना *manā* forbidden; मना करना *manā karnā*^N to forbid, prohibit

मनाना *manānā*^N to celebrate (birthday, festival etc.)

मनुष्य *manuṣya*^M man, person, human being

मनोरंजन *manoranjan*^M entertainment

मरज़ी *marzī*^F preference, choice, wish

मरना *marnā* to die

मरम्मत *marammat*^F repair; (की) मरम्मत करना *(kī) marammat karnā*^N to mend, repair; to beat up

मरीज़ *marīz*^M patient

मरुस्थल *marusthal*^M desert

मर्द *mard* (adj. & noun) male;^M male, man

मर्म *marm*^M heart, core; inner meaning; मर्म-स्पर्शी *marm-sparśī* touching, affecting

मलत्याग *maltyāg*^M defecation

मलबा *malbā*^M rubble

मलाई *malāī*^F cream (dairy)

मशहूर *maśhūr* famous

मसजिद *masjid*^F mosque

मसलन *maslan* for example

मसरूफ़ *masrūf* busy, occupied

मसाला *masālā*^M spice; मसालेदार *masāledār* spicy, 'hot'

मस्त *mast* intoxicated (with happiness, delight, etc.), blithely happy

मस्ताना *mastānā* drunken, carefree, spirited

मस्ती *mastī*^F intoxication, delight, passion, enjoyment

महँगा *mahãgā* expensive

महत्त्व *mahattva*^M importance

महत्त्वपूर्ण *mahattvapūrṇ* important

महफ़िल *mahfil*^F gathering (for music, dance, poetry etc.)

महबूब *mahbūb* (adj. & noun)^M beloved

महल *mahal*^M palace

महसूस *mahsūs* felt, perceived

महा- *mahā-* (prefix) great

महाद्वीप *mahādvīp*^M continent

महान् *mahān* great

महानगर *mahānagar*^M city, metropolis

महायुद्ध *mahāyuddh*^M great war, world war

महाराष्ट्र *mahārāṣṭra*^M Maharashtra

महिला *mahilā*^F lady

महीन *mahīn* fine, delicate

महीना *mahīnā*^M month; menstruation; महीना लगना *mahīnā lagnā* to have a monthly period

महोदय *mahoday*[M] sir (honorific used in letters)

महोदया *mahodayā*[F] madam (honorific used in letters)

माँ *mā̃*[F] mum

माँ-बाप *mā̃-bāp*[MPL] parents

माँग[1] *mā̃g*[F] demand

माँग[2] *mā̃g*[F] hair parting

माँगना *mā̃gnā*[N] to ask for, demand

माँजना *mā̃jnā*[N] to scrub, scour, clean, polish up

मांस *mā̃s*[M] meat, flesh

मांस-पेशी *mā̃s-peśī*[F] muscle

माचिस *mācis*[F] match, matchstick

माता *mātā*[F] mother; माता-पिता *mātā-pitā*[MPL] parents

मातृभाषा *mātṛbhāṣā*[F] mother tongue

मात्रा *mātrā*[F] amount, quantity; a beat (in music or verse rhythm)

माथा *māthā*[M] forehead

मादा *mādā* female

मानना *mānnā*[N] to accept, believe

मानव *mānav*[M] human, man

माने *māne* (adverb & noun) that is, i.e.;[M] meaning, sense

मानों *mānõ* as if, as though

मापना *māpnā*[N] to measure

माफ़ करना *māf karnā*[N] to forgive

माफ़ी *māfī*[F] forgiveness; माफ़ी माँगना *māfī mā̃gnā*[N] to apologize

मामला *māmlā*[M] matter, affair

मामा *māmā*[M] maternal uncle

मामी *māmī*[F] aunt (maternal uncle's wife)

मामूली *māmūlī* ordinary, usual

मायका *māykā*[M] married woman's parental home

मायने *māyne* (adverb & noun) that is, i.e.;[M] meaning, sense

मार *mār*[F] beating; मार खाना *mār khānā*[N] to suffer a beating

मारना *mārnā*[N] to hit, beat, strike, kill

मार्ग *mārg*[M] road, street (common in street names)

मार्च *mārc*[M] March

माल *māl*[M] goods, property, possessions

मालगाड़ी *mālgāṛī*[F] goods train

माला *mālā*[F] garland

मालिक *mālik*[M] boss, owner, proprietor; मालिक-मकान *mālik-makān*[M] householder, landlord

माली *mālī*[M] gardener

मालूम *mālūm* (is) known; मालूम नहीं *mālūm nahī̃* (I) don't know; मालूम करना *mālūm karnā*[N] to find out, ascertain

मास *mās*ᴹ month
मासूम *māsūm* innocent
माहिर *māhir* expert, skilled
माहौल *māhaul*ᴹ atmosphere
मिचली *miclī*ᶠ nausea
मिज़ाज *mizāj*ᴹ temperament
मिटना *miṭnā* to be erased, obliterated
मिटाना *miṭānā*ᴺ to erase, obliterate
मिट्टी *miṭṭī*ᶠ earth, soil; dust; मिट्टी का तेल *miṭṭī kā tel*ᴹ kerosene
मिठाई *miṭhāī*ᶠ sweet, sweet dish, sweetmeat
मिठास *miṭhās*ᶠ sweetness
मित्र *mitr*ᴹ friend
मित्रता *mitratā*ᶠ friendship
मिनट *minaṭ*ᴹ minute
मिर्च *mirc*ᶠ pepper, chilli; शिमला मिर्च *śimlā mirc*ᶠ capsicum, green pepper; हरी मिर्च *harī mirc*ᶠ green chilli
मिलकर *milkar* together, united
मिलनसार *milansār* sociable, friendly
मिलना *milnā* to meet (with, से *se*); to be available; to resemble; मिलना-जुलना *milnā-julnā* to meet, to get on with, to resemble
मिलाना *milānā*ᴺ to bring together; to mix; to dial (a number); to join (hands); to tune (a musical instrument)
मिश्रण *miśraṇ*ᴹ mixture
मिश्रित *miśrit* mixed
मिसाल *misāl*ᶠ example
मिस्तरी *mistrī*ᴹ mechanic, artisan, skilled worker
मीठा *mīṭhā* sweet
मीनार *mīnār*ᶠ tower, minaret
मुंबई *mumbaī*ᶠ Mumbai, Bombay
मुँह *mũh*ᴹ mouth; face
मुक़दमा *muqadmā*ᴹ lawsuit, case
मुक़ाबला *muqāblā*ᴹ challenge, competition, rivalry, comparison
मुख *mukh*ᴹ mouth; face
मुख्य *mukhya* principal, chief, main
मुग़ल *mugal* (adj. & noun)ᴹ Mughal
मुझ *mujh* oblique of मैं *maĩ*
मुट्ठी *muṭṭhī*ᶠ fist
मुड़ना *muṛnā* to turn
मुबारक *mubārak* blessed; नया साल मुबारक! *nayā sāl mubārak!* happy new year!
मुफ़्त (का) *muft (kā)* free; मुफ़्त में *muft mẽ* for nothing, free, gratis

मुमकिन *mumkin* possible

मुसीबत *musībat*$^{F}$ trouble, calamity, misfortune

मुर्ग़ *murg*$^{M}$ cock, cockerel

मुर्ग़ी *murgī*$^{F}$ hen, chicken

मुलाक़ात *mulāqāt*$^{F}$ meeting, encounter

मुलायम *mulāyam* soft, tender

मुश्किल *muśkil* (adj. & noun) difficult;$^{F}$ difficulty; मुश्किल से *muśkil se* with difficulty, hardly, barely

मुसलमान *musalmān* (adj. & noun)$^{M}$ Muslim

मुसीबत *musībat*$^{F}$ trouble, difficulty, crisis

मुस्कराना *muskarānā*$^{n}$ to smile

मूर्च्छित *mūrcchit* fainted, unconscious

मूल *mūl*$^{M}$ origin, root

मूली *mūlī*$^{F}$ mooli, a white radish

मूल्य *mūlya*$^{M}$ value, price

मूल्यवान *mūlyavān* valuable

मृग *mṛg*$^{M}$ deer

मृत्यु *mṛtyu*$^{F}$ death

में *mẽ* in; में से *mẽ se* from among, out of

मेंढक *mẽḍhak*$^{M}$ frog

मेज़ *mez*$^{F}$ table

मेज़बान *mezbān*$^{M}$ host

मेज़बानी *mezbānī*$^{F}$ hospitality

मेमसाहब *memsāhab*$^{F}$ memsahib

**Insight**

मेमसाहब *memsāhab* derives from English 'ma'am' (Madam) plus *sāhab* 'master' (from Arabic through Persian).

मुहब्बत *muhabbat*$^{F}$ love

मुहावरा *muhāvrā*$^{M}$ saying, idiom

मूँगफली *mūgphalī*$^{F}$ peanut, groundnut

मूँछ *mūch*$^{F}$ moustache

मूर्ख *mūrkh*$^{M}$ fool

मूर्खता *mūrkhtā*$^{F}$ foolishness

मूर्ति *mūrti*$^{F}$ statue, image

मूर्च्छा *mūrcchā*$^{F}$ faint, swoon

मेरा *merā* my, mine

मेला *melā*$^{M}$ fair; मेला लगना *melā lagnā* a fair to be held

मेहनत *mehnat*$^{F}$ hard work

मेहनती *mehntī* hard working

मेहमान *mehmān*$^{M}$ guest

मेहरबानी *mehrbānī*$^{F}$ kindness; आपकी मेहरबानी है *āpkī mehrbānī hai* thank you

मैं *maĩ* I

मैदा *maidā*^M fine-ground flour

मैदान *maidān*^M open area, playing field, plain

मैल *mail*^F dirt

मैला *mailā* dirty

मोज़ा *mozā*^M sock

मोटा *moṭā* fat, thick; rough, course

मोड़ *moṛ*^M turn, turning

मोड़ना^N *moṛnā* to turn

मोती *motī*^M pearl

मोम *mom*^M wax

मोमबत्ती *mombattī*^F candle

मोर *mor*^M peacock

मौत *maut*^F death

मौलिक *maulik* original

मौसम *mausam*^M weather

मौसा *mausā*^M uncle (husband of mother's sister)

मौसी *mausī*^F aunt (mother's sister)

## य ***ya***

यक़ीन *yaqīn*^M confidence, faith; मुझे यक़ीन है *mujhe yaqīn hai* I'm certain

यथार्थ *yathārth* (adj. & noun) real, realistic;^M reality

यथार्थवाद *yathārthvād*^M realism

यदि *yadi* if

यद्यपि *yadyapi* although

**Insight**

यद्यपि *yadyapi* combines two Sanskrit words: यदि *yadi* 'if' (also used in Hindi) and अपि *api*, an emphatic similar in sense to Hindi भी *bhī*.

मोरचा *morcā*^M front (military, political)

मोल *mol*^M price, value; मोल लेना *mol lenā*^M to buy, to take on, buy into, to get into something (with all its consequences)

मोल-तोल *mol-tol*^M, मोल-भाव *mol-bhāv*^M haggling, bargaining

मौक़ा *mauqā*^M chance, opportunity

यश *yaś*^M fame, renown

यह *yah* he, she, it, this

यहाँ *yahā̃* here; यहाँ तक कि... *yahā̃ tak ki*... so much so that...

यहीं *yahī̃* right here, in this very place

या *yā* or; या तो... या *yā to*... *yā* either... or

यातायात *yātāyāt*^M traffic

यात्रा *yātrā*$^{F}$ journey

यात्री *yātrī*$^{M}$ traveller, passenger

याद *yād*$^{F}$ memory; याद आना *yād ānā* to come to mind, be remembered; याद करना *yād karnā*$^{N}$ to remember; to recall, to commit to memory; to think of, summon (e.g. an employee); याद दिलाना *yād dilānā*$^{N}$ to remind; याद रखना *yād rakhnā*$^{N}$ to keep in mind

यादगार *yādgār*$^{F}$ memorial; souvenir

याददाश्त *yāddāśt*$^{F}$ memory, power of memory

यानी *yānī* that is to say, i.e.

यार *yār*$^{M}$ friend, pal

युग *yug*$^{M}$ historical age, period

युद्ध *yuddh*$^{M}$ war

युवक *yuvak*$^{M}$ a youth, young man

यूँ *yū̃*: see यों *yõ*

ये *ye* they, these; he, she (honorific plural)

यों *yõ* thus, like this; यों तो *yõ to* actually, as a matter of fact; while, although

योग *yog*$^{M}$ yoga

योगदान *yogdān*$^{M}$ contribution (to a cause)

योग्य *yogya* worthy, suitable

योग्यता *yogyatā*$^{F}$ suitability, ability

योजना *yojnā*$^{F}$ scheme, plan

यौन *yaun* sexual, venereal

## र ***ra***

रंग *raṅg*$^{M}$ colour; dye

रँगरेज़ *rãgrez*$^{M}$ dyer

रंगीन *raṅgīn* coloured

रँगीला *rãgīlā* colourful, bright, vivacious

रंडी *raṇḍī*$^{F}$ prostitute

रईस *raīs*$^{M}$ aristocrat, nobleman, wealthy or landed person

रक्त *rakt*$^{M}$ blood

रक्तचाप *raktacāp*$^{M}$ blood pressure

रक्षा *rakṣā*$^{F}$ protection, security, preservation, defence; (की) रक्षा करना *(kī) rakṣā karnā*$^{N}$ to protect, preserve, defend

रखना *rakhnā*$^{N}$ to put, keep

रचना[1] *racnā*$^{F}$ creation, artistic work

रचना[2] *racnā*$^{N}$ to create

रज़ाई *razāī*$^{F}$ quilt

रत्न *ratna*$^{M}$ jewel, gem

रद्द *radd* cancelled

रफ़्तार *raftār*$^{F}$ speed

रवानी *ravānī*$^{F}$ fluency; रवानी से *ravānī se* fluently

रविवार *ravivār*$^{M}$ Sunday

रवैया *ravaiyā*^M attitude, conduct, manner

रस *ras*^M juice; essence; aesthetic delight, pleasure

रसिक *rasik*^M one who takes delight in something, a connoisseur, aficionado

रसीद *rasīd*^F receipt

रसीला *rasīlā* juicy

रसोइया *rasoiyā*^M cook

रसोई *rasoī*^F kitchen

रस्ता *rastā*: see रास्ता *rāstā*

रस्सी *rassī*^F string, rope

रहना *rahnā* to live, to stay; (in the negative, न रहना *na rahnā* to be no more, to die — रवि कुमार नहीं रहे *ravi kumār nahī̃ rahe* Ravi Kumar has passed away)

रहस्य *rahasya*^M secret, mystery

रहस्यमय *rahasyamay* mysterious

राख *rākh*^F ash, ashes

राज *rāj*^M rule; realm, empire

राज़ *rāz*^M secret

राजदूत *rājdūt*^M ambassador

राजदूतावास *rājdūtāvās*^M embassy

राजधानी *rājdhānī*^F capital city

राजनीति *rājnīti*^F politics

राजनीतिज्ञ *rājnītijña* (pronounced 'rājnītigya')^M politician

राजनेता *rājnetā*^M politician

राजा *rājā*^M king, raja

राज़ी *rāzī* agreeable, content (with a suggestion)

रात *rāt*^F night; रात का खाना *rāt kā khānā*^M dinner; रात भर *rāt bhar* all night long; रातोंरात *rātõrāt* overnight

रानी *rānī*^F queen

राम-कहानी *rām-kahānī*^F long rambling story, tale of woe

राय *rāy*^F opinion

राशि *rāśi*^F sum, amount; sign of the zodiac

राष्ट्र *rāṣṭra*^M state, nation

राष्ट्रभाषा *raṣṭrabhāṣā*^F national language

राष्ट्रवाद *rāṣṭravād*^M nationalism

राष्ट्रवादी *rāṣṭravādī* (adj. & noun)^M nationalist

राष्ट्रीय *rāṣṭrīy* national

राष्ट्रीयता *rāṣṭrīyatā*^F nationality

रास्ता *rāstā* (often pronounced 'rastā')^M road, way; पाँच मिनट का रास्ता *pā̃c minaṭ kā rāstā* five minutes' journey; रास्ते में *rāste mẽ* on the way, en route

राहत *rāhat*^F relief, ease

रिक्शा *rikśā*^M rickshaw

रिक्शे-वाला *rikśe-vālā*$^{M}$ rickshaw driver

रियाज़ *riyāz*$^{F}$ practice, training

रिवाज *rivāj*$^{M}$ custom, practice

रिश्ता *riśtā*$^{M}$ connection, relationship

रिश्तेदार *riśtedār*$^{M}$ relation, relative

रिश्वत *riśvat*$^{F}$ bribe; रिश्वत लेना *riśvat lenā*$^{N}$ to take a bribe

रिहा करना *rihā karnā* (*-ā* invariable in *rihā*)$^{N}$ to release

रुकना *ruknā* to stop

रुखाई *rukhāī*$^{F}$ dryness, roughness, harshness, bluntness

रुचि *ruci*$^{F}$ taste, liking, interest

रुपया *rupayā*$^{M}$ rupee; money

रूबरू *rūbarū* face to face

रूमाल *rūmāl*$^{M}$ handkerchief

रूस *rūs*$^{M}$ Russia

रूसी *rūsī* (adj. & noun)$^{M}$ Russian;$^{F}$ the Russian language

रेखा *rekhā*$^{F}$ line

रेगिस्तान *registān*$^{M}$ desert

रेज़गारी *rezgārī*$^{F}$ change, small change

रेडियो *rediyo*$^{M}$ radio

रेत *ret*$^{F}$ sand

रेतीला *retīlā* sandy

रेलगाड़ी *relgāṛī*$^{F}$ train

रेशम *reśam*$^{M}$ silk

रेशमी *reśmī* silken, made of silk

रोक *rok*$^{F}$ restriction, limitation, bar

**Insight**

रुपया *rupayā* – the rupee (the word originally connoted a silver coin) consists of 100 पैसा *paise* (singular पैसे *paisā*). Before decimalization in 1957 it consisted of 16 आने *āne* (singular आना *ānā*), each of which was divided into four 'old' पैसे *paise*.

रुलाना *rulānā*$^{N}$ to make (someone) cry

रूखा *rūkhā* rough, dry, harsh

रूठना *rūṭhnā* to sulk

रूप *rūp*$^{M}$ form, beauty; के रूप में *ke rūp mē* in the form of

रोकना *roknā*$^{N}$ to stop

रोग *rog*$^{M}$ illness

रोगी *rogī*$^{M}$ patient

रोचक *rocak* interesting

रोज़ *roz* (adv. & noun) every day, daily;$^{M}$ day

रोज़ाना *rozānā* daily

रोटी *roṭī*^F bread; a chapati or other type of flatbread; food; daily bread, livelihood

रोना *ronā*^n to cry, weep; रोना-धोना *ronā-dhonā* to weep and wail

रोशन *rośan* bright, lit

रोशनी *rośnī*^F light, brightness

रौनक *raunak*^F brightness of mood, liveliness of atmosphere (of a place)

## ल *la*

लँगड़ा *lãgṛā* (adj. & noun) lame;^M a lame person

लंगूर *laṅgūr*^M langur, a species of long-tailed monkey

लंदन *landan*^M London

लंबा *lambā* long, tall; लंबा-चौड़ा *lambā-cauṛā* of large proportions, huge, endless

लंबाई *lambāī*^F length; height

लकड़ी *lakṛī*^F wood; a piece of wood, stick

लकीर *lakīr*^F line, rut; लकीर का फ़कीर *lakīr kā faqīr*^M someone who treads an established path

लखपति *lakhpati*^M owner of lakhs, i.e. a 'millionaire'

लगना *lagnā* to seem; to be related, attached; to catch (of fire); to be caught (of illness); to gather (of crowds); to begin to (with oblique infinitive: वह रोने लगी *vah rone lagī* she began to cry); time to be taken: घर जाने में १० मिनट लगते हैं/एक घंटा लगता है *ghar jāne mẽ 10 minaṭ lagte haĩ/ ek ghaṇṭā lagtā hai* it takes 10 minutes/one hour to get home

लगभग *lagbhag* about, approximately

लगाना *lagānā* to connect, apply, fix, set up

लघु *laghu* small, light

लघुशंका *laghuśaṅkā*^F (euphemism for) urination

लज़ीज़ *lazīz* delicious

लज्जा *lajjā*^F shame; shyness, modesty, bashfulness

लटकना *laṭaknā* to hang, be suspended, dangle

लटकाना *laṭkānā*^N to hang up, suspend

लड़कपन *laṛakpan*^M boyhood, childhood; childishness

लड़का *laṛkā*^M boy

लड़की *laṛkī*^F girl

लड़ना *laṛnā*^N to fight

लड़ाई *laṛāī*^F fighting, battle, war

लदना *ladnā* to be loaded, laden; to be over (of one's days, life)

लपेटना *lapeṭnā*^N to wrap

लस्सी *lassī*^F a drink made of yoghurt

लहर *lahar*^F wave, billow; frenzy, wave of emotion

लहसुन *lahsun*^M garlic

लाइट *lāiṭ*^F light; electricity, current

लाख *lākh* lakh, one hundred thousand

लाजवाब *lājavāb* beyond compare

लाज़िमी *lāzimī* obligatory; proper

लाठी *lāṭhī*^F stick, truncheon

लादना *lādnā*^N to load

लाना *lānā* to bring, fetch

लापता *lāpatā* (-*ā* invariable) missing

लापरवाह *lāparvāh* careless

लापरवाही *lāparvāhī*^F carelessness

लाभ *lābh*^M profit, advantage

लाभकर *lābhkar* beneficial, advantageous

लायक़ *lāyaq* worthy, suitable

लाल *lāl* red

लालच *lālac*^M greed

लालची *lālcī* greedy

लालसा *lālsā*^F longing, desire

लाश *lāś*^F dead body, corpse

लिंग *liṅg*^M gender (in grammar)

लिखना *likhnā*^N to write

लिखाना *likhānā*^N to dictate

लिखावट *likhāvaṭ*^F writing, handwriting

लिखित *likhit* written; in writing, in written form

लिटाना *liṭānā*^N to make lie down

लिपटना *lipaṭnā* to stick, to cling

लिपटाना *lipṭānā*^N to make cling, to wrap

लिपि *lipi*^F script, alphabet

लिफ़ाफ़ा *lifāfā*^M envelope

लीद *līd*^F dung

लीपना *līpnā*^N to plaster, smear, whitewash

लुढ़कना *luṛhaknā* to topple over, roll down, tumble

लुत्फ़ *lutf*^M enjoyment, pleasure

लूटना *lūṭnā*^N to loot, rob, rip off

ले आना *le ānā* to bring

ले जाना *le jānā* to take away

लेकिन *lekin* but

लेख *lekh*^M article (written)

लेखक *lekhak*^M writer, author

लेखन *lekhan*^M writing

लेखिका *lekhikā*^F writer, authoress

लेटना *leṭnā* to lie down

लेना *lenā*N to take; लेना-देना *lenā-denā*M dealings, connection

लोक- *lok-* folk~, to do with 'the people'

लोकगीत *lokgīt*M folksong

लोकप्रिय *lokpriy* popular

लोग *log*MPL people

लोटपोट *loṭpoṭ* rolling about, convulsed (with pain or laughter)

लोभ *lobh*M greed

लोमड़ी *lomṛī*F fox

लोहा *lohā*M iron; metal

लौटना *lauṭnā* to return, to come/go back

लौटाना *lauṭānā*N to give back, return

## व ***va***

वक़ालत *vaqālat*F law practice

वक़ील *vaqīl*M lawyer

वक़्त *vaqt*M time

वजह *vajah*F reason; की वजह से *kī vajah se* because of

वट *vaṭ*M banyan (tree)

वन *van*M wood, forest, jungle

वयस्क *vayask* adult

वरदी *vardī*F uniform

वर्जित *varjit* prohibited

वर्ण *varṇ*M category, type, colour, caste

वर्णन *varṇan*M description; (का) वर्णन करना N *(kā) varṇan karnā* to describe

वर्णमाला *varṇmālā*F syllabary, alphabet

वर्तनी *vartanī*F spelling, orthography

वर्तमान *vartmān* current, present

वर्ष *varṣ*M year

वर्षा *varṣā*F rain; rainy season

वसंत *vasant*M spring (season)

**Insight**

वसंत *vasant* – like many other Sanskrit loanwords such as वन *van* 'forest' and वीर *vīr* 'hero', this word has parallel vernacular pronunciations and spellings in ब- *ba-* (बसंत, बन, बीर). Compare also बरस *baras* < बर्ष *varṣ*.

वग़ैरह *vagairah* etc., and so on

वचन *vacan*M word, promise

वज़न *vazan*M weight

वसीयत *vasīyat*F will, testament

वसूल करना *vasūl karnā*N to collect (payment)

वस्तु *vastu*^F thing, object

वह *vah* he, she, it, that

वहाँ *vahā̃* there

वहीं *vahī̃* right there, in that very place

वाक्य *vākya*^M sentence

वाणी *vāṇī*^F speech, utterance; voice; (sacred) text

वातावरण *vātāvaraṇ*^M atmosphere

वाद-विवाद *vād-vivād*^M debate, discussion

वादा *vādā*^M promise

वाद्य *vādya*^M musical instrument

वापस *vāpas* back; वापस आना *vāpas ānā* to come back; वापस जाना *vāpas jānā* to go back; वापस देना *vāpas denā*^N to give back

वाराणसी *vārāṇasī*^F Varanasi, Banaras

वार्षिक *vārṣik* annual

-वाला *vālā a* suffix forming nouns and adjectives, e.g. गाँववाला *gā̃vvālā*^M villager; पीछेवाली सीट *pīchevālī sīṭ*^F the rear seat; with oblique infinitive verb it has the sense 'the one who does/is about to do' — जानेवाले *jānevāle* those who are leaving, about to leave

वासना *vāsnā*^F desire, passion

वास्तव *vāstav* real, actual; वास्तव में *vāstav mẽ* in fact, in reality

वाह *vāh* ah!, bravo! (expresses admiration – or sarcastic scorn)

वाहन *vāhan*^M vehicle

विकलांग *vikalāṅg* disabled

विकल्प *vikalp*^M option, alternative

विकसित *vikasit* developed (of an economy etc.)

विकार *vikār*^M change, deviation, deterioration

विकास *vikās*^M development

विकासशील *vikāsśīl* developing (of an economy etc.)

विक्रम संवत् *vikram samvat*^M dating system beginning 57 years BC with the reign of Vikramāditya (thus 2068 VS = AD 2011)

विचार *vicār*^M thought, idea, opinion

विचार-विमर्श करना *vicār-vimarś karnā*^N to discuss, debate

विजय *vijay*^F victory

विज्ञान *vijñān* (pronounced 'vigyān')^M science

विज्ञानी *vijñānī* (pronounced 'vigyānī')^M scientist

विज्ञापन *vijñāpan* (pronounced 'vigyāpan')^M advertisement

विदा *vidā*F departure, leave taking; विदा करना *vidā karnā*N to bid goodbye, to see off

विदेश *videś* (adv. & noun) abroad;M foreign country

विदेशी *videśī* (adj. & noun) foreign;M foreigner

विद्या *vidyā*F knowledge, learning; a discipline

विद्यार्थी *vidyārthī*M student

विद्यालय *vidyālay*M college

विधवा *vidhvā*F widow

विधि *vidhi*F rule, law; manner

विनम्र *vinamra* modest, humble

विभाग *vibhāg*M department, division, section

विरह *virah*M separation; the pain of parting

विरासत *virāsat*F inheritance; विरासत में पाना *virāsat mẽ pānā*N to inherit

विरोध *virodh*M opposition

विवाह *vivāh*M marriage, wedding

विवाहित *vivāhit* married

विशाल *viśāl* huge, expansive

विशेष *viśeṣ* special, particular

विशेषण *viśeṣaṇ*M adjective

विश्लेषण *viśleṣaṇ*M analysis

विश्व *viśva*M universe

विश्वविद्यालय *viśvavidyālay*M university

विश्वास *viśvās*M belief

विष *viṣ*M poison

विषय *viṣay*M subject

विस्तार *vistār*M expanse, extent; विस्तार से *vistār se* at length, in detail

वीर *vīr* (adj. & noun) valiant, brave, heroic;M hero, warrior

वीरान *vīrān* deserted, desolate

वे *ve* they, those; he, she (honorific plural)

वेतन *vetan*M pay, wage, salary

वेश्या *veśyā*F prostitute

वैर *vair*M enmity, hostility

वैवाहिक *vaivāhik* marital

वैसा *vaisā* of that kind

वैसे *vaise* actually, in fact, as it happens, although

वोट *voṭ*M vote; वोट देना *voṭ denā*N to vote (for, को *ko*)

व्यंग्य *vyaṅgya*M sarcasm

व्यंजन *vyanjan*M consonant; cooked food, dish

व्यक्ति *vyakti*M person, individual

व्यक्तिगत *vyaktigat* individual; व्यक्तिगत रूप से *vyaktigat rūp se* individually, personally

व्यक्तित्व *vyaktitva*M personality

व्यर्थ *vyarth* useless, vain
व्यवसाय *vyavasāy*[M] business, trade
व्यवस्था *vyavasthā*[F] arrangement
व्यवहार *vyavahār*[M] behaviour, manner (towards someone)
व्यस्त *vyast* busy, occupied
व्याकरण *vyākaraṇ*[M] grammar
व्यापार *vyāpār*[M] trade, business
व्यापारी *vyāpārī*[M] trader
व्यायाम *vyāyām*[M] exercise (physical)
व्यावहारिक *vyāvahārik* practical
व्रत *vrat*[M] vow; fast

## श *śa*

शंका *śaṅkā*[F] doubt, hesitation, suspicion
शक *śak*[M] doubt, suspicion
शक्ति *śakti*[F] power
शख़्स *śakhs*[M] person, individual, fellow
शतरंज *śatranj*[M] chess
शताब्दी *śatābdī*[F] century; name of various intercity trains in India
शत्रु *śatru*[M] enemy
शनिवार *śanivār*[M] Saturday
शपथ *śapath*[F] oath
शब्द *śabd*[M] word
शब्दकोश *śabdkoś*[M] dictionary
शरण *śaraṇ*[F] refuge, shelter
शरणार्थी *śaraṇārthī*[M] refugee
शरद् *śarad*[F] autumn
शरबत *śarbat*[F] a sweet drink
शरम *śarm,* शर्म *śarm*[F] shame; शर्म आना *śarm ānā* to feel ashamed
शरमाना *śarmānā* (intr.) to be ashamed, embarrassed
शरमिंदा *śarmindā* (-*ā* invariable) ashamed, embarrassed, bashful
शराब *śarāb*[F] alcoholic drink
शराबी *śarābī*[M] drunkard, boozer
शरारत *śarārat*[F] mischief
शरारती *śarāratī* mischievous
शरीफ़ *śarīf* noble, upstanding, very decent
शरीर *śarīr*[M] body
शर्त *śart*[F] condition, terms (of agreement etc.)
शव *śav*[M] corpse
शस्त्र *śastra*[M] weapon
शहद *śahad*[M] honey
शहर *śahar*[M] town, city
शहीद *śahīd*[M] martyr; शहीद होना *śahīd honā* to be martyred
शाकाहारी *śākāhārī* (adj. & noun)[M] vegetarian
शाखा *śākhā*[F] branch (of tree or organization)
शागिर्द *śāgird*[M] pupil, disciple (of an *ustād*)

शादी *śādī*^F wedding, marriage; शादी-शुदा *śādī-śudā* (*-ā* invariable) married

शानदार *śāndār* splendid, magnificent

शान्त *śānt* peaceful

शान्ति *śānti*^F peace

शाबाश *śābāś* well done! (NB: patronizing if used with peers and superiors)

शाम *śām*^F evening

शामिल *śāmil* included, taking part

शायद *śāyad* maybe, perhaps; शायद ही *śāyad hī* barely, hardly likely

शायर *śāyar*^M poet

शायरी *śāyrī*^F poetry

शारीरिक *śārīrik* physical, bodily

शाल *śāl*^F shawl

शासन *śāsan*^M ruling, government

शास्त्र *śāstra*^M a work of scripture or learning; treatise

शास्त्रीय *śāstrīy* classical

शिकायत *śikāyat*^F complaint; मुझसे उनकी शिकायत करना *mujhse unkī śikāyat karnā*^N to complain to me about them

शिकार *śikār*^M hunting; prey; victim

शिक्षा *śikṣā*^F education

शिक्षित *śikṣit* educated

शिखर *śikhar*^M summit, apex

शिथिल *śithil* lax, slack

शिमला मिर्च *śimlā mirc*^F capsicum, green pepper

शिष्ट *śiṣṭ* civil, decent, polite

शिष्टता *śiṣṭtā*^F decency, politeness

शिष्टाचार *śiṣṭācār*^M good manners, civil behaviour

शिष्य *śiṣya*^M pupil, disciple (of a guru)

शीत *śīt* (adj. & noun)^M cold, coldness; शीत-लहर *śīt-lahar*^F a cold wave, cold snap

शीतल *śītal* cool

शीशम *śīśam*^M rosewood

शीशा *śīśā*^M glass (the substance); bottle; mirror

शीशी *śīśī*^F small bottle, phial

शुक्रवार *śukravār*^M Friday

शुक्रिया *śukriyā* thank you

शुद्ध *śuddh* pure, ummixed

शुभ *śubh* auspicious; शुभ कामनाएँ *śubh kāmnāē*^FPL best wishes

शुरुआत *śuruāt*^F beginning, inception

शुरू *śurū*^M beginning; शुरू होना *śurū honā* to start; शुरू करना *śurū karnā*^N to start

शुल्क *śulk*ᴹ fee, payment, subscription

शून्य *śūnya* (adj. & noun) void;ᴹ void; zero

शेष *śeṣ* (adj. & noun) remaining, left;ᴹ the remainder, everything else

शैतान *śaitān*ᴹ devil

शैली *śailī*ᶠ style (in art etc.)

शोध *śodh*ᴹ research, investigation; शोध-कार्य *śodh-kārya*ᴹ research work; शोध-प्रबंध *śodh-prabandh*ᴹ dissertation

शोर *śor*ᴹ noise, din, tumult; शोर मचाना *śor macānā*ᴺ to create a noise, kick up a row

शोला *śolā*ᴹ flame

शोषण *śoṣaṇ*ᴹ exploitation

शौक़ *śauq*ᴹ liking, hobby, interest

शौचालय *śaucālay*ᴹ toilet, lavatory

श्रम *śram*ᴹ labour, toil, exertion

श्री *śrī* Mr

श्रीमती *śrīmatī* Mrs

श्रेणी *śreṇī*ᶠ class, grade

श्रेय *śrey*ᴹ credit (due to someone for achievement), recognition

## ष **ṣa**

षड्यंत्र *ṣaḍyantra*ᴹ plot, conspiracy

## स **sa**

संकट *saṅkaṭ*ᴹ crisis, state of emergency

संक्षिप्त *saṅkṣipt* concise, short

संक्षेप में *saṅkṣep mē* in brief

संख्या *saṅkhyā*ᶠ number (total)

संगत *saṅgat*ᶠ accompaniment (musical etc.)

संगमर्मर *saṅgmarmar*ᴹ marble

संगी *saṅgī*ᴹ companion

संगीत *saṅgīt*ᴹ music

संगीतकार *saṅgītkār*ᴹ musician

संग्रह *saṅgrah*ᴹ collection (e.g. of poems)

संग्रहालय *saṅgrahālay*ᴹ museum

संचार *sancār*ᴹ communication

संचालक *sancālak*ᴹ manager

संजीदा *sanjīdā* serious, grave

संज्ञा *sanjñā* (pronounced 'sangyā')ᶠ noun

संत *sant* (adj. & noun) good, pious, saintly;ᴹ an ascetic, 'saint'

संतरा *santarā*ᴹ orange

संतुलन *santulan*ᴹ balance

संतुलित *santulit* balanced

संतुष्ट *santuṣṭ* satisfied, content

संतोष *santoṣ*ᴹ satisfaction

संतोषजनक *santoṣjanak* satisfactory

संदर्भ *sandarbh*[M] context

संदिग्ध *sandigdh* suspect, suspected, doubtful

संदूक़ *sandūq*[M] box

संदेश *sandeś*[M] message

संदेह *sandeh*[M] doubt, suspicion

संपत्ति *sampatti*[F] property

संपर्क *sampark*[M] contact, link; संपर्क करना *sampark karnā*[N] to contact

संपादक *sampādak*[M] editor

संपादकीय *sampādakīy*[M] editorial

संपादित *sampādit* edited

संपूर्ण *sampūrṇ* complete, entire

संबंध *sambandh*[M] connection, relationship

संबंधित *sambandhit* related to, concerning

संभव *sambhav* possible

सँभलना *sãbhalnā* to manage, be supported; to regain control or health; to be cautious

सँभालना *sãbhālnā*[N] to take care of, deal with

संभावना *sambhāvnā*[F] possibility

संभोग *sambhog*[M] sexual intercourse

संयुक्त *sanyukt* joint; संयुक्त परिवार *sanyukt parivār*[M] joint family

संयुक्ताक्षर *sanyuktākṣar*[M] conjunct character (e.g. क्त *kta*, a conjunct of क् *k* and त *ta*)

संवाद *samvād*[M] dialogue

संसद *sansad*[M] parliament

संसदीय *sansadīy* parliamentary

संस्कार *sanskār*[M] a life cycle event or its ritual; an innate instinct or capacity (reflecting previous experiences or births)

संस्कृत *sanskṛt*[F] Sanskrit

संस्कृति *sanskṛti*[F] culture

संस्था *sansthā*[F] institution

सकना *saknā* to be able (with verb stem: तुम जा सकते हो *tum jā sakte ho* you can go)

सख़्त *sakht* hard; strict, stern, tough

सख़्ती *sakhtī*[F] hardness, strictness

सगा *sagā* born of the same parents (सगा भाई *sagā bhāī* specifies 'real brother', while भाई *bhāī* alone can also mean 'cousin'); सगे-संबंधी *sage-sambandhī*[MPL] relatives

सच *sac* (adj. & noun) true;[M] truth

सचमुच *sacmuc* really, truly

सचाई *sacāī*[F] truthfulness, honesty

सच्चा *saccā* true, honest (सच्चा दोस्त *saccā dost*ᴹ a true friend)

सच्चाई *saccāī*: see सचाई *sacāī*

सज़ा *sazā*ᶠ punishment; सज़ा देना *sazā denā*ᴺ to punish

सजाना *sajānā*ᴺ to decorate, adorn, arrange

सज्जन *sajjan*ᴹ gentleman

सड़क *saṛak*ᶠ road, street

सतहत्तर *sat'hattar* seventy-seven

सत्ताईस *sattāīs* twenty-seven

सत्तानवे *sattānve* ninety-seven

सत्तावन *sattāvan* fifty-seven

सत्तासी *sattāsī* eighty-seven

सत्र *satra*ᴹ session, term, semester

सत्रह *satrah* seventeen

सदस्य *sadasya*ᴹ member

सदा *sadā* ever, always

सदी *sadī*ᶠ century

सन् *san* year (of calendar or era)

सनकी *sankī* eccentric

सपना *sapnā*ᴹ dream; सपना देखना *sapnā dekhnā*ᴺ to dream, have a dream (about, का *kā*)

सप्तक *saptak*ᴹ octave (in music)

सप्ताह *saptāh*ᴹ week

सफ़र *safar*ᴹ journey, travel; सफ़र करना *safar karnā*ᴺ to travel

सफल *saphal* successful, fruitful

सफलता *saphaltā*ᶠ success

सफ़ाई *safāī*ᶠ cleaning, cleanness

सफ़ेद *safed* white

सब *sab* all; सब कुछ *sab kuch* everything

सबक़ *sabaq*ᴹ lesson

सबूत *sabūt*ᴹ evidence, proof

सब्ज़ी *sabzī*ᶠ vegetable

सब्ज़ीमंडी *sabzīmaṇḍī*ᶠ vegetable market

सभी *sabhī* (emphatic form of सब *sab*) all

सभ्य *sabhya* civilized

सभ्यता *sabhyatā*ᶠ civilization

समझ *samajh*ᶠ understanding; समझ में आना *samajh mẽ ānā* to be understood

**Insight**

समझ *samajh*ᶠ 'understanding' – like most nouns deriving from verb stems, this is feminine. Others include पहुँच *pahũc*ᶠ 'reach, scope', रोक *rok*ᶠ 'restriction, impediment', and बक or बकबक *bak, bakbak*ᶠ 'chatter, nonsense' (from बकना *baknā* 'to gabble').

समझदार *samajhdār* discerning, understanding, wise, sympathetic

समझना *samajhnā*$^{n}$ to understand

समझाना *samjhānā*$^{N}$ to make understand, to explain, console

समतल *samtal* level, even

समय *samay*$^{M}$ time

समय-सारणी *samay-sāraṇī*$^{F}$ timetable

समर्थ *samarth* capable

समर्थन *samarthan*$^{M}$ support

समस्या *samasyā*$^{F}$ problem

समाचार *samācār*$^{M}$ news

समाचार-पत्र *samācār-patra*$^{M}$ newspaper

समाज *samāj*$^{M}$ society

समाजवाद *samājvād*$^{M}$ socialism

समाजवादी *samājvādī* (adj. & noun)$^{M}$ socialist

समाधान *samādhān*$^{M}$ solution, resolution (of a problem)

समाधि *samādhi*$^{F}$ meditation, state of yogic trance; memorial, place of cremation or burial

समान *samān* equal, like, similar

समानता *samāntā*$^{F}$ likeness, similarity

समाप्त *samāpt* concluded, finished, completed

समारोह *samāroh*$^{M}$ function, event, ceremony

समुद्र *samudra*$^{M}$ sea, ocean

समोसा *samosā*$^{M}$ samosa, a deep-fried stuffed pastry

सम्मान *sammān*$^{M}$ honour

सम्मान्य *sammānya* honourable, respected (used in formal letters for 'Dear . . .')

सम्मेलन *sammelan*$^{M}$ conference, congress

सर$^{1}$ *sar*: see सिर *sir*

सर$^{2}$ *sar* sir (the English word)

सरकार *sarkār*$^{F}$ government

सरकारी *sarkārī* governmental

सरदार *sardār*$^{M}$ leader; a term of respect used with Sikh men; a Sikh

सरदारनी *sardārnī*$^{F}$ a Sikh woman

सरल *saral* simple

सरसठ *sarsaṭh* sixty-seven

सरसों *sarsõ*$^{F}$ mustard (plant, seed)

सरासर *sarāsar* complete, utter, sheer, out-and-out

सर्दी *sardī*$^{F}$ cold; a head cold; winter (used in plural: सरदियों में *sardiyõ mẽ* in the winter)

सर्वथा *sarvathā* completely

सर्वनाम *sarvanām*$^{M}$ pronoun

सलवार क़मीज़ *salvār qamīz*ᶠ woman's suit of loose trousers (salwar) and qameez (shirt, kurta)

सलाम *salām*ᴹ salutation, salute

सलाह *salāh*ᶠ advice

सलूक *salūk*ᴹ conduct, behaviour

सवा *savā* quarter more than a full unit (e.g. सवा चार किलो *savā cār kilo* 4.25 kilos, सवा चार बजे *savā cār baje* a quarter past four; सवा चार सौ *savā cār sau* 425)

सवार *savār* riding, mounted, aboard

सवारी *savārī*ᶠ passenger, rider

सवाल *savāl*ᴹ question

सवेरा *saverā*ᴹ morning

ससुर *sasur*ᴹ father-in-law

ससुराल *sasurāl*ᴹ in-laws' house

सस्ता *sastā* cheap

सहकर्मी *sahakarmī*ᴹ colleague

सहनशील *sahanśīl* tolerant

सहना *sahnā*ᴺ to bear, endure, tolerate

सहमत *sahmat* in agreement

सहमति *sahmati*ᶠ agreement, consent

सहयोग *sahyog*ᴹ cooperation

सहसा *sahsā* suddenly

सहानुभूति *sahānubhūti*ᶠ sympathy

सहायक *sahāyak*ᴹ assistant

सहायता *sahāytā*ᶠ assistance

सहारा *sahārā*ᴹ support

सही *sahī* correct, right

सहेली *sahelī*ᶠ friend (female's female friend)

साँचा *sā̃cā*ᴹ mould

सांत्वना *sāntvanā*ᶠ consolation

साँप *sā̃p*ᴹ snake

साँवला *sā̃vlā* dusky, dark (of complexion)

साँस *sā̃s*ᶠ breath, breathing

सांसद *sānsad*ᴹ member of parliament

सांस्कृतिक *sā̃skṛtik* cultural

-सा *-sā* suffix meaning '-ish', as in बड़ा-सा *baṛā-sā* biggish

साइकिल *sāikil*ᶠ bicycle

साक्षात्कार *sākṣātkār*ᴹ interview

साक्षी *sākṣī*ᴹ witness

साग *sāg*ᴹ greens, vegetables

सागर *sāgar*ᴹ ocean

साड़ी *sāṛī*ᶠ sari

साढ़े *sāṛhe* a half more than the full unit (e.g. साढ़े चार किलो *sāṛhe cār kilo* 4.5 kilos; साढ़े चार बजे *sāṛhe cār baje* four thirty; साढ़े चार सौ *sāṛhe cār sau* 450)

सात *sāt* seven

साथ *sāth* (adv. & noun) together; ᴹ company, being together

साथी *sāthī*ᴹ companion

सादर *sādar* respectful (in the letter-writing formula सादर नमस्ते *sādar namaste*)

सादा *sādā* plain

साधन *sādhan*ᴹ means

साधारण *sādhāraṇ* ordinary, normal

साधु *sādhu* (adj. & noun) pious; ᴹ holy man, ascetic

साफ़ *sāf* clean, clear

साबित करना *sābit karnā*ᴺ to prove

साबुत *sābut* whole (as of unground spice); undamaged

साबुन *sābun*ᴹ soap

सामना *sāmnā*ᴹ confrontation, encounter; का सामना करना *kā sāmnā karnā*ᴺ to confront, to face up to

सामने *sāmne* opposite

सामाजिक *sāmājik* social

सामान *sāmān*ᴹ luggage, goods, furniture

सामान्य *sāmānya* ordinary, common

साया *sāyā*ᴹ shade, shadow, shelter

सारा *sārā* whole, entire, all

सार्थक *sārthak* meaningful

साल *sāl*ᴹ year

साल-गिरह *sāl-girah*ᶠ anniversary, birthday

साला *sālā*ᴹ brother-in-law (wife's brother); it also serves as a vulgar term of abuse, implying 'I have carnal knowledge of your sister'

सालाना *sālānā* annual

साली *sālī*ᴹ sister-in-law (wife's sister)

सावधान *sāvdhān* careful, cautious

सावधानी *sāvdhānī*ᶠ care, caution; सावधानी से *sāvdhānī se* carefully

सास *sās*ᶠ mother-in-law

साहब *sāhab*ᴹ sahib (used as honorific with male names and relationship terms, as in भाई साहब *bhāī sāhab*)

साहस *sāhas*ᴹ courage

साहसी *sāhasī* courageous, brave, bold

साहित्य *sāhitya*ᴹ literature

साहित्यिक *sāhityik* literary

सिक्का *sikkā*ᴹ coin

सिख *sikh* (adj. & noun) Sikh; ᴹ a Sikh

सिग्रेट *sigreṭ*ᴹ cigarette

सितंबर *sitambar*ᴹ September

सितार *sitār*ᴹ sitar

सितारा *sitārā*ᴹ star

सिद्ध *siddh* proved, perfected; सिद्ध करना *siddh karnā*ᴺ to prove

सिद्धांत *siddhānt*ᴹ principle

सिनेमा *sinemā*ᴹ cinema

सिपाही *sipāhī*ᴹ constable; soldier

सिर *sir* (also सर *sar*)ᴹ head

सिरदर्द *sirdard*ᴹ headache

सिर्फ़ *sirf* only

सिलवट *silvaṭ*ᶠ fold, crease, wrinkle

सिलवाना *silvānā*ᴺ to cause to be sewn, to get sewn

सिलसिला *silsilā*ᴹ connection

सिसकना *sisaknā* to sob

सीखना *sīkhnā*ᴺ to learn

सीट *sīṭ*ᶠ seat

सीटी *sīṭī*ᶠ whistle, whistling; सीटी बजाना *sīṭī bajānā* ᴺ to whistle

सीढ़ी *sīṛhī*ᶠ step, stair, staircase, ladder

सीधा *sīdhā* straight, straightforward

सीधे *sīdhe* straight; सीधे हाथ *sīdhe hāth* to the right (hand)

सीना[1] *sīnā*ᴺ to sew

सीना[2] *sīnā*ᴹ chest (part of body)

सीमा *sīmā*ᶠ border, frontier; limit, bounds

सीमा शुल्क *sīmā śulk*ᴹ customs (tax)

सीमित *sīmit* limited

सुंदर *sundar* beautiful, handsome, nice

सुंदरता *sundartā*ᶠ beauty

सुखद *sukhad* pleasant

सुखाना *sukhānā*ᴺ to dry

सुगंध *sugandh*ᴹ fragrance

सुझाव *sujhāv*ᴹ suggestion; सुझाव देना *sujhāv denā*ᴺ to suggest

सुधरना *sudharnā* to improve, to be corrected

सुधार *sudhār*ᴹ reform, correction

सुधारना *sudharnā*ᴺ to improve, correct

सुनना *sunnā*ᴺ to hear, to listen (to)

सुनहरा *sunahrā* golden

सुनाई देना *sunāī denā,* सुनाई पड़ना *sunaī parna* to be heard; to be audible

सुनाना *sunānā*ᴺ to recite, tell

सुन्न *sunn* still, silent, numb

सुबह *subah*ᶠ morning

सुर[1] *sur*[M] god, deity

सुर[2] *sur*[M] musical note, tone

सुरक्षा *surakṣā*[F] security, safety

सुरक्षित *surakṣit* protected, safe

सुलझना *sulajhnā* to be solved, become untangled

सुलझाना *suljhānā*[N] to solve, untangle

सुलाना[N] *sulānā* to make sleep, put to sleep

सुविधा *suvidhā*[F] convenience

सुविधाजनक *suvidhājanak* convenient

सुस्त *sust* languid, slow, in low spirits

सुस्ताना *sustānā* to relax, take a little rest

सुहावना *suhāvnā* charming, pleasant, lovely

सूँड़ *sũṛ*[F] elephant's trunk

सूअर *sūar*[M] pig; सूअर का माँस/गोश्त *sūar kā mās/gośt*[M] pork

सूई *suī*[F] needle; the hand of a watch; injection; सूई लगाना *sūī lagānā*[N] to give an injection

सूक्ष्म *sūkṣma* subtle, fine

सूखना *sūkhnā* to dry

सूखा *sūkhā* (adj. & noun) dry;[M] drought

सूचना *sūcnā*[F] information

सूचित करना *sūcit karnā*[N] to inform, tell

सूची *sūcī*[F] list

सूजन *sūjan*[F] swelling

सूजना *sūjnā* to swell

सूझना *sūjhnā* to occur (to the mind)

सूती *sūtī* made of cotton

सूद *sūd*[M] interest (financial)

सूना *sūnā* deserted, desolate, empty

सूनापन *sūnāpan*[M] desolation, emptiness

सूरज *sūraj*[M] sun

सूरत *sūrat*[F] face, appearance; condition

सूर्ख़ी *sūrkhī*[F] headline

सूर्य *sūrya*[M] sun

सेंकना *sẽknā*[N] to warm, heat, roast, bake

से *se* from; than; with; by; since

सेना *senā*[F] army

सेनापति *senāpati*[M] general (military)

सेब *seb*[M] apple

सेवा *sevā*[F] service

सेहत *sehat*[F] health

सैंतालीस *saĩtālīs* forty-seven

सैंतीस *saĩtīs* thirty-seven

सैनिक *sainik* (adj. & noun) military;$^{M}$ soldier

सैर *sair*$^{F}$ trip, walk

सो *so* so, therefore

सोचना *socnā*$^{N}$ to think

सोना[1] *sonā*$^{M}$ gold

सोना[2] *sonā* to sleep

सोमवार *somvār*$^{M}$ Monday

सोलह *solah* sixteen

सौंदर्य *saundarya*$^{M}$ beauty

सौंफ *saũph*$^{F}$ aniseed, fennel

सौ *sau* hundred

सौतेला *sautelā* step- (e.g. सौतेली माँ *sautelī mā̃*$^{F}$ stepmother)

स्कूल *skūl*$^{M}$ school

स्टेशन *sṭeśan*$^{M}$ station

स्तंभ *stambh*$^{M}$ pillar; column (architectural, or in newspaper)

स्त्री *strī*$^{F}$ woman

स्त्रीलिंग *strīliṅg*$^{M}$ feminine (in grammatical gender)

स्थगित *sthagit* postponed

स्थल *sthal*$^{F}$ site, place

स्थान *sthān*$^{M}$ place

स्थापित *sthāpit* established

स्थायी *sthāyī* fixed, permanent; स्थायी रूप से *sthāyī rūp se* permanently

स्थित *sthit* situated, located

स्थिति *sthiti*$^{F}$ situation

स्थिर *sthir*$^{F}$ fixed, steady, constant

स्नातक *snātak*$^{M}$ graduate

स्नातकोत्तर *snātakottar* postgraduate

स्नान *snān*$^{M}$ bathing

स्नेह *sneh*$^{M}$ affection

स्पष्ट *spaṣṭ* clear, apparent

स्याही *syāhī*$^{F}$ ink

स्वतंत्र *svatantra* independent

स्वतंत्रता *svatantratā*$^{F}$ independence

स्वप्न *svapn*$^{M}$ dream; स्वप्न देखना *svapn dekhnā*$^{N}$ to dream, to have a dream (about, का *kā*)

स्वभाव *svabhāv*$^{M}$ character

स्वयं *svayaṃ* oneself

स्वर *svar*$^{M}$ voice; musical note

स्वराज्य *svarājya*$^{M}$ self-rule, independence

स्वर्ग *svarg*$^{M}$ heaven, paradise

स्वर्गवास *svargvās*$^{M}$ death, demise

स्वर्गीय *svargīy*$^{M}$ deceased, the late

स्वस्थ *svasth* healthy, fit, well

स्वागत *svāgat*$^{M}$ welcome; (का) स्वागत करना *(kā) svāgat karnā*$^{N}$ to welcome

स्वाद *svād*$^{M}$ taste

स्वादिष्ट *svādiṣṭ* tasty, delicious

स्वार्थ *svārth*[M] selfishness, self-interest

स्वार्थी *svārthī* selfish

स्वास्थ्य *svāsthya*[M] health

स्वीकार करना *svīkār karnā*[N] to accept

## ह ***ha***

हंटर *haṇṭar*[M] whip, lash

हँसना *hãsnā*[n] to laugh

हँसी *hãsī*[F] laugh; हँसी-मज़ाक़ *hãsī-mazāq*[M] laughter, fun, joking

हक़ *haq*[M] right, privilege

हगना *hagnā* to shit (impolite)

हज़ार *hazār* thousand

हटना *haṭnā* to withdraw, recede, move out of the way

हटाना *haṭānā*[N] to drive away, remove, get rid of

हड़ताल *haṛtāl*[F] strike, lockout

हड्डी *haḍḍī*[F] bone

हताश *hatāś* dejected

हथकड़ी *hathkaṛī*[F] handcuff

हद *had*[F] limit, boundary, extent; कुछ हद तक *kuch had tak* to some extent; हद हो गई! *had ho gaī!* that's going too far!

हथियार *hathiyār*[M] weapon

हथेली *hathelī*[F] palm (of hand)

हथौड़ी *hathauṛī*[F] hammer

हफ़्ता *haftā*[M] week

हम *ham* we; us

हमदर्द *hamdard* (adj. & noun) sympathetic;[M] sympathetic person

हमदर्दी *hamdardī*[F] sympathy

हमला *hamlā*[M] attack

हमारा *hamārā* our, ours

हमेशा *hameśā* always

हर *har* every, each; हर कोई *har koī* everyone; हर क़ीमत पर *har qīmat par* at any cost; हर हाल में *har hāl mẽ* definitely, for sure

हरा *harā* green

हराना *harānā*[N] to defeat

हराम *harām* forbidden

हरामज़ादा *harāmzādā* (adj. & noun) ill begotten;[M] bastard

हरियाली *hariyālī*[F] greenery, greenness, verdure

हरेक *harek* each, every

हर्ष *harṣ*[M] joy, happiness

हल[1] *hal*[M] solution (to a problem)

हल[2] *hal*[M] plough

हलका *halkā* light

हवा *havā*[F] air, breeze

हवाई जहाज़ *havāī jahāz*[M] aeroplane

हवाई डाक *havāī ḍāk*[F] airmail

हस्ताक्षर *hastākṣar*[M] signature

हाँ *hā̃* yes

हाँफना *hā̃phnā* to puff, pant

हाथ *hāth*[M] hand; हाथ आना *hāth ānā* to come to hand; हाथ बँटाना *hāth bā̃ṭānā*[N] to lend a hand

हाथी *hāthī*[M] elephant

हाथी-दाँत *hāthī-dā̃t*[M] ivory

हादसा *hādsā*[M] accident

हानि *hāni*[F] loss, damage; हानि पहुँचाना *hāni pahũcānā*[N] to cause damage

हारना *hārnā*[n] to lose, be defeated

हाल *hāl*[M] condition, circumstances (क्या हाल है? *kyā hāl hai?* 'How's things?'); हाल में *hāl mẽ* recently; हर हाल में *har hāl mẽ* definitely, for sure

हालत *hālat*[F] condition, state (e.g. of a road, or of health)

हालाँकि *hālā̃ki* although

हासिल करना *hāsil karnā*[N] to obtain, gain

हास्यास्पद *hāsyāspad* ridiculous

हिंसा *hinsā*[F] violence

हिंसात्मक *hinsātmak* violent

हिचकी *hickī*[F] hiccup, sob

हिज्जे *hijje*[M] spelling

हिन्द *hind*[M] India; हिन्द महासागर *hind mahāsāgar*[M] the Indian Ocean

हिन्दी *hindī*[F] Hindi

हिन्दुस्तानी *hindustānī* (adj. & noun) Indian;[F] the Hindustani language (the common ground between Hindi and Urdu)

हिन्दू *hindū* (adj. & noun) Hindu;[M] a Hindu

हिफ़ाज़त *hifāzat*[F] protection, safety, security

हिम्मत *himmat*[F] courage, nerve

हिरन *hiran*[M] deer

हिलना *hilnā* to move, shake, wave

हिलाना[N] *hilānā* to move, shake, wave

हिसाब *hisāb*[M] account, accounts

हिस्सा *hissā*[M] part, portion

ही *hī* only (emphatic; follows emphasized word, as in मैं ही *maĩ hī* only I, I myself)

हीरा *hīrā*[M] diamond

हीरो *hīro*[M] hero, film star

हुआ *huā* (perfective of होना *honā*) happened; क्या हुआ? *kyā huā*? what happened; (rhetorically) so what?

हूँ *hū̃* am

हृदय *hṛday*ᴹ heart

हृष्ट-पुष्ट *hṛṣṭ-puṣṭ* stout, robust

हैं *haĩ* are; is (honorific plural)

है *hai* is; are (with तू *tū* you)

हैरान *hairān* amazed, perplexed

होनहार *honhār* promising, full of potential

होना *honā* to be; हो चलना *ho calnā* to begin to be, to set in; हो जाना *ho jānā* to become

**Insight**

होना *honā* derives from the Sanskrit verb root *bhū-*, which is ultimately cognate with English 'be'.

हैरानी *hairānī*ᶠ amazement, surprise

हैसियत *haisiyat*ᶠ capacity; की हैसियत से *kī haisiyat se* in the capacity of

होंठ *hõṭh*ᴹ lip

हो *ho* are (with तुम *tum* you)

होकर *hokar* via (e.g. दिल्ली से होकर *dillī se hokar* via Delhi)

होटलᴹ *hoṭal* hotel; restaurant

होली *holī*ᶠ Holi, springtime festival of colours

होश *hoś*ᴹ consciousness; होश सँभालना *hoś sãbhālnā*ᴺ to become aware, to be of an age to understand things

होशियार *hośiyār* clever

होशियारी *hośiyārī*ᶠ cleverness

हौज़ *hauz*ᴹ reservoir, tank

हौसला *hauslā*ᴹ courage, morale

ह्विस्की *hviskī*ᶠ whisky

# English–Hindi Dictionary

## A

**a** एक *ek*; (a certain) कोई *koī* — a man is asking where you are कोई आदमी पूछ रहा है कि तुम कहाँ हो *koī ādmī pūch rahā hai ki tum kahā̃ ho*

**abandon, to** छोड़ना *choṛnā*[N] — abandon this idea इस ख़याल को छोड़ो [छोड़ दो] *is khyāl ko choṛo [choṛ do]*

this matter इस बात को लेकर *is bāt ko lekar;* to be about to do something: the oblique infinitive takes a वाला *vālā* suffix — she was just about to go वह अभी जानेवाली थी *vah abhī jānevālī thī*

**above** के ऊपर *ke ūpar* — above the door दरवाज़े के ऊपर *darvāze ke ūpar*

**Insight**

> **ABC** – in Hindi, the 'ABC' of a subject is its 'क-ख-ग' – referencing the first three consonants in the syllabary.

**able** (capable) समर्थ *samarth*; to be able सकना *saknā* (follows verb stem) — he is able to go, can go वह जा सकता है *vah jā saktā hai*; (to know how to, to have the skill of doing: use infinitive + आना *ānā*) — can you cook? क्या आपको खाना बनाना आता है? *kyā āpko khānā banānā ātā hai?*

**about** (approximately) लगभग *lagbhag*; (with a number) कोई *koī* — about ten people कोई दस लोग *koī das log*; (concerning) के बारे में *ke bāre mẽ* — about this इसके बारे में *iske bāre mẽ*; (in relation to) को लकर *ko lekar* — about

**abroad** विदेश *videś* — we're going abroad हम विदेश जा रहे हैं *ham videś jā rahe haĩ*

**absent** (not attending) ग़ैरहाज़िर *gairhāzir*

**abstain from, to** से परहेज़ होना *se parhez honā,* से परहेज़ करना *se parhez karnā*[N] — I abstain from this 💣 मुझे इस चीज़ से परहेज़ है *mujhe is cīz se parhez hai;* you should abstain from smoking 💣 तुम्हें सिग्रेट पीने से परहेज़ करना चाहिए *tumhẽ sigreṭ pīne se parhez karnā cāhie*

**abuse** (verbal) गाली *gālī*[F]

**abuse, to** (verbally) गाली देना *gālī denā*[N] — they began abusing me वे मुझे गालियाँ देने लगे *ve mujhe gāliyā̃ dene lage*

**accept, to** स्वीकार करना *svīkār karnā*[N] — please accept this gift यह भेंट स्वीकार कीजिए *yah bhẽṭ svīkār kījie*; (to admit, acknowledge) मानना *mānnā*[N]

**accident** दुर्घटना *durghaṭnā*[F], हादसा *hādsā*[M] — an accident happened एक दुर्घटना हुई *ek durghaṭnā huī*, एक हादसा हुआ *ek hādsā huā*

**accompany, to** के साथ चलना *ke sāth calnā* — I'll accompany you मैं आपके साथ चलूँगा *maĩ āpke sāth calū̃gā*

**according to** के अनुसार *ke anusār* — according to the government सरकार के अनुसार *sarkār ke anusār*

**account** (financial) हिसाब *hisāb*[M]; (narrative) वृत्तांत *vr̥ttānt*[M]

**accurate** सही *sahī*

**accuse, to** (पर) दोष लगाना *(par) doṣ lagānā*[N] — we'll accuse them of theft हम उनपर चोरी का दोष लगाएँगे *ham unpar corī kā doṣ lagāẽge*

**ache** दर्द *dard*[M]

**ache, to** दर्द करना *dard karnā*[M] — my leg is aching मेरी टाँग दर्द कर रही है *merī ṭā̃g dard kar rahī hai*

**acquaintance** परिचय *paricay*[M] — I have no acquaintance with him/her, don't know him/her ❁ उनसे मेरा परिचय नहीं है *unse merā paricay nahī̃ hai*; (a person who is known) परिचित व्यक्ति *paricit vyakti*[M]

**across** के पार *ke pār* — across the river नदी के पार *nadī ke pār*

**act, to** (in a drama) अभिनय करना *abhinay karnā*[N]; (to take action) अदा करना *adā karnā*[N]

**actor** अभिनेता *abhinetā*[M]

**actress** अभिनेत्री *abhinetrī*[F]

**actually** वैसे *vaise*; in fact दरअसल *dar'asal*, असल में *asal mẽ*, वास्तव में *vāstav mẽ*

**add, to** जोड़ना *joṛnā*[N] — add my name to the list सूची में मेरा नाम जोड़ो [जोड़ दो] *sūcī mẽ merā nām joṛo [joṛ do]*

**address** पता *patā*[M]

**adjective** विशेषण *viśeṣaṇ*[M]

**admission** (to a college etc.) दाख़िला *dā<u>kh</u>ilā*[M], भरती *bhartī*[F]

**admit, to** (to acknowledge) मानना *mānnā*[N] — I must admit that ❁ मुझे मानना पड़ेगा कि . . . *mujhe mānnā paṛegā* *ki* . . .; (to let in) अंदर आने देना *andar āne dena*[N] – admit him/her उसको अंदर आने दो *use andar āne do*; (to enrol) भरती करना *bhartī karnā*[N]; to be admitted (to a college etc.) भरती होना *bhartī honā*, दाख़िल होना *dākhil honā* – she'll be admitted to the same school वह उसी स्कूल में दाख़िल होगी *vah usī skūl mẽ dākhil hogī*

**adopt, to** (to make one's own) अपनाना *apnānā*[N]; (to foster a child) गोद लेना *god lenā*[N]

**adult** वयस्क *vayask*

**advance, to** बढ़ना *baṛhnā*

**advantage** फ़ायदा *fāydā*[M], लाभ *lābh*[M]

**adverb** क्रिया-विशेषण *kriyā-viśeṣaṇ*[M]

**advertisement** विज्ञापन *vijñāpan*[M] (pronounced 'vigyāpan')

**advice** सलाह *salāh*[F] – you gave me good advice आपने मुझे अच्छी सलाह दी *āpne mujhe acchī salāh dī*

**advise, to** सलाह देना *salāh denā*[N] – I can advise you on this subject मैं आपको इस विषय पर सलाह दे सकता हूँ *maĩ āpko is viṣay par salāh de saktā hũ*

**aeroplane** हवाई जहाज़ *havāī jahāz*[M]

**affect, to** असर पड़ना *asar paṛnā* – your work will affect him a lot आपके काम का उसपर बहुत असर पड़ेगा *āpke kām kā uspar bahut asar paṛegā*

**affection** प्यार *pyār*[M], स्नेह *sneh*[M]; affectionately प्यार से *pyār se*

**afraid, to be** डरना *ḍarnā* – I'm afraid of dogs मैं कुत्तों से डरता हूँ *maĩ kuttõ se ḍartā hũ*; she's always afraid वह हमेशा डरी रहती है *vah hameśā ḍarī rahtī hai*; (to regret) अफ़सोस होना *afsos honā* – I'm afraid I can't come मुझे अफ़सोस है कि मैं नहीं आ सकता *mujhe afsos hai ki maĩ nahī̃ ā saktā*

**after** के बाद *ke bād* – after today आज के बाद *āj ke bād*

**afternoon** दोपहर *dopahar*[M] – in the afternoon दोपहर को *dopahar ko*

**afterwards** बाद में *bād mẽ*

**again** दुबारा *dubārā*; फिर *phir*, फिर से *phir se*

**against** के ख़िलाफ़ *ke khilāf*, के विरुद्ध *ke viruddh* – he won't speak against you वह आपके

ख़िलाफ़ नहीं बोलेगा *vah āpke khilāf nahī̃ bolegā*

**age** (of person) उम्र *umra*[F] (often pronounced 'umar'); at this age इस उम्र में *is umra mẽ*; at the age of ten दस साल की उम्र में *das sāl kī umra mẽ*; (historical period) युग *yug*[M], ज़माना *zamānā*[M] — in the age of the Mughals मुग़लों के ज़माने में *mugalõ ke zamāne mẽ*

**ago** पहले *pahle* — ten years ago दस साल पहले *das sāl pahle*

**agree, to** (to accept) मानना *mānnā*[N] — you'll have to agree आपको मानना पड़ेगा *āpko mānnā paṛegā*; (to be in agreement) सहमत होना *sahmat honā* ('with', से *se*) — I agree with you मैं आपसे सहमत हूँ *maĩ āpse sahmat hū̃*; राज़ी होना *rāzī honā* — he/she agrees to my suggestion वह मेरे सुझाव से राज़ी है *vah mere sujhāv se rāzī hai*

**ahead** आगे *āge* — she moved ahead वह आगे बढ़ी *vah āge baṛhī*; look ahead आगे देखो *āge dekho*

**aid** सहायता *sahāytā*[F] (see also 'help'); financial aid आर्थिक सहायता *ārthik sahāytā*[F]

**AIDS** एड्स का रोग *eḍs kā rog*[M]

**aim** (intention) इरादा *irādā*[M], उद्देश्य *uddeśya*[M]

**air** हवा *havā*[F]; air letter हवाई पत्र *havāī patra*[M]

**airmail** हवाई डाक *havāī ḍāk*[F]

**airport** हवाई अड्डा *havāī āḍḍā*[M]

**alcoholic drink** शराब *śarāb*[F]

**alight, to** उतरना *utarnā*

**alike** एक-जैसा *ek-jaisā* — they're all alike वे सब एक-जैसे हैं *ve sab ek-jaise haĩ*

**alive** ज़िन्दा *zindā* (-*ā* invariable), जीवित *jīvit* — are they alive? क्या वे ज़िन्दा/जीवित हैं? *kyā ve zindā/jīvit haĩ?*

**all** सब *sab*, (emphatic) सभी *sabhī*; all right ठीक *ṭhīk*; all round चारों तरफ़ *cārõ taraf*; all day दिन भर *din bhar*; all night रात भर *rāt bhar*; (with numbers, e.g. 'all three', use an aggregative form, ending *-õ* — *all three boys* तीनों लड़के *tīnõ laṛke*, all seven books सातों किताबें *sātõ kitābẽ*)

**alley** गली *galī*[F]

**allow, to** देना *denā*[N] (follows oblique infinitive) — allow us to go हमको जाने दो *hamko jāne do*

**almond** बादाम *bādām*[M]

**alone** अकेला *akelā* — I'm alone मैं अकेला हूँ *maĩ akelā hū̃*; (adverb) अकेले *akele* — come alone अकेले आना *akele ānā*

**alphabet** वर्णमाला *varṇmālā*[F]; (script) लिपि *lipi*[F] — the Devanagari alphabet देवनागरी वर्णमाला *devnāgarī varṇmālā*

**already** (use the verb चुकना *cuknā* 'to have done', following stem of main verb: खा चुकना *khā cuknā* 'to have already eaten' (no ने *ne* construction) — we have already eaten हम खाना खा चुके हैं *ham khānā khā cuke haĩ*)

**also** भी *bhī* (follows the emphasized item) — I too speak Hindi मैं भी हिन्दी बोलता हूँ *maĩ bhī hindī boltā hū̃*; I speak Hindi, and I speak Panjabi too मैं हिन्दी बोलता हूँ, और पंजाबी भी बोलता हूँ *maĩ hindī boltā hū̃, aur panjābī bhī boltā hū̃*

**alter, to**: see 'change'

**alteration** परिवर्तन *parivartan*[M]

**alternative** (option) विकल्प *vikalp*[M] — you have no alternative आपके पास और कोई विकल्प नहीं हैं *āpke pās aur koī vikalp nahī̃ hai*

**although** हालाँकि *hālā̃ki*

**always** हमेशा *hameśā*; as always हमेशा की तरह *hameśā kī tarah*

**amend, to** (to change) बदलना *badalnā*[N]; (to correct) सुधारना *sudhārnā*[N]

**America** अमरीका *amrīkā*[M]

**American** (adj. & noun) अमरीकन *amrīkan*[M]

**among** (between) में *mẽ* — to divide the money among the children बच्चों में पैसा बाँटना *baccõ mẽ paisā bā̃ṭnā*; (from among a group) में से *mẽ se* — who is the best among them? उनमें से सबसे अच्छा कौन है ? *unmẽ se sabse acchā kaun hai?*

**amuse, to** जी बहलाना *jī bahlānā*[N]

**amusement** मनोरंजन *manoranjan*[M]

**amusing** मनोरंजक *manoranjak*

**ancestor** पूर्वज *pūrvaj*[M]

**ancient** प्राचीन *prācīn*

**and** और *aur*

**anger** ग़ुस्सा *gussā*[M], क्रोध *krodh*[M]

**angry** ग़ुस्से *gusse*; (displeased) नाराज़ *nārāz* — she got angry with me वह मुझसे नाराज़ हुई *vah mujhse nārāz huī*

**animal** जानवर *jānvar*ᴹ

**ankle** टखना *ṭakhnā*ᴹ

**annual** सालाना *sālānā,* वार्षिक *vārṣik*

**another** (second, different) दूसरा *dūsrā*; (one more) एक और *ek aur* — take another banana एक और केला लीजिए *ek aur kelā lījie*

**answer** जवाब *javāb*ᴹ, उत्तर *uttar*ᴹ; to answer (का) जवाब/उत्तर देना *(kā) javāb/uttar denā*ᴺ — please answer my letter मेरे पत्र का जवाब/उत्तर दीजिए *mere patra kā javāb/uttar dījie*

**ant** चींटी *cĩṭī*ᶠ

**anxiety** परेशानी *pareśānī*ᶠ, चिन्ता *cintā*ᶠ

**anxious** परेशान *pareśān* — you're looking anxious तुम परेशान लग रहे हो *tum pareśān lag rahe ho*

**anxiousness**: see 'anxiety'

**any** कोई *koī* — this sentence doesn't have any meaning ☛ इस वाक्य का कोई मतलब नहीं है *is vākya kā koī matlab nahī̃ hai*; (with uncountables) कुछ *kuch* — do you have any flour/sugar? ☛ आपके पास कुछ आटा/चीनी है? *āpke pās kuch āṭā/cīnī hai?*; any . . . at all कोई भी — take any book कोई भी किताब लो *koī bhī kitāb lo*

**anyhow**: see 'anyway'

**anyone** कोई *koī* — is anyone there? कोई है? *koī hai?*; anyone at all कोई भी *koī bhī*

**anyway** (in any way) किसी भी तरह *kisī bhī tarah*; (regardless of the circumstances) हर हालत में *har hālat mẽ*; (changing the topic, 'well anyway . . .') ख़ैर *khair*

**anywhere** कहीं *kahī̃*; anywhere at all कहीं भी *kahī̃ bhī*

**apart** (distant) दूर *dūr*; (separate) अलग *alag*; (separated) जुदा *judā* (*-ā* invariable)

**apart from** (in addition to) के सिवाय *ke sivāy* — what do I need apart from money? ☛ पैसे के सिवाय मुझे क्या चाहिए? *paise ke sivāy mujhe kyā cāhie?*; (leaving aside, excluding) को छोड़कर *ko choṛkar* — apart from me मुझको छोड़कर *mujhko choṛkar*

**apologize, to** माफ़ी माँगना *māfī mā̃gnā*ᴺ ('to' someone,

से *se*) — I apologized to them मैंने उनसे माफ़ी माँगी *maĩne unse māfī mā̃gī*

**appeal, to** (to be pleasing) भाना *bhānā*, पसंद आना/होना *pasand ānā/honā* — this place appeals to me a lot यह जगह मुझे बहुत भाती है *yah jagah mujhe bahut bhātī hai*; (to supplicate) अनुरोध करना *anurodh karnā*ᴺ

**appear, to** (to come into view) दिखाई देना *dikhāī denā* (no ने *ne* construction) — Ram and Bharat appeared राम और भरत दिखाई दिए *rām aur bharat dikhāī die*; (to seem) लगना *lagnā* — they appear happy वे ख़ुश लगते हैं *ve khuś lagte haĩ*

**appearance** (the way someone looks) रूप-रंग *rūp-raṅg*ᴹ

**apple** सेब *seb*ᴹ

**application** अर्ज़ी *arzī*ᶠ; to apply अर्ज़ी देनाᴺ *arzī denā* — we applied for a loan हमने उधार के लिए अर्ज़ी दी *hamne udhār ke lie arzī dī*

**appoint, to** नियुक्त करना *niyukt karnā*ᴺ

**appointment** (to a job) नियुक्ति *niyukti*ᶠ — I was appointed last year ☛ मेरी नियुक्ति पिछले साल हुई *merī niyukti pichle sāl huī*

**appropriate** ठीक *ṭhīk*; उचित *ucit*

**approximately** लगभग *lagbhag*

**April** अप्रैल *aprail*ᴹ

**area** इलाक़ा *ilāqā*ᴹ; (abstract senses) क्षेत्र *kṣetra* ᴹ — in the area of politics राजनीति के क्षेत्र में *rājnīti ke kṣetra mẽ*

**argue, to** बहस करना *bahas karnā*ᴺ ('with', से *se*); (to discuss, argue a point) तर्क-वितर्क करना *tark-vitark karnā*ᴺ ('with', से *se*)

**argument** (dispute) बहस *bahas*ᶠ, झगड़ा *jhagṛā*ᴹ; (reasoning) दलील *dalīl*ᶠ, तर्क *tark*ᴹ

**arise, to** उठना *uṭhnā* — the question doesn't arise सवाल नहीं उठता *savāl nahī̃ uṭhtā*; (to appear) प्रकट होना *prakaṭ honā*

**aristocrat** रईस *raīs*ᴹ

**arm** बाँह *bā̃h*ᶠ

**armchair** आराम-कुरसी *ārām-kursī*ᶠ

**armpit** बग़ल *bagal*ᶠ

**army** सेना *senā*ᶠ; फ़ौज *fauj*ᶠ

**around** (near) के आस-पास *ke ās-pās*, (surrounding) के चारों ओर/तरफ़ *ke cārõ or/ taraf*

**arrange, to** का इंतज़ाम करना *kā intazām karnā*ᴺ — we'll arrange the meeting हम मीटिंग

का इंतज़ाम करेंगे *ham mīṭiṅg kā intazām karẽge*

**arrangement** इंतज़ाम *intazām*[M], व्यवस्था *vyavasthā*[F]

**arrest, to** गिरफ़्तार करना *giraftār karnā* [N] — the police arrested them पुलिस ने उन्हें गिरफ़्तार किया *pulis ne unhẽ giraftār kiyā*

**arrive, to** पहुँचना *pahũcnā*

**arrogance** घमंड *ghamaṇḍ*[M]

**art** कला *kalā*[F]

**article** (in newspaper) लेख *lekh*[M]; (thing, item) चीज़ *cīz*[F], वस्तु *vastu*[F]

**artificial** कृत्रिम *kṛtrim*

**artist** कलाकार *kalākār*[M]

**artistic** कलात्मक *kalātmak*

**as** (like) जैसे *jaise*, की तरह *kī tarah* — as always हमेशा की तरह *hameśā kī tarah*; (in the capacity of ) की हैसियत से *kī haisiyat se*, के रूप में *ke rūp mẽ* — as a guest मेहमान के रूप में *mehmān ke rūp mẽ*; (because) क्योंकि *kyõki*

**as if, as though** मानों *mānõ*; as if he were ill मानों वह बीमार हो *mānõ vah bīmār ho*

**as soon as** जैसे ही *jaise hī*, ज्यों ही *jyõ hī* (often correlates with वैसे ही *vaise hī* / त्यों ही *tyõ hī*) — as soon as I saw her I phoned you जैसे ही मैंने उसको देखा वैसे ही मैंने आपको फ़ोन किया *jaise hī maĩne usko dekhā vaise hī maĩne āpko fon kiyā*; (an alternative construction is oblique imperfective participle + ही *hī*, e.g. देखते ही *dekhte hī* 'immediately on seeing')

**as well**: see 'also'

**ash, ashes** राख *rākh*[F]

**ashamed**: see 'shame'

**ask, to** (से) पूछना *(se) pūchnā*[N] — ask his name उसका नाम पूछो *uskā nām pūcho*; ask Ram राम से पूछो *rām se pūcho*

**ask for, to** (से) माँगना *(se) mā̃gnā*[N] — ask Ram for money राम से पैसा माँगो *rām se paisā mā̃go*

**aspect** पहलू *pahlū*[M] — there are two aspects to this matter इस बात के दो पहलू हैं *is bāt ke do pahlū haĩ*

**assemble, to** इकट्ठा होना *ikaṭṭhā honā*

**assist, to** (की) सहायता करना *(kī) sahāytā karnā*[N] — we shall assist you हम आपकी सहायता करेंगे *ham āpkī sahāytā karẽge*

**assistance** सहायता *sahāytā*[F]

**assistant** सहायक *sahāyak*ᴹ

**astonishment:** see 'surprise'

**at** (a place) पर *par* — at home घर पर *ghar par*; at the place of के यहाँ *ke yahā̃* — at my place मेरे यहाँ *mere yahā̃*; (time: use the oblique case) — at one o'clock एक बजे *ek baje*; at doing something करने में *karne mẽ* — he's very good at refusing वह इनकार करने में माहिर है *vah inkār karne mẽ māhir hai*; at last आख़िर *ākhir*; at once तुरंत *turant*, अभी *abhī*; at night रात को *rāt ko*

**atheist** नास्तिक *nāstik*ᴹ

**atmosphere** वातावरण *vātāvaraṇ*ᴹ, माहौल *māhaul*ᴹ — an atmosphere of fear डर का माहौल *ḍar kā māhaul*

**attack** हमला *hamlā*ᴹ, आक्रमण *ākramaṇ*ᴹ; to attack हमला/ आक्रमण करना *hamlā/ ākramaṇ karnā*ᴺ (object takes पर *par*) — we attacked the enemy हमने दुश्मन पर हमला किया *hamne duśman par hamlā kiyā*

**attempt** प्रयास *prayās*ᴹ; see also 'to try'

**attention** ध्यान *dhyān*ᴹ

**attentively** ध्यान से *dhyān se*

**attract, to** आकर्षित करना *ākarṣit karnā*ᴺ

**attraction** आकर्षण *ākarṣaṇ*ᴹ

**aubergine** बैंगन *baĩgan*ᴹ

**August** अगस्त *agast*ᴹ

**aunt** (father's sister) बुआ *buā*ᶠ; फूफी *phūphī*ᶠ; (mother's sister) मौसी *mausī*ᶠ; (father's brother's wife) चाची *cācī*ᶠ; (mother's brother's wife) मामी *māmī*ᶠ

**author** लेखक *lekhak*ᴹ; (female) लेखिका *lekhikā*ᶠ

**autobiography** आत्मकथा *ātmakathā*ᶠ

**autumn** शरद् *śarad*ᶠ

**available** उपलब्ध *uplabdh*; to be available मिलना *milnā* — is coffee available? क्या कॉफ़ी मिलेगी? *kyā kāfī milegī?*

**average** औसत *ausat* — the average age of the children बच्चों की औसत उम्र *baccõ kī ausat umra*

**avoid, to** (से) बचे रहना *(se) bace rahnā* — you should avoid such problems आप ऐसी समस्याओं से बचे रहें *āp aisī samasyāõ se bace rahẽ*; (to abstain from: see 'abstain from')

## B

**baby** शिशु *śiśu*ᴹ, बच्चा *baccā*ᴹ

**back** (part of body) पीठ *pīṭh*ᴹ; (of building) पिछवाड़ा *pichvāṛā*ᴹ – at the back of the house घर के पिछवाड़े में *ghar ke pichvāṛe mẽ*; (returned: see 'next')

**back** (return) वापस *vāpas*: to come back वापस आना *vāpas ānā*; to go back वापस जाना *vāpas jānā*; to give back वापस देना *vāpas denā*ᴺ

**background** पृष्ठभूमि *pṛṣṭhbhūmi*ᶠ

**backwards** (in motion) पीछे *pīche*, पीछे की तरफ़ *pīche kī taraf*; (reversed) उलटा *ulṭā* – the picture is backwards तस्वीर उलटी है *tasvīr ulṭī hai*

**bad** बुरा *burā*; ख़राब *kharāb*

**badly** बुरी तरह से *burī tarah se*

**badness** बुराई *burāī*ᶠ

**bag** बैग *baig*ᴹ; थैला *thailā*ᴹ – plastic bag प्लास्टिक का थैला *plāsṭik kā thailā*; cloth shoulder bag झोला *jholā*ᴹ

**balance** संतुलन *santulan*ᴹ – one should maintain a balance ❧ संतुलन बनाए रखना चाहिए *santulan banāe rakhnā cāhie*

**balance, to** संतुलित करना *santulit karnā*ᴺ

**balanced** संतुलित *santulit*

**bald** गंजा *ganjā*

**ball** गेंद *gẽd*ᶠ

**balloon** गुब्बारा *gubbārā*ᴹ

**banana** केला *kelā*ᴹ

**bandage** पट्टी *paṭṭī*ᶠ

**bandage, to** पट्टी बाँधना *paṭṭī bā̃dhnā*ᴺ

**bandit** डाकू *ḍākū*ᴹ

**bangle** चूड़ी *cūṛī*ᶠ

**bank**¹ (shore) किनारा *kinārā*ᴹ; (riverbank) घाट *ghāṭ*ᴹ

**bank**² (financial) बैंक *baink*ᴹ

**banyan** बरगद *bargad*ᴹ, वट *vaṭ*ᴹ

**barbarism** बरबरता *barbartā*ᶠ

**barber** नाई *nāī*ᴹ

**bare** नंगा *naṅgā*

**bargain, to:** see 'haggle'

**bark, to** भौंकना *bhaũknā*

**barley** जौ *jau*ᴹ

**base** (basis) बुनियाद *buniyād*ᶠ, आधार *ādhār*ᴹ

**based** आधारित *ādhārit* – this story is based on real events यह कहानी असली घटनाओं पर

आधारित है *yah kahānī aslī ghaṭnāõ par ādhārit hai*

**basic** (language etc.) बुनियादी *buniyādī* — basic Urdu बुनियादी उर्दू *buniyādī urdū*

**basis** आधार *ādhār*ᴹ — on this basis इस आधार पर *is ādhār par*

**basket** टोकरी *ṭokrī*ᶠ

**bastard** (adj. & noun) हरामज़ादा *harāmzādā*ᴹ

**bathe, to** नहाना *nahānā*, स्नान करना *snān karnā*ᴺ

**bathroom** गुसलख़ाना *gusal<u>kh</u>ānā*ᴹ, बाथरूम *bāthrūm*ᴹ; (toilet) शौचालय *śaucālay*ᴹ

**be, to** होना *honā*; to become, act, behave as बनना *bannā* — don't be an ass! गधा मत बनो! *gadhā mat bano!*; I want to be a doctor मैं डाक्टर बनना चाहता हूँ *maĩ ḍākṭar bannā cāhtā hū̃*

**bear** (animal) भालू *bhālū*ᴹ

**bear, to** (to endure) सहना *sahnā*ᴺ

**beard** दाढ़ी *dāṛhī*ᶠ; to grow a beard दाढ़ी बढ़ाना *dāṛhī baṛhānā*ᴺ

**beat, to** (strike) मारना *mārnā*ᴺ; (to thrash) पीटना *pīṭnā*ᴺ; (to defeat) हराना *harānā*ᴺ; (to palpitate) धड़कना *dhaṛaknā*

**beautiful** सुन्दर *sundar*, ख़ूबसूरत *<u>kh</u>ūbsūrat*

**beauty** सुन्दरता *sundartā*ᶠ, ख़ूबसूरती *<u>kh</u>ūbsūrtī*ᶠ

**because** क्योंकि *kyõki*; because of की वजह से *kī vajah se*, के कारण *ke kāraṇ*; because of this इस लिए *is lie*; (when cause precedes consequence, चूँकि *cū̃ki* may be used — because he's very weak, he should rest चूँकि वह बहुत कमज़ोर है, इसलिए उसे आराम करना चाहिए *cū̃ki vah bahut kamzor hai, islie use ārām karnā cāhie*)

**become, to** बनना *bannā*, बन जाना *ban jānā* — he'll become a politician वह राजनेता बनेगा *vah rājnetā banegā*; होना *honā*, हो जाना *ho jānā* — what will become of me? मेरा क्या होगा? *merā kyā hogā?*; the situation has become serious स्थिति गंभीर हो गई है *sthiti gambhīr ho gaī hai*

**bed** (bedstead) पलंग *palaṅg*ᴹ; (bedding) बिस्तर *bistar*ᴹ; to get out of bed बिस्तर से उठना *bistar se uṭhnā*; to go to bed सो जाना *so jānā*; please make the bed बिस्तर लगाइए *bistar lagāie*

**bedding** बिस्तर *bistar*$^{M}$

**bedroom** सोने का कमरा *sone kā kamrā*$^{M}$ — the house has three bedrooms घर में तीन सोने के कमरे हैं *ghar mẽ tīn sone ke kamre haĩ*

**beer** बियर *biyar*$^{M\ (F)}$

**before** पहले *pahle* — why didn't you tell me before? तुमने मुझे पहले क्यों नहीं बताया? *tumne mujhe pahle kyõ nahī̃ batāyā?*; (before a specified time) के पहले *ke pahle* — before tomorrow कल के पहले *kal ke pahle*; (before an action) से पहले *se pahle* — before leaving जाने से पहले *jāne se pahle*

**beg, to** भीख माँगना *bhīkh mā̃gnā*$^{N}$

**beggar** भिखारी *bhikhārī*$^{M}$

**begin, to** शुरू करना *śurū karnā* — you begin work तुम काम शुरू करो *tum kām śurū karo*; to begin spontaneously: use oblique infinitive + लगना *lagnā* — it began raining पानी पड़ने लगा *pānī paṛne lagā*; to break out (war etc.) छिड़ना *chiṛnā*

**beginning** शुरू *śurū*$^{M}$ — in the beginning शुरू में *śurū mẽ*; from the very beginning शुरू से ही *śurū se hī*; (a beginning) शुरुआत *śuruāt*$^{F}$ — a new beginning एक नई शुरुआत *ek naī śuruāt*

**behave, to** सलूक/व्यवहार करना *salūk/vyavahār karnā*$^{N}$, पेश आना *peś ānā* — he/she behaved well towards me उसने मेरे प्रति अच्छा सलूक/व्यवहार किया *usne mere prati acchā salūk/vyavahār kiyā*

**behaviour** व्यवहार *vyavahār*$^{M}$; dealings, treatment of someone बरताव *bartāv*$^{M}$ — I didn't like his behaviour with me मेरे साथ उसका बरताव मुझे अच्छा नहीं लगा *mere sāth uskā bartāv mujhe acchā nahī̃ lagā*

**behind** पीछे *pīche* — we're being left behind हम पीछे छूट रहे हैं *ham pīche chūṭ rahe haĩ*; (behind something) के पीछे *ke pīche* — behind the house घर के पीछे *ghar ke pīche*; from behind पीछे से *pīche se*

**belch** डकार *ḍakār*$^{F}$; to belch डकार लेना *ḍakār lenā*$^{N}$

**belief** विश्वास *viśvās*$^{M}$; (trust) भरोसा *bharosā*$^{M}$

**believe, to** विश्वास करना *viśvās karnā*[N] (object takes पर *par*) — I don't believe him/her मैं उसपर विश्वास नहीं करता *maĩ uspar viśvās nahī̃ kartā*; to believe (an opinion etc.) मानना[N] — believe what I say मेरी बात मानो *merī bāt māno*

**bell** घंटा *ghaṇṭā*[M], (small) घंटी *ghaṇṭī*[F]

**below:** see 'beneath'

**belt** पेटी *peṭī*[F]

**bend, to** (intr.) झुकना *jhuknā*; (to turn, as road) मुड़ना *muṛnā* — the road bends सड़क मुड़ती है *saṛak muṛtī hai*; (tr.) मोड़ना *moṛnā*

**beneath** के नीचे *ke nīce* — beneath the sheet चादर के नीचे *cādar ke nīce*

**beneficial** लाभकर *lābhkar*

**Bengali** (adj. & noun) बंगाली *baṅgālī*[M]; Bengali language बंगाली *baṅgālī*[F]

**bent** (crooked) टेढ़ा *ṭeṛhā*

**beside** (next to) की बग़ल में *kī bagal mẽ*

**besides** (apart from) को छोड़कर *ko choṛkar*; (as well as) के अलावा *ke alāvā*

**best** सबसे अच्छा *sabse acchā* — the best cars सबसे अच्छी गाड़ियाँ *sabse acchī gāṛiyā̃*

**better** बेहतर *behtar*, ज़्यादा अच्छा *zyādā acchā* — better than them उनसे ज़्यादा अच्छा *unse zyādā acchā*

**between** के बीच *ke bīc*; between two trees दो पेड़ों के बीच *do peṛõ ke bīc*; (in 'the difference between') में *mẽ* — what's the difference between the two books? दोनों किताबों में क्या फ़र्क़ है? *donõ kitābõ mẽ kyā farq hai?*

**beware** ख़बरदार *k͟habardār*, सावधान *sāvdhān* — beware of the dog! कुत्ते से सावधान! *kutte se sāvdhān!*

**beyond** आगे *āge*, के आगे *ke āge*, से आगे *se āge* — beyond the last house आख़िरी मकान से आगे *āk͟hirī makān se āge*; (in abstract senses) से परे *se pare* — beyond doubt संदेह से परे *sandeh se pare*

**bicycle** साइकिल *sāikil*[F]; he was riding a bicycle वह साइकिल पर सवार था *vah sāikil par savār thā*

**big** बड़ा *baṛā*

**bind, to** बाँधना *bā̃dhnā*[N]

**bird** चिड़िया *ciṛiyā*$^{F}$, पक्षी *pakṣī*$^{M}$

**birth** जन्म *janma*$^{M}$

**birthday** साल-गिरह *sāl-girah*$^{F}$, जन्मदिन *janmadin*$^{M}$; to celebrate a birthday साल-गिरह/जन्मदिन मनाना *sāl-girah/janmadin manānā*$^{N}$

**bit** (small piece) टुकड़ा *ṭukṛā*$^{M}$

**bite, to** (दांत से) काटना *(dā̃t se) kāṭnā*$^{N}$ — the dog bit me कुत्ते ने मुझे काटा *kutte ne mujhe kāṭā*

**bitter** कड़वा *karvā*

**black** काला *kālā*

**blame, to** दोष लगाना *doṣ lagānā*$^{N}$ (object takes पर *par*) — they blamed me उन्होंने मुझपर दोष लगाया *unhõne mujhpar doṣ lagāyā*

**bland** फीका *phīkā*

**blank** (of paper etc.) कोरा *korā*; (empty, as space) ख़ाली *khālī* — let's leave this page blank इस पन्ने को ख़ाली छोड़ें *is panne ko khālī choṛẽ*

**blanket** कंबल *kambal*$^{M}$

**bless, to** आशीर्वाद देना *āśīrvād denā*$^{N}$ — grandfather blessed us affectionately दादा ने हमें प्यार से आशीर्वाद दिया *dādā ne hamẽ pyār se āśīrvād diyā*

**blessing** आशीर्वाद *āśīrvād*$^{M}$

**blind**[1] (sightless) अंधा *andhā*; blind man अंधा *andhā*$^{M}$

**blind**[2] (for window) चिक़ *ciq*$^{F}$

**bliss** आनंद *ānand*$^{M}$; (in religious context) परमानंद *paramānand*$^{M}$

**blister** फफोला *phapholā*$^{M}$

**blood** ख़ून *khūn*$^{M}$, रक्त *rakt*$^{M}$

**blow** (shock) धक्का *dhakkā*$^{M}$

**blow, to** (intr., of wind) चलना *calnā,* बहना *bahnā*; (tr.) फूँकना *phū̃knā* — blow the fire आग को फूँको *āg ko phū̃ko*

**blue** नीला *nīlā*

**boat** नाव *nāv*$^{F}$; small boat कश्ती *kaśtī*$^{F}$

**bodily** शारीरिक *śārīrik*

**body** शरीर *śarīr*$^{M}$; dead body, corpse लाश *lāś*$^{F}$

**boil, to** (intr.) उबलना *ubalnā* — boiled water उबला हुआ पानी *ublā huā pānī*; (tr.) उबालना *ubālnā*$^{N}$ — please boil the water पानी को उबालिए [उबाल दीजिए] *pānī ko ubālie [ubāl dījie]*

**bomb** बम *bam*$^{M}$ — a bomb exploded बम का विस्फोट हुआ *bam kā visphoṭ huā*

**bone** हड्डी *haḍḍī*$^{F}$

**book** किताब *kitāb*$^{F}$, पुस्तक *pustak*$^{F}$

**bookish** किताबी

**border** (frontier) सीमा *sīmā*$^{F}$; (of cloth etc.) किनारा *kinārā*$^{M}$

**bore, to** बोर करना *bor karnā*$^{N}$ — he'll bore us वह हमें बोर करेगा *vah hamẽ bor caregā*; to become bored बोर होना *bor honā*, ऊबना *ūbnā* — I began to get bored writing the dictionary शब्दकोश लिखते लिखते मैं ऊबने लगा *śabdkoś likhte likhte maĩ ūbne lagā*

**boredom** ऊब *ūb*$^{F}$, बोरियत *boriyat*$^{F}$

**borrow, to** उधार लेना *udhār lenā*$^{N}$ — I borrowed 100 rupees from Ram मैंने राम से १०० रुपये उधार लिए *maĩne rām se 100 rupaye udhār lie*

**boss** मालिक *mālik*$^{M}$

**both** दोनों *donõ* — look both ways दोनों तरफ़ देखो *donõ taraf dekho*; both . . . and भी . . . भी *bhī . . . bhī* — I both eat meat and drink alcohol मैं गोश्त भी खाता हूँ और शराब भी पीता हूँ *maĩ gośt bhī khātā hũ aur śarāb bhī pītā hũ*

**bottle** बोतल *botal*$^{F}$, शीशी *śīśī*$^{F}$

---

**Insight**

Boredom – बोरियत *boriyat*$^{F}$ — such a combination of an English loanword and an Arabic-origin suffix (*-iyat* forms abstract nouns) is rare in Hindi.

---

**boring** उबाऊ *ubāū*; (dull) नीरस *nīras*, फीका *phīkā*

**born, to be** (का) जन्म होना *(kā) janma honā*; पैदा होना *paidā honā* (*-ā* invariable in पैदा *paidā*) — she was born in India वह भारत में पैदा हुई *vah bhārat mẽ paidā huī*, उसका जन्म भारत में हुआ *uskā janma bhārat mẽ huā*

**bottom** (base) निचला भाग *niclā bhāg*$^{M}$; (bum, buttocks) चूतड़ *cūtaṛ*$^{M}$

**boundary** सीमा *sīmā*$^{F}$

**bowl** (large) कटोरा *kaṭorā*$^{M}$; (small) कटोरी *kaṭorī*$^{F}$

**box** डिब्बा *ḍibbā*$^{M}$, बक्सा *baksā*$^{M}$

**boy** लड़का *laṛkā*$^{M}$

**brain** (intellect) बुद्धि *buddhi*[F]; (organ) दिमाग़ *dimāg*[M], मस्तिष्क *mastiṣk*[M]

**branch** (of tree) डाल *ḍāl*[F]; (also of bank, shop etc.) शाखा *śākhā*[F]

**brass** पीतल *pītal*[M] – brass statues पीतल की मूर्तियाँ[F] *pītal kī mūrtiyā̃*

**brave** बहादुर *bahādur*; (plucky) साहसी *sāhasī*

**bravery** बहादुरी *bahādurī*[F]

**bread** रोटी *roṭī*[F]; loaf डबल रोटी *ḍabal roṭī*[F]

**breadth** चौड़ाई *cauṛāī*[F]

**break, to** (intr.) टूटना *ṭūṭnā* – the window broke खिड़की टूटी [टूट गई] *khiṛkī ṭūṭī [ṭūṭ gaī]*; (tr.) तोड़ना *toṛnā*[N] – I broke a window मैंने खिड़की तोड़ी [तोड़ दी] *maĩne khiṛkī toṛī [toṛ dī]*; to break down बिगड़ना *bigaṛnā*, ख़राब हो जाना *kharāb ho jānā* – the car broke down गाड़ी ख़राब हो गई *gāṛī kharāb ho gaī*; to break out, start (war etc.) छिड़ना *chiṛnā*

**breakfast** नाश्ता *nāśtā*[M]; to have breakfast नाश्ता करना *nāśtā karnā*[N] – they've already had breakfast वे नाश्ता कर चुके हैं *ve nāśtā kar cuke haĩ*

**breath** साँस *sā̃s*[F]

**breathe, to** साँस लेना *sā̃s lenā*[N]

**bribe** घूँस *ghū̃s*[F]; रिश्वत *riśvat*[F]; to bribe रिश्वत देना *riśvat denā*[N]; to take a bribe रिश्वत लेना *riśvat lenā*[N]

**brick** ईंट *ĩṭ*[F] – a brick wall ईंटों की दीवार *ĩṭõ kī dīvār*

**bridge** पुल *pul*[M]

**brief** संक्षिप्त *saṅkṣipt*; in brief संक्षेप में *saṅkṣep mẽ*

**bright** (well lit) रोशन *rośan*; (clever) तेज़ *tez*

**bring, to** लाना *lānā*; ले आना *le ānā* (no ने *ne* construction in either) – she brought a gift वह तोहफ़ा लाई / ले आई *vah tohfā lāī / le āī*

**broken** टूटा हुआ *ṭūṭā huā* – a broken window टूटी हुई खिड़की *ṭūṭī huī khiṛkī*

**brothel** कोठा *koṭhā*[M]

**brother** भाई *bhāī*[M]

**brother-in-law** (wife's brother) साला *sālā*[M] (this is also used as an abusive insult meaning 'I have carnal knowledge of your sister', so it must be used carefully!); (sister's husband) बहनोई *bahnoī*[M]; (husband's elder brother) जेठ *jeṭh*[M]; (husband's younger brother) देवर *devar*[M]

**brown** भूरा *bhūṛā* — brown coloured cloth भूरे रंग का कपड़ा *bhūre raṅg kā kapṛā*

**brush** बुरुश *buruś*[M]; (broom) झाड़ू *jhāṛū*[M]

**bubble** बबूला *babūlā*[M]

**bucket** बालटी *bālṭī*[F]

**Buddha (the)** बुद्ध *buddh*

**Buddhist** बौद्ध *baudh*[M]

**build, to** बनाना *banānā*[N]

**building** इमारत *imārat*[F] — tall buildings ऊँची इमारतें *ũcī imāratẽ*

**bullet** गोली *golī*[F]; to be hit by a bullet गोली लगना *golī lagnā* — he/she was hit by a bullet उसे गोली लगी *use golī lagī*; to fire a bullet गोली चलाना *golī calānā*[N]

**bullock** बैल *bail*[M]; bullock cart बैलगाड़ी *bailgāṛī*[F]

**burial** दफ़न *dafan*[M]

**burn, to** (intr., to be on fire) जलना *jalnā* — burning wood जलती हुई लकड़ी *jaltī huī lakṛī*; burned food जला हुआ खाना *jalā huā khānā*; (tr., to set alight) जलाना *jalānā*[N] — we burned the sticks हमने लकड़ियाँ जलाईं *hamne lakṛiyā̃ jalāī̃*

**burst, to** (intr.) फूटना *phūṭnā*, (tr.) फोड़ना *phoṛnā*

**bury, to** दफ़नाना *dafnānā*[N]

**bus** बस *bas*[F] — we go to school by bus हम बस से स्कूल जाते हैं *ham bas se skūl jāte haĩ*

**bush** झाड़ी *jhāṛī*[F]; (scrubland) जंगल *jaṅgal*[M]

**business** व्यवसाय *vyavasāy*[M] — what business does he do? वह क्या व्यवसाय करता है? *vah kyā vyavasāy kartā hai?*

**busy** मसरूफ़ *masrūf*, व्यस्त *vyast*

**but** लेकिन *lekin*, पर *par*, मगर *magar*

**butcher** क़साई *qasāī*[M] (carries negative or abusive image)

**butter** मक्खन *makkhan*[M]

**butterfly** तितली *titlī*[F]

**buy, to** ख़रीदना *kharīdnā*[N] — we bought a car हमने गाड़ी ख़रीदी *hamne gāṛī kharīdī*

**by** से *se*; by post डाक से *ḍāk se*; (with passive) के द्वारा *ke dvārā* — this book was written by my uncle यह पुस्तक मेरे चाचाजी के द्वारा लिखी गई *yah pustak mere cācājī ke dvārā likhī gaī*; (by a certain time) तक *tak* — by tomorrow कल तक *kal tak*

# C

**cabbage** गोभी *gobhī*[F]

**cage** पिंजरा *pinjrā*[M]

**call, to** बुलाना *bulānā*[N]; (call out) पुकारना *pukārnā*[N]; (to name, refer to as) कहना *kahnā*[N] — what's this called? इसको क्या कहते हैं? *isko kyā kahte haĩ?*; (to give nickname to, dub) कहकर बुलाना *kahkar bulānā*[N] — what do you call Anuradha at home? घर में आप अनुराधा को क्या कहकर बुलाते हैं? *ghar mẽ āp anurādhā ko kyā kahkar bulāte haĩ?*

**called** (named, known as) नाम का *nām kā* — a village called Rajpur राजपुर नाम का गाँव *rājpur nām kā gā̃v*

**camel** ऊंट *ū̃ṭ*[M]

**camera** कैमरा *kaimrā*[M]

**can**: see 'able'

**cancel, to** रद्द करना *radd karnā*[N]

**candidate** उम्मीदवार *ummīdvār*[M]

**candle** मोमबत्ती *mombattī*[F] — light this candle यह मोमबत्ती जलाओ [जला दो] *yah mombattī jalāo [jalā do]*

**capable** समर्थ *samarth*

**capacity** (ability to act; or amount that can be held) क्षमता *kṣamtā*[F]; (role) हैसियत *haisiyat*[F] — I'm speaking in the capacity of lawyer मैं वक़ील की हैसियत से बोल रहा हूँ *maĩ vaqīl kī haisiyat se bol rahā hū̃*

**capital** (city) राजधानी *rājdhānī*[F]; (money) पूंजी *pū̃jī*[F]

**car** गाड़ी *gāṛī*[F], कार *kār*[F]

**cardamom** इलायची *ilāycī*[F]

**cards** (game) ताश *tāś*[M] — shall we play cards? ताश खेलें? *tāś khelẽ?*; (an individual playing card) ताश का पत्ता *tāś kā pattā*[M]

**care** परवाह *parvāh*[F]; to care about की परवाह करना / होना *kī parvāh karnā*[N]*/honā* — what do I care about that? मुझे उसकी क्या परवाह है? *mujhe uskī kyā parvāh hai?*; (carefulness) सावधानी *sāvdhānī*[F]

**careful** सावधान *sāvdhān*

**carefully** सावधानी से *sāvdhānī se*; (attentively) ध्यान से *dhyān se*

**careless** लापरवाह *lāparvāh*

**carelessly** लापरवाही से *lāparvāhī se*

**carpenter** बढ़ई *baṛhaī*[M]

**carrot** गाजर *gājar*[F]

**carry, to** (to convey) ले जाना *le jānā*; (to lug) ढोना *ḍhonā*[N]

**cart** (handcart) ठेला *ṭhelā*[M]; (bullock cart) बैलगाड़ी *bailgāṛī*[F]

**case** (matter) मामला *māmlā*[M]; (lawsuit) मुक़दमा *muqadmā*[M]; (sufferer from an illness) मरीज़ *marīz*[M]

**caste** जाति *jāti*[F], वर्ण *varṇ*[M]

**cat** बिल्ली *billī*[F]

**catch, to** पकड़ना *pakaṛnā*[N]; (to trap) फँसाना *phãsānā*[N]; (to become infected) लगना *lagnā* — I caught flu मुझे फ़्लू लगा *mujhe flū lagā*

**cauliflower** फूल-गोभी *phūl-gobhī*[F]

**cause** कारण *kāraṇ*[M]

**caution** (carefulness) सावधानी *sāvdhānī*[F]; (warning) चेतावनी *cetāvnī*[F]

**cautious** सावधान *sāvdhān*

**cave** गुफा *guphā*[F]

**celebrate, to** मनाना *manānā*[N] — we celebrate this festival every year यह उत्सव हम हर साल मनाते हैं *yah utsav ham har sāl manāte haĩ*; (to have a celebration) खुशियाँ मनाना *khuśiyā̃ manānā*[N] — when you come home we'll celebrate जब आप घर आएँगे तो हम खुशियाँ मनाएँगे *jab āp ghar āẽge to ham khuśiyā̃ manāẽge*

**centre** केन्द्र *kendra*[M]

**century** शताब्दी *śatābdī*[F] — the twenty-first century इक्कीसवीं शताब्दी *ikkīsvī̃ śatābdī*

**certain** पक्का *pakkā*, निश्चित *niścit*; (decided) तय *tay*; a certain one कोई *koī* — in a certain city lived a certain man किसी शहर में कोई आदमी रहता था *kisī śahar mẽ koī ādmī rahtā thā*

**certainly** ज़रूर *zarūr*, अवश्य *avaśya*

**chair** कुरसी *kursī*[F]

**challenge** चुनौती *cunautī*[F]

**chance**: see 'opportunity'; by chance संयोग से *sãyog se*

**change**[1] (innovation) परिवर्तन *parivartan*[M] — to bring change परिवर्तन लाना *parivartan lānā*

**change**[2] (coins) रेज़गारी *rezgārī*[F] — change for 50 rupees ५० रुपये की रेज़गारी *50 rupaye kī rezgārī*

**change, to** (intr. & tr.[N]) बदलना *badalnā* — the weather changes मौसम बदलता है [बदल जाता है] *mausam badaltā hai [badal jātā hai]*; I want to change tomorrow's plan मैं कल का प्रोग्राम बदलना चाहता हूँ *maĩ kal kā progrām badalnā cāhtā* *hū̃*; to change money पैसा चेंज करना *paisā cẽj karnā*$^{N}$ — I need to change money मुझे पैसा चेंज करना है *mujhe paisā cẽj karnā hai*

**chapati** चपाती *capātī*$^{F}$, फुलका *phulkā*$^{M}$

**chapter** अध्याय *adhyāy*$^{M}$

**character** (nature) स्वभाव *svabhāv*$^{M}$; (in drama) पात्र *pātra*$^{M}$; (of script, alphabet) अक्षर *akṣar*$^{M}$

**cheap** सस्ता *sastā*; (inferior) घटिया *ghaṭiyā* (-*ā* invariable)

**cheek** (face) गाल *gāl*$^{M}$; (impertinence) गुस्ताख़ी *gustā<u>kh</u>ī*$^{F}$

**cheeky** गुस्ताख़ *gustā<u>kh</u>*

**cheese** (cottage cheese) पनीर *panīr*$^{M}$

**chess** शतरंज *śatranj*$^{M}$

**chest**[1] (part of body) सीना *sīnā*$^{M}$

**chest**[2] (box) पेटी *peṭī*$^{F}$

**chew, to** चबाना *cabānā*$^{N}$

**chicken** मुर्ग़ी *murġī*$^{F}$, मुर्ग़ *murġ*$^{M}$

**child** बच्चा *baccā*$^{M}$, बच्ची *baccī*$^{F}$

**childhood** बचपन *bacpan*$^{M}$

**chilli** (green) हरी मिर्च *harī mirc*$^{F}$, (red) लाल मिर्च *lāl mirc*$^{F}$

**China** चीन *cīn*$^{M}$

**Chinese** (adj. & noun) चीनी *cīnī*$^{M}$

**choice** (act of choosing) चुनाव *cunāv*$^{M}$; (favourite) पसंद *pasand*$^{F}$; (option) विकल्प *vikalp*$^{M}$

**choose, to** चुनना *cunnā*$^{N}$ — she can choose any subject वह कोई भी विषय चुन सकती है *vah koī bhī viṣay cun saktī hai*; (to take one's pick) पसंद करना *pasand karnā*$^{M}$ — choose any colour कोई भी रंग पसंद करो [कर लो] *koī bhī raṅg pasand karo [kar lo]*

**Christian** (adj. & noun) ईसाई *īsāī*$^{M}$

**Christianity** ईसाई धर्म *īsāī dharm*$^{M}$

**Christmas Day** बड़ा दिन *baṛā din*$^{M}$

**church** गिरजाघर *girjāghar*$^{M}$

**cigarette** सिग्रेट *sigreṭ*$^{M (F)}$

**cinema** सिनेमा *sinemā*$^{M}$

**cinnamon** दालचीनी *dālcīnī*$^{F}$

**circle** गोला *golā*$^{M}$, वृत्त *vṛtt*$^{M}$

**circumstance** परिस्थिति$^{F}$ *paristhiti* — considering the circumstances परिस्थितियों को देखते हुए *paristhitiyõ ko dekhte hue*

**citizen** नागरिक *nāgarik*$^{M}$; (inhabitant) निवासी *nivāsī*$^{M}$, रहनेवाला *rahnevālā*$^{M}$

**city** शहर *śahar*ᴹ

**civilization** सभ्यता *sabhyatā*ᶠ

**civilized** सभ्य *sabhya*

**claim, to** दावा करना *dāvā karnā*ᴺ — he claims to be a good poet वह अच्छा कवि होने का दावा करता है *vah acchā kavi hone kā dāvā kartā hai*

**clap, to** ताली बजाना *tālī bajānā*ᴺ — we clapped loudly हमने ज़ोर से तालियाँ बजाईं *hamne zor se tāliyā̃ bajāī̃*

**clarify, to** (to explain) स्पष्ट करना *spaṣṭ karnā*ᴺ

**clash** टकराव *ṭakrāv*ᴹ

**class** (in school) क्लास *klās*ᶠ, कक्षा *kakṣā*ᶠ; (in grade or level) दर्जा *darjā*ᴹ; (in society) वर्ग *varg*ᴹ; (in train) श्रेणी *śreṇī*ᶠ

**classical** शास्त्रीय *śāstrīy*

**clean** साफ़ *sāf*

**clean, to** साफ़ करना *sāf karnā*ᴺ — clean your room अपने कमरे को साफ़ करो *apne kamre ko sāf karo*

**cleanness** सफ़ाई *safāī*ᶠ

**clear** साफ़ — the sky is clear आसमान साफ़ है *āsmān sāf hai*; (apparent) ज़ाहिर *zāhir*, स्पष्ट *spaṣṭ* — it's clear that… ज़ाहिर/स्पष्ट है कि… *zāhir/spaṣṭ hai ki . . .*

**clerk** बाबू *bābū*ᴹ

**clever** (intelligent) होशियार *hośiyār*; (cunning) चालाक *cālāk*

**climate** आबोहवा *ābohavā*ᶠ, जलवायु *jalvāyu*ᴹ; (weather) मौसम *mausam*ᴹ

**climb, to** चढ़ना *caṛhnā* — she climbed onto the wall वह दीवार पर चढ़ी [चढ़ गई] *vah dīvār par caṛhī [caṛh gaī]*

**cling, to** चिपकना *cipaknā*

**clock** घड़ी *ghaṛī*ᶠ; clock tower घंटा-घर *ghaṇṭā-ghar*ᴹ

**close** (near) (adj.) पास/नज़दीक *pās/nazdīk* — the road is very close सड़क पास ही है *saṛak pās hī hai*; (close to something) के पास *ke pās* — the temple is close to the village मंदिर गाँव के पास है *mandir gā̃v ke pās hai*; close, intimate घनिष्ठ *ghaniṣṭh*

**close, to** (intr.) बंद होना *band honā* — today the bank closed early आज बैंक जल्दी बंद हुआ *āj baink jaldī band huā*; (tr.) बंद करना *band karnā*ᴺ — please close the door दरवाज़ा बंद कीजिए *darvāzā band kījie*

**closed** बंद *band* — the shops are closed दुकानें बंद हैं *dukānẽ band haĩ*

**closely** ग़ौर से *gaur se* — please read this closely इसको ग़ौर से पढ़िए *isko gaur se paṛhie*

**cloth** कपड़ा *kapṛā*[M]; cloth shop कपड़े की दुकान *kapṛe kī dukān*[F]

**clothes** कपड़े *kapṛe*[M PL]

**cloud** बादल *bādal*[M]

**clown** (in circus) जोकर *jokar*[M]

**coal** कोयला *koylā*[M]

**coast** समुद्र का किनारा *samudra kā kinārā*[M]

**coat** कोट *koṭ*[M]

**coconut** नारियल *nāriyal*[M]

**coffee** कॉफ़ी *kāfī*[F]

**coin** सिक्का *sikkā*[M]

**cold** (noun) ठंड *ṭhaṇḍ*[F], सरदी *sardī*[F] — it's cold today आज ठंड है *āj ṭhaṇḍ hai*; I'm feeling cold 💣 मुझे ठंड लग रही है *mujhe ṭhaṇḍ lag rahī hai*; (adj.) ठंडा *ṭhaṇḍā* — cold water ठंडा पानी *ṭhaṇḍā pānī*[M]; (a head cold) ज़ुकाम *zukām*[M] — I've got a cold 💣 मुझे ज़ुकाम है *mujhe zukām hai*

**colleague** (companion) साथी *sāthī*[M], (co-worker) सहकर्मी *sahkarmī*[M]

**collect, to** (to gather together) इकट्ठा करना *ikaṭṭhā karnā*; (to collect tax, subscriptions etc.) वसूल करना *vasūl karnā*[N]

**collection** (of poems etc.) संग्रह *saṅgrah*[M]

**college** कालेज *kālej*[M]; विद्यालय *vidyālay*[M]

**collide, to** टकराना *ṭakrānā* — the bicycle collided with a handcart साइकिल ठेले से टकराई [टकरा गई] *sāikil ṭhele se ṭakrāī [ṭakrā gaī]*

**colour** रंग *raṅg*[M]

**coloured** रंगीन *raṅgīn*

**colourful** रंगीला *raṅgīlā*

**column** (architectural, or in newspaper) स्तंभ *stambh*[M]

**come, to** आना *ānā*; to come along, accompany चलना *calnā* — you come along too तुम भी चलो *tum bhī calo*; to come out निकलना *nikalnā*

**comfort** आराम *ārām*[M]

**comfortable** (in a state of comfort) आराम से *ārām se* — are you comfortable? आप आराम से हैं? *āp ārām se haĩ?*; (providing comfort) आरामदेह *ārāmdeh* — comfortable houses आरामदेह मकान *ārāmdeh makān*

**comfortably** आराम से *ārām se* — sit comfortably आराम

से बैठो *ārām se baiṭho*; we'll finish comfortably by five o'clock हम पाँच बजे तक आराम से ख़त्म करेंगे *ham pā̃c baje tak ārām se khatm karẽge*

**command** (order) आदेश *ādeś*ᴹ; to command आदेश देना *ādeś denā*ᴺ — he commanded me to shoot उसने मुझे गोली चलाने का आदेश दिया *usne mujhe golī calāne kā ādeś diyā*

**common** आम *ām*, सामान्य *sāmānya* — this is a common problem यह तो आम समस्या है *yah to ām samasyā hai*

**companion** साथी *sāthī*ᴹ — these elephants are my companions ये हाथी मेरे साथी हैं *ye hāthī mere sāthī haĩ*

**company** (firm) कंपनी *kampanī*ᶠ; (companionship) साथ *sāth*ᴹ — will you keep me company? तुम मेरा साथ दोगे? *tum merā sāth doge?*

**compare, to** की तुलना करना *kī tulnā karnā*ᴺ — we can compare our country to China हम अपने देश की चीन से तुलना कर सकते हैं *ham apne deś kī cīn se tulnā kar sakte haĩ*

**compartment** (in train) डिब्बा *ḍibbā*ᴹ

**compassion** दया *dayā*ᶠ; to feel compassion दया आना *dayā ānā* — I felt compassion for them ☀ मुझे उनपर दया आई *mujhe unpar dayā āī*

**compassionate** दयालु *dayālu*

**compel, to:** see 'force'

**competition** (rivalry) प्रतिस्पर्धा *pratispardhā*ᶠ; (contest) प्रतियोगिता *pratiyogitā*ᶠ

**complain, to** शिकायत करना *śikāyat karnā*ᴺ ('to', से *se*; 'about Ram': say राम की शिकायत करना *rām kī śikāyat karnā*) — I complained to Uma about Ram मैंने उमा से राम की शिकायत की *maĩne umā se rām kī śikāyat kī*

**complaint** शिकायत *śikāyat*ᶠ

**complete** पूरा *pūrā* — the work is complete काम पूरा हुआ है [हो गया है] *kām pūrā huā hai [ho gayā hai]*

**completely** पूरी तरह से *pūrī tarah se*

**complex** पेचीदा *pecīdā*, जटिल *jaṭil*

**compliment, to:** see 'praise'

**computer** कम्प्यूटर *kampyūṭar*ᴹ

**concise** संक्षिप्त *saṅkṣipt*

**condemn, to** (to criticize) (की) निंदा करना *(kī) nindā karnā*ᴺ;

(to find guilty) दोषी ठहराना *doṣī ṭhaharānā*[N]

**condition** हालत *hālat*[F] — the condition of the road सड़क की हालत *saṛak kī hālat*; (term of agreement) शर्त *śart*[F] — on one condition एक शर्त पर *ek śart par*

**condom** निरोध *nirodh*[M]

**conduct** (behaviour) व्यवहार *vyavahār*[M]

**conference** सम्मेलन *sammelan*[M]; (seminar) गोष्ठी *goṣṭhī*[F]

**confidence** विश्वास *viśvās*[M]

**confused** गड़बड़ *gaṛbaṛ*

**confusion** गड़बड़ *gaṛbaṛ*[F (M)]

**congratulate, to** बधाई देना *badhāī denā*[N] — they congratulated me उन्होंने मुझे बधाइयाँ दीं *unhõne mujhe badhāiyā̃ dī̃*; many congratulations! बहुत बधाइयाँ! *bahut badhāiyā̃!*

**connection** रिश्ता *riśtā*[M], संबंध *sambandh*[M] — I have no connection with the government 💣 सरकार से मेरा कोई संबंध नहीं *sarkār se merā koī sambandh nahī̃*

**consider, to** मानना *mānnā*[N] — I consider you my friend मैं आपको अपना दोस्त मानता हूँ *maĩ āpko apnā dost māntā hū̃*; (to bear in mind ) ख़याल रखना *khyāl rakhnā*[N] — you shouldn't consider the expense 💣 तुम्हें ख़रचे का ख़याल नहीं रखना चाहिए *tumhẽ kharce kā khyāl nahī̃ rakhnā cāhie*

**consideration, for/out of** की ख़ातिर *kī khātir* — for consideration of people living nearby पास में रहनेवाले लोगों की ख़ातिर *pās mẽ rahnevāle logõ kī khātir*

**consolation** दिलासा *dilāsā*[M], तसल्ली *tasallī*[F]

**console, to** दिलासा देना *dilāsā denā*[N] — we tried to console them हमने उन्हें दिलासा देने की कोशिश की *hamne unhẽ dilāsā dene kī kośiś kī*

**consonant** व्यंजन *vyanjan*[M]

**constipation** कब्ज़ *kabz*[F]

**construct, to** बनाना *banānā*[N]

**contact** (connection) संपर्क *sampark*[M] — we'll contact the director हम निर्देशक साहब से संपर्क करेंगे *ham nirdeśak sāhab se sampark karẽge*

**content** (satisfied) संतुष्ट *santuṣṭ* — the customers are not content ग्राहक संतुष्ट नहीं हैं *grāhak santuṣṭ nahī̃ haĩ*

**contentment** संतोष *santoṣ*[M]

**context** संदर्भ *sandarbh*[M]

**continent** महाद्वीप *mahādvīp*[M]

**continue, to** (to go on) आगे चलना *āge calnā*; (to go on doing) करते रहना *karte rahnā* — please continue watching देखते रहिए *dekhte rahie*

**contract** ठेका *ṭhekā*[M]

**contractor** ठेकेदार *ṭhekedār*[M]

**contribution** योगदान *yogdān*[M] — your contribution to this work is very important इस काम में आपका योगदान बहुत महत्त्वपूर्ण है *is kām mẽ āpkā yogdān bahut mahattvapūrṇ hai*; (subscription) चंदा *candā*[M]

**control** (capacity to act) बस bas[M] — this is beyond my control यह मेरे बस के बाहर है *yah mere bas ke bāhar hai*; (restraint) क़ाबू *qābū*[M] — keep the kids under control! बच्चों को क़ाबू में रखो! *baccõ ko qābū mẽ rakho!*

**convenience** सुविधा *suvidhā*[F]

**convenient** सुविधाजनक *suvidhājanak*

**conversation** बातचीत *bātcīt*[F]

**converse, to** बातचीत करना *bātcīt karnā*[N]

**convince, to** मनवा लेना *manvā lenā*[N]

**cook** रसोइया *rasoiyā*[M]

**cook, to** पकाना *pakānā*[N], (खाना) बनाना *(khānā) banānā*[N]

**cool** ठंडा *ṭhaṇḍā* — a cool breeze was blowing ठंडी हवा चल रही थी *ṭhaṇḍī havā cal rahī thī*

**copy** (of book etc.) प्रति *prati*[F]

**copy, to** (to imitate) नक़ल करना *naqal karnā*[N]

**corner** कोना *konā*[M]

**correct** (right) ठीक *ṭhīk*, सही *sahī*; (proper) उचित *ucit*

**correct, to** सुधारना *sudhārnā*[N]

**correction** सुधार *sudhār*[M]; (of errors in written work) भूल-सुधार *bhūl-sudhār*[M]

**correspondence** (written) पत्र-व्यवहार *patra-vyavahār*[M]

**corrupt** भ्रष्ट *bhraṣṭ*

**corruption** भ्रष्टाचार *bhraṣṭācār*[M]

**cost** दाम *dām*[M], क़ीमत *qīmat*[F], मूल्य *mūlya*[M]; what does this cost? इसका दाम क्या है? *iskā dām kyā hai?*, यह कितने का है? *yah kitne kā hai?*; at any cost हर क़ीमत पर *har qīmat par*

**costly** महँगा *mahãgā*

**cotton** (adj., made of cotton) सूती *sūtī* — this cotton cloth is beautiful यह सूती कपड़ा सुंदर है *yah sūtī kapṛā sundar hai*

**cough** खाँसी *khãsī*$^{F}$ — she's got a cough 💣 उसे खाँसी (आती) है *use khãsī (ātī) hai*

**cough, to** खाँसना *khãsnā*

**could:** see 'able'

**count, to** गिनना *ginnā*$^{N}$

**country** (nation) देश *deś*$^{M}$; (countryside) देहात *dehāt*$^{M}$

**couple** (married) दंपति *dampati*$^{M}$; a couple of एकाध *ekādh*, दो-तीन *do-tīn*

**courage** हिम्मत *himmat*$^{F}$, साहस *sāhas*$^{M}$ — I didn't have the courage to ask 💣 मुझे पूछने की हिम्मत नहीं हुई *mujhe pūchne kī himmat nahī̃ huī*

**court** (royal) दरबार *darbār*$^{M}$; (court of law) अदालत *adālat*$^{F}$

**courthouse** कचहरी *kacahrī*$^{F}$

**courtyard** आँगन *ãgan*$^{M}$

**cousin** (child of father's brother) चचेरा भाई *cacerā bhāī*$^{M}$, चचेरी बहिन *cacerī bahin*$^{F}$; (child of father's sister) फुफेरा भाई *phūpherā bhāī*$^{M}$, फुफेरी बहिन *phūpherī bahin*$^{F}$; (child of mother's brother) ममेरा भाई *mamerā bhāī*$^{M}$, ममेरी बहिन *mamerī bahin*$^{F}$; (child of mother's sister) मौसेरा भाई *mauserā bhāī*$^{M}$, मौसेरी बहिन *mauserī bahin*$^{F}$

**cover, to** ढकना *ḍhaknā*$^{N}$ — cover the food with a lid खाने को ढक्कन से ढकना *khāne ko ḍhakkan se ḍhaknā*

**cow** गाय *gāy*$^{F}$

**cream** मलाई *malāī*$^{F}$

**crease** सिलवट *silvaṭ*$^{F}$

**credit** (recognition for something done) श्रेय *śrey*$^{M}$; — my father has the credit for doing this 💣 यह करने का श्रेय मेरे पिताजी को है *yah karne kā śrey mere pitājī ko hai*

**cricket**$^{1}$ (insect) झींगुर *jhī̃gur*$^{M}$

**cricket**$^{2}$ (game) क्रिकेट *krikeṭ*$^{M}$

**crisis** संकट *saṅkaṭ*$^{M}$; to get into a crisis संकट में पड़ना *saṅkaṭ mẽ paṛnā*

**crocodile** मगर *magar*$^{M}$, मगरमच्छ *magarmacch*$^{M}$

**crop** फ़सल *fasal*$^{F}$

**crore** (10 million) करोड़ *karoṛ*$^{M}$

**cross** (angry) नाराज़ *nārāz*

**cross, to** (a road, river) पार करना *pār karnā*$^{N}$ — turn left after crossing the road सड़क को पार करके बायें मुड़ना *saṛak ko pār karke bāyẽ muṛnā*

**cross-legged** (posture) पालथी *pālthī*$^{F}$ — to sit cross-legged पालथी मारकर बैठना *pālthī mārkar baiṭhnā*

**crow**$^{1}$ (bird) कौवा *kauvā*$^{M}$

**crow**$^{2}$ (cock's call) बांग *bā̃g*$^{F}$

**crow, to** बांग देना *bā̃g denā*$^{N}$

**crowd** भीड़ *bhīṛ*$^{F}$ — a big crowd gathered बड़ी भीड़ जमा हुई [हो गई] *baṛī bhīṛ jamā huī [ho gaī]*

**cruel** निर्दय *nirday*

**cry, to** (weep) रोना *ronā*, आँसू आना *ā̃sū ānā* ('tears come') — he/she began to cry उसे आँसू आने लगे *use ā̃sū āne lage*; (to call out) चिल्लाना$^{N}$ *cillānā*

**cunning** (adj.) चालाक *cālāk*; (noun) चालाकी *cālākī*$^{F}$

**cup** प्याला *pyālā*$^{M}$, कप *kap*$^{M}$

**cupboard** अलमारी *almārī*$^{F}$

**cure, to** का इलाज करना *kā ilāj karnā*$^{N}$ — to heal the sick is a doctor's duty मरीज़ों का इलाज करना डाक्टर का कर्तव्य होता है *marīzõ kā ilāj karnā ḍākṭar kā kartavya hotā hai*

**curious** (strange) अजीब *ajīb*; (inquisitive) जिज्ञासु *jijñāsu* (pronounced 'jigyāsu')

**current** (stream) धारा *dhārā*$^{F}$; (flow) प्रवाह *pravāh*$^{M}$; (adj., of the present) वर्तमान *vartmān* — the current circumstances वर्तमान परिस्थितियाँ *vartmān paristhitiyā̃*; (widespread) प्रचलित *pracalit*

**curtain** परदा *pardā*$^{M}$

**Insight**

Curtain: many such words of Persian origin can be spelt with or without conjunct: परदा / पर्दा *pardā*, कुर्सी / कुरसी *kursī*, गर्म / गरम *garm*, etc.

**cucumber** खीरा *khīrā*$^{M}$

**cultural** सांस्कृतिक *sā̃skṛtik*

**culture** संस्कृति *sanskṛti*$^{F}$

**custom** रिवाज *rivāj*$^{M}$, प्रथा *prathā*$^{F}$

**customer** ग्राहक *grāhak*$^{M}$

**customs** (tax) सीमा शुल्क *sīmā śulk*$^{M}$

**cut, to** (tr.) काटना *kāṭnā*$^{N}$ — cut the string with scissors रस्सी को कैंची से काटो *rassī ko kaĩcī se kāṭo*; (to reduce) कम करना *kam karnā*$^{N}$ — cut the price of this इसका दाम कम करो *iskā dām kam karo*

**cut, to be** कटना *kaṭnā* — the string was cut into two pieces रस्सी दो हिस्सों में कटी थी *rassī ko do hissõ mẽ kaṭī thī*

## D

**daal** दाल *dāl*$^{F}$ — the daal has come out really well today! आज दाल बहुत बढ़िया बनी है! *āj dāl bahut baṛhiyā banī hai!*

**daily** (adv.) रोज़ *roz*, हर रोज़ *har roz*, प्रतिदिन *pratidin*; (adj.) रोज़ाना *rozānā*

**dam** बाँध *bā̃dh*$^{M}$

**damage** नुक़सान *nuqsān*$^{M}$, हानि *hāni*$^{F}$

**damp** (adj.) नम *nam*; (noun) नमी *namī*$^{F}$

**dance** नृत्य *nṛtya*$^{M}$, नाच *nāc*$^{M}$

**dance, to** नाचना *nācnā*

**danger** ख़तरा *khatrā*$^{M}$

**dangerous** ख़तरनाक *khatarnāk*

**dare, to** (to have courage) साहस होना *sāhas honā* — I didn't dare tell him/her मुझे उसे बताने का साहस नहीं हुआ *mujhe use batāne kā sāhas nahī̃ huā*

**dark** (adj.) अँधेरा *ā̃dherā*; a dark night अँधेरी रात *ā̃dherī rāt*; (of colours) गहरा *gahrā* — dark red cloth गहरे लाल रंग का कपड़ा *gahre lāl raṅg kā kapṛā*; (of complexion) साँवला *sā̃vlā* — a dark-skinned woman साँवली औरत *sā̃vlī aurat*; (noun, 'darkness') अँधेरा *ā̃dherā*$^{M}$

**date** तारीख़ *tārīkh*$^{F}$ — what's the date today? आज तारीख़ क्या है? *āj tārīkh kyā hai?*; (date in festival calendar, i.e. lunar date) तिथि *tithi*$^{F}$

**daughter** बेटी *beṭī*$^{F}$

**daughter-in-law** बहू *bahū*$^{F}$

**dawn** प्रातः *prātaḥ*$^{M}$; प्रातःकाल *prātaḥkāl*$^{M}$

**day** दिन *din*$^{M}$; daytime दिन का समय$^{M}$ *din kā samay* — in the daytime दिन के समय *din ke samay*, दिन में *din mẽ*; every day रोज़ *roz*; all day दिन भर *din bhar*; the day before yesterday, the day after tomorrow परसों *parsõ*; day by day दिन-ब-दिन *din-ba-din*

**dead** मरा हुआ *marā huā* – a dead bird मरी हुई चिड़िया *marī huī ciṛiyā*; is he dead? (has he died?) क्या वह मर गया है? *kyā vah mar gayā hai?*

**deaf** बहरा *bahrā*

**dear** प्रिय *priy*; (in an informal letter) प्रिय *priy* – Dear Sujata प्रिय सुजाता *priy sujātā*; (formal) आदरणीय *ādarṇīy* ('respected') – Dear Sir आदरणीय महोदय *ādarṇīy mahoday*

**death** मौत *maut*ᶠ, मृत्यु *mṛtyu*ᶠ, देहान्त *dehānt*ᴹ

**deceive, to** धोखा देना *dhokhā denā*ᴺ – they deceived us उन्होंने हमको धोखा दिया *unhõne hamko dhokhā diyā*; to be deceived धोखा खाना *dhokhā khānā*ᴺ – we were deceived हमने धोखा खाया *hamne dhokhā khāyā*

**December** दिसंबर *disambar*ᴹ

**decide, to** (का) फ़ैसला / निश्चय करना *(kā) faislā/ niścay karnā*ᴺ – I've decided to go abroad मैंने विदेश जाने का फ़ैसला/निश्चय किया है *maĩne videś jāne kā faislā/ niścay kiyā hai*

**Insight**

Death: like most languages, Hindi has many euphemisms for dying. Examples are: गुज़र जाना *guzar jānā* 'to pass on', *dehānt honā* 'the body to come to an end', चल बसना *cal basnā* 'to move to a new abode'.

**debate** वाद-विवाद *vād-vivād*ᴹ

**debt** कर्ज़ा *karzā*ᴹ, ऋण *ṛṇ*ᴹ; to settle a debt कर्ज़ा/ऋण चुकाना *karzā/ṛṇ cukānā*ᴺ

**decade** दशक *daśak*ᴹ – in the decade of the sixties साठ के दशक में *sāṭh ke daśak mẽ*

**deceit, deception** धोखा *dhokhā*ᴹ

**decided** (settled) निश्चित *niścit*, तय *tay* – the schedule has been decided प्रोग्राम तय हुआ है [हो गया है] *progrām tay huā hai [ho gayā hai]*

**decision** (resolve) निश्चय *niścay*ᴹ; (arbitration) निर्णय *nirṇay*ᴹ

**decline, to** (to go down, of the sun etc.) ढलना *ḍhalnā*;

(to refuse, turn down) ना कहना *'nā' kahnā*ᴺ, इनकार करना *inkār karnā*ᴺ

**decorate, to** सजाना *sajānā*ᴺ

**decrease, to** (intr.) घटना *ghaṭnā*; (tr.) घटाना *ghaṭānā*ᴺ, कम करना *kam karnā*ᴺ

**deep** गहरा *gahrā*

**deer** हिरन *hiran*ᴹ

**defeat** हार *hār*ᶠ

**defeat, to** हराना *harānā*ᴺ

**defecate, to** मलत्याग करना *maltyāg karnā*ᴺ; (less polite) हगना *hagnā*

**defence** रक्षा *rakṣā*ᶠ

**defend, to** की रक्षा करना *kī rakṣā karnā*ᴺ — we shall defend our country हम अपने देश की रक्षा करेंगे *ham apne deś kī rakṣā karẽge*

**definite** पक्का *pakkā* — my schedule isn't definite yet मेरा प्रोग्राम अभी तक पक्का नहीं है *merā progrām abhī tak pakkā nahī̃ hai*

**degree** डिगरी *ḍigrī*ᶠ — a BA degree बी.ए. की डिगरी *bī.e. kī ḍigrī*; (title) उपाधि *upādhi*ᶠ

**dejected** हताश *hatāś*

**delay** देर *der*ᶠ; to be delayed देर होना *der honā* — I was delayed ● मुझे देर हुई [हो गई] *mujhe der huī [ho gaī]*; to delay देर करना *der karnā*ᴺ — don't delay देर मत करो *der mat karo*

**Delhi** दिल्ली *dillī*ᶠ

**deliberately** जान-बूझकर *jān-būjhkar*

**delicious** लज़ीज़ *lazīz*, स्वादिष्ट *svādiṣṭ*

**delight** आनंद *ānand*ᴹ

**delighted:** see 'pleased'

**demand** माँग *mā̃g*ᶠ

**demand, to** माँगना *mā̃gnā*ᴺ — they're demanding money from us वे हमसे पैसा माँग रहे हैं *ve hamse paisā mā̃g rahe haĩ*

**democracy** लोकतंत्र *loktantra*ᴹ

**democratic** लोकतांत्रिक *loktāntrik*

**dense** घना *ghanā*

**depart, to:** see 'leave'

**department** विभाग *vibhāg*ᴹ

**depend, to** निर्भर करना/होना *nirbhar karnā*ᴺ*/honā* — it depends on my brother मेरे भाई पर निर्भर करता है *mere bhāī par nirbhar kartā hai*

**depressed** (sad) दुःखी *duḥkhī*, उदास *udās*; (dejected) हताश *hatāś*

**depth** गहराई *gahrāī*ᶠ — the depth of this well is ten metres

इस कुएँ की गहराई दस मीटर है *is kuẽ kī gahrāī das mīṭar hai*

**descend, to** उतरना *utarnā*

**describe, to** (का) वर्णन करना *(kā) varṇan karnā*ᴺ — I'll describe the room मैं कमरे का वर्णन करूँगा *maĩ kamre kā varṇan karũgā*

**description** वर्णन *varṇan*ᴹ

**desert** रेगिस्तान *registān*ᴹ, मरुस्थल *marusthal*ᴹ

**deserted** (uninhabited) वीरान *vīrān*

**desire** इच्छा *icchā*ᶠ; (passion) वासना *vāsnā*ᶠ, कामना *kāmnā*ᶠ

**desire, to** चाहना *cāhnā*ᴺ, इच्छा करना *icchā karnā*ᴺ

**desolate** (deserted) वीरान *vīrān*

**despair** निराशा *nirāśā*ᶠ — I felt deep despair when I heard this news 💣 यह ख़बर सुनकर मुझे गहरी निराशा हुई *yah khabar sunkar mujhe gahrī nirāśā huī*

**despair, to** निराश होना *nirāś honā* — don't despair! निराश न होओ! *nirāś na ho'o!*

**despite** के बावजूद *ke bāvajūd* — despite his absence उसकी ग़ैरहाज़िरी के बावजूद *uskī gairhāzirī ke bāvajūd*

**destiny** नियति *niyati*ᶠ

**destroy, to** नष्ट करना *naṣṭ karnā*ᴺ, बरबाद करना *barbād karnā*ᴺ — he destroyed our work उसने हमारे काम को नष्ट/ बरबाद किया *usne hamāre kām ko naṣṭ/ barbād kiyā*

**detail** ब्योरा *byorā*ᴹ — in detail ब्योरे के साथ *byore ke sāth*

**detest, to** घृणा करना *ghṛṇā karnā*ᴺ, सख़्त नफ़रत करना *sakht nafrat karnā*ᴺ

**Devanagari** देवनागरी *devnāgarī*ᶠ

**developed** विकसित *vikasit*

**developing** विकासशील *vikāsśīl*

**development** विकास *vikās*ᴹ

**devil** शैतान *śaitān*ᴹ

**dew** ओस *os*ᶠ

**dialect** बोली *bolī*ᶠ

**dialogue** संवाद *saṃvād*ᴹ

**diamond** हीरा *hīrā*ᴹ

**diarrhoea** दस्त *dast*ᴹ — I've got diarrhoea 💣 मुझे दस्त लगे हैं *mujhe dast lage haĩ* (note plural usage)

**dictate, to** (to make write) लिखाना *likhānā*ᴺ

**dictator** तानाशाह *tānāśāh*ᴹ

**dictatorship** तानाशाही *tānāśāhī*ᶠ

**dictionary** शब्दकोश *śabdkoś*ᴹ

**die, to** मरना *marnā*, मर जाना *mar jānā*; का देहान्त होना *kā dehānt honā* — someone has died कोई मर गया है *koī mar gayā hai*, 💣 किसी का देहान्त हुआ है [हो गया है] *kisī kā dehānt huā hai [ho gayā hai]*

**difference** फ़र्क़ *farq*ᴹ, अंतर *antar*ᴹ — what difference does it make? क्या फ़र्क़ पड़ता है? *kyā farq paṛtā hai?*; (difference between: use में *mẽ* for 'between') — what's the difference between Hindi and Urdu? हिन्दी और उर्दू में क्या फ़र्क़/अंतर है? *hindī aur urdū mẽ kyā farq/antar hai?*

**different** भिन्न *bhinn*; (separate) अलग *alag*; (often repeated to stress diversity — in (various) different places अलग-अलग जगहों में *alag-alag jagahõ mẽ)*

**difficult** मुश्किल *muśkil*, कठिन *kaṭhin*

**difficulty** मुश्किल *muśkil*ᶠ, कठिनाई *kaṭhinaī*ᶠ

**dig, to** खोदना *khodnā*ᴺ

**dim** (of light, memory) धुँधला *dhũdhlā*

**diplomacy** कूटनीति *kūṭnīti*ᶠ

**diplomat** कूटनीतिज्ञ *kūṭnītijña*ᴹ (pronounced 'kūṭnītigya')

**direct** सीधा *sīdhā*

**direct, to** निर्देशन करना *nirdeśan karnā*ᴺ

**direction** तरफ़ *taraf*ᶠ, ओर *or*ᶠ, दिशा *diśā*ᶠ — in this direction इस तरफ़ *is taraf*; to ask for / to give directions रास्ता पूछना / बताना *rāstā pūchnā*ᴺ / *batānā*ᴺ

**directly** सीधे *sīdhe*

**director** निर्देशक *nirdeśak*ᴹ, निदेशक *nideśak*ᴹ

**dirt** मैल *mail*ᴹ; (mud) कीचड़ *kīcaṛ*ᴹ; (American usage, meaning 'soil, earth') मिट्टी *miṭṭī*ᶠ

**dirty** मैला *mailā* — dirty hands/clothes मैले हाथ/कपड़े *maile hāth/kapṛe*; (also in abstract) गंदा *gandā* — dirty work गंदा काम *gandā kām*, dirty habits गंदी आदतें *gandī ādatẽ*

**disabled** विकलांग *vikalāṅg*

**disagree, to** असहमत होना *asahmat honā*, सहमत न होना *sahmat na honā* — I disagree with you मैं आपसे सहमत नहीं हूँ *maĩ āpse sahmat nahī̃ hū̃*

**disagreement** (difference of opinion) असहमति *asahmati*ᶠ; (dispute, argument) बहस *bahas*ᶠ

**disappear:** see 'vanish'

**disappoint, to** निराश करना *nirāś karnā*ᴺ; I was very disappointed 💣 मुझे बहुत निराशा हुई *mujhe bahut nirāśā huī*

**disappointment** निराशा *nirāśā*ᶠ

**discipline** (control) अनुशासन *anuśāsan*ᴹ; (subject area, e.g. history) विषय *viṣay*ᴹ

**discover, to** (to come to know) पता चलना *patā calnā* — I discovered that he was lying 💣 मुझे पता चला कि वह झूठ बोल रहा था *mujhe patā calā ki vah jhūṭh bol rahā thā*; (to ascertain) मालूम करना *mālūm karnā*ᴺ — I discovered his real name मैंने उसका असली नाम मालूम किया [कर लिया] *maĩne uskā aslī nām mālūm kiyā [kar liyā]*

**discovery** खोज *khoj*ᶠ; आविष्कार *āviṣkār*ᴹ; to make a new discovery नई खोज करना *naī khoj karnā*ᴺ

**discrimination** भेदभाव *bhedbhāv*ᴹ

**discuss, to** बहस करना *bahas karnā*ᴺ, विचार-विमर्श करना *vicār-vimarś karnā*ᴺ — we were discussing the subject of poverty हम ग़रीबी के विषय पर बहस/विचार-विमर्श कर रहे थे *ham garībī ke viṣay par bahas/vicār-vimarś kar rahe the*

**disease** रोग *rog*ᴹ, बीमारी *bīmārī*ᶠ

**dishonest** बेईमान *beīmān*

**dishonesty** बेईमानी *beīmānī*ᶠ

**dislike, to** नापसंद करना *nāpasand karnā*ᴺ — I dislike him/her मैं उसे नापसंद करता हूँ *maĩ use nāpasand kartā hū̃*; (stronger aversion) नफ़रत करना *nafrat karnā*ᴺ (object takes से *se*)

**disrespect** अनादर *anādar*ᴹ

**dissatisfied** असंतुष्ट *asantuṣṭ*

**dissertation** शोध-प्रबंध *śodh-prabandh*ᴹ

**distance** दूरी *dūrī*ᶠ

**distant** दूर *dūr* (see also 'far')

**distress** (trouble, harassment) परेशानी *pareśānī*ᶠ; (suffering) दुःख *duḥkh*ᴹ

**distress, to** परेशान करना *pareśān karnā*ᴺ, दुःख देना *duḥkh denā*ᴺ

**dive** ग़ोता *gotā*ᴹ

**dive, to** ग़ोता लगाना *gotā lagānā*ᴺ — he/she dived into the pond उसने तालाब में ग़ोता लगाया *usne tālāb mẽ gotā lagāyā*

**divide, to** (tr.) बाँटना *bā̃ṭnā*[N]

**divorce** तलाक़ *talāq*[M]

**divorce, to** तलाक़ देना *talāq denā*[N] — he/she divorced me उसने मुझे तलाक़ दिया *usne mujhe talāq diyā*

**divorced** तलाक़-शुदा *talāq-śudā* (*-ā* invariable) — I'm divorced मैं तलाक़-शुदा हूँ *maĩ talāq-śudā hū̃*

**do, to** करना *karnā*[N] — what are you doing? तुम क्या कर रहे हो? *tum kyā kar rahe ho?*; — what (work) do you do? आप क्या काम करते हैं? *āp kyā kām karte haĩ?*; (to suffice) काम चलना *kām calnā* — will coffee do? क्या कॉफ़ी से काम चलेगा? *kyā kāfī se kām calegā?*

**doctor** डाक्टर *ḍākṭar*[M] — to go to the doctor डाक्टर को दिखाना *ḍākṭar ko dikhānā*

**document** दस्तावेज़ *dastāvez*[F]

**dog** कुत्ता *kuttā*[M]

**dollar** डॉलर *ḍālar*[M]

**domestic** घरेलू *gharelū*, घर का *ghar kā*

**donkey** गधा *gadhā*[M]

**don't** (imperative) मत *mat*, न *na* — don't go मत जाओ *mat jāo*, please don't touch my computer मेरे कंप्यूटर पर हाथ न लगाएँ *mere kampyūṭar par hāth na lagāẽ*

**door** दरवाज़ा *darvāzā*[M]; at the door दरवाज़े पर *darvāze par*

**dot** बिन्दु *bindu*[M]; (mark worn on forehead) बिन्दी *bindī*[F]

**double** दुगुना *dugunā* — the price has doubled दाम दुगुना हुआ है [हो गया है] *dām dugunā huā hai [ho gayā hai]*

**doubt** संदेह *sandeh*[M]; to doubt संदेह करना/होना *sandeh karnā*[N]*/honā* — I doubt 💣 मुझे संदेह है *mujhe sandeh hai*

**down** नीचे *nīce* — put it down उसे नीचे रखो *use nīce rakho*

**downstairs** (adverb) नीचे *nīce* — we live downstairs हम नीचे रहते हैं *ham nīce rahte haĩ*; (adj.) नीचेवाला *nīcevālā* — in the downstairs room नीचेवाले कमरे में *nīcevāle kamre mẽ*

**dowry** दहेज *dahej*[M]

**dozen** दर्जन *darjan*[F] — two dozen chairs दो दर्जन कुरसियाँ *do darjan kursiyā̃*; dozens of monkeys दर्जनों बंदर *darjanõ bandar*

**drag, to** घसीटना *ghasīṭnā*[N]

**drain** नाली *nālī*[F]

**drama** नाटक *nāṭak*ᴹ

**draw, to** (तस्वीर/चित्र) बनाना *(tasvīr/citra) banānā*ᴺ — I'm drawing a picture of you मैं तुम्हारी तस्वीर बना रहा हूँ *maĩ tumhārī tasvīr banā rahā hū̃*

**drawer** दराज़ *darāz*ᶠ

**dream** सपना *sapnā*ᴹ

**dream, to** सपना देखना *sapnā dekhnā*ᴺ — I dream of distant places मैं दूर जगहों के सपने देखता हूँ *maĩ dūr jagahõ ke sapne dekhtā hū̃*

**dress** (clothing) पोशाक *pośāk*ᶠ

**dress, to** (कपड़े) पहनना *(kapṛe) pahannā*ᴺ — dress quickly! जल्दी से कपड़े पहनो [पहन लो]! *jaldī se kapṛe pahno [pahan lo]!*

**drink** (alcohol) शराब *śarāb*ᶠ — I don't drink मैं शराब नहीं पीता *maĩ śarāb nahī̃ pītā*

**drink, to** पीना *pīnā*ᴺ

**drinking water** पीने का पानी *pīne kā pānī*ᴹ

**drive (car), to** चलाना *calānā*ᴺ

**driver** ड्राइवर *ḍrāivar*ᴹ, चालक *cālak*ᴹ

**drop** बूँद *bū̃d*ᶠ

**drop, to** (intr.) गिरना *girnā* — the cup dropped to the floor प्याला ज़मीन पर गिरा [गिर गया, गिर पड़ा] *pyālā zamīn par girā [gir gayā, gir paṛā]*; (tr.) गिराना *girānā*ᴺ; he/she dropped the cup उसने प्याले को गिराया [गिरा दिया] *usne pyāle ko girāyā [girā diyā]*; (to let fall) गिरने देना *girne denā*ᴺ

**drought** सूखा *sūkhā*ᴹ — a drought has set in सूखा पड़ा है [पड़ गया है] *sūkhā paṛā hai [paṛ gayā hai]*

**drown, to** डूबना *ḍūbnā* — he was drowning in work वह काम में डूब रहा था *vah kām mẽ ḍūb rahā thā*; (to die by drowning) डूब मरना *ḍūb marnā* — he drowned in the river वह नदी में डूब मरा *vah nadī mẽ ḍūb marā*

**drug** (medicine) दवा *davā*ᶠ; (intoxicant) नशीली दवा *naśīlī davā*ᶠ; drug addict नशीली दवाओं का आदी *naśīlī davāõ kā ādī*ᴹ; drug addiction नशीली दवाओं की आदत *naśīlī davāõ kī ādat*ᶠ

**drunk, to be** (to be inebriated), नशे में होना *naśe mẽ honā,* पिया हुआ होना *piyā huā honā* — uncle is drunk! चाचाजी पिए हुए हैं! *cācājī pie hue haĩ!*

**dry** सूखा *sūkhā*; (uninteresting) नीरस *nīras*

**dry, to** (intr.) सूखना *sūkhnā* — let the clothes dry कपड़ों को सूखने दो *kapṛõ ko sūkhne do*; (tr.) सुखाना *sukhānā*$^N$ — she was drying her hair वह अपने बाल सुखा रही थी *vah āpne bāl sukhā rahī thī* (बाल *bāl* is plural here)

**dull** (in colour) फीका *phīkā*; (boring) नीरस *nīras*; (insipid) फीका *phīkā*

**dumb** गूंगा *gū̃gā*; (American sense, 'stupid') बेवक़ूफ़ *bevaqūf*

**durable** टिकाऊ *ṭikāū*; (strong) मज़बूत *mazbūt*

**during** के दौरान *ke daurān*; during the holidays छुट्टियों के दौरान *chuṭṭiyõ ke daurān*

**dusk** संध्या समय *sandhyā samay*$^M$

**dust** धूल *dhūl*$^F$ — layers of dust धूल की परतें *dhūl kī partẽ*

**duty** कर्तव्य *kartavya*$^M$, फ़र्ज़ *farz*$^M$ — it's my duty to do this यह करना मेरा कर्तव्य है *yah karnā merā kartavya hai*; to carry out a duty कर्तव्य का पालन करना *kartavya kā pālan karnā*$^N$

**dye** रंग *raṅg*$^M$

**dyeing** रँगाई *rãgāī*$^F$

**dyer** रँगरेज़ *rãgrez*$^M$

# E

**each** हर *har*; to each other एक दूसरे को *ek dūsre ko*

**ear** कान *kān*$^M$

**early** जल्दी *jaldī* — we'll arrive early हम जल्दी पहुँचेंगे *ham jaldī pahũcẽge*

**earn, to** कमाना *kamānā*$^N$

**earnings** कमाई *kamāī*$^F$

**earth** (planet) पृथ्वी *pṛthvī*$^F$; (soil) मिट्टी *miṭṭī*$^F$

**earthquake** भूकंप *bhūkamp*$^M$

**easily** आसानी से *āsānī se*; (comfortably) आराम से *ārām se*

**east** पूर्व *pūrv*$^M$

**eastern** पूर्वी *pūrvī*

**easy** आसान *āsān*; (simple) सरल *saral*

**eat, to** खाना *khānā*$^N$ — I ate an egg मैंने अंडा खाया *maĩne aṇḍā khāyā*; (to have a meal) खाना खाना *khānā khānā*$^N$ — we'll eat at one हम एक बजे खाना खाएँगे *ham ek baje khānā khāẽge*; we've already eaten हम खाना खा चुके हैं *ham khānā khā cuke haĩ*

**eccentric** सनकी *sankī*

**echo** गूंज *gū̃j*$^F$, प्रतिध्वनि *pratidhvani*$^F$

**economics** अर्थशास्त्र *arthaśāstra*$^M$

**economize, to** किफ़ायत करना *kifāyat karnā*[N]

**edge** (border, rim) किनारा *kinārā*[M]; (of blade) धार *dhār*[F]

**educate, to** शिक्षित करना *śikṣit karnā*[N]

**educated** शिक्षित *śikṣit*; (literate) पढ़ा-लिखा *paṛhā-likhā* — educated people पढ़े-लिखे लोग *paṛhe-likhe log*; I was educated in India मेरी शिक्षा भारत में हुई *merī śikṣā bhārat mẽ huī*

**education** शिक्षा *śikṣā*[F]

**effect** असर *asar*[M], प्रभाव *prabhāv*[M]; to have an effect असर पड़ना *asar paṛnā* — the film 'Devdas' had a great effect on me 'देवदास' फ़िल्म का मुझपर बहुत असर पड़ा '*Devdās' film kā mujhpar bahut asar paṛā*

**effort** प्रयास *prayās*[M]

**either** (either one) दोनों में से कोई एक *donõ mẽ se koī ek*; either...or... या तो . . . या *yā to...yā* — either today or tomorrow या तो आज या कल *yā to āj yā kal*

**elbow** कुहनी *kuhnī*[F], कोहनी *kohnī*[F]

**elder** ज्येष्ठ *jyeṣṭh*

**election** चुनाव *cunāv*[M] — to fight the general election आम चुनाव लड़ना *ām cunāv laṛnā*[N]

**electrician** बिजलीवाला *bijlīvālā*[M]

**electricity** बिजली *bijlī*[F], (colloquially, as 'power supply') लाइट *lāiṭ*[F] — the electricity went off बिजली/लाइट बंद हुई [हो गई] *bijlī/lāiṭ band huī [ho gaī]*

**element** तत्त्व *tattva*[M]

**elephant** हाथी *hāthī*[M]

**Insight**

Elephant: the हाथी *hāthī* is an animal with a 'hand' (हाथ *hāth*) – its trunk!

**egg** अंडा *aṇḍā*[M]

**eight** आठ *āṭh*

**eighteen** अठारह *aṭhārah*

**eighty** अस्सी *assī*

**eleven** ग्यारह *gyārah*

**else** what else और क्या *aur kyā*; something else कुछ और *kuch aur*; or else नहीं तो *nahī̃ to*

**embarrass, to** शरमिंदा करना *śarmindā karnā*ᴺ (-*ā* in *śarmindā* invariable) — don't embarrass me! मुझे शरमिंदा न करना ! *mujhe śarmindā na karnā!*

**embarrassed, to be** शरमिंदा होना *śarmindā honā* (-*ā* in *śarmindā* invariable)

**embarrassment** शरम, शर्म *śarm*ᶠ

**embassy** राजदूतावास *rājdūtāvās*ᴹ

**emblem** (symbol) प्रतीक *pratīk*ᴹ; (sign) चिह्न *cihn*ᴹ

**embrace, to** (to hug) गले लगाना *gale lagānā*ᴺ — he/she embraced me affectionately उसने मुझे प्यार से गले लगाया *usne mujhe pyār se gale lagāya*

**emerge, to** निकलना *nikalnā*

**emotion** (feeling) भावना *bhāvnā*ᶠ — many kinds of emotion तरह तरह की भावनाएँ *tarah tarah kī bhāvnāẽ*

**emotional** भावुक *bhāvuk* — he's very emotional by nature वह स्वभाव से बहुत भावुक है *vah svabhāv se bahut bhāvuk hai*

**emphasize, to** ज़ोर देना *zor denā*ᴺ (object takes पर *par*) — please emphasize this point इस बात पर ज़ोर दीजिए *is bāt par zor dījie*

**empire** साम्राज्य *sāmrājya*ᴹ

**employee** कर्मचारी *karmcārī*ᴹ

**employment** (service) नौकरी *naukrī*ᶠ; (position) पद *pad*ᴹ

**empty** ख़ाली *khālī*; empty-handed ख़ाली-हाथ *khālī-hāth*

**encourage, to** प्रोत्साहित करना *protsāhit karnā*ᴺ; प्रोत्साहन देना *protsāhan denā*ᴺ

**encouragement** प्रोत्साहन *protsāhan*ᴹ

**end** अन्त *ant*ᴹ; in the end अंत में *ant mẽ,* आख़िर में *ākhir mẽ*

**end, to:** see 'finish'

**endure, to** (to tolerate, suffer) सहना *sahnā*ᴺ; (to last) टिकना *ṭiknā,* चलना *calnā*

**enemy** दुश्मन *duśman*ᴹ

**English** (adj.) अँग्रेज़ी *ãgrezī* — English food is famous throughout the world अँग्रेज़ी खाना दुनिया भर में मशहूर है *ãgrezī khānā duniyā bhar mẽ maśhūr hai*; (noun) English person अँग्रेज़ *ãgrez*ᴹ — are you English? क्या आप अँग्रेज़ हैं? *kyā āp ãgrez haĩ?*; the English language अँग्रेज़ी *ãgrezī*ᶠ

**enjoyment** मज़ा *mazā*[M], आनंद *ānand*[M]; to enjoy मज़ा/आनंद आना *mazā/ānand ānā* – I enjoyed it a lot 💣 मुझे बहुत मज़ा आया *mujhe bahut mazā āyā*; (tr.) मज़ा करना *mazā karnā*[N] – enjoy yourself! ख़ूब मज़ा कीजिए! *khūb mazā kījie!*

**enmity** दुश्मनी *duśmanī*[F], वैर *vair*[M]

**enough** काफ़ी *kāfī* – enough time/money काफ़ी समय/पैसा *kāfī samay/paisā*; that's enough! (i.e. don't give/do/ say any more!) बस! *bas!*

**enquire, to** पूछताछ करना *pūchtāch karnā*[N] – we'll go to the station and enquire हम स्टेशन जाकर पूछताछ करेंगे *ham steśan jākar pūchtāch karẽge*

**enquiries** पूछताछ *pūchtāch*[F]

**enter, to** (में) प्रवेश करना *(mẽ) praveś karnā*[N] – the minister entered the room मंत्री ने कमरे में प्रवेश किया *mantrī ne kamre mẽ praveś kiyā*; (to enter illicitly, sneak in, force way in) (में) घुसना *(mẽ) ghusnā* – the thief entered the house चोर घर में घुसा [घुस आया/गया] *cor ghar mẽ ghusā [ghus āyā/gayā]*

**entertaining** मनोरंजक *manoranjak*

**entertainment** मनोरंजन *manoranjan*[M]

**enthusiasm** जोश *joś*[M], उत्साह *utsāh*[M]

**enthusiastically** जोश से *joś se*

**entire:** see 'whole'

**entrance** (way in) प्रवेश *praveś*[M]

**entrance, to** (to charm) मोहित करना *mohit karnā*[N]

**entrust, to** (to put into the care of) सौंपना *saũpnā*[N] – they entrusted me with the diamonds उन्होंने मुझे हीरे सौंपे [सौंप दिए] *unhõne mujhe hīre saũpe [saũp die]*

**entry** प्रवेश *praveś*[M]

**envelope** लिफ़ाफ़ा *lifāfā*[M]

**environment** पर्यावरण *paryāvaraṇ*[M]

**episode** (of serial) क़िस्त *qist*[F]

**equal** समान *samān*, बराबर *barābar*

**erase, to** मिटाना *miṭānā*[N]

**erased, to be** मिटना *miṭnā*

**error** भूल *bhūl*[F], ग़लती *galtī*[F]

**escape, to** बचना *bacnā*; (to flee) भागना *bhāgnā*

**especially** ख़ास तौर पर *khās taur par*

**essay** निबंध *nibandh*[M] — I have to write two essays by tomorrow ☀ मुझे कल तक दो निबंध लिखने हैं *mujhe kal tak do nibandh likhne haĩ*

**establish, to** स्थापित करना *sthāpit karnā*[N]

**estimate, to** अनुमान करना *anumān karnā*[N]

**etc.** वग़ैरह *vagairah,* आदि *ādi,* इत्यादि *ityādi*

**ethical** नैतिक *naitik*

**even**[1] (emphatic) भी *bhī* (follows the word it qualifies) — even Ram राम भी *Rām bhī*; even more और भी *aur bhī*; even better और भी अच्छा *aur bhī acchā*

**even**[2] (adj.: level, having an even surface) बराबर *barābar*, समतल *samtal* — the ground isn't even ज़मीन बराबर/समतल नहीं है *zamīn barābar/samtal nahī̃ hai*

**evening** शाम *śām*[F]; in the evening शाम को *śām ko*; this evening आज शाम को *āj śām ko*

**event** घटना *ghaṭnā*[F]; (a function) कार्यक्रम *kāryakram*[M], प्रोग्राम *progrām*[M]

**every** हर *har*, हर एक *har ek*; every day रोज़ *roz*, हर रोज़ *har roz*; everyone सब लोग *sab log* (plural), हर कोई *har koī* (singular); everything सब कुछ *sab kuch*; everywhere हर जगह *har jagah*, सब कहीं *sab kahī̃*

**evidence** (proof) सबूत *sabūt*[M], प्रमाण *pramāṇ*[M]; (testimony) गवाही *gavāhī*[F]

**exact** सही *sahī*

**exactly** (agreeing with someone) yes, exactly! हाँ, सही बात है! *hā̃, sahī bāt hai!*; (precisely) ठीक *ṭhīk* — at exactly three o'clock ठीक तीन बजे *ṭhīk tīn baje*

**exaggerate, to** बढ़ा-चढ़ाकर कहना *baṛhā-caṛhākar kahnā*[N], अतिशयोक्ति से कहना *atiśayokti se kahnā*[N]

**exaggeration** अतिशयोक्ति *atiśayokti*[F]

**examination** परीक्षा *parīkṣā*[F], इम्तहान *imtahān*[M]; to take an exam परीक्षा/इम्तहान देना *parīkṣā/imtahān denā*[N] (NB: ***not*** लेना *lenā*[N] !) — the students have to take an exam ☀ विद्यार्थियों को परीक्षा देनी है *vidyārthiyõ ko parīkṣā denī hai*

**example** उदाहरण *udāharaṇ*[M]; for example मसलन *maslan,* उदाहरण के लिए *udāharaṇ ke lie*

**except** के सिवा *ke sivā*

**exchange** आदान-प्रदान *ādān-pradān*ᴹ — an exchange of ideas took place विचारों का आदान-प्रदान हुआ *vicārõ kā ādān-pradān huā*

**excited, to be** जोश में आना *joś mẽ ānā*

**excrement** मल *mal*ᴹ

**excuse** बहाना *bahānā*ᴹ — he's making excuses वह बहाने बना रहा है *vah bahāne banā rahā hai*

**excuse, to** माफ़/क्षमा करना *māf/kṣamā karnā*ᴺ — excuse me (apology) माफ़ कीजिए *māf kījie*; excuse me (getting someone's attention) सुनिए! *sunie!*

**exercise** (physical) कसरत kasratᶠ; व्यायाम *vyāyām*ᴹ; to take exercise कसरत करना *kasrat karnā*ᴺ; (drilling, practice) अभ्यास *abhyās*ᴹ

**exercise book** कॉपी *kāpī*ᶠ

**exhibition** प्रदर्शनी *pradarśanī*ᶠ

**expel, to** निकालना *nikālnā*ᴺ, निकाल देना *nikāl denā*ᴺ

**expense** (s) ख़रच, ख़र्च *kharc*ᴹ; to bear expense ख़रच उठाना *kharc uṭhānā*ᴺ — who will bear the expense of the journey? सफ़र का ख़रच कौन उठाएगा? *safar kā kharc kaun uṭhāegā?*

**expensive** महँगा *mahãgā*

**experience** अनुभव *anubhav*ᴹ

**experience, to** अनुभव करना *anubhav karnā*ᴺ

**experienced** अनुभवी *anubhavī* — an experienced teacher अनुभवी अध्यापक *anubhavī adhyāpak*

**experiment** प्रयोग *prayog*ᴹ

**expert** (adj.) माहिर *māhir* — you're expert at cooking तुम खाना बनाने में माहिर हो *tum khānā banāne mẽ māhir ho*

**explain, to** समझाना *samjhānā*ᴺ

**exploit, to** फ़ायदा उठाना *fāydā uṭhānā*ᴺ — we exploited his generosity हमने उसकी उदारता का फ़ायदा उठाया *hamne uskī udārtā kā fāydā uṭhāyā*

**exploitation** शोषण *śoṣaṇ*ᴹ

**explosion** विस्फोट *visphoṭ*ᴹ

**extract, to** निकालना *nikālnā*ᴺ

**extremely** बहुत ही *bahut hī*, निहायत *nihāyat*

**extremism** अतिवाद *ativād*ᴹ

**extremist** अतिवादी *ativādī*ᴹ

**eye** आँख *ãkh*ᶠ — their eyes met उनकी आँखें चार हुईं *unkī ãkhẽ cār huī̃*

# F

**face** मुख *mukh*[M], मुँह *mũh*[M] (both also mean 'mouth'); चेहरा *cehrā*[M]; face-to-face रूबरू *rūbarū*

**face, to** (का) सामना करना *(kā) sāmnā karnā*[N] — I had to face several difficulties ● मुझे कई कठिनाइयों का सामना करना पड़ा *mujhe kaī kaṭhināiyõ kā sāmnā karnā paṛā*

**factory** कारख़ाना *kār<u>kh</u>ānā*[M], फ़ैक्टरी *faikṭarī*[F] — factory-made goods फ़ैक्टरी का बना हुआ सामान *faikṭarī kā banā huā sāmān*

**fail, to** (to be unsuccessful) असफल होना *asaphal honā* — all our efforts failed हमारे सारे प्रयास असफल रहे *hamāre sāre prayās asaphal rahe* (lit. 'remained unsuccessful'); (in exam) फ़ेल होना *fel honā* — he failed वह फ़ेल हुआ [हो गया] *vah fel huā [ho gayā]*

**faint** (dim) धुँधला *dhũdhlā*

**faint, to** (to swoon) बेहोश हो जाना *behoś ho jānā* — he fainted वह बेहोश हो गया *vah behoś ho gayā*

**fair**[1] (of complexion) गोरा *gorā* — a fair-skinned boy गोरी चमड़ी का लड़का *gorī camṛī kā laṛkā*

**fair**[2] (impartial) निष्पक्ष *niṣpakṣ*

**fair**[3] (festival) मेला *melā*[M]; to go to a fair मेले में जाना *mele mẽ jānā*

**fairy** परी *parī*[F]

**fairytale** परी-कथा *parī-kathā*[F]

**faith** विश्वास *viśvās*[M] — I have faith in God ● मुझे ईश्वर में विश्वास है *mujhe īśvar mẽ viśvās hai*; (trust) भरोसा *bharosā*[M]

**fake** (adj.) (artificial) नक़ली *naqlī*; (counterfeit) खोटा *khoṭā*

**fall, to** पड़ना *paṛnā* — rain was falling पानी पड़ रहा था *pānī paṛ rahā thā*; (to drop, fall) गिरना *girnā* — prices are falling दाम गिर रहे हैं *dām gir rahe haĩ*; she fell from the roof वह छत से गिरी [गिर पड़ी] *vah chat se girī [gir paṛī]*

**false** झूठा *jhūṭhā* (see also 'fake')

**fame** यश *yaś*[M]

**family** परिवार *parivār*[M]; (referring generally to family unit) बीवी-बच्चे *bīvī-bacce*[M PL] — how's the family? बीवी-बच्चे कैसे हैं? *bīvī-bacce kaise haĩ?*

**famous** मशहूर *maśhūr*, प्रसिद्ध *prasiddh*

**fan** पंखा *paṅkhā*ᴹ — this fan doesn't work यह पंखा काम नहीं करता *yah paṅkhā kām nahī̃ kartā*

**far** दूर *dūr* — Agra is quite far from here आगरा यहाँ से काफ़ी दूर है *āgrā yahā̃ se kāfī dūr hai*; as far as, up to तक *tak* — we're only going as far as Delhi हम दिल्ली तक ही जा रहे हैं *ham dillī tak hī jā rahe haī̃*; as far as I know 💣 जहाँ तक मुझे मालूम है *jahā̃ tak mujhe mālūm hai*

**fare:** see 'rent'

**farm, to** खेती-बाड़ी करना *khetī-bāṛī karnā*ᴺ

**farmer** (peasant) किसान *kisān*ᴹ

**farming** खेती-बाड़ी *khetī-bāṛī*ᶠ

**fast**[1] (quick) तेज़ *tez,* तीव्र *tīvra*; (of colour, dye) पक्का *pakkā*

**fast**[2] (abstinence from food) उपवास *upvās*ᴹ; to fast उपवास करना/रखना *upvās karnā*ᴺ/*rakhnā*ᴺ

**fat** (adj.) मोटा *moṭā*; (noun: the fatty part of meat) चरबी *carbī*ᶠ

**fate** क़िस्मत *qismat*ᶠ

**father** पिता *pitā*ᴹ; (less formal) बाप *bāp*ᴹ, पापा *pāpā*ᴹ

**father-in-law** ससुर *sasur*ᴹ

**fault** (offence) क़सूर *qasūr*ᴹ — it's not my fault मेरा क़सूर नहीं है *merā qasūr nahī̃ hai*; (defect) ख़राबी *<u>kh</u>arābī*ᶠ

**favourite** पसंदीदा *pasandīdā* (-*ā* invariable), प्रिय *priy* — these are my favourite stories ये मेरी प्रिय कहानियाँ हैं *ye merī priy kahāniyā̃ haī̃*

**fear** डर *ḍar*ᴹ

**fear, to** डरना *ḍarnā* (see also 'be afraid')

**features** (facial) चेहरा *cehrā*ᴹ

**February** फरवरी *farvarī*ᶠ

**fee** फ़ीस *fīs*ᶠ (singular noun) — how much is/was the fee? फ़ीस कितनी हुई? *fīs kitnī huī?*

**feed** (serve food), to खिलाना *khilānā*ᴺ

**feel, to** महसूस होना/करना *mahsūs honā/karnā*ᴺ — I felt nothing 💣 मुझे कुछ नहीं महसूस हुआ *mujhe kuch nahī̃ mahsūs huā*; (several expressions use the verb लगना *lagnā* 'to strike') — to feel at home मन/दिल लगना *man/dil lagnā* — I feel at home here 💣 यहाँ मेरा मन/दिल लगता है *yahā̃ merā man/dil lagtā hai*; to feel hungry/thirsty भूख /प्यास लगना *bhūkh/pyās lagnā* — I'm feeling hungry/

thirsty मुझे भूख/प्यास लगी है *mujhe bhūkh/pyās lagī hai*; to feel like (doing something) मन करना *man karnā*[N], मन होना *man honā* — I feel like going to the cinema मन करता है कि मैं सिनेमा जाऊँ *man kartā hai ki maĩ sinemā jāũ*; I don't feel like working today आज काम करने का मन नहीं है *āj kām karne kā man nahī̃ hai*

**female** मादा *mādā* (*-ā* invariable) — female animal मादा जानवर *mādā jānvar*

**feminine** (in grammar) स्त्रीलिंग *strīliṅg*

**fennel** सौंफ *saũph*[F]

**fertile** उपजाऊ *upjāū*

**festival** उत्सव *utsav*[M]; (in religious calendar) त्यौहार *tyauhar*[M]

**fetch, to** लाना *lānā*; ले आना *le ānā*; to go and fetch जाकर लाना *jākar lānā*

**fever** बुख़ार *bukhār*[M] — I have a fever मुझे बुख़ार है *mujhe bukhār hai*

**few** कम *kam* — few people कम लोग *kam log*; very few houses बहुत कम मकान *bahut kam makān*; a few कुछ *kuch*, थोड़े-से *thoṛe se*

**field** (piece of land) खेत *khet*[M]; (abstract sense) क्षेत्र *kṣetra*[M] — in the field of education शिक्षा के क्षेत्र में *śikṣā ke kṣetra mẽ*

**fifteen** पंद्रह *pandrah*

**fifty** पचास *pacās*

**fight, to** (से) लड़ना *(se) laṛnā*[N]; he won't fight me वह मुझसे नहीं लड़ेगा *vah mujhse nahī̃ laṛegā*

**fighting** लड़ाई *laṛāī*[F]

**fill, to** (intr., to be filled) भरना *bharnā* — in the rains this reservoir fills with water बरसात में यह हौज़ पानी से भरता है [भर जाता है] *barsāt mẽ yah hauz pānī se bhartā hai [bhar jātā hai]*; (tr.) भरना *bharnā*[N] — fill this bottle यह बोतल भरो [भर दो] *yah botal bharo [bhar do]*; we ate our fill हमने भर-पेट खाना खाया *hamne bhar-peṭ khānā khāyā*

**Insight**

Fill: भरना *bharnā* is rare among Hindi verbs in being both intransitive and transitive (as in English 'to fill': 'the bucket fills' versus 'I fill the bucket').

**film** फ़िल्म *film*[F]

**final** आख़िरी *ākhirī*, अंतिम *antim*

**financial** आर्थिक *ārthik*

**find, to** पाना *pānā*[N] — I found him/her working in the garden मैंने उसे बग़ीचे में काम करते हुए पाया *maĩne use bagīce mẽ kām karte hue pāyā*

**fine**[1] (of good quality) बढ़िया *baṛhiyā*; (thin) पतला *patlā*; (delicate) महीन *mahīn*

**fine**[2] (penalty) जुरमाना *jurmānā*[M]

**finger** उँगली *ũglī*[F]

**fingernail** नाख़ून *nākhūn*[F]

**finish, to** (intr., to be finished) ख़त्म होना *khatm honā* — the movie hasn't finished yet फ़िल्म अभी ख़त्म नहीं हुई *film abhī khatm nahī̃ huī*; (tr.) ख़त्म करना *khatm karnā*[N], समाप्त करना *samāpt karnā*[N] — finish your work अपना काम ख़त्म करो *apnā kām khatm karo*; (to complete) पूरा करना *pūrā karnā*[N]

**finite** सीमित *sīmit*

**fire** आग *āg*[F]; to catch fire आग लगना *āg lagnā* — the house caught fire मकान में आग लगी [लग गई] *makān mẽ āg lagī [lag gaī]*

**firefly** जुगनू *jugnū*[M]

**firework** पटाखा *paṭākhā*[M]

**firm**[1] (adj: stable, resolute) दृढ़ *dṛṛh*

**firm**[2] (noun: commercial company) कंपनी *kampanī*[F]

**first** पहला *pahlā* — the first book पहली किताब *pahlī kitāb*; are you going to India for the first time? आप पहली बार भारत जा रहे हैं? *āp pahlī bār bhārat jā rahe haĩ?*; first of all सबसे पहले *sabse pahle*; at first शुरू में *śurū mẽ*; the first of May/June पहली मई/जून *pahlī maī/jūn*

**first(ly)** पहले *pahle* — first(ly) finish this work पहले यह काम ख़त्म करो *pahle yah kām khatm karo*

**fish** मछली *machlī*[F]

**fist** मुट्ठी *muṭṭhī*[F]

**fit**[1] (well, healthy) तंदुरुस्त *tandurust*, ठीक-ठाक *ṭhīk-ṭhāk*, स्वस्थ *svasth*

**fit**[2] (attack, seizure) दौरा *daurā*[M]

**fit, to** (to be of right shape, e.g a peg in a hole) ठीक बैठना *ṭhīk baiṭhnā* — it doesn't fit properly वह ठीक से नहीं बैठता *vah ṭhīk se nahī̃ baiṭhtā*; (of clothing) ठीक होना *ṭhīk honā;* (to have space) आना

*ānā* — my box won't fit in this cupboard मेरा बक्सा इस अलमारी में नहीं आएगा *merā baksā is almārī mẽ nahī̃ āegā*

**five** पाँच *pā̃c*

**fix, to** (mend) ठीक करना *ṭhīk karnā*[N], की मरम्मत करना *kī marammat karnā*[N] — fix the car गाड़ी को ठीक करो *gāṛī ko ṭhīk karo*, गाड़ी की मरम्मत करो *gāṛī kī marammat karo*

**flag** झंडा *jhaṇḍā*[M]

**flame** (of candle) लौ *lau*[F]; (flare, blaze) ज्वाला *jvālā*[F]

**flat**[1] (level) समतल *samtal*; (dull) फीका *phīkā*

**flat**[2] (apartment) फ़्लैट *flaiṭ*[M]

**flavour** स्वाद *svād*[M]

**flee, to** भागना — we fled from there हम वहाँ से भागे [भाग गए] *ham vahā̃ se bhāge [bhāg gae]*

**flesh** मांस *mā̃s*[M]

**flight** (of plane etc.) उड़ान *uṛān*[F]

**flood** बाढ़ *bāṛh*[F] — last year the Yamuna flooded पिछले साल यमुना में बाढ़ आई *pichle sāl yamunā mẽ bāṛh āī*

**floor** फ़र्श *farś*[F (M)]; (ground) ज़मीन *zamīn*[F] — sit on the floor ज़मीन पर बैठो *zamīn par baiṭho*, नीचे बैठो *nīce baiṭho*; (level in building: see 'storey')

**flour** आटा *āṭā*[M]; (fine flour) मैदा *maidā*[M]

**flow** बहाव *bahāv*[M]; to flow बहना *bahnā*

**flower** फूल *phūl*[M]

**flower, to** फूलना *phūlnā*; to pick a flower फूल चुनना *phūl cunnā*[N]

**flowerpot** गमला *gamlā*[M]

**fluency** रवानी *ravānī*[F]

**fluently** रवानी से *ravānī se* — you speak fluently आप रवानी से बोलते हैं *āp ravānī se bolte haĩ*

**flute** बाँसुरी *bā̃surī*[F]

**fly** (insect) मक्खी *makkhī*[F]

**fly, to** उड़ना *uṛnā*; (to travel by plane) हवाई जहाज़ से सफ़र करना *havāī jahāz se safar karnā*[N]

**fog** धुंध *dhundh*[F], कुहरा *kuhrā*[M] — the fog is spreading/clearing कुहरा छा रहा है/छँट रहा है *kuhrā chā rahā hai/chā̃ṭ rahā hai*

**fold** (in cloth etc.) तह *tah*[F]

**fold, to** तह करना *tah karnā*[N] — fold these clothes and put them away इन कपड़ों को तह करके रखना *in kapṛõ ko tah karke rakhnā*

**folksong** लोकगीत *lokgīt*[M]

**follow, to** (to pursue) का पीछा करना *kā pīchā karnā*[N] — follow that car उस गाड़ी का पीछा करो *us gāṛī kā pīchā karo*; (to tag along) (के) पीछे-पीछे चलना *(ke) pīche-pīche calnā* — the tall man began following me लंबा आदमी मेरे पीछे-पीछे चलने लगा *lambā ādmī mere pīche-pīche calne lagā*; (to imitate, emulate) का अनुकरण करना *kā anukaraṇ karnā*[N]

**follower** अनुयायी *anuyāyī*[M]

**fond of, to be** चाहना *cāhnā* — he's very fond of me वह मुझे बहुत चाहता है *vah mujhe bahut cāhtā hai*; (to have fondness for an activity) शौक़ होना *śauq honā* — I'm very fond of reading मुझे पढ़ने का बहुत शौक़ है *mujhe paṛhne kā bahut śauq hai*

**food** खाना *khānā*[M]

**fool** मूर्ख *mūrkh*[M]; (court jester) विदूषक *vidūṣak*[M]

**foolish** मूर्ख *mūrkh*, बेवक़ूफ़ *bevaqūf*; (unwise) नासमझ *nāsamajh*

**foot** पैर *pair*[M]; on foot पैदल *paidal* — let's walk, go on foot हम पैदल चलें *ham paidal calẽ*

**for** के लिए *ke lie* — for me मेरे लिए *mere lie*; for now, for the time being फ़िलहाल *filhāl*; for example मसलन *maslan*, उदाहरण के लिए *udāharaṇ ke lie*; 'for' a sum of money: use में *mẽ* — I got this shawl for 1500 (rupees) मुझे यह शाल डेढ़ हज़ार में मिली *mujhe yah śāl ḍeṛh hazār mẽ milī*

**forbid, to** मना करना *manā karnā*[N] ('to do' something: use से *se*) — he forbids me to speak वह मुझे बोलने से मना करता है *vah mujhe bolne se manā kartā hai*

**forbidden** मना *manā* — drinking is forbidden here यहाँ शराब पीना मना है *yahā̃ śarāb pīnā manā hai*

**force** (strength) ज़ोर *zor*[M], शक्ति *śakti*[F]

**force, to** (पर) मजबूर करना *(par) majbūr karnā*[N] — Uncle forced me to sing चाचाजी ने मुझे गाने पर मजबूर किया *cācājī ne mujhe gāne par majbūr kiyā*

**forehead** माथा *māthā*[M]

**foreign** विदेशी *videśī*

**foreigner** विदेशी *videśī*[M]

**forest** वन *van*[M], जंगल *jaṅgal*[M]

**forget, to** भूलना *bhūlnā*, भूल जाना *bhūl jānā* — she forgot to give me her address वह मुझे अपना पता देना भूल गई *vah mujhe apnā patā denā bhūl gaī*

**forgive, to** माफ़/क्षमा करना *māf/kṣamā karnā*[N] — please forgive me मुझे माफ़/क्षमा कीजिए *mujhe māf/kṣamā kījie*

**forgiveness** माफ़ी *māfī*[F], क्षमा *kṣamā*[F]

**fork** (cutlery, flatware) काँटा[M] *kā̃ṭā*

**form** (shape) रूप *rūp*[M] — in the form of के रूप में *ke rūp mẽ*; (a paper form) फ़ॉर्म *fārm*[M] — fill in this form इस फ़ॉर्म को भरो [भर दो] *is fārm ko bharo [bhar do]*

**formal** औपचारिक *aupcārik*

**formality** औपचारिकता *aupcāriktā*[F]

**formally** औपचारिक रूप से *aupcārik rūp se*

**former** भूतपूर्व *bhūtpūrv* — some former prime minister कोई भूतपूर्व प्रधानमंत्री *koī bhūtpūrv pradhān-mantrī*

**fort** क़िला *qilā*[M], गढ़ *garh*[M] — the Red Fort in Delhi दिल्ली का लाल क़िला *dillī kā lāl qilā*

**fortunate** ख़ुशक़िस्मत *khuśqismat*, भाग्यवान *bhāgyavān*

**forty** चालीस *cālīs*

**forward** आगे *āge*

**found, to be** मिलना *milnā*; are there snakes to be found here? क्या यहाँ साँप मिलते हैं? *kyā yahā̃ sā̃p milte haĩ?*

**four** चार *cār*

**fourteen** चौदह *caudah*

**fourth** चौथा *cauthā*

**fox** लोमड़ी *lomṛī*[F]

**fragrance** ख़ुशबू *khuśbū*[F], सुगंध *sugandh*[M]

**framework** ढाँचा *ḍhā̃cā*[M]

**fraud** (fraudulent act) धोखा *dhokhā*[M], छल *chal*[M]; (the practice of fraud) धोखेबाज़ी *dhokhebāzī*[M]

**fraudster** धोखेबाज़ *dhokhebāz*[M]

**free** (gratis) मुफ़्त (में) *muft (mẽ)* — I got these books free ☞ मुझे ये किताबें मुफ़्त में मिलीं *mujhe ye kitābẽ muft mẽ milī̃*; (independent) आज़ाद — in 1947 India became free सन् १९४७ में भारत आज़ाद हुआ *san 1947 mẽ bhārat āzād huā*; (vacant; not busy) ख़ाली *khālī* — is the room/boss free?

क्या कमरा/मालिक ख़ाली है? *kyā kamrā/mālik khālī hai?*; free time, leisure फ़ुरसत *fursat*$^{F}$ — I'll be free this evening आज शाम को मुझे फ़ुरसत होगी *āj śām ko mujhe fursat hogī* (see also 'leisure')

**freedom** आज़ादी *āzādī*$^{F}$, स्वतंत्रता *svatantratā*$^{F}$

**fresh** ताज़ा *tāzā* (-*ā* sometimes used as invariable)

**Friday** शुक्रवार *śukravār*$^{M}$

**friend** दोस्त *dost*$^{M}$, मित्र *mitra*$^{M}$; woman/girl's female friend सहेली *sahelī*$^{F}$

**friendly** मिलनसार *milansār*

**friendship** दोस्ती *dostī*$^{F}$, मित्रता *mitratā*$^{F}$

**frighten, to** डराना *ḍarānā*$^{N}$ — why do you deliberately frighten him/her? तुम उसे जान-बूझकर क्यों डराते हो? *tum use jān-būjhkar kyõ ḍarāte ho?*; (see also 'startle')

**frog** मेंढक *mẽḍhak*$^{M}$

**from** से *se* — where are you from? आप कहाँ से हैं? *āp kahā̃ se haĩ?*; (resulting 'from' a feeling) के मारे *ke māre* — he was speechless from fear वह डर के मारे बोल नहीं पा रहा था *vah ḍar ke māre bol nahī̃ pā rahā thā*

**front** (military, political) मोरचा *morcā*$^{M}$; (front part) आगे का हिस्सा *āge kā hissā*$^{M}$; (in front) आगे *āge*; he's standing in front वह आगे खड़ा है *vah āge khaṛā hai*; (in front of) के आगे *ke āge* — in front of the shop दुकान के आगे *dukān ke āge*

**fruit** फल *phal*$^{M}$

**fruit, to** (to bear fruit) फलना *phalnā*

**fry, to** तलना *talnā*$^{N}$ — fried fish तली हुई मछली *talī huī machlī*

**frying pan** कड़ाही *kaṛāhī*$^{F}$

**fuel** ईंधन *īdhan*$^{M}$

**full** (replete) भरा हुआ *bharā huā*; I'm full (can't eat any more)! मेरा पेट भर गया! *merā peṭ bhar gayā!*

**fun** मज़ा *mazā*$^{M}$; to have fun मज़ा आना *mazā ānā* — I had a lot of fun मुझे बहुत मज़ा आया *mujhe bahut mazā āyā*

**function (event)** समारोह *samāroh*$^{M}$ प्रोग्राम *progām*

**fundamentalist** (adj. & noun) कट्टरपंथी *kaṭṭarpanthī*$^{M}$

**funeral** अंत्येष्टि *antyeṣṭi*$^{F}$

**furniture** सामान *sāmān*[M]

**further** आगे *āge,* और आगे *aur āge*

**future** भविष्य *bhaviṣya*[M]; in the future भविष्य में *bhaviṣya mẽ*; (from now on) आगे चलकर *āge calkar*

## G

**gambit** चाल *cāl*[F]

**gamble, to** जुआ खेलना *juā khelnā*[N]

**gambling** जुआ *juā*[M]

**game** खेल *khel*[M]

**Ganges** गंगा *gaṅgā*[F]

**garden** (small) बग़ीचा *bagīcā*[M]; (big, public) बाग़ *bāg*[M]

**gardener** माली *mālī*[M]

**garland** माला *mālā*[F]

**garland, to** गले में माला डालना *gale mẽ mālā ḍālnā*[N]

**garlic** लहसुन *lahsun*[M]

**garrulous** बातूनी *bātūnī*

**gas** गैस *gais*[M]

**gather, to** (intr.) जमा होना *jamā honā* (*-ā* invariable in जमा *jamā*); everyone gathered in my room सब लोग मेरे कमरे में जमा हुए [हो गए] *sab log mere kamre mẽ jamā hue [ho gae]*; (tr.) जमा करना *jamā karnā*[N]

**gay:** see 'homosexual', 'lesbian'

**gender** लिंग *liṅg*[M]

**general**[1] (ordinary, public) आम *ām,* साधारण *sādhāraṇ*; general election आम चुनाव *ām cunāv*[M]

**general**[2] (army officer) सेनापति *senāpati*[M]

**generation** पीढ़ी *pīṛhī*[F]

**generosity** उदारता *udārtā*[F]

**generous** उदार *udār*

**genius** (talent) प्रतिभा *pratibhā*[F]

**gentle** (kind) दयालु *dayālu*; (light, delicate) हलका *halkā*

**get, to** मिलना *milnā* ('to be got') — can you get books there? क्या वहाँ किताबें मिलती हैं ? *kyā vahā̃ kitābẽ miltī haĩ?*; we got this video in Mumbai हमें यह विडियो मुंबई में मिला *hamẽ yah viḍiyo mumbaī mẽ milā*; to get out of (a vehicle) उतरना *utarnā* — I got out of the taxi मैं टैक्सी से उतरा [उतर गया] *maĩ ṭaiksī se utarā [utar gayā]*; to get up उठना *uṭhnā* — I got up early मैं जल्दी उठा *maĩ jaldī uṭhā*; to get rid of: see 'remove'

**get down, to** उतरना *utarnā* — we got down from the train हम ट्रेन से उतरे *ham ṭren se utare*

**ghost** भूत *bhūt*[M]

**Insight**

Ghost: the word भूत *bhūt* meaning 'ghost' means also 'the past', as in भूत-काल *bhūt-kāl* 'past tense' (in grammar).

**ginger** अदरक *adrak*[F]

**girl** लड़की *laṛkī*[F]

**give, to** देना *denā*[N]; to give back वापस देना *vāpas denā*[N], लौटाना *lauṭānā*[N]; to give up छोड़ देना *choṛ denā*[N] — you should give up this habit तुम्हें इस आदत को छोड़ना चाहिए [छोड़ देना चाहिए] *tumhē is ādat ko choṛnā cāhie [choṛ denā cāhie]*

**glad** ख़ुश *khuś*, प्रसन्न *prasann*

**glance** नज़र *nazar*[F], दृष्टि *dṛṣṭi*[F]

**glance, to** नज़र डालना *nazar ḍālnā*[N] — he/she glanced at me उसने मेरी तरफ़ नज़र डाली *usne merī taraf nazar ḍālī*; (to peep) झाँकना *jhā̃knā*[N]

**glass**[1] (the substance) काँच *kā̃c*[M]

**glass**[2] (tumbler, made of glass or metal) गिलास *gilās*[M]

**glasses** चश्मा *caśmā*[M] (singular) — where are my glasses? मेरा चश्मा कहाँ है? *merā caśmā kahā̃ hai?*; to put on glasses चश्मा लगाना *caśmā lagānā*[N]

**globalization** भूमंडलीकरण *bhūmaṇḍalīkaraṇ*[M]

**globe** भूमंडल *bhūmaṇḍal*[M]

**glove** दस्ताना *dastānā*[M]

**glue** गोंद *gõd*[F], सरेस *sares*[M]

**go, to** जाना *jānā*; (to progress) चलना *calnā* — the work is going well काम ठीक चल रहा है *kām ṭhīk cal rahā hai*; (NB: जाना *jānā* has a focus on a destination, as in घर जाओ *ghar jāo* 'go home', while चलना *calnā* has a focus on motion from a static state, as in चलें *calē* 'let's go!, let's be off!'); to go to do something: use oblique infinitive + जाना *jānā* — we're going to see a film हम फ़िल्म देखने जा रहे हैं *ham film dekhne jā rahe haĩ*

**go out, to** (to be extinguished) बुझना *bujhnā*

**goat** बकरी *bakrī*[F]; billygoat बकरा *bakrā*[M]

**god** देवता *devtā*[M]; God भगवान *bhagvān*[M], ख़ुदा *khudā*; God knows! भगवान/ख़ुदा जाने! *bhagvān/khudā jāne!*

**goddess** देवी *devī*ᶠ

**gold** सोना *sonā*ᴹ

**golden** सुनहरा *sunaharā*

**good** अच्छा *acchā*; (decent) नेक *nek* – he's a very good man वह बड़ा नेक आदमी है *vah baṛā nek ādmī hai*

**goodbye** नमस्ते *namaste*, नमस्कार *namaskār*; (casual, 'see you!') फिर मिलेंगे *phir milẽge*

**goodness** भलाई *bhalāī*ᶠ

**goods** माल *māl*ᴹ; goods train मालगाड़ी *mālgāṛī*ᶠ

**gossip** गप-शप *gap-śap*ᶠ

**gossip, to** गप-शप करना *gap-śap karnā*ᴺ

**governance** शासन *śāsan*ᴹ

**government** सरकार *sarkār*ᶠ – the Indian government भारत सरकार *bhārat sarkār*

**governmental** सरकारी *sarkārī* – government buildings सरकारी इमारतें *sarkārī imāratẽ*

**grab, to** पकड़ना *pakaṛnā*ᴺ

**gradually** धीरे-धीरे *dhīre-dhīre*

**graduate** स्नातक *snātak*ᴹ

**grammar** व्याकरण *vyākaraṇ*ᴹ

**grand** (magnificent) भव्य *bhavya*

**grand** granddaughter (son's daughter) पोती *potī*ᶠ; (daughter's daughter) नातिन *nātin*ᶠ; grandfather (paternal) दादा *dādā*ᴹ; (maternal) नाना *nānā*ᴹ; grandmother (paternal) दादी *dādī*ᶠ; (maternal) नानी *nānī*ᶠ; grandson (daughter's son) नाती *nātī*ᴹ; (son's son) पोता *potā*ᴹ

**grape** अंगूर *aṅgūr*ᴹ

**grass** घास *ghās*ᶠ

**grateful** कृतज्ञ *kṛtajña* (pronounced 'kṛtagya'); (indebted) आभारी *ābhārī* – if you help us I'll be very grateful अगर आप हमारी मदद करेंगे तो मैं बहुत आभारी रहूँगा *agar āp hamārī madad karẽge to maĩ bahut ābhārī rahũgā*

**grating** जंगला *jaṅglā*ᴹ

**gratitude** कृतज्ञता *kṛtajñatā*ᶠ (pronounced 'kṛtagyatā')

**grave**[1] (serious) गंभीर *gambhīr*

**grave**[2] (burial place) कब्र *kabra*ᶠ, समाधि *samādhi*ᶠ

**graze, to** चरना *carnā* n

**great** महान् *mahān*

**greed** लोभ *lobh*ᴹ, लालच *lālac*ᴹ

**greedy** लालची *lālcī*

**green** हरा *harā*

**greenery** हरियाली *hariyālī*$^{F}$

**greet, to** नमस्कार करना *namaskār karnā*$^{N}$ (see also 'welcome')

**grey** धूसर *dhūsar*, भूरा *bhūrā* (the latter also means 'brown')

**grind, to** पीसना *pīsnā*$^{N}$

**ground**$^{1}$ (from 'to grind') पीसा हुआ *pīsā huā*

**ground**$^{2}$ (earth, land) ज़मीन *zamīn*$^{F}$

**groundnut** मूँगफली *mū̃gphalī*$^{F}$

**group** दल *dal*$^{M}$, ग्रुप *grup*$^{M}$ — in our group there are ten boys हमारे ग्रुप में दस लड़के हैं *hamāre grup mẽ das laṛke haĩ*

**grow, to** (intr., of plants) उगना *ugnā* — mangoes don't grow here आम यहाँ नहीं उगते *ām yahā̃ nahī̃ ugte*; (to get bigger) बढ़ना *baṛhnā* — unemployment is growing बेरोज़गारी बढ़ रही है *berozgārī baṛh rahī hai*; (to grow up) बड़ा होना *baṛā honā* — the children grew up बच्चे बड़े हुए [हो गए] *bacce baṛe hue [ho gae];* (tr., to grow a crop) उगाना *ugānā*$^{N}$ — we grow potatoes हम आलू उगाते हैं *ham ālū ugāte haĩ*

**guard, to** (to protect) की रक्षा करना *kī rakṣā karnā*$^{N}$; (to stand on guard) पहरा देना *pahrā denā*$^{N}$

**guava** अमरूद *amrūd*$^{M}$

**guess** अंदाज़ा *andāzā*$^{M}$

**guess, to** अंदाज़ा करना/लगाना *andāzā karnā*$^{N}$/*lagānā*$^{N}$ — I'd guessed that he must be alive मैंने अंदाज़ा लगाया था कि वह ज़िंदा होगा *maĩne andāzā lagāyā thā ki vah zindā hogā*

**guest** मेहमान *mehmān*$^{M}$, अतिथि *atithi*$^{M}$

**guesthouse** अतिथि-गृह *atithi-gṛh*$^{M}$

**guile** छल-कपट *chal-kapaṭ*$^{M}$

**guilt** दोष *doṣ*$^{M}$

**guilty** दोषी *doṣī*

**gun** बंदूक़ *bandūq*$^{F}$; (field gun) तोप *top*$^{F}$

**guru** गुरु *guru*$^{M}$

## H

**habit** आदत *ādat*$^{F}$ — I got into the habit of smoking मुझे सिग्रेट पीने की आदत पड़ी [पड़ गई] *mujhe sigreṭ pīne kī ādat paṛī [paṛ gaī]*

**habitually** आदतन *ādatan*, आदत से *ādat se*

**haggle, to** मोल-भाव करना *mol-bhāv karnā*ᴺ

**hail** (frozen rain) ओला *olā*ᴹ

**hair** बाल *bāl*ᴹ — her hair is very long/short उसके बाल बहुत लंबे/छोटे हैं *uske bāl bahut lambe/choṭe haĩ* (note plural usage); to have hair cut/done बाल कटवाना/बनवाना *bāl kaṭvānā*ᴺ/*banvānā*ᴺ — I had my hair cut मैंने अपने बाल कटवाए *maĩne apne bāl kaṭvāe*

**half** (adj. & noun) आधा *ādhā*ᴹ; half of this इसका आधा *iskā ādhā*; half of the people आधे लोग *ādhe log*

**hammer** हथौड़ी *hathauṛī*ᶠ

**hand** हाथ *hāth*ᴹ; to lend a hand हाथ बँटाना *hāth bãṭānā*ᴺ; to come to hand हाथ आना *hāth ānā*; (hand of clock) सूई *sūī*ᶠ

**hand in, to** जमा करना *jamā karnā*ᴺ (*-ā* invariable in *jamā*)

**hand over, to** (to pass) थमाना *thamānā*ᴺ; (to entrust) सुपुर्द करना *supurd karnā*ᴺ

**handcuff** हथकड़ी *hathkaṛī*ᶠ

**handkerchief** रूमाल *rūmāl*ᴹ

**handle (manage), to** सँभालना *sãbhālnā*ᴺ — how should I handle this matter? मैं इस मामले को कैसे सँभालूँ ? *maĩ is māmle ko kaise sãbhālū̃?*

**handsome** सुन्दर *sundar*

**hang, to** (intr., to dangle, be suspended) लटकना *laṭaknā* — my clothes were hanging on the tree मेरे कपड़े पेड़ पर लटके हुए थे *mere kapṛe peṛ par laṭke hue the*; (tr., to hang up) लटकानाᴺ *laṭkānā* — hang your coat on the door अपना कोट दरवाज़े पर लटकाओ [लटका दो] *apnā koṭ darvāze par laṭkāo [laṭkā do]*; (to execute, kill by hanging) फाँसी देना *phā̃sī denā*ᴺ

**happen, to** होना *honā*, हो जाना *ho jānā*; what happened? क्या हुआ? *kyā huā?*; what happened to you? तुम्हें क्या हो गया? *tumhẽ kyā ho gayā?*

**happiness** सुख *sukh*ᴹ

**happy** ख़ुश, *khuś*, सुखी *sukhī*

**harass, to** तंग करना *taṅg karnā*ᴺ; परेशान करना *pareśān karnā*ᴺ — don't harass me! मुझे तंग/परेशान मत करना! *mujhe taṅg/pareśān mat karnā!*

**hard** (stiff) कठोर *kaṭhor*, सख़्त *sakht*; (difficult) मुश्किल *muśkil*; hard work मेहनत *mehnat*ᶠ

**hardly** (being very unlikely) शायद ही *śāyad hī* — he's

hardly going to agree! वह शायद ही मानेगा! *vah śāyad hī mānegā!*

**hard working** मेहनती *mehntī* — he's a very hard-working boy वह बहुत मेहनती लड़का है *vah bahut mehntī laṛkā hai*

**harm** नुक़सान *nuqsān*[M], हानि *hāni*[F]; to harm someone किसी को नुक़सान/हानि पहुँचाना *kisī ko nuqsān/hāni pahũcānā*[N]

**harshness** रुखाई *rukhāī*[F]

**haste** (impetuousness) जल्दबाज़ी *jaldbāzī*[F]

**hat** टोपी *ṭopī*[F]

**hate** नफ़रत *nafrat*[F]

**hate, to** (से) नफ़रत करना[N] *(se) nafrat karnā* — he hates me वह मुझसे नफ़रत करता है *vah mujhse nafrat kartā hai*

**have, to** (Hindi has no direct equivalent; for possession of things, time, money etc., use के पास *ke pās)* — we have no food/time/money हमारे पास खाना/समय/पैसा नहीं है *hamāre pās khānā/samay/paisā nahī̃ hai*; (for relatives and real estate, use possessive pronoun) — I have two sons/houses मेरे दो बेटे/मकान हैं *mere do beṭe/makān haī̃*; (for afflictions, use को *ko*) — I have a cold मुझको ज़ुकाम है *mujhko zukām hai*; (for the sense 'have to, must', see 'must')

**he** वह *vah*

**head**[1] (adj.: chief) मुख्य *mukhya*

**head**[2] (part of body) सिर *sir*[M]

**headache** सिरदर्द *sirdard*[M]

**health** तबियत *tabiyat*[F], सेहत *sehat*[F], स्वास्थ्य *svāsthya*[M] — my health is better/worse than before मेरी तबियत पहले से अच्छी/ख़राब है *merī tabiyat pahle se acchī/<u>kh</u>arāb hai*

**healthy** स्वस्थ *svasth*

**heap** ढेर *ḍher*[M] — heaps of (lots of) ढेरों *ḍherõ*

**hear, to** सुनना *sunnā*[N]

**heard, to be** सुनाई देना *sunāī denā* (no ने *ne* construction) — the sound of a car was heard गाड़ी की आवाज़ सुनाई दी *gāṛī kī āvāz sunāī dī*

**heart** दिल *dil*[M], हृदय *hṛday*[M]; heart attack दिल का दौरा *dil kā daurā*[M]

**heat** गरमी *garmī*[F]

**heaven** स्वर्ग *svarg*[M]

**heavy** भारी *bhārī*

**heel** एड़ी *eṛī*[F]

**height** ऊँचाई *ũcāī*[F] — she was measuring the height of the wall

वह दीवार की ऊँचाई नाप रही थी *vah dīvār kī ũcāī nāp rahī thī*; (height of a person) लंबाई *lambāī*[F]

**hell** नरक *narak*[M]; go to hell! भाड़ में जाओ! *bhāṛ mẽ jāo!*

**hello** नमस्ते *namaste*, नमस्कार *namaskār*; (casual, 'hi!') कहो, क्या हाल है? *kaho, kyā hāl hai?*

**help** मदद *madad*[F]; 'help!' ('save me') बचाओ! *bacāo!*

**help, to** की मदद करना *kī madad karnā*[N] — Amrik ji helped me a lot अमरीक जी ने मेरी बहुत मदद की *amrīk jī ne merī bahut madad kī*

**helper** मददगार *madadgār*[M], सहायक *sahāyak*[M]

**helpful** मददगार *madadgār*

**helpless** (having no choice, compelled) मजबूर *majbūr* — what can I do? I am helpless क्या करूँ? मैं मजबूर हूँ *kyā karũ? maĩ majbūr hũ*; (powerless) बेबस *bebas*

**her** (possessive) उसका *uskā*

**herb** जड़ी-बूटी *jaṛī-būṭī*[F]

**here** यहाँ *yahā̃*; right here यहीं *yahī̃*; over here इधर *idhar* — come over here! इधर आओ! *idhar āo!*

**hiccup** हिचकी *hickī*[F] — I got hiccups मुझे हिचकी आई *mujhe hickī āī*

**hidden** छिपा हुआ *chipā huā*; (secret) गुप्त *gupt*

**hide, to** (intr.) छिपना *chipnā* — we hid in the jungle हम जंगल में छिपे [छिप गए] *ham jaṅgal mẽ chipe [chip gae]*; (tr.) छिपाना *chipānā*[N] — let's hide the money here पैसे को यहाँ छिपाएँ [छिपा लें] *paise ko yahā̃ chipāẽ [chipā lẽ]*

**high** ऊँचा *ũcā*

**hill** पहाड़ *pahāṛ*[M] — high hills ऊँचे पहाड़ *ũce pahāṛ*

**hillock** पहाड़ी *pahāṛī*[F], टीला *ṭīlā*[M]

**hilly** पहाड़ी *pahāṛī*

**hinder, to** रोकना *roknā*[N]

**Hindi** हिन्दी *hindī*[F]; Hindi-speaking people हिन्दी-भाषी लोग *hindī-bhāṣī log*

---

**Insight**

Hindi: हिन्दी *hindī* and हिन्दू *hindū* both derive from हिन्द *hind*, the Persian name for India, which, in turn, derives from the name of the river सिंधु *sindhu*, 'Indus'.

---

**Hindu** (adj. & noun) हिन्दू *hindū*ᴹ

**Hinduism** हिन्दू धर्म *hindū dharm*ᴹ

**hire, to:** see 'rent'

**his** उसका *uskā*

**historical** ऐतिहासिक *aitihāsik*

**history** इतिहास *itihās*ᴹ

**hit, to** मारना *mārnā*ᴺ

**hoarse, to be** (of the throat) गला बैठना *galā baiṭhnā* — my throat is hoarse मेरा गला बैठ गया है *merā galā baiṭh gayā hai*

**hobby** शौक़ *śauq*ᴹ — I have many hobbies ● मेरे बहुत-से शौक़ हैं *mere bahut-se śauq haĩ*

**hold, to** पकड़ना *pakaṛnā*ᴺ — just hold this, will you? ज़रा इसको पकड़ो न? *zarā isko pakṛo na?*; (on phone) होल्ड करना *holḍ karnā*ᴺ

**hole** छेद *ched*ᴹ; (pit in the ground) गड्ढा *gaḍḍhā*ᴹ; (rodent's or snake's lair) बिल *bil*ᴹ

**holiday** छुट्टी *chuṭṭī*ᶠ — summer holidays गरमी की छुट्टियाँ *garmī kī chuṭṭiyā̃*

**hollow**[1] (adj.) छिछला *chichlā*

**hollow**[2] (a pit) गड्ढा *gaḍḍhā*ᴹ

**home** घर *ghar*ᴹ — let's go home घर चलें *ghar calẽ*; at home घर पर *ghar par*; home minister गृह मंत्री *gṛh mantrī*ᴹ

**homework** गृहकार्य *gṛhakārya*ᴹ

**homosexual** (adj. & noun) समलिंगी *samliṅgī*ᴹ

**honest** ईमानदार *īmāndār*

**honesty** ईमानदारी *īmāndārī*ᶠ

**honey** शहद *śahad*ᴹ — as sweet as honey शहद की तरह मीठा *śahad kī tarah mīṭhā*

**honour** सम्मान *sammān*ᴹ; in honour of के सम्मान में *ke sammān mẽ*

**honour, to** (का) सम्मान करना *(kā) sammān karnā*ᴺ — we honour the soldiers हम जवानों का सम्मान करते हैं *ham javānõ kā sammān karte haĩ*

**hope** उम्मीद *ummīd*ᶠ, आशा *āśā*ᶠ; (the following expressions can use either word) to hope आशा करना *āśā karnā*ᴺ; I hope that... मैं आशा करता हूँ कि... *maĩ āśā kartā hū̃ ki...*, आशा होना *āśā honā* — I hope that... ● मुझे आशा है कि... *mujhe āśā hai ki...*; my hopes were fulfilled मेरी आशाएँ पूरी हुईं [हो गईं] *merī āśāẽ pūrī huī̃ [ho gaī̃]*

**hopeless** (causing despair) निराशाजनक *nirāśājanak*; (useless) बेकार *bekār*; (in vain) व्यर्थ *vyarth*

**horse** घोड़ा *ghoṛā*$^{M}$

**hospital** अस्पताल *aspatāl*$^{M}$

**host** मेज़बान *mezbān*$^{M}$

**hostility** दुश्मनी *duśmanī*$^{F}$

**hot** गरम *garam*; (spicy) मसालेदार *masāledār*

**hour** घंटा *ghaṇṭā*$^{M}$; an hour and a half डेढ़ घंटा *ḍeṛh ghaṇṭā* (gramm. singular) — it'll take an hour and a half to prepare the food खाना तैयार करने में डेढ़ घंटा लगेगा *khānā taiyār karne mẽ ḍeṛh ghaṇṭā lagegā*

**house** मकान *makān*$^{M}$, घर *ghar*$^{M}$ (NB: only घर *ghar* has the more abstract sense of 'home')

**how** कैसे *kaise*

**how much** कितना *kitnā* — how much is this? यह कितने का है? *yah kitne kā hai?*; how much are these saris? ये साड़ियाँ कितने की हैं? *ye sāṛiyā̃ kitne kī haĩ?*

**however** (even so) फिर भी *phir bhī*; (but) लेकिन *lekin*; (in any way at all) किसी भी तरह *kisī bhī tarah*; however much जितना भी *jitnā bhī*; however many people जितने भी लोग *jitne bhī log*

**huge** विशाल *viśal*

**human** इनसान *insān*$^{M}$, मनुष्य *manuṣya*$^{M}$

**humanity** (humaneness) इनसानियत *insāniyat*$^{F}$

**humble** विनम्र *vinamra*

**humid** नम *nam*

**humidity** आर्द्रता *ārdratā*$^{F}$; humid heat उमस *umas*$^{F}$

**humiliate, to** नीचा दिखाना *nīcā dikhānā*$^{N}$

**humiliation** ज़िल्लत *zillat*$^{F}$ — it was a humiliation for me (I was humiliated) मेरी ज़िल्लत हुई *merī zillat huī*

**hundred** सौ sau$^{M}$; 150 डेढ़ सौ *ḍeṛh sau*, 250 ढाई सौ *ḍhāī sau;* a hundred (group of a hundred) सैकड़ा$^{M}$ — hundreds of children सैकड़ों बच्चे *saikṛõ bacce*

**hunger** भूख *bhūkh*$^{F}$; to be hungry भूख लगना *bhūkh lagnā* — I'm hungry मुझे भूख लगी है *mujhe bhūkh lagī hai*

**hurry** जल्दी *jaldī*$^{F}$ — there's no hurry कोई जल्दी नहीं है *koī jaldī nahī̃ hai*; we're in a hurry हम जल्दी में हैं *ham jaldī mẽ haĩ*, हमें जल्दी है *hamẽ jaldī hai*; to hurry जल्दी करना *jaldī karnā*$^{N}$ — hurry up! जल्दी करो! *jaldī karo!*

**hurt** (injury) चोट *coṭ*$^{F}$

**hurt, to be** or **get** चोट लगना *coṭ lagnā* — I got hurt मुझे

चोट लगी [लग गई] *mujhe coṭ lagī [lag gaī]*; (mental) दुःख *duḥkh* — I was deeply hurt मुझे बहुत दुःख हुआ *mujhe bahut duḥkh huā*; to hurt (tr.) दुःख देना *duḥkh denā*[N]; (to cause grief, to offend) ठेस पहुँचाना *ṭhes pahũcānā*[N] — what's the point in hurting them? उन्हें ठेस पहुँचाने में क्या फ़ायदा है? *unhẽ ṭhes pahũcāne mẽ kyā fāydā hai?*

**husband** पति *pati*[M]

**husk** छिलका *chilkā*[M]

**hut** झोंपड़ी *jhõpṛī*[F]

## I

**I** मैं *maĩ*

**ice** बर्फ़ *barf*[F]

**idea** विचार *vicār*[M]

**ideal** (adj.) आदर्श *ādarś* — he'll make the ideal husband वह आदर्श पति बनेगा *vah ādarś pati banegā*; (noun) आदर्श *ādarś*[M] — according to one's ideals अपने आदर्शों के अनुसार *apne ādarśõ ke anusār*

**i.e.** यानी *yānī*

**if** अगर *agar*; यदि *yadi*; if only.... काश कि *kās ki* — if only you were here too! काश कि तुम भी यहाँ होते! *kāś ki tum bhī yahā̃ hote!*

**ignore, to** अनदेखा करना *andekhā karnā*[N], (की) उपेक्षा करना *(kī) upekṣā karna*[N] — they ignored me उन्होंने मेरी उपेक्षा की *unhõne merī upekṣā kī*

**ill** बीमार *bīmār*

**illegal** ग़ैर-क़ानूनी *gair-qānūnī*, अवैध *avaidh*

**illness** बीमारी *bīmārī*[F]

**imaginary** काल्पनिक *kālpanik*

**imagination** कल्पना *kalpanā*[F]

**imagine, to** कल्पना करना *kalpanā karnā*[N] — I'd never imagined that this government would fall मैंने कभी कल्पना नहीं की थी कि यह सरकार गिरेगी *maĩne kabhī kalpanā nahī̃ kī thī ki yah sarkār giregī*

**imitate, to** (की) नक़ल करना *(kī) naqal karnā*[N] — I'll imitate his writing मैं उसके लेखन की नक़ल करूँगा *maĩ uske lekhan kī naqal karū̃gā*

**immediately** तुरंत *turant*; (right now) अभी *abhī*

**impertinence** गुस्ताख़ी *gustākhī*[F]

**impertinent** गुस्ताख़ *gustākh*

**important** महत्त्वपूर्ण *mahattva-pūrṇ*, अहम *aham* — the important thing is... अहम बात यह है कि... *aham bāt yah hai ki*

...; (essential) ज़रूरी *zarūrī* — some important work/ letters कुछ ज़रूरी काम/पत्र *kuch zarūrī kām/patra*; an important man बड़ा आदमी *baṛā ādmī*

**impossible** नामुमकिन *nāmumkin*, असंभव *asambhav*

**impress, to** प्रभाव डालना *prabhāv ḍālnā*[N] (object takes पर *par*) — he/she impressed me a lot उसने मुझपर बहुत प्रभाव डाला *usne mujhpar bahut prabhāv ḍālā*

**impressed** प्रभावित *prabhāvit* — we were very impressed by their suggestion हम उनके सुझाव से बहुत प्रभावित हुए *ham unke sujhāv se bahut prabhāvit hue*

**improve, to** सुधारना *sudhārnā*[N] — we're trying to improve the environment हम पर्यावरण को सुधारने की कोशिश कर रहे हैं *ham paryāvaraṇ ko sudhārne kī kośiś kar rahe haĩ*

**improvement** सुधार *sudhār*[M]

**in** में *mẽ*; is Saroj in? क्या सरोज है? *kyā saroj hai?*

**in spite of** के बावजूद *ke bavjūd*

**in vain** व्यर्थ में *vyarth mẽ*

**incense stick** अगरबत्ती *agarbattī*[F]

**incident** घटना *ghaṭnā*[F] — today a rather strange incident happened आज एक अजीब-सी घटना हुई *āj ek ajīb-sī ghaṭnā huī*

**include, to** शामिल करना *śāmil karnā*[N]

**included** शामिल *śāmil* — we're included in this too हम भी इसमें शामिल हैं *ham bhī ismẽ śāmil haĩ*

**including** को शामिल करके *ko śāmil karke*; (more commonly, use भी *bhī* 'also')

**income** आमदनी *āmdanī*[F], आय *āy*[F]; income tax आय-कर *āy-kar*[M]

**inconvenience** तकलीफ़ *taklīf*[F], असुविधा *asuvidhā*[F] — you didn't have any inconvenience getting here? यहाँ आने में आपको कोई असुविधा तो नहीं हुई ? *yahā̃ āne mẽ āpko koī asuvidhā to nahī̃ huī?*

**increase, to** (intr.) बढ़ना *baṛhnā* — the price increases दाम बढ़ता है *dām baṛhtā hai*; (tr.) बढ़ाना *baṛhānā*[N] — please increase my pay मेरा वेतन बढ़ाइए [बढ़ा दीजिए] *merā vetan baṛhāie [baṛhā dījie]*

**indeed** (really) सच में *sac mẽ* — the house is indeed very cheap मकान सच में बहुत सस्ता है *makān sac mẽ bahut sastā hai*; (emphatic) ही *hī* — very cheap indeed बहुत ही सस्ता *bahut hī sastā*

**independence** स्वतंत्रता *svatantratā*[F]; Independence Day स्वतंत्रता दिवस *svatantratā divas*[M]; (freedom) आज़ादी *āzādī*[F]

**independent** स्वतंत्र *svatantra*; (free) आज़ाद *āzād*

**India** भारत *bhārat*[M], हिन्दुस्तान *hindustān*[M], (formal) भारतवर्ष *bhāratvarṣ*[M]

**Indian** (adj. & noun) हिन्दुस्तानी *hindustānī*[M], भारतीय *bhārtīy*[M]

**individual**[1] (adj.: separate) अलग *alag*

**individual**[2] (noun: an individual) व्यक्ति *vyakti*[M]

**inferior** घटिया *ghaṭiyā* (*-ā* invariable)

**influence** असर *asar*[M], प्रभाव *prabhāv*[M]; to influence असर/प्रभाव डालना *asar/prabhāv ḍālnā*[N] (object takes पर *par*) — he/she influenced me a lot उसने मुझपर बहुत असर/प्रभाव डाला *usne mujhpar bahut asar/prabhāv ḍālā*

**influential** प्रभावशाली *prabhāvśālī*

**inform, to** बताना *batānā*[N], (formal) सूचित करना *sūcit karnā*[N]

**informal** अनौपचारिक *anaupcārik*

**informally** अनौपचारिक रूप से *anaupcārik rūp se*

**information** सूचना *sūcnā*[F]

**inherit, to** विरासत में पाना *virāsat mẽ pānā*[N]

**inheritance** विरासत *virāsat*[F]

**injection, to give** सूई लगाना *sūī lagānā*[N]

**injure, to** चोट पहुँचाना *coṭ pahũcānā*[N]

**injury** चोट *coṭ*[F]

**ink** स्याही *syāhī*[F]

**innocent** (free of guilt) निर्दोष *nirdoṣ*; (naive) भोला *bholā*, मासूम *māsūm* — an innocent child भोला-सा बच्चा *bholā-sā baccā*

**inquire, to** पूछना *pūchnā*[N] (of, से *se*); (to make inquiries) पूछताछ करना *pūchtāch karnā*[N] — let's inquire in the office हम दफ़्तर में पूछताछ करें *ham daftar mẽ pūchtāch karẽ*

**inquisitive** जिज्ञासु *jijñāsu* (pronounced 'jigyāsu')

**insect** कीड़ा *kīṛā*[M]

**inside** अन्दर *andar* — go inside अन्दर जाओ *andar jāo*; (inside something) के अन्दर — inside the house घर के अन्दर *ghar ke andar*

**insist, to** आग्रह करना *āgrah karnā*[N] (on, पर *par*) — we should insist on staying here हमें यहाँ रहने पर आग्रह करना चाहिए *hamẽ yahā̃ rahne par āgrah karnā cāhie*

**inspect, to** (का) निरीक्षण करना *(kā) nirīkṣaṇ karnā*[N] — the school will be inspected स्कूल का निरीक्षण किया जाएगा *skūl kā nirīkṣaṇ kiyā jāegā*

**inspiration** प्रेरणा *preraṇā*[F]

**inspire, to** प्रेरित करना *prerit karnā*[N]

**instalment** क़िस्त *qist*[F]

**instead of** के बजाय *ke bajāy* instead of going out let's eat at home बाहर जाने के बजाय हम घर पर ही खाना खाएँ *bāhar jāne ke bajāy ham ghar par hī khānā khāẽ*; (substituting one thing for another) की जगह *kī jagah* — we bought a car instead of a bicycle साइकिल की जगह हमने गाड़ी ख़रीदी *sāikil kī jagah hamne gāṛī <u>kh</u>arīdī*

**institution** संस्था *sansthā*[F] — a government institution सरकारी संस्था *sarkārī sansthā*

**instrument** (mechanical) औज़ार *auzār*[M]; (musical) वाद्य *vādya*[M]

**insult** (abuse) गाली *gālī*[F]; (disrespect) अपमान *apmān*[M]

**insult, to** गाली देना *gālī denā*[N] — they began insulting me वे मुझे गालियाँ देने लगे *ve mujhe gāliyā̃ dene lage*

**intellect** बुद्धि *buddhi*[F]

**intellectual** (adj. & noun) बुद्धिजीवी *buddhijīvī*[M]

**intelligent** होशियार *hośiyār*, ज़हीन *zahīn*

**intend:** see 'intention'

**intense** तीव्र *tīvra*

**intention** इरादा *irādā*[M]; I intend to go to India 💣 मुझे भारत जाने का इरादा है *mujhe bhārat jāne kā irādā hai*

**interest**[1] (curiosity) दिलचस्पी *dilcaspī*[F], रुचि *ruci*[F] — I'm very interested in history 💣 इतिहास में मेरी बहुत दिलचस्पी/ रुचि है *itihās mẽ merī bahut dilcaspī/ ruci hai*

**interest**[2] (financial) सूद *sūd*[M] — to pay interest सूद देना *sūd denā*[N]

**interested:** see 'interest'[1]

**interesting** दिलचस्प *dilcasp*, रोचक *rocak*

**interfere, to** दख़ल देना *dakhal denā*[N] — you shouldn't interfere in other people's work आपको दूसरों के काम में नहीं दख़ल देना चाहिए *āpko dūsrõ ke kām mẽ nahī̃ dakhal denā cāhie*

**interference** हस्तक्षेप *hastakṣep*[M]

**intermediate** माध्यमिक *mādhyamik*

**internal** अंदर का *andar kā,* आंतरिक *āntarik*

**international** अंतर्राष्ट्रीय *antarrāṣṭrīy*

**interrupt, to** (in speech) बात काटना *bāt kāṭnā*[N] — he keeps interrupting me वह मेरी बात काटता रहता है *vah merī bāt kāṭtā rahtā hai*

**interview** साक्षात्कार *sākṣātkār*[M]

**intimacy** आत्मीयता *ātmīytā*[F]

**intimate** घनिष्ठ *ghaniṣṭh,* आत्मीय *ātmīy*

**intimidate, to** डराना *ḍarānā*[N]

**intoxicated:** see 'drunk'

**intoxication** नशा *naśā*[M] — love is a kind of intoxication प्रेम एक प्रकार का नशा होता है *prem ek prakār kā naśā hotā hai*

**invisible** अदृश्य *adṛśya*

**invite, to** बुलाना *bulānā*[N] — we invited some friends for a meal हमने कुछ दोस्तों को खाना खाने बुलाया *hamne kuch dostõ ko khānā khāne bulāyā*; दावत देना *dāvat denā*[F] — Ramesh has invited us today रमेश ने आज हमें दावत दी है *rameś ne āj hamẽ dāvat dī hai*; (formal) निमंत्रण देना *nimantraṇ denā*[N]

**involve, to** (to include) शामिल करना *śāmil karnā*[N]

**iron**[1] (metal) लोहा *lohā*[M]

**iron**[2] (appliance) इस्तरी *istarī*[F]

**iron, to** इस्तरी करना *istarī karnā*[N]*,* प्रेस करना *pres karnā*[N]

**irritate, to** चिढ़ाना *ciṛhānā*[N]

**-ish** -सा *-sā* — biggish houses बड़े-से मकान *baṛe-se makān,* yellowish walls पीली-सी दीवारें *pīlī-sī dīvarẽ*

**Islam** इसलाम *islām*[M]

**island** टापू *ṭāpū*[M], द्वीप *dvīp*[M]

**it** वह *vah*

**itch** खुजली *khujlī*[F] — I've got an itch मुझे खुजली हो रही है *mujhe khujlī ho rahī hai*

**its** उसका *uskā*

**ivory** हाथी-दाँत *hāthī-dā̃t*[M]

## J

**jail** जेल *jel*[M] — I was sentenced to jail मुझे जेल की सज़ा दी गई *mujhe jel kī sazā dī gaī*

**January** जनवरी *janvarī*^F

**jaw** जबड़ा *jabṛā*^M

**jealous, to be** जलना *jalnā* – he's jealous of me वह मुझसे जलता है *vah mujhse jaltā hai*

**jealousy** ईर्ष्या *īrṣyā*^F, जलन *jalan*^F

**jewel** रत्न *ratna*^M

**jewellery** (item of) ज़ेवर *zevar*^M (plural: ज़ेवर *zevar* or ज़ेवरात *zevarāt*)

**job** (piece of work) काम *kām*^M – do these two or three jobs ये दो-तीन काम करो *ye do-tīn kām karo*; (employment) नौकरी *naukarī*^F – you'll get a good job तुम्हें अच्छी नौकरी मिलेगी *tumhẽ acchī naukarī milegī*

**join, to** (to fix together) जोड़ना *joṛnā*^N; (become member) सदस्य बनना *sadasya bannā* – I'll join Congress मैं कांग्रेस का सदस्य बनूँगा *maĩ kãgres kā sadasya banū̃gā*; (to take up a place) ज्वाइन करना *jvāin karnā*^N – I joined my new school मैंने अपना नया स्कूल ज्वाइन किया *maĩne apnā nayā skūl jvāin kiyā*

**joint family** संयुक्त परिवार *sãyukt parivār*^M

**joke** मज़ाक़ *mazāq*^M

**joke, to** मज़ाक़ करना *mazāq karnā*^N – you shouldn't joke about them तुम्हें उनके बारे में मज़ाक़ नहीं करना चाहिए *tumhẽ unke bāre mẽ mazāq nahī̃ karnā cāhie*

**journal** (magazine) पत्रिका *patrikā*^F; (diary) दैनिकी *dainikī*^F

**journalism** पत्रकारिता *patrakāritā*^F

**journalist** पत्रकार *patrakār*^M

**journey** सफ़र *safar*^M, यात्रा *yātrā*^F – during the journey सफ़र के दौरान *safar ke daurān*; *a* journey to/in the Himalayas हीमालय की यात्रा *hīmālay kī yātrā*

**joy** हर्ष *harṣ*^M

**joyfully** हर्ष से *harṣ se*

**juice** रस *ras*^M – orange juice संतरे का रस *santare kā ras*

**juicy** रसीला *rasīlā*

**July** जुलाई *julāī*^F

**jump, to** कूदना *kūdnā*; (to leap) छलाँग मारना *chalā̃g mārnā*^N – he/she leaped into the pond उसने तालाब में छलाँग मारी *usne tālāb mẽ chalā̃g mārī*; (to be startled) चौंकना *caũknā*, चौंक उठना *caũk uṭhnā* – they jumped up in surprise when they saw me मुझे देखकर वे चौंक उठे *mujhe dekhkar ve caũk uṭhe*

**June** जून *jūn*ᴹ

**jungle** जंगल *jaṅgal*ᴹ, वन *van*ᴹ

**Insight**

Jungle: this is one of the first Hindi words to have been assimilated into English. The Hindi adjective जंगली *janglī* means 'wild' (of animals) and 'boorish, crude' (of behaviour).

**just** (only) सिर्फ़ *sirf*; (exactly) ठीक *ṭhīk* — just below the line लकीर के ठीक नीचे *lakīr ke ṭhīk nīce*; ('just' do this and no more) ज़रा *zarā* — just wait/listen ज़रा ठहरो/सुनो *zarā ṭhahro/suno*; just now अभी-अभी *abhī-abhī*; just as (immediately as) जैसे ही *jaise hī* — just as I sat down जैसे ही मैं बैठ गया *jaise hī maĩ baiṭh gayā*; just as you like जैसा आप चाहें *jaisā āp cāhẽ*; just like that (for no particular purpose) ऐसे ही *aise hī*

# K

**keen** (eager) उत्सुक *utsuk*; to be keen on शौक़ होना *śauq honā* — I'm very keen on Indian music ✹ मुझे हिन्दुस्तानी संगीत का बहुत शौक़ है *mujhe hindustānī saṅgīt kā bahut śauq hai*

**keep, to** रखना *rakhnā*ᴺ; to keep on doing करता रहना *kartā rahnā* — they keep forgetting वे भूलते रहते हैं *ve bhūlte rahte haĩ*; to keep quiet चुप रहना *cup rahnā* — keep quiet! चुप रहो! *cup raho!*

**kerosene** मिट्टी का तेल *miṭṭī kā tel*ᶠ

**key** चाबी *cābī*ᶠ

**khadi** (homespun cloth) खादी *khādī*ᶠ

**kill, to** मारना *mārnā*ᴺ, मार देना/डालना *mār denā*ᴺ/*ḍālnā*ᴺ — they killed ten people उन्होंने दस लोगों को मार डाला *unhõne das logõ ko mār ḍālā*

**kind**[1] (gracious) दयालु *dayālu*, भला *bhalā* — he was very kind to me वह मुझपर बहुत दयालु था *vah mujhpar bahut dayālu thā*; it's very kind of you आपकी बड़ी मेहरबानी है *āpkī baṛī meharbānī hai*

**kind**[2] (sort) प्रकार *prakār*ᴹ, क़िस्म *qism*ᴹ, तरह *tarah*ᶠ — a kind of grass एक प्रकार की घास *ek prakār kī ghās*; many kinds of people तरह तरह के लोग *tarah tarah ke log*; what kind of man is your neighbour? आपका पड़ोसी किस क़िस्म का आदमी है? *āpkā paṛosī kis qism kā ādmī hai?*

**kindness** (abstract quality) दयालुता *dayālutā*$^{F}$, (kindness or act of kindness) मेहरबानी *meharbānī*$^{F}$

**king** राजा *raja*$^{M}$ — three kings तीन राजा *tīn rājā*

**kiss** चुंबन *cumban*$^{M}$

**kiss, to** चूमना *cūmnā*$^{N}$

**kitchen** रसोई *rasoī*$^{F}$, रसोईघर *rasoīghar*$^{M}$

**kite** (flying toy) पतंग *pataṅg*$^{M}$ — to fly a kite पतंग उड़ाना *pataṅg uṛānā*$^{N}$

**know, to** जानना *jānnā*$^{N}$, मालूम होना *mālūm honā* — they knew his name वे उसका नाम जानते थे *ve uskā nām jānte the,* 💣 उनको उसका नाम मालूम था *unko uskā nām mālūm thā*; do you know where the bank is? 💣 क्या आपको मालूम है कि बैंक किधर है? *kyā āpko mālūm hai ki baink kidhar hai?*; who knows? (rhetorical) कौन जाने? *kaun jāne?*; to know how to: see 'be able'

**knowledge** (practical) जानकारी *jānkārī*$^{F}$; (abstract, spiritual) ज्ञान *jñān* (pronounced 'gyān')$^{M}$

**kurta** (loose shirt) कुरता *kurtā*$^{M}$

**Insight**

Kite: kite flying is a highly popular competitive sport in India. The strings of the paper kites are rubbed with an abrasive paste to help cut the strings of rivals in flight.

**kite flying** पतंगबाज़ी *pataṅgbāzī*$^{F}$

**kitten** बिल्ली का बच्चा *billī kā baccā*$^{M}$

**knee** घुटना *ghuṭnā*$^{M}$

**kneel, to** घुटनों के बल बैठना *ghuṭnõ ke bal baiṭhnā*

**knife** (table knife) छुरी *churī*$^{F}$; (pocket knife) चाक़ू *cāqū*$^{M}$

**knot** गांठ *gā̃ṭh*$^{F}$

## L

**labour** (hard work) मेहनत *mehnat*$^{F}$, परिश्रम *pariśram*$^{M}$; (manual work) मज़दूरी *mazdūrī*$^{F}$

**labour, to** (to work as labourer) मज़दूरी करना *mazdūrī karnā*$^{N}$; (to toil) मेहनत/परिश्रम करना *mehnat/pariśram karnā*$^{N}$

**labourer** मज़दूर *mazdūr*$^{M}$

**lack** कमी *kamī*[F], अभाव[M] *abhāv* — a lack of time समय का अभाव *samay kā abhāv*

**ladder** सीढ़ी *sīṛhī*[F]

**laden, to be** लदना *ladnā* — the taxi was laden with luggage टैक्सी सामान से लदी हुई थी *ṭaiksī sāmān se ladī huī thī*

**lady** महिला *mahilā*[F]

**lake** झील *jhīl*[F]

**lakh** (100,000) लाख *lākh*[M] — lakhs of rupees लाखों रुपये *lākhõ rupaye*

**lame** लंगड़ा *lãgṛā*

**lamp** बत्ती *battī*[F] — the lamp is on बत्ती जल रही है *battī jal rahī hai*; (clay lamp) दीया *dīyā*[M]

**land** ज़मीन *zamīn*[F]

**landlord** (domestic) मकान-मालिक *makān-mālik*[M]; (landowner) ज़मींदार *zamī̃dār*[M]

**lane** (urban) गली *galī*[F]; (rural) रास्ता *rāstā*[M]

**language** भाषा *bhāṣā*[F]

**lap** गोद *god*[F] — the mother lifted the child into her lap माँ ने बच्चे को गोद में उठाया [उठा लिया] *mā̃ ne bacce ko god mẽ uṭhāyā [uṭhā liyā]*

**large** बड़ा *baṛā*

**last** (final) आख़िरी *ākhirī*, अन्तिम *antim* — today is our last day आज हमारा आख़िरी दिन है *āj hamārā ākhirī din hai*; (previous) पिछला *pichlā* — last week/year पिछले हफ़्ते/साल *pichle hafte/sāl*; last night (yesterday night) कल रात *kal rāt*

**last, to** (to endure) टिकना *ṭiknā* — this way of thinking won't last long यह सोचने का ढंग ज़्यादा देर नहीं टिकेगा *yah socne ka ḍhaṅg zyādā der nahī̃ ṭikegā*; चलना *calnā* — cheap cloth doesn't last long सस्ता कपड़ा ज़्यादा देर नहीं चलता *sastā kapṛā zyādā der nahī̃ caltā*

**lasting** टिकाऊ *ṭikāū*; (strong) मज़बूत *mazbūt*

**late** देर से *der se* — we'll arrive late हम देर से पहुँचेंगे *ham der se pahũcẽge*; we were late हमें देर हो गई *hamẽ der ho gaī*; (until a late hour) देर तक *der tak* — we'll work late हम देर तक काम करेंगे *ham der tak kām karẽge*; the late, deceased स्वर्गीय *svargīy*

**lately** हाल में *hāl mẽ*, इधर *idhar*

**later** बाद *bad* — three years later तीन साल बाद *tīn sāl bād*;

(later on) बाद में *bād mẽ* — think about this later इसके बारे में बाद में सोचना *iske bāre mẽ bād mẽ socnā*

**lathi** (stick, long truncheon) लाठी *lāṭhī*[F]

**laugh, to** हँसना *hãsnā*[n]; to burst out laughing हँस पड़ना *hãs paṛnā* — she burst out laughing वह हँस पड़ी *vah hãs paṛī*; to laugh at someone किसी पर हँसना *kisī par hãsnā*

**laughter** हँसी *hãsī*[F]

**lavatory** शौचालय *śaucālay*[M]

**law** क़ानून *qānūn*[M]; (rule) नियम *niyam*[M]

**lawyer** वकील *vakīl*[M]

**layer** परत *parat*[F]

**lazy** आलसी *ālsī*; (lethargic) सुस्त *sust*

**leader**[1] (politician) नेता *netā*[M] — three important leaders तीन बड़े बड़े नेता *tīn baṛe baṛe netā*

**leader**[2] (editorial essay) संपादकीय *sampādakīy*[M]

**leaf** पत्ता *pattā*[M]

**lean** (thin) दुबला-पतला *dublā-patlā*

**lean, to** झुकना *jhuknā*

**leap, to** कूदना *kūdnā*

**learn, to** सीखना *sīkhnā*[N] — what did you learn today? आज तुमने क्या सीखा? *āj tumne kyā sīkhā?*; to learn a lesson सबक़ सीखना *sabaq sīkhnā*[N]; (to study) पढ़ना *paṛhnā*

**least** सबसे कम *sabse kam*; the least clever boy सबसे कम होशियार लड़का *sabse kam hośiyār laṛkā*; at least कम से कम *kam se kam* — for at least ten years कम से कम दस साल तक *kam se kam das sāl tak*

**leather** चमड़ा *camṛā*[M]; (made) of leather चमड़े का *camṛe kā* — a real leather shoe असली चमड़े का जूता *aslī camṛe kā jūtā*

**leave** (time off work) छुट्टी *chuṭṭī*[F] — you should take one month's leave आपको एक महीने की छुट्टी लेनी चाहिए *āpko ek mahīne kī chuṭṭī lenī cāhie*

**leave, to** (to abandon, quit) छोड़ना *choṛnā*[N] — I left my job मैंने अपनी नौकरी को छोड़ा [छोड़ दिया] *maĩne apnī naukrī ko choṛā [choṛ diyā]*; (to go away) चला जाना *calā jānā* — he left just like that वह ऐसे ही चला गया *vah aise hī calā gayā*; (to set off) चलना *calnā* — we left at two हम दो बजे चले *ham* *do baje cale*; (formal) प्रस्थान करना *prasthān karnā*$^{N}$ – the minister left at three मंत्री जी ने तीन बजे प्रस्थान किया *mantrī jī ne tīn baje prasthān kiyā*; may I leave?, please let me leave आज्ञा/इजाज़त दीजिए *ājñā/ ijāzat dījie* (*ājñā* is pronounced 'āgyā'); to leave behind (by mistake), use 'to be left behind', छूट जाना *chūṭ jānā* – I left my coat in the hotel 💣 मेरा कोट होटल में छूट गया *merā koṭ hoṭal mẽ chūṭ gayā*

**lecture** भाषण *bhāṣaṇ*$^{M}$

**lecturer** (college teacher) प्राध्यापक *prādhyāpak;* (speaker) वक्ता *vaktā*$^{M}$

**left**$^{1}$ (opposite of right) बायाँ *bāyā̃* – turn left बायें मुड़ना *bāyẽ muṛnā*

**left**$^{2}$ (remaining) बाक़ी *bāqī* – how much money is left? कितना पैसा बाक़ी है? *kitnā paisā bāqī hai?*; to be left behind: see 'leave'

**leg** टाँग *ṭā̃g*$^{F}$; (of journey) पड़ाव *paṛāv*$^{M}$

**legacy** (bequest) वसीयत *vasīyat*$^{F}$

**legend** दंतकथा *dantkathā*$^{F}$

**leisure** फ़ुरसत *fursat*$^{F}$ – leisure time फ़ुरसत का समय *fursat kā samay* – how do you spend your leisure time? आप अपना फ़ुरसत का समय कैसे गुज़ारते हैं? *āp apnā fursat kā samay kaise guzārte haĩ?*; I'm not free at the moment 💣 अभी मुझे फ़ुरसत नहीं है *abhī mujhe fursat nahī̃ hai*

**lemon** निंबू *nimbū*$^{M}$

**lend, to** उधार देना *udhār denā*$^{N}$ – please lend me a thousand rupees मुझे हज़ार रुपये उधार दीजिए *mujhe hazār rupaye udhār dījie*

**length** लंबाई *lambāī*$^{F}$

**lentil(s)** दाल *dāl*$^{F}$

**leopard** चीता *cītā*$^{M}$

**leper** कोढ़ी *koṛhī*$^{M}$

**leprosy** कोढ़ *koṛh*$^{M}$

**Lesbian** (adj.) समलिंगी *samliṅgī*; (noun) समलिंगी स्त्री *samliṅgī strī*$^{F}$

**less** कम *kam*; much less बहुत कम *bahut kam*; even less और भी कम *aur bhī kam*; less than this इससे कम *isse kam*; less than before पहले से कम *pahle se kam*; less expensive कम महँगा *kam mahā̃gā*

**lessen, to** कम करना *kam karnā*$^{N}$

**lesson** सबक़ *sabaq*$^{M}$ – to learn a lesson सबक़ सीखना *sabaq sīkhnā*$^{N}$; (part of book or course) पाठ *pāṭh*$^{M}$

**let** see 'rent', 'allow'; let alone (leave out of consideration) तो दूर *to dūr* — I don't even know English, let alone German जर्मन तो दूर, मैं तो अँग्रेज़ी भी नहीं जानता *jarman to dūr, maĩ to ãgrezī bhī nahī̃ jāntā*

**lethargic** सुस्त *sust*

**lethargy** सुस्ती *sustī*$^{F}$

**letter**[1] (correspondence) ख़त *khat*$^{M}$, पत्र *patra*$^{M}$, चिट्ठी *ciṭṭhī*$^{F}$

**letter**[2] (of alphabet) अक्षर *akṣar*$^{M}$

**life** ज़िन्दगी *zindagī*$^{F}$, जीवन *jīvan*$^{M}$; (one of a succession of lives/births) जन्म *janma*$^{M}$ — in my previous/next life मेरे पिछले/अगले जन्म में *mere pichle/agle janma mẽ*; (liveliness of spirit) दम *dam*$^{M}$ — there's no life in this poem! इस कविता में दम नहीं है! *is kavitā mẽ dam nahī̃ hai!*

**Insight**

Letter: the word अक्षर *akṣar* alludes to the 'irreducible' aspect of a syllable, stressing the fact that Devanagari is a syllabic script.

**library** लाइब्रेरी *lāibrerī*$^{F}$, पुस्तकालय *pustakālay*$^{M}$

**lick, to** चाटना *cāṭnā*$^{N}$

**lid** ढक्कन *ḍhakkan*$^{M}$

**lie** झूठ *jhūṭh*$^{M}$; to tell a lie झूठ बोलना *jhūṭh bolnā*$^{N}$; you shouldn't lie तुम्हें झूठ नहीं बोलना चाहिए *tumhẽ jhūṭh nahī̃ bolnā cāhie*

**lie, to** (to recline), लेटना *leṭnā*; to lie down लेट जाना — we lay down on the ground हम ज़मीन पर लेट गए *ham zamīn par leṭ gae*; lie down! लेट जाओ! *leṭ jāo!*; (to rest on something) पड़ना *paṛnā* — your clothes are lying on the big chair तुम्हारे कपड़े बड़ी कुरसी पर पड़े हुए हैं *tumhāre kapṛe baṛī kursī par paṛe hue haĩ*

**lift, to** उठाना *uṭhānā*$^{N}$

**light**[1] (in weight or colour) हलका *halkā* — you should eat light food only आपको हलका खाना ही खाना चाहिए *āpko halkā khānā hī khānā cāhie*

**light**[2] (lamp) बत्ती *battī*$^{F}$ — the lights are on बत्तियाँ जल रही हैं *battiyā̃ jal rahī haĩ*; put the light on/off बत्ती को जलाओ/बुझाओ *battī ko jalāo/bujhāo*

**light, to** (to set alight) जलाना *jalānā*$^{N}$

**lightning** बिजली *bijlī*$^{F}$ — lightning flashes, clouds thunder बिजली कौंधती है, बादल गरजते हैं *bijlī kaũdhtī hai, bādal garajte haĩ*

**like** (similar to) जैसा *jaisā* – what could be done about people like them? उन जैसे लोगों के बारे में क्या किया जाए? *un jaise logõ ke bāre mẽ kyā kiyā jāe?*; (adv.) की तरह *kī tarah* — he speaks like you वह आपकी तरह बोलता है *vah āpkī tarah boltā hai*; like this इस तरह *is tarah*

**like, to** पसंद होना *pasand honā* ('to be liked') — I like old films ◆ मुझे पुरानी फ़िल्में पसंद हैं *mujhe purānī filmẽ pasand haĩ*; (with a specific item in past or future tense) पसंद आना *pasand ānā* — I liked your new film ◆ मुझे अपकी नई फ़िल्म पसंद आई *mujhe āpkī naī film pasand āī*; (to have as a hobby) शौक़ होना *śauq honā* — I like singing ◆ मुझे गाने का शौक़ है *mujhe gāne kā śauq hai*

**likeness** समानता *samāntā*[F]

**limb** अंग *aṅg*[M]

**limit** सीमा *sīmā*[F], हद *had*[F]

**limit, to** सीमित करना *sīmit karnā*[N]

**line** (mark) रेखा *rekhā*[F] — lines on the face/hand चेहरे/हाथ की रेखाएँ *cehre/hāth kī rekhāẽ*; (row) पंक्ति *paṅkti*[F] — a line of birds पक्षियों की पंक्ति *pakṣiyõ kī paṅkti*; (queue) लाइन *lāin*[F] — we were standing in line हम लाइन में खड़े थे *ham lāin mẽ khaṛe the*

**link** (in chain) कड़ी *kaṛī*[F]; (contact) संपर्क *sampark*[M]

**link, to** (intr., to be linked) जुड़ना *juṛnā*; (tr.) जोड़ना *joṛnā*[N]

**lion** शेर *śer*[M], सिंह *sĩh*[M]

**lip** होंठ *hõṭh*[M]

**liquid** (adj.) द्रव; (liquid substance) द्रव पदार्थ *drav padārth*[M]

**list** सूची *sūcī*[F]

**listen, to** सुनना *sunnā*[N] — please listen carefully ध्यान से सुनिए *dhyān se sunie*; listen to me मेरी बात सुनिए *merī bāt sunie;* listen to the music संगीत को सुनिए *saṅgīt ko sunie*

**literacy** साक्षरता *sākṣartā*[F]

**literary** साहित्यिक *sāhityik*

**literate** पढ़ा-लिखा *paṛhā-likhā,* साक्षर *sākṣar*

**literature** साहित्य *sāhitya*[M]

**little** छोटा *choṭā*; a little थोड़ा *thoṛā*, थोड़ा-सा *thoṛā-sā* — a little more ghee थोड़ा और घी *thoṛā aur ghī*

**live, to**[1] (to reside) रहना *rahnā* — I live in London मैं लंदन में रहता हूँ *maĩ landan mẽ rahtā hū̃*

**live, to**[2] (to be alive) जीना *jīnā* — we live and die हम जीते हैं और मरते हैं *ham jīte haĩ aur marte haĩ*

**liveliness:** see 'life'

**load, to** लादना *lādnā*[N] — load all the luggage into the car सारे सामान को कार में लादना *sāre sāmān ko kār mẽ lādnā*

**loaded, to be** लदना *ladnā*

**loan** उधार *udhār*[M]

**local** स्थानीय *sthānīy* — a local newspaper स्थानीय अख़बार *sthānīy a<u>kh</u>bār*

**lock** ताला *tālā*[M]

**lock, to** ताले से बंद करना *tāle se band karnā*[N], ताला लगाना *tālā lagānā*[N] — did you lock the room? क्या तुमने कमरे में ताला लगाया? *kyā tumne kamre mẽ tālā lagāyā?*

**logic** तर्क *tark*[M]; (science of logic) तर्कशास्त्र *tarkśāstra*[M]

**logical** तर्कसंगत *tarksaṅgat*

**loneliness** अकेलापन *akelāpan*[M]

**lonely** (alone) अकेला *akelā*; (deserted) वीरान *vīrān* — a lonely road वीरान सड़क *vīrān saṛak;* to feel lonely अकेलापन महसूस करना *akelāpan mahsūs karnā*[N] — Grandmother feels lonely दादीजी अकेलापन महसूस करती हैं *dādījī akelāpan mahsūs kartī haĩ*

**long** लंबा *lambā*; for a long time लंबे अरसे से/तक *lambe arse se/tak*; as long as (in time sense): see 'until'

**long, to** लालसा होना *lālsā honā*; — I long to go home मुझे घर जाने की लालसा है *mujhe ghar jāne kī lālsā hai*

**longing** लालसा *lālsā*[F]

**look, to** देखना *dekhnā*[N]; to look at someone किसी की तरफ़ देखना *kisī kī taraf dekhnā*[N] — look at me मेरी तरफ़ देखो *merī taraf dekho*; to have a look देख लेना *dekh lenā*[N]; to look like मिलना-जुलना *milnā-julnā* — she looks a lot like you वह तुमसे बहुत मिलती-जुलती है *vah tumse bahut miltī-jultī hai*; (to seem) लगना *lagnā* — she looks rather ill वह बीमार-सी लगती है *vah bīmār-sī lagtī hai*; to look for: see 'search for'

**loose** ढीला *ḍhīlā* — loose clothes ढीले कपड़े *ḍhīle kapṛe*; (untied) खुला *khulā*

**loosen, to** ढीला करना *ḍhīlā karnā*[N]; (to untie) खोलना *kholnā*[N]

**lose, to** (to be defeated) हारना *hārnā*[N] – she won, I lost वह जीत गई, मैं हार गया *vah jīt gaī, maī̃ hār gayā*; (to lose possession of) खोना *khonā*[N], खो देना *kho denā*[N] – I lost my purse मैंने अपना बटुआ खो दिया *maī̃ne apnā baṭuā kho diyā*; (to lose, misplace: see 'to be misplaced'); to lose weight वज़न घटाना *vazan ghaṭānā*[N], वज़न कम करना *vazan kam karnā*[N] – you should lose weight 💣 तुमको अपना वज़न घटाना चाहिए *tumko apnā vazan ghaṭānā cāhie*

**loss** नुक़सान *nuqsān*[M] – they had a big (financial) loss 💣 उन्हें (पैसे का) भारी नुक़सान हुआ *unhẽ (paise ka) bhārī nuqsān huā*

**lost** खोया हुआ *khoyā huā*; (missing) गुम *gum*; (of unknown whereabouts) लापता *lāpatā* (-*ā* invariable)

**lots of** बहुत-सा *bahut-sā*, बहुत-सारा *bahut-sārā* – we'll invite lots of friends हम बहुत-सारे दोस्तों को बुलाएँगे *ham bahut-sāre dostõ ko bulāẽge*

**lotus** कमल *kamal*[M]

**loud** (of voice) ऊँचा *ū̃cā*; (of noise) ज़ोर का *zor kā*

**loudly** ज़ोर से *zor se* – speak loudly! ज़ोर से बोलो! *zor se bolo!*

**love** प्यार *pyār*[M], प्रेम *prem*[M], मुहब्बत *muhabbat*[F]; to love प्यार होना *pyār hona,* प्यार करना *pyār karnā*[N] (person loved takes से *se*) – she loves you 💣 उसे तुमसे प्यार है *use tumse pyār hai,* वह तुमसे प्यार करती है *vah tumse pyār kartī hai*; I fell in love with him/her 💣 मुझे उससे प्यार हो गया *mujhe usse pyār ho gayā*

**lover** प्रेमी *premī*[M]

**low** नीचा *nīcā*; (quiet, as of voice) मंद *mand*

**luck** (fortune) भाग्य *bhāgya*[M]; (fate) नियति *niyati*[F]

**luggage** सामान *sāmān*[M]

**lumber** (timber) लकड़ी *lakṛī*[F]

**lunch** दोपहर का खाना *dopahar kā khānā*[M]

**lung** फेफड़ा *phephṛā*[M]

**lure, to** लुभाना *lubhānā*[N]

**luxury** ऐश *aiś*[M] – to live in luxury ऐश से जीना *aiś se jīnā*

**lying** (placed on something) पड़ा हुआ *paṛā huā* – your book is lying on the table आपकी किताब मेज़ पर पड़ी हुई है *āpkī kitāb mez par paṛī huī hai*; (lying down, reclining) लेटा हुआ *leṭā huā* — she was lying on the grass वह घास पर लेटी हुई थी *vah ghās par leṭī huī thī*

## M

**machine** मशीन *maśīn*^F^ — washing machine कपड़े धोने की मशीन *kapṛe dhone kī maśīn*

**mad** पागल *pāgal*

**made, to be** बनना *bannā* — where are saris made? साड़ियाँ कहाँ बनती हैं? *sāṛiyā̃ kahā̃ bantī haĩ?*; what's this toy made of? यह खिलौना किस चीज़ का बना हुआ है? *yah khilaunā kis cīz kā banā huā hai?*; ready made बना-बनाया *banā-banāyā* — ready-made clothes बने-बनाए कपड़े *bane-banāe kapṛe*

**magazine** पत्रिका *patrikā*^F^

**magic** जादू *jādū*^M^

**magical** जादुई *jāduī*

**magician** जादूगर *jādūgar*^M^

**magnificent** शानदार *śāndār*

**mail** डाक *ḍāk*^F^

**mail, to** डाक से भेजना *ḍāk se bhejnā*^N^

**main** मुख्य *mukhya*, प्रमुख *pramukh*

**maintain, to** बनाए रखना *banāe rakhnā*^N^ — maintain your connection with them उनसे अपना संबंध बनाए रखना *unse apnā sambandh banāe rakhnā*

**make, to** बनाना *banānā*^N^; to make noise, rumpus शोर मचाना *śor macānā*^N^; to make time समय निकालना *samay nikālnā*^N^ — please make a little time for me too मेरे लिए भी थोड़ा समय निकालिए *mere lie bhī thoṛā samay nikālie*

**make-do** काम-चलाऊ *kām-calāū*

**malaria** मलेरिया *maleriyā*^M^

**male** मर्द *mard* — male animal मर्द जानवर *mard jānvar*

**man** आदमी *ādmī*^M^; (human being) इनसान *insān*^M^, मनुष्य *manuṣya*^M^; (one who does a job, e.g. 'postman') -वाला *-vālā*^M^ (often follows oblique noun, as in रिक्शेवाला *rikśevālā* rickshaw man)

**manage, to** (to take care of) संभालना *sambhālnā*^N^ — you manage this work yourself यह काम तुम ख़ुद संभालो *yah kām tum khud sambhālo*; to manage to do: use verb stem + पाना *pānā* (no ने *ne* construction) — my sister didn't manage to finish her work मेरी बहिन अपना काम ख़त्म नहीं कर पाई *merī bahin apnā kām khatm nahī̃ kar pāī*

**manager** मैनेजर *mainejar*[M], संचालक *sancālak*[M]

**mango** आम *ām*[M]

**manner** (method) ढंग *ḍhaṅg*[M] — in this manner इस ढंग से *is ḍhaṅg se*

**manners** आचरण *ācaraṇ*[M]

**many** बहुत *bahut*, बहुत-से *bahut-se*

**marble** संगमर्मर *saṅgmarmar*[M]

**March** मार्च *mārc*[M]

**marital** वैवाहिक *vaivāhik*

**mark** (imprint, indication) निशान *niśān*[M]; (blot, stain) धब्बा *dhabbā*[M]; (number, score) अंक *aṅk*[M] — he/she has got good marks 💣 उसे अच्छे अंक मिले हैं *use acche aṅk mile haĩ*; (sign) चिह्न *cihn*[M]

**market** बाज़ार *bāzār*[M]

**marriage** शादी *śādī*[F], विवाह *vivāh*[M]

**married** शादी-शुदा *śādī-śudā* (-*ā* invariable) — is your sister married? क्या आपकी बहिन शादी-शुदा है? *kyā āpkī bahin śādī-śudā hai?*

**marry, to** शादी करना *śādī karnā*[N] (partner takes से *se*) — he married Savitri उसने सावित्री से शादी की *usne sāvitrī se śādī kī*; शादी होना *śādī honā* — he married Savitri 💣 उसकी शादी सावित्री से हुई *uskī śādī sāvitrī se huī*; (to marry off, cause to marry) शादी कराना[N] *śādī karānā* — we married our daughter to Sohan हमने अपनी बेटी की शादी सोहन से कराई [करा दी] *hamne apnī beṭī kī śādī sohan se karāī [karā dī]*

**martyr** शहीद *śahīd*[M]

**masculine** (in grammar) पुल्लिंग *pulliṅg*

**match**[1] (matchstick) दीयासलाई *dīyāsalāī*[F], माचिस *mācis*[M]

**match**[2] (sport event) मैच *maic*[F]

**material**[1] (adj. 'physical') भौतिक *bhautik*

**material**[2] (cloth) कपड़ा *kapṛā*[M]; (goods) सामान *sāmān*[M]; (ingredients, data) सामग्री *sāmagrī*[F]

**mathematics** गणित *gaṇit*[M]

**matter** (problem, issue) बात *bāt*[F] — what's the matter?

क्या बात है? *kyā bāt hai?*; it doesn't matter कोई बात नहीं *koī bāt nahī̃*; (topic, question) मामला *māmlā*ᴹ — Father's a traditionalist in the matter of marriage शादी के मामले में पिताजी परंपरावादी हैं *śādī ke māmle mē̃ pitājī paramparā-vādī haĩ*

**mattress** गद्दा *gaddā*ᴹ

**may** (have permission to): see 'able'; for 'perhaps' sense use शायद *śāyad* + subjunctive verb — perhaps I may go too शायद मैं भी जाऊँ *śāyad maĩ bhī jāū̃*

**May** मई *maī*ꟳ

**maybe** शायद *śāyad*

**meal** खाना *khānā*ᴹ — evening meal रात का खाना *rāt kā khānā*; to prepare a meal खाना तैयार करना *khānā taiyār karnā*ᴺ

**mean** (miserly) कंजूस *kanjūs* — he's a very mean man वह बड़ा कंजूस आदमी है *vah baṛā kanjūs ādmī hai*

**mean, to** (to indicate): see 'meaning'; (to do intentionally) जान-बूझकर करना *jān-būjhkar karnā*ᴺ — I didn't mean to hit him/her मैंने उसे जान-बूझकर तो नहीं मारा *maĩne use jān-būjhkar to nahī̃ mārā*

**meaning** मतलब *matlab*ᴹ, अर्थ *arth*ᴹ — what does this sentence mean? ☛ इस वाक्य का अर्थ क्या है? *is vākya kā arth kyā hai?*

**meaningful** सार्थक *sārthak*

**means** साधन *sādhan*ᴹ (used in plural) — I don't have the means to build a house ☛ मेरे पास घर बनाने के साधन नहीं हैं *mere pās ghar banāne ke sādhan nahī̃ haĩ*; by means of के द्वारा *ke dvārā*

**Insight**

Maybe: a clause containing the word शायद *śāyad* is very likely to feature a subjunctive verb as further indication of inherent 'uncertainty'.

**meanwhile** इस बीच (में) *is bīc (mē̃)*; in the meantime फ़िलहाल *filhāl*

**measure, to** नापना *nāpnā*ᴺ — I measured the length of the cloth मैंने कपड़े की लंबाई नापी [नाप ली] *maĩne kapṛe kī lambāī nāpī [nāp lī]*

**measurement** नाप *nāp*ꟳ

**meat** गोश्त *gośt*ᴹ, माँस *mā̃s*ᴹ

**mechanic** मिस्तरी *mistarī*$^{M}$

**medicine** दवा *davā*$^{F}$ — I've taken the medicine मैंने दवा खाई है *maĩne davā khāī hai*; (medical practice or profession) डाक्टरी *ḍākṭarī*$^{F}$ — my daughter wants to practise medicine मेरी बेटी डाक्टरी करना चाहती है *merī beṭī ḍākṭarī karnā cāhtī hai*

**medieval** मध्यकालीन *madhyakālīn*

**meditation** समाधि *samādhi*$^{F}$; to meditate समाधि लगाना$^{N}$ *samādhi lagānā*

**medium**$^{1}$ (adj.) मँझला *mãjhlā* — a girl of medium height मँझले क़द की लड़की *mãjhle qad kī laṛkī*

**medium**$^{2}$ (noun) माध्यम *mādhyam*$^{M}$

**meet, to** मिलना *milnā* — I'll meet them today मैं उनसे आज ही मिलूँगा *maĩ unse āj hī milū̃gā*; I met (chanced to meet) Uma yesterday कल मुझे उमा मिली *kal mujhe umā milī*

**meeting** (encounter) मुलाक़ात *mulāqāt*$^{F}$ — our first meeting happened in Jaipur हमारी पहली मुलाक़ात जयपुर में हुई थी *hamārī pahlī mulāqāt jaypur mẽ huī thī*; (assembly, gathering) मीटिंग *mīṭiṅg*$^{F}$ — we're going to the meeting हम मीटिंग में जा रहे हैं *ham mīṭiṅg mẽ jā rahe haĩ*

**melon** (water melon) तरबूज़ *tarbūz*$^{M}$

**melt, to** पिघलना *pighalnā*; (to dissolve) घुलना *ghulnā*

**member** सदस्य *sadasya*$^{M}$

**membership** सदस्यता *sadasyatā*$^{F}$

**memorial** (monument) स्मारक *smārak*$^{M}$

**memory** याद *yād*$^{F}$, स्मृति *smṛti*$^{F}$ — childhood memories बचपन की यादें *bacpan kī yādẽ*; in memory of Bapu बापू की स्मृति में *bāpū kī smṛti mẽ*; (power of memory) याददाश्त *yāddāśt*$^{F}$ — my memory is quite sharp मेरी याददाश्त काफ़ी तेज़ है *merī yāddāśt kāfī tez hai*

**mend, to** ठीक करना *ṭhīk karnā*$^{N}$, की मरम्मत करना *kī marammat karnā*$^{N}$ — I mended my bicycle मैंने अपनी साइकिल की मरम्मत की [कर ली] *maĩne apnī sāikil kī marammat kī [kar lī]*

**mental** मानसिक *mānsik*

**mention** चर्चा *carcā*$^{F}$, ज़िक्र *zikra*$^{M}$; to mention की चर्चा करना *kī carcā karnā*$^{N}$, का ज़िक्र करना

*kā zikra karnā*ᴺ — don't mention the war! युद्ध का ज़िक्र मत करना! *yuddh kā zikra mat karnā!*

**message** संदेश *sandeś*ᴹ — I got your message ☞ मुझे आपका संदेश मिला *mujhe āpkā sandeś milā*

**metal** लोहा *lohā*ᴹ (lit. 'iron') — metal box लोहे का बक्सा *lohe kā baksā*

**metre**[1] (100 cm) मीटर *mīṭar*ᴹ

**metre**[2] (in prosody) छंद *chand*ᴹ

**method** तरीक़ा *tarīqā*ᴹ, प्रणाली *praṇālī*ᶠ, विधि *vidhi*ᶠ

**microphone** माइक *māik*ᴹ

**middle** बीच *bīc*ᴹ; (centre) केन्द्र *kendra*ᴹ; (adj., the middle one) बीचवाला *bīcvālā* — I like the middle picture ☞ मुझे बीचवाली तस्वीर पसंद है *mujhe bīcvālī tasvīr pasand hai*; in the middle (of) (के) बीच में *(ke) bīc mẽ* — I was standing in the middle of the crowd मैं भीड़ के बीच में खड़ा था *maĩ bhīṛ ke bīc mẽ khaṛā thā*

**middle aged** अधेड़ *adheṛ*

**middle class** (adj.) मध्यवर्गीय *madhyavargīy*; (noun) मध्य वर्ग *madhya varg*ᴹ

**midnight** आधी रात *ādhī rāt*ᶠ

**midwife** दाई *dāī*ᶠ

**might** (often expressed by a subjunctive verb — he might burst into tears वह शायद रो पड़े *vah śāyad ro paṛe*)

**milk** दूध *dūdh*ᴹ

**Milky Way** आकाश गंगा *ākāś gaṅgā*ᶠ

**million** दस लाख *das lākh*

**millionaire** लखपति *lakhpati*ᴹ, करोड़पति *karoṛpati*ᴹ

**minaret** मीनार *mīnār*ᶠ

**mind** (intellect) बुद्धि *buddhi*ᶠ — your mind is very sharp तुम्हारी बुद्धि बहुत तेज़ है *tumhārī buddhi bahut tez hai*; (abode of intellect) मन *man*ᴹ — various kinds of thought were coming to my mind मेरे मन में तरह तरह के विचार आ रहे थे *mere man mẽ tarah tarah ke vicār ā rahe the*

**mind, to** (to look after) (की) देखभाल करना *kī dekhbhāl karnā*ᴺ; (to take offence) बुरा मानना *burā mānnā*ᴺ

**mine**[1] (possessive) मेरा *merā*

**mine**[2] (quarry) खान *khān*ᶠ

**minister** (govt.) मंत्री *mantrī*ᴹ

**ministry** (govt.) मंत्रालय *mantrālay*ᴹ

**minute**[1] (tiny) बहुत छोटा *bahut choṭā*

**minute**[2] (60 seconds) मिनट *minaṭ*[M]

**mirror** शीशा *śīśā*[M], आइना *āinā*[M]

**mischief** शैतानी *śaitānī*[F]

**mischievous** शैतान *śaitān*, नटखट *naṭkhaṭ*

**misconception** भ्रांति *bhrānti*[F]

**misplaced, to be** खो जाना *kho jānā* (intr.) — I've lost my watch मेरी घड़ी खो गई है *merī ghaṛī kho gaī hai*

**miss, to** (an aim, opportunity) चूकना *cūknā,* चूक जाना *cūk jānā* ('to be missed') — the opportunity was missed मौक़ा चूक गया *mauqā cūk gayā,* (to feel absence of) याद आना *yād ānā* — I miss you a lot मुझे तुम्हारी याद बहुत आती है *mujhe tumhārī yād bahut ātī hai*; मिस करना *mis karnā*[N] — she misses you a lot वह तुम्हें बहुत मिस करती है *vah tumhẽ bahut mis kartī hai*

**mistake** ग़लती *ġaltī*[F]; by mistake ग़लती से *ġaltī se*; to make a mistake ग़लती करना *ġaltī karnā*[N]; I made a big mistake मैंने बड़ी ग़लती की *maĩne baṛī ġaltī kī,* मुझसे बड़ी ग़लती हुई [हो गई] *mujhse baṛī ġaltī huī [ho gaī]*

**mix, to** (intr.) मिलना *milnā*; (to socialize) मिलना-जुलना *milnā-julnā*; (tr.) मिलाना *milānā*[N] — mix the salt and the flour नमक और आटे को मिलाना *namak aur āṭe ko milānā*

**mock, to** हँसी उड़ाना *hãsī uṛānā*[N] — you're mocking me तुम मेरी हँसी उड़ा रही हो *tum merī hãsī uṛā rahī ho*

**modern** आधुनिक *ādhunik*

**modernity** आधुनिकता *ādhuniktā*[F]

**modernization** आधुनिकीकरण *ādhunikīkaraṇ*[M]

**modest** (of temperament) विनम्र *vinamra*; (trivial) लघु *laghu* — a modest endeavour लघु प्रयास *laghu prayās*[M]

**moment** पल *pal*[M], क्षण *kṣaṇ*[M]; at the moment अभी *abhī*; at that very moment तभी *tabhī*, उसी क्षण *usī kṣaṇ*; wait a moment एक मिनट ठहरो *ek minaṭ ṭhahro*

**Monday** सोमवार *somvār*[M]

**money** पैसा *paisā*[M]

**monkey** बंदर *bandar*[M]; (langur, long-tailed species) लंगूर *laṅgūr*[M]

**monsoon** (season) बरसात का मौसम^M *barsāt kā mausam*; in the monsoon बरसात में *barsāt mẽ*

**month** महीना *mahīnā*^M – three months later तीन महीने बाद *tīn mahīne bād*; last/next month पिछले/अगले महीने *pichle/agle mahīne*

**monument** (memorial) स्मारक *smārak*^M

**mood** मिज़ाज़ *mizāz*^M – he/she's in a bad mood 💣 उसका मिज़ाज़ बिगड़ा हुआ है *uskā mizāz bigaṛā huā hai*

**moon** चाँद *cā̃d*^M, चन्द्र *candra*^M

**moonlight** चाँदनी *cā̃dnī* – a moonlit night चाँदनी रात *cā̃ndnī rāt*

**mop, to** पोंछना *põchnā*^N

**moral** नैतिक *naitik*

**morality** नैतिकता *naitiktā*^F

**more** (comparative) और *aur*, ज़्यादा *zyādā*, अधिक *adhik* – more expensive than this इससे (ज़्यादा) महँगा *isse (zyādā) mahā̃gā*; (additional) और *aur* – have some more! और लीजिए! *aur lījie!*; we need more money 💣 हमको और पैसा चाहिए *hamko aur paisā cāhie*

**morning** सुबह *subah*^F – we arrived yesterday morning हम कल सुबह पहुँचे *ham kal subah pahũce*

**mosque** मसजिद *masjid*^F

**mosquito** मच्छर *macchar*^M

**mosquito net** मच्छरदानी *macchardānī*^F

**most** (superlative) सबसे *sabse* + adj. – the most expensive car सबसे महँगी गाड़ी *sabse mahā̃gī gāṛī*; (majority of ) ज़्यादातर *zyādātar* – most people ज़्यादातर लोग *zyādātar log*

**mostly** ज़्यादातर *zyādātar* – we mostly stay at home हम ज़्यादातर घर पर ही रहते हैं *ham zyādātar ghar par hī rahte haĩ*

**moth** पतंगा *pataṅgā*^M

**mother** माता *mātā*^F; (less formal) माँ *mā̃*^F

**mother-in-law** सास *sās*^F

**mother tongue** मातृभाषा *mātṛbhāṣā*^F

**motive** (aim) प्रयोजन *prayojan*^M

**mountain** पहाड़ *pahāṛ*^M

**mountainous** पहाड़ी *pahāṛī*

**mouse** चूहा *cūhā*^M; (for computer) माउस *māus*^M

**mouth** मुँह *mũh*^M, मुख *mukh*^M (both words also mean 'face')

**move, to** (to wobble, budge) हिलना *hilnā* – the luggage won't move सामान नहीं हिलेगा *sāmān nahī̃ hilegā*; (to be on the move) चलना *calnā* – the train was moving slowly गाड़ी धीरे धीरे चल रही थी *gāṛī dhīre dhīre cal rahī thī*; to move house घर बदलना *ghar badalnā*[N], शिफ़्ट करना *śifṭ karnā*[N] – we're moving house हम घर बदल रहे हैं *ham ghar badal rahe haĩ*, हम शिफ़्ट कर रहे हैं *ham śifṭ kar rahe haĩ*; to move away/aside (intr.) हटना *haṭnā* – the car moved out of the way गाड़ी हट गई *gāṛī haṭ gaī*; (tr.) हटाना *haṭānā*[N] – move the car away! गाड़ी को हटाओ [हटा दो]! *gāṛī ko haṭāo [haṭā do]!*

**movement** (social etc.) आंदोलन *āndolan*[M]; to start a movement आंदोलन चलाना *āndolan calānā*[N]

**Mr** श्री *śrī*; जी *jī* (after name) – Mr Khanna श्री खन्ना *śrī khannā*, खन्ना जी *khannā jī*

**Mrs** श्रीमती *śrīmatī*

**much** बहुत *bahut*, अधिक *adhik*, ज़्यादा *zyādā* – I don't know much about this मैं इसके बारे में बहुत नहीं जानता *maĩ iske bāre mẽ bahut nahī̃ jāntā*; much too बहुत ज़्यादा *bahut zyādā* – this hotel is much too expensive यह होटल बहुत ज़्यादा महँगा है *yah hoṭal bahut zyādā mahãgā hai*

**mud** कीचड़ *kīcaṛ*[M]

**muddle** गड़बड़ *gaṛbaṛ*[F] – there was quite a muddle about the hotel होटल को लेकर काफ़ी गड़बड़ हुई *hoṭal ko lekar kāfī gaṛbaṛ huī*

**mule** खच्चर *khaccar*[M]

**murder, to** की हत्या करना *kī hatyā karnā*[N] – he murdered his neighbour उसने अपने पड़ोसी की हत्या की [कर दी] *usne apne paṛosī kī hatyā kī [kar dī]*

**muscle** माँसपेशी *mā̃speśī*[F]

**museum** संग्रहालय *saṅgrahālay*[M]

**music** संगीत *saṅgīt*[M]

**musician** संगीतकार *saṅgītkār*[M]

**Muslim** मुसलमान *musalmān*[M]

**must** (use infinitive verb + होना *honā*) – we must go 💣 हमको जाना है *hamko jānā hai*; (for stronger compulsion use पड़ना *paṛnā*) – we'll have to go 💣 हमको जाना पड़ेगा *hamko jānā paṛegā*

**mustard** (plant) सरसों *sarsõ*[F]

**mutual** परस्पर *paraspar*

**my** मेरा *merā*

**mysterious** रहस्यमय *rahasyamay*

**mystery** रहस्य^M *rahasya*; to solve a mystery रहस्य खोलना *rahasya kholnā*^N

## N

**nail** (fastening) कील *kīl*^F; (fingernail) नाख़ून *nā<u>kh</u>ūn*^M

**naked** नंगा *naṅgā*

**nakedness** नंगापन *naṅgāpan*^M

**name** नाम *nām*^M

**name, to** नाम देना /रखना *nām denā*^N/ *rakhnā*^N

**named** नाम का *nām kā* — a girl named Radha राधा नाम की लड़की *rādhā nām kī laṛkī*; (more formal) नामक — a gentleman named Krishna Kumar कृष्णकुमार नामक सज्जन *kṛṣṇakumār nāmak sajjan*

**narrow** पतला *patlā*; (constricting) तंग *taṅg*

**nation** राष्ट्र *rāṣṭra*^M

**national** राष्ट्रीय *rāṣṭrīy*; national language राष्ट्रभाषा *rāṣṭrabhāṣā*^F

**nationalism** राष्ट्रवाद *rāṣṭravād*^M

**nationalist** (adj. & noun) राष्ट्रवादी *rāṣṭravādī*^M

**nationality** राष्ट्रीयता *rāṣṭrīytā*^F

**natural** (of landscape etc.) प्राकृतिक *prākṛtik* — natural beauty प्राकृतिक सौंदर्य *prākṛtik saundarya*^M; (spontaneous, not artificial) सहज *sahaj* — she's very natural वह बहुत ही सहज स्वभाव की है *vah bahut hī sahaj svabhāv kī hai*

**naturally** (without contrivance) सहज ढंग से *sahaj ḍhaṅg se*; (of course) ज़रूर *zarūr*, अवश्य *avaśya*

**nature** (the natural world) प्रकृति *prakṛti*^F; (disposition) स्वभाव *svabhāv*^M — she was kind by nature वह स्वभाव से ही दयालु थी *vah svabhāv se hī dayālu thī*

**naughty** नटखट *naṭkhaṭ*

**navy** नौसेना *nausenā*^F

**near, nearby** पास *pās*, नज़दीक *nazdīk* — the village is quite near गाँव काफ़ी पास/नज़दीक है *gā̃v kāfī pās/nazdīk hai*; (near something) के पास/नज़दीक *ke pās/nazdīk* — our village is near the town हमारा गाँव शहर के पास/नज़दीक है *hamārā gā̃v śahar ke pās/nazdīk hai*

**nearly** क़रीब क़रीब *qarīb qarīb*

**necessary** ज़रूरी *zarūrī*, आवश्यक *āvaśyak*

**neck** गरदन *gardan*[F]

**need, to** की ज़रूरत होना *kī zarūrat honā* — I need money मुझे पैसे की ज़रूरत है *mujhe paise kī zarūrat hai*; needed चाहिए — they need money उनको पैसा चाहिए *unko paisā cāhie*; your brother needed this medicine तुम्हारे भाई को यह दवा चाहिए थी *tumhāre bhāī ko yah davā cāhie thī*

**needle** सूई *sūī*[F]; needle and thread सूई-धागा *sūī-dhāgā*[M]

**neglect, to** (की) उपेक्षा करना *(kī) upekṣā karnā*[N], की अवहेलना करना *kī avhelnā karnā*[N] — we neglected him/her for years हमने कई साल तक उसकी उपेक्षा की *hamne kaī sāl tak uskī upekṣā kī*

**negligence** (carelessness) लापरवाही *lāparvāhī*[F]

**negligent** (careless) लापरवाह *lāparvāh*[F]

**neighbour** पड़ोसी *paṛosī*[M]; (female) पड़ोसिन *paṛosin*[F]

**neighbourhood** पड़ोस *paṛos*[M]

**neither** दोनों में से कोई नहीं *donõ mẽ se koī nahī̃*; neither…nor…. न *na…na* — I neither write nor read poetry मैं कविता न लिखता हूँ न पढ़ता हूँ *maĩ kavitā na likhtā hū̃ na paṛhtā hū̃*

**Nepal** नेपाल *nepāl*[M]

**Nepali** (adj. & noun) नेपाली *nepālī*[M]; Nepali language नेपाली *nepālī*[F]

**nephew** भतीजा *bhatījā*[M]

**nerve** (body fibre) नस *nas*[F]; (courage) हिम्मत *himmat*[F]; to get on someone's nerves तंग करना *taṅg karnā*[N], परेशान करना *pareśān karnā*[N]

**nest** घोंसला *ghõslā*[M]

**nest, to** घोंसला बसाना *ghõslā basānā*[N]

**net** जाल *jāl*[M]

**never** कभी नहीं *kabhī nahī̃* — I never read the papers these days आजकल मैं अख़बार कभी नहीं पढ़ता *ājkal maĩ akhbār kabhī nahī̃ paṛhtā*; never mind कोई बात नहीं *koī bāt nahī̃*

**nevertheless** फिर भी *phir bhī*

**new** नया *nayā* (note how spelling changes with gender) — new kurta नया कुरता *nayā kurtā*, new things नई चीज़ें *naī cīzẽ*, new clothes नए कपड़े *nae kapṛe*

**newness** नयापन *nayāpan*ᴹ

**news** ख़बर *khabar*ᶠ, समाचार *samācār*ᴹ — I read the news every day मैं रोज़ खबरें/समाचार पढ़ता हूँ *maĩ roz khabrẽ/samācār paṛhtā hũ*; hello, any news? कहिए, कोई नई ख़बर? *kahie, koī naī khabar?*

**newspaper** अख़बार *akhbār*ᴹ, समाचार-पत्र *samācār-patra*ᴹ

**next** अगला *aglā* — next week/month/year अगले हफ़्ते/महीने/साल *agle hafte/mahīne/sāl*

**nice** अच्छा *acchā*; (nice looking) सुंदर *sundar*; (lovely) सुहावना *suhāvnā* — a nice evening सुहावनी शाम *suhāvnī śām*; (of food, delicious) लज़ीज़ *lazīz*

**niece** भतीजी *bhatījī*ᶠ

**night** रात *rāt*ᶠ — at night रात को *rāt ko*; all night रात भर *rāt bhar*; tonight आज रात (को) *āj rāt (ko)*

**nine** नौ *nau*; ninth नवाँ *navā̃*

**nineteen** उन्नीस *unnīs*

**ninety** नब्बे *nabbe*

**no** नहीं, *nahī̃*; (more polite) जी नहीं *jī nahī̃*; I have no time मेरे पास समय नहीं है *mere pās samay nahī̃ hai*

**nobody** कोई नहीं *koī nahī̃* — there's nobody in the house घर में कोई नहीं है *ghar mẽ koī nahī̃ hai*; nobody here speaks Gujarati यहाँ कोई गुजराती नहीं बोलता *yahā̃ koī gujarātī nahī̃ boltā*

**noise** (disturbance) शोर *śor*ᴹ — there's a lot of noise in the street at night रात को सड़क में बहुत शोर होता है *rāt ko saṛak mẽ bahut śor hotā hai*; to make noise शोर मचाना *śor macānā*ᴺ; (see also 'sound')

**none** (referring to people or countables) कोई नहीं *koī nahī̃*; (referring to substances) कुछ नहीं *kuch nahī̃*

**nonsense** बकवास *bakvās*ᴹ; to talk nonsense बकवास करना *bakvās karnā*ᴺ

---

**Insight**

Nineteen: the 'nine' numbers in each decade (19, 29, 39 etc.) all begin *un-*, meaning 'less than', followed by a form of the following decade number.

**noon** दोपहर *dopahar*[F]; at noon दोपहर को *dopahar ko*

**normal** सामान्य *sāmānya*

**north** उत्तर *uttar*[M]; northwards उत्तर की तरफ़/ओर *uttar kī taraf/or*

**northern** उत्तरी *uttarī*

**nose** नाक *nāk*[F]

**not** नहीं *nahī̃*; (with subjunctive and with imperative, use न *na*) — don't you go there alone तुम वहाँ अकेले न जाओ *tum vahā̃ akele na jāo*

**note**[1] (letter) चिट्ठी *ciṭṭhī*[F]

**note**[2] (musical) स्वर *svar*[M], सुर *sur*[M]

**note**[3] (currency) नोट *noṭ*[M]

**nothing** कुछ नहीं *kuch nahī̃*; nothing at all कुछ भी नहीं *kuch bhī nahī̃*

**notice** (announcement) सूचना *sūcnā*[F]

**notice, to** (to pay heed; 'to' is पर *par*) ध्यान देना *dhyān denā*[N] — he/she didn't notice what I said उसने मेरी बात पर ध्यान नहीं दिया *usne merī bāt par dhyān nahī̃ diyā*

**notice board** सूचना-पट *sūcnā-paṭ*[F]

**noun** संज्ञा *sanjñā*[F] (pronounced 'sangyā')

**novel** (work of fiction) उपन्यास *upanyās*[M]

**novelist** उपन्यासकार *upanyāskār*[M]

**November** नवंबर *navambar*[M]

**now** अब *ab*; right now अभी *abhī*; now and then कभी कभी *kabhī kabhī,* समय समय पर *samay samay par*

**nowadays** आजकल *ājkal*

**nowhere** कहीं नहीं *kahī̃ nahī̃*; nowhere at all कहीं भी नहीं *kahī̃ bhī nahī̃*

**numb** सुन्न *sunn*

**number** (total) संख्या *saṅkhyā*[F] — the number of states in India is increasing भारत के प्रदेशों की संख्या बढ़ रही है *bhārat ke pradeśõ kī saṅkhyā baṛh rahī hai*; (digit) अंक *aṅk*[M] — there were several numbers written on the paper काग़ज़ पर कई अंक लिखे हुए थे *kāgaz par kaī aṅk likhe hue the*; (phone number etc.) नंबर *nambar*[M]

**nurse** नर्स *nars*[F]

## O

**obey, to** मानना *mānnā*[N]; to obey a rule नियम का पालन करना *niyam kā pālan karnā*[N]

**object**$^{1}$ (thing) चीज़ *cīz*$^{F}$, वस्तु *vastu*$^{F}$

**object**$^{2}$ (purpose) उद्देश्य *uddeśya*$^{M}$

**object, to** आपत्ति करना *āpatti karnā*$^{N}$ – we objected to their coming हमने उनके आने पर आपत्ति की *hamne unke āne par āpatti kī*

**objection** आपत्ति *āpatti*$^{F}$, एतराज़ *etrāz*$^{M}$ – we have no objection हमें कोई आपत्ति/एतराज़ नहीं है *hamẽ koī āpatti/etrāz nahī̃ hai*

**obligatory** अनिवार्य *anivārya*$^{M}$

**obscene** अश्लील *aślīl*

**obstacle** बाधा *bādhā*$^{F}$

**obstinacy** ज़िद *zid*$^{F}$

**obstinate** ज़िद्दी *ziddī*

**obstruction** बाधा *bādhā*$^{F}$

**obtain, to** पाना *pānā*$^{N}$, (more formal) प्राप्त करना *prāpt karnā*$^{N}$ (see 'get' for the more common usage with मिलना *milnā*)

**obvious** ज़ाहिर *zāhir*, स्पष्ट *spaṣṭ*

**obviously** ज़ाहिर तौर पर *zāhir taur par*

**occasion** मौक़ा *mauqā*$^{M}$, अवसर *avsar*$^{M}$; on such an occasion ऐसे मौक़े/अवसर पर *aise mauqe/avsar par*; (time) बार *bār*$^{F}$ – on three occasions, three times तीन बार *tīn bār*

**occupation** पेशा *peśā*$^{M}$ – what is your occupation? आपका पेशा क्या है? *āpkā peśā kyā hai?*

**occur, to** होना *honā* – when did all this occur? यह सब कब हुआ? *yah sab kab huā?*

**ocean** सागर *sāgar*$^{M}$, समुद्र *samudra*$^{M}$

**o'clock** बजा *bajā* – it's one o'clock एक बजा है *ek bajā hai*, it's two o'clock दो बजे हैं *do baje haĩ*; at three o'clock तीन बजे *tīn baje*

**October** अक्तूबर *aktūbar*$^{M}$

**of** का *kā* (this works like English apostrophe 's', coming between the possessor and the thing possessed; it agrees with the latter) – the name of the girl (= 'the girl's name') लड़की का नाम *laṛkī kā nām*)

**of course** ज़रूर *zarūr* (the sense can also be expressed with future tense and emphatics – they have a car, of course? उनके पास गाड़ी तो होगी ही? *unke pās gāṛī to hogī hī?*)

**off** (of electricity, water etc.) बंद *band*

**offence** अपराध *aprādh*$^{M}$; to commit an offence अपराध करना *aprādh karnā*$^{N}$;

(bad feeling, hurt) ठेस *ṭhes*[F] —
to cause offence ठेस पहुँचाना
*ṭhes pahũcānā*[N]

**offend, to** बुरा लगना *burā lagnā*
— what you said offended him/
her आपकी बात उसको बुरी
लगी *āpkī bāt usko burī lagī*
(see also 'offence')

**office** दफ़्तर *daftar*[M], कार्यालय
*kāryālay*[M]

**officer** अफ़सर *afsar*[M]; (an
official) अधिकारी *adhikārī*[M]

**often** अक्सर *aksar*; (many
times) कई बार *kaī bār*

**oil** तेल *tel*[M]

**oil, to** तेल लगाना *tel lagānā*[N]

**oily** चिकना *ciknā*

**old** (of animates) बूढ़ा *būṛhā* —
I'm getting old मैं बूढ़ा हो रहा
हूँ *maĩ būṛhā ho rahā hū̃*; (of
inanimates) पुराना *purānā* —
old pictures पुरानी तस्वीरें
*purānī tasvīrẽ*; old friend
(i.e. a friend of long standing)
पुराना दोस्त *purānā dost*

**old age** (of animates) बूढ़ापन
*būṛhāpan*[M]

**on** पर *par*; on time ठीक समय
पर *ṭhīk samay par*; on top of
के ऊपर *ke ūpar*; on a particular
day of the week को *ko* — on
Monday सोमवार को *somvār ko*

**once** एक बार *ek bār*; at once
तुरंत *turant*

**one** एक *ek*; one or two एकाध
*ekādh*; one by one एक एक करके
*ek ek karke*; one and a half डेढ़
*ḍeṛh* (grammatically singular) —
it will take one and a half hours
☀ डेढ़ घंटा लगेगा *ḍeṛh ghaṇṭā
lagegā*; one another एक दूसरे
को *ek dūsre ko* — we know one
another हम एक दूसरे को जानते
हैं *ham ek dūsre ko jānte haĩ*;
('one' as impersonal pronoun:
use passive voice) — one does
not eat roti with a fork रोटी को
काँटे से नहीं खाया जाता *roṭī ko
kā̃ṭe se nahī̃ khāyā jātā*

**oneself** ख़ुद *khud* — I'll go myself
मैं ख़ुद जाऊँगा *maĩ khud jāū̃gā*

**onion** प्याज़ *pyāz*[M (F)]

**only** सिर्फ़ *sirf*, केवल *keval*;
I only know Hindi मैं सिर्फ़
हिन्दी जानता हूँ *maĩ sirf hindī
jāntā hū̃*; ही *hī* (follows the
emphasized word) — I only
know Hindi मैं हिन्दी ही जानता
हूँ *maĩ hindī hī jāntā hū̃*

**open** खुला *khulā*

**open, to** (intr.) खुलना
*khulnā* — the office will
open at six o'clock दफ़्तर छह
बजे खुलेगा *daftar chah baje*

*khulegā*; to open (tr.) खोलना *kholnā*[N] – should I open the door? मैं दरवाज़ा खोलूँ? *maĩ darvāzā kholū̃?*

**openly** खुलकर *khulkar*

**openness** खुलापन *khulāpan*[M]

**opinion** राय *rāy*[F], ख़याल *khyāl*[M], विचार *vicār*[M] – in my opinion, to my way of thinking मेरे ख़याल में *mere khyāl mẽ*; tell me your opinion मुझे अपनी राय बताइए *mujhe apnī rāy batāie*

**opportunity** मौक़ा *mauqā*[M], अवसर *avsar*[M]; you'll get a good opportunity to travel 💣 तुमको सफ़र करने का अच्छा मौक़ा मिलेगा *tumko safar karne kā acchā mauqā milegā*

**oppose, to** (का) विरोध करना *(kā) virodh karnā*[N] – we'll oppose this plan हम इस योजना का विरोध करेंगे *ham is yojnā kā virodh karẽge*

**opposite** (facing) सामने *sāmne* – my shop is opposite मेरी दुकान सामने है *merī dukān sāmne hai*; (opposite something) के सामने – my shop is opposite your house मेरी दुकान तुम्हारे घर के सामने है *merī dukān tumhāre ghar ke sāmne hai*

**option** विकल्प *vikalp*[M] – isn't there any another option? कोई दूसरा विकल्प नहीं है? *koī dūsrā vikalp nahī̃ hai?*

**or** या *yā*; (between two simple alternatives) कि *ki* – are you going or not? तुम जा रहे हो कि नहीं? *tum jā rahe ho ki nahī̃?*

**oral** मौखिक *maukhik*

**orange** (loose skinned) संतरा *santarā*[M]; (tight skinned) नारंगी *nāraṅgī*[F]; (adj., colour) नारंगी *nāraṅgī*

**order**[1] (sequence) क्रम *kram*[M] – please do these three jobs in order ये तीन काम क्रम से कीजिए *ye tīn kām kram se kījie*; in order that ताकि *tāki* (+ subjunctive) – in order that they understand ताकि वे समझें *tāki ve samjhẽ*

**Insight**

Order: the word क्रम *kram* is a component in कार्यक्रम *kāryakram*[M] 'programme', lit. 'order of work'.

**order**[2] (command) आदेश *ādeś*[M]

**order**[3] (in restaurant) आर्डर *ārḍar*[M]

**order, to** (to command) आदेश देना *ādeś denā*[N] — he/she ordered us to come उसने हमें आने का आदेश दिया *usne hamẽ āne kā ādeś diya*; (to ask for) मँगाना *mãgānā*[N] — I ordered coffee मैंने कॉफ़ी मँगाई *maĩne kāfī mãgāī*

**ordinary** (unremarkable) मामूली *māmūlī* — it's an ordinary matter मामूली-सी बात है *māmūlī-sī bāt hai*; (everyday, plain) साधारण *sādhāraṇ* — ordinary clothes साधारण कपड़े *sādhāraṇ kapṛe*

**origin** मूल *mūl*[M] — people of Indian origin भारतीय मूल के लोग *bhāratīy mūl ke log*

**original** मौलिक *maulik* — an original poem मौलिक कविता *maulik kavitā*

**originality** मौलिकता *mauliktā*[F]

**ostentation** आडंबर *āḍambar*[M]

**other** दूसरा *dūsrā*, अन्य *anya* — other people दूसरे लोग *dūsre log*; of another kind दूसरे प्रकार का *dūsre prakār kā*; just the other day कुछ ही दिन पहले *kuch hī din pahle*

**otherwise** नहीं तो *nahī̃ to*

**ought:** see 'should'

**our, ours** हमारा *hamārā*

**out** बाहर *bāhar*; to go out बाहर जाना *bāhar jānā*

**outside** बाहर *bāhar* — let's sleep outside हम बाहर सोएँ *ham bāhar soẽ*; (outside something) के बाहर *ke bāhar* — outside the window खिड़की के बाहर *khiṛkī ke bāhar*

**over** (across) के पार *ke pār* — over the fields खेतों के पार *khetõ ke pār*; (finished) ख़त्म *khatm* — it's over ख़त्म हो गया है *khatm ho gayā hai*; (more than) से ज़्यादा *se zyādā* — over a thousand हज़ार से ज़्यादा *hazār se zyādā*

**own** (belonging to self) अपना *apnā* — my own room मेरा अपना कमरा *merā apnā kamrā*

**own, to** (Hindi has no direct equivalent, so use होना *honā*, and see also 'have' — he owns/has two houses उसके दो घर हैं *uske do ghar haĩ*)

**owner** मालिक *mālik*[M]

## P

**pace** (step) क़दम *qadam*[M] — two paces forward दो क़दम आगे *do qadam āge*; (speed: see 'speed')

**packet** लिफ़ाफ़ा *lifāfā*ᴹ, पुलिंदा *pulindā*ᴹ

**page** पन्ना *pannā*ᴹ, पृष्ठ *pṛṣṭh*ᴹ; a book of 250 pages ढाई सौ पन्नों की किताब *ḍhāī sau pannõ kī kitāb*

**pain** दर्द *dard*ᴹ — I have a pain in my leg ☞ मेरी टाँग में दर्द है *merī ṭā̃g mẽ dard hai*; (anguish) पीड़ा *pīṛā*ᶠ

**paint, to** (a wall etc.) रंग लगाना *raṅg lagānā*ᴺ; (a picture) चित्र बनाना *citra banānā*ᴺ

**painter** (artist) चित्रकार *citrakār*ᴹ

**pair** जोड़ा *joṛā*ᴹ — a pair of socks एक जोड़ा मोज़े *ek joṛā moze*

**Pakistan** पाकिस्तान *pākistān*ᴹ

**Pakistani** (adj. & noun) पाकिस्तानी *pākistānī*ᴹ

**palace** महल *mahal*ᴹ

**palm** (of hand) हथेली *hathelī*ᶠ

**palm tree** ताड़ *tāṛ*ᴹ

**pandit** पंडित *paṇḍit*ᴹ

**pant, to** हाँफना *hā̃phnā*

**paper** (both 'a sheet of paper' and the substance itself) कागज़ *kāgaz*ᴹ — write your name on this paper इस कागज़ पर अपना नाम लिखो *is kāgaz par apnā nām likho*; paper flowers कागज़ के फूल *kāgaz ke phūl*; see also 'newspaper'

**pardon, to:** see 'forgive'

**pare, to** छीलना *chīlnā*ᴺ

**parental** (ancestral) पैतृक *paitṛk*

**parents** माता-पिता *mātā-pitā*ᴹ ᴾᴸ, (less formal) माँ-बाप *mā̃-bāp*ᴹ ᴾᴸ — what will your parents say? आपके माता-पिता क्या कहेंगे? *āpke mātā-pitā kyā kahẽge?*

**park** बाग़ *bāg*ᴹ

**park, to** (a car) खड़ा करना *khaṛā karnā*ᴺ — parking is strictly forbidden गाड़ी खड़ी करना सख़्त मना है *gāṛī khaṛī karnā sa<u>kh</u>t manā hai*

**parliament** संसद *sansad*ᴹ

**parliamentary** संसदीय *sansadīy*

**parrot** तोता *totā*ᴹ

**part** हिस्सा *hissā*ᴹ, भाग *bhāg*ᴹ; to take part हिस्सा/भाग लेना *hissā/bhāg lenā*ᴺ — I will take part in the meeting मैं मीटिंग में हिस्सा लूँगा *maĩ mīṭiṅg mẽ hissā lū̃gā*; part (component) of a machine पुरज़ा *purzā*ᴹ

**part, to:** see 'to separate'

**particular** ख़ास *<u>kh</u>ās*, विशेष *viśeṣ* (see also 'special')

**parting**[1] (separation) जुदाई *judāī*^F

**parting**[2] (in hair) माँग *mãg*^F

**party** (event) पार्टी *pārṭī*^F — to go to a party पार्टी में जाना *pārṭī mẽ jānā*; (political party) पार्टी *pārṭī*^F, दल *dal*^M

**pass, to** (to pass time) बिताना *bitānā*^N, गुज़ारना *guzārnā*^N; how do you pass your time ? आप अपना समय कैसे गुज़ारते/बिताते हैं? *āp apnā samay kaise guzārte/bitāte haĩ?*; (to hand over) थमाना^N *thamānā*; (to pass exam) पास होना *pās honā* — Radha will pass, Ram will fail राधा पास होगी, राम फ़ेल होगा *rādhā pās hogī, rām fel hogā*; (to overtake) आगे निकल जाना *āge nikal jānā* — their car passed us उनकी गाड़ी हमसे आगे निकल गई *unkī gāṛī hamse āge nikal gaī*

**passage** (piece of prose text) गद्यांश *gadyā̃ś*^M

**passenger** (traveller) मुसाफ़िर *musāfir*^M, यात्री *yātrī*^M — passengers are requested to remain seated ☛ यात्रियों से निवेदन है कि वे बैठे रहें *yātriyõ se nivedan hai ki ve baiṭhe rahẽ*; (in vehicle) सवारी *savārī*^F

**passport** पासपोर्ट *pāsporṭ*^M

**past** (the past) भूत *bhūt*^M

**patience** धैर्य *dhairya*^M

**patient**[1] (tolerant) सहनशील *sahanśīl*

**patient**[2] (sick person) मरीज़ *marīz*^M, रोगी *rogī*^M

**patriot** देश-भक्त *deś-bhakt*^M

**patriotic** देश-भक्त *deś-bhakt*

**patriotism** देश-भक्ति *deś-bhakti*^F

**pay, to** पैसा देना *paisā denā*^N; (to settle a bill) चुकाना *cukānā*^N — pay the electricity bill बिजली का बिल चुकाओ [चुका दो] *bijlī kā bil cukāo [cukā do]*; to pay attention ध्यान देना *dhyān denā*^N (object takes पर *par*) — pay attention to what I'm saying मेरी बात पर ध्यान दो *merī bāt par dhyān do*

**pea** मटर *maṭar*^M

**peace** शान्ति *śānti*^F

**peaceful** शान्त *śānt*

**peacock** मोर *mor*^M

**peanut** मूँगफली *mū̃gphalī*^F

**pearl** मोती *motī*^M

**pee, to** पेशाब करना *peśāb karnā*^N

**peel, to** छीलना *chīlnā*^N

**peg** खूँटी *khū̃ṭī*^F

**pen** क़लम *qalam*$^{M\ (F)}$, पेन *pen*$^{M}$

**pencil** पेंसिल *pensil*$^{F}$

**people** लोग *log*$^{M\ PL}$ – tell these people इन लोगों को बताओ *in logõ ko batāo*; the people (the public) जनता *jantā*$^{F}$ (singular) – the people want to know जनता जानना चाहती है *jantā jānnā cāhtī hai*

**pepper** (black pepper) काली मिर्च *kālī mirc*$^{F}$; (green pepper, capsicum) शिमला मिर्च *śimlā mirc*$^{F}$

**perceive, to** महसूस करना *mahsūs karnā*$^{N}$

**percent** प्रतिशत *pratiśat* – 15% of the people १५प्रतिशत लोग *15 pratiśat log*

**perhaps** शायद *śāyad*

**period** (age) ज़माना *zamānā*$^{M}$ – in the Muslim period मुसलमानों के ज़माने में *musalmānõ ke zamāne mẽ*; (monthly period) महीना *mahīnā*$^{M}$ I am having my monthly period मुझे महीना लगा हुआ है *mujhe mahīnā lagā huā hai*

**permanent** स्थायी *sthāyī*

**permanently** स्थायी रूप से *sthāyī rūp se* – I live permanently in America मैं स्थायी रूप से अमरीका में रहता हूँ *maĩ sthāyī rūp se amrīkā mẽ rahtā hū̃*

**permission** इजाज़त *ijāzat*$^{F}$, अनुमति *anumati*$^{F}$ – please give me permission to go abroad this year मुझे इस साल विदेश जाने की अनुमति दीजिए *mujhe is sāl videś jāne kī anumati dījie*; permission to leave आज्ञा *ājñā*$^{F}$ (pronounced 'āgyā'), इजाज़त *ijāzat*$^{F}$ – may I take my leave? (please give me permission) आज्ञा/इजाज़त दीजिए *ājñā/ ijāzat dījie*

**person** व्यक्ति *vyakti*$^{M}$

**personal** (individual) व्यक्तिगत *vyaktigat*; (private) निजी *nijī* – this is a private matter यह निजी मामला है *yah nijī māmlā hai*

**personality** व्यक्तित्व *vyaktitva*$^{M}$

**personally** व्यक्तिगत रूप से *vyaktigat rūp se* – I know them personally मैं उन्हें व्यक्तिगत रूप से जानता हूँ *maĩ unhẽ vyaktigat rūp se jāntā hū̃*

**perspire, to:** see 'sweat'

**persuade (to), to** (के लिए) राज़ी करना *(ke lie) rāzī karnā*$^{N}$ – we persuaded him/her to leave हमने उसको जाने के लिए राज़ी किया *hamne usko jāne ke lie rāzī kiyā*

**pharmacy** दवाख़ाना *davākhānā*ᴹ

**phone:** see 'telephone'

**photograph** फ़ोटो *foṭo*ᴹ ⁽ᶠ⁾; to take a photograph फ़ोटो खींचना *foṭo khĩcnā*ᴺ – take a photo of the Taj Mahal ताज महल का फोटो खींचो *tāj mahal kā foṭo khĩco*

**physical** (bodily) शारीरिक *śārīrik*

**pick:** see 'choose'; to pick a flower फूल चुनना *phūl cunnā*ᴺ

**pick up, to** उठाना *uṭhānā*ᴺ

**pickle** अचार *acār*ᴹ

**pickpocket** जेबकतरा *jebkatrā*ᴹ

**picture** तस्वीर *tasvīr*ᶠ, चित्र *citra*ᴹ

**piece** टुकड़ा *ṭukṛā*ᴹ – a piece of wood लकड़ी का टुकड़ा *lakṛī kā ṭukṛā*

**pig** सूअर *sūar*ᴹ

**pigeon** कबूतर *kabūtar*ᴹ

**pile** ढेर *ḍher*ᴹ – a pile of bricks ईंटों का ढेर *ĩṭõ kā ḍher*

**piles** (haemorrhoids) बवासीर *bavāsīr*ᶠ

**pilgrim** तीर्थ-यात्री *tīrth-yātrī*ᴹ

**pilgrimage** तीर्थ-यात्रा *tīrth-yātrā*ᶠ; pilgrimage place तीर्थ *tīrth*ᴹ

**pill** गोली *golī*ᶠ to take a pill गोली खाना/लेना *golī khānā*ᴺ / *lenā*ᴺ

**pillar** स्तंभ *stambh*ᴹ

**pillow** तकिया *takiyā*ᴹ

**pink** गुलाबी *gulābī* – pink clothes गुलाबी रंग के कपड़े *gulābī raṅg ke kapṛe*

**pipe** (for water) नल *nal*ᴹ; (for tobacco) पाइप *pāip*ᴹ

**pity** (compassion) दया *dayā*ᶠ; to have pity दया करना *dayā karnā*ᴺ – have pity on me मुझपर दया कीजिए *mujhpar dayā kījie*; (regret) अफ़सोस *afsos*ᴹ – it's a pity he can't come to the wedding अफ़सोस की बात है कि वह शादी में नहीं आ सकता *afsos kī bāt hai ki vah śādī mẽ nahī̃ ā saktā*

**place** जगह *jagah*ᶠ, स्थान *sthān*ᴹ

**plain**[1] (ordinary) सादा *sādā* – plain food सादा खाना *sādā khānā*

**plain**[2] (flat land, open space) मैदान *maidān*ᴹ

**plan** प्रोग्राम *progrām*ᴹ; (scheme) योजना *yojnā*ᶠ – government plans सरकारी योजनाएँ *sarkārī yojnāẽ*

**plan, to** प्रोग्राम बनाना *progrām banānā*ᴺ – we're planning a trip to India हम भारत जाने का प्रोग्राम बना रहे हैं *ham bhārat jāne kā progrām banā rahe haĩ*

**plant** पौधा *paudhā*[M]

**plant, to** लगाना *lagānā*[N], रोपना *ropnā*[N]

**plaster, to** पोतना *potnā*[N]

**plate** प्लेट *pleṭ*[F] — broken plates टूटी हुई प्लेटें *ṭūṭī huī pleṭẽ*

**play** (drama) नाटक *nāṭak*[M]

**play, to** (a game) खेलना *khelnā*[N]; (music) बजाना *bajānā*[N]

**pleasant** सुखद *sukhad*

**please** कृपया *kṛpayā*; मेहरबानी से *meharbānī se*; ('please' is implicit in आप *āp* requests — please sit, बैठिए *baiṭhie*)

**please, to** ख़ुश करना *khuś karnā*[N], प्रसन्न करना *prasann karnā*[N]

**pleased** ख़ुश *khuś* — I am/was very pleased to meet you (use noun ख़ुशी *khuśī* 'pleasure') आपसे मिलकर बड़ी ख़ुशी हुई *āpse milkar baṛī khuśī huī*

**pleasure** ख़ुशी *khuśī*[F]; (happiness) सुख *sukh*[M]

**plot**[1] (story) कथानक *kathānak*[M]

**plot**[2] (piece of land) ज़मीन का टुकड़ा *zamīn kā ṭukṛā*[M]

**plot**[3] (conspiracy) षड्यंत्र *ṣaḍyantra*[M]

**plough** हल *hal*[M]

**plough, to** हल चलाना *hal calānā*[N]

**plumber** प्लंबर *plambar*[M]

**plural** बहुवचन *bahuvacan*

**pocket** जेब *jeb*[F]

**poem** कविता *kavitā*[F]

**poet** कवि *kavi*[M]; (female) कवयित्री *kavayitrī*[F]

**poetry** कविता *kavitā*[F]; to write poetry कविता लिखना/करना *kavitā likhnā*[N]*/karnā*[N]

**point** (advantage) फ़ायदा *fāydā*[M] — what's the point in this? इसमें क्या फ़ायदा है? *ismẽ kyā fāydā hai?*; (sharp end) नोक *nok*[F]; (dot) बिंदु *bindu*[F]; (idea, thought) बात *bāt*[F] — I have a point to make मुझे एक बात कहनी है *mujhe ek bāt kahnī hai*; point of view दृष्टिकोण *dṛṣṭikoṇ*[M]

**point, to** (to gesture) इशारा करना *iśārā karnā*[N] — he is pointing at us वह हमारी तरफ़ इशारा कर रहा है *vah hamārī taraf iśārā kar rahā hai*

**poison** ज़हर *zahar*[M], विष *viṣ*[M]

**pole**[1] (stick) डंडा *ḍaṇḍā*[M]

**pole**[2] (north/south) ध्रुव *dhruv*[M]

**police** पुलिस *pulis*[F] — the police are coming पुलिस आ रही है

*pulis ā rahī hai* (note singular number)

**policeman** पुलिसवाला *pulisvālā*ᴹ; (constable) सिपाही *sipāhī*ᴹ

**police station** थाना *thānā*ᴹ

**political** राजनीतिक *rājnītik*

**politician** राजनेता *rājnetā*ᴹ

**politics** राजनीति *rājnīti*ᶠ

**polluted** प्रदूषित *pradūṣit*

**pollution** प्रदूषण *pradūṣaṇ*ᴹ

**pond** तालाब *tālāb*ᴹ

**poor** ग़रीब *garīb*; (in quality) घटिया *ghaṭiyā* (-*ā* invariable)

**popular** लोकप्रिय *lokpriy*

**population** आबादी *ābādī*ᶠ – the population is growing/declining आबादी बढ़/घट रही है *ābādī baṛh/ghaṭ rahī hai*

**pork** सूअर का माँस /गोश्त *sūar kā mā̃s*ᴹ /*gośt*ᴹ – we don't eat pork हम लोग सूअर का माँस नहीं खाते *ham log sūar kā mā̃s nahī̃ khāte*

**position** (situation) स्थिति *sthiti*ᶠ; (place) स्थान *sthān*ᴹ; (in employment) पद *pad*ᴹ, नौकरी *naukrī*ᶠ; (yoga posture) आसन *āsan*ᴹ

**possibility** संभावना *sambhāvnā*ᶠ

**possible** मुमकिन *mumkin*, संभव *sambhav*

**post** (mail) डाक *ḍāk*ᶠ

**post, to** (to send by mail) डाक से भेजना *ḍāk se bhejnā*ᴺ

**postage stamp** डाक-टिकट *ḍāk-ṭikaṭ*ᴹ ⁽ᶠ⁾

**postman** डाकिया *ḍākiyā*ᴹ, डाकवाला *ḍākvālā*ᴹ

**post office** डाक-घर *ḍāk-ghar*ᴹ

**postpone, to** स्थगित करना *sthagit karnā*ᴺ – the meeting will be postponed मीटिंग को स्थगित किया जाएगा *mīṭiṅg ko sthagit kiyā jāegā*

**pot**[1] (container) बरतन *bartan*ᴹ; (flowerpot) गमला *gamlā*ᴹ

**pot**[2] (cannabis) चरस *caras*ᶠ

**potato** आलू *ālū*ᴹ

**pound** पाउंड *pāuṇḍ*ᴹ

**pour, to** डालना *ḍālnā*ᴺ

**poverty** ग़रीबी *garībī*ᶠ

**powder** चूर्ण *cūrṇ*ᴹ; (talcum etc.) पाउडर *pāuḍar*ᴹ

**power** शक्ति *śakti*ᶠ, बल *bal*ᴹ; (capacity, sphere of influence) बस *bas*ᴹ – this isn't in my power यह मेरे बस की बात नहीं है *yah mere bas kī bāt nahī̃ hai*; (legal right) अधिकार *adhikār*ᴹ

**practical** व्यावहारिक *vyāvahārik*

**practice** (behaviour, usage) व्यवहार *vyavahār*[M]; (custom) रिवाज *rivāj*[M], प्रथा *prathā*[F]; (exercise, as on a musical instrument) रियाज़ *riyāz*[F], अभ्यास *abhyās*[M]

**practise, to** (का) अभ्यास करना *(kā) abhyās karnā*[N] — it's vital to practise speaking Hindi हिन्दी बोलने का अभ्यास करना बहुत ज़रूरी है *hindī bolne kā abhyās karnā bahut zarūrī hai*

**praise, to** (की) तारीफ़/प्रशंसा करना *(kī) tārīf /praśansā karnā*[N] — we were praising you हम आपकी तारीफ़/प्रशंसा कर रहे थे *ham āpkī tārīf/praśansā kar rahe the*

**pray, to** प्रार्थना करना *prārthanā karnā*[N] — to pray to God भगवान से प्रार्थना करना *bhagvān se prārthanā karnā*[N]; I pray that… मेरी प्रार्थना है कि . . . *merī prārthanā hai ki . . .*

**prayer** प्रार्थना *prārthanā*[F]

**precious** क़ीमती *qīmatī*

**prefer, to** पसंद करना *pasand karnā*[N]

**pregnant** गर्भवती *garbhvatī*, गर्भ से *garbh se*

**prejudice** पूर्वाग्रह *pūrvāgrah*[M]

**preparation** तैयारी *taiyārī*[F]; to make preparations (की) तैयारियाँ करना *(kī) taiyāriyā̃ karnā*[N] — we're making preparations for the holidays हम छुट्टियों की तैयारियाँ कर रहे हैं *ham chuṭṭiyõ kī taiyāriyā̃ kar rahe haĩ*

**prepare, to** तैयार करना *taiyār karnā*[N] — please prepare the food खाना तैयार कीजिए [कर दीजिए] *khānā taiyār kījie [kar dījie]*

**presence** उपस्थिति *upasthiti*[F]

**present**[1] (gift) तोहफ़ा *tohfā*[M]

**present**[2] (time: adj. & noun) वर्तमान *vartamān*[M] — at the present time वर्तमान समय में *vartamān samay mẽ*

**present**[3] (not absent) हाज़िर *hāzir*, उपस्थित *upasthit*

**present, to** (a gift) भेंट करना *bhẽṭ karnā*[N]; (a performance) पेश करना *peś karnā*[N] — Panditji will present a folksong पंडितजी एक लोकगीत पेश करेंगे *paṇḍitjī ek lokgīt peś karẽge*

**press, to** दबाना *dabānā*[N] — to press the button बटन दबाना *baṭan dabānā*; (to press clothes: see 'iron')

**pressure** दबाव *dabāv*[M]

**pretext** बहाना *bahānā*$^{M}$ — on the pretext of helping us हमारी मदद करने के बहाने *hamārī madad karne ke bahāne*

**prevent, to** रोकना *roknā*$^{N}$ — how can we prevent him from going? हम उसे जाने से कैसे रोक सकते हैं? *ham use jāne se kaise rok sakte haĩ?*

**previous** पिछला *pichlā* — in the previous ten days पिछले दस दिनों में *pichle das dinõ mẽ*

**previously** पहले *pahle* — previously Deven lived in Berkeley पहले तो देवेन बर्कली में रहता था *pahle to deven barklī mẽ rahtā thā*

**price** दाम *dām*$^{M}$ — what's the price of this? इसका दाम क्या है? *iskā dām kyā hai?*; (rate per unit of weight) भाव *bhāv*$^{M}$

**pride** (conceit) घमंड *ghamaṇḍ*$^{M}$; (egotism) अहंकार *ahankār*$^{M}$; (conceit or proper pride) गर्व *garv*$^{M}$ — we're very proud of Rina हमें रीना पर बहुत गर्व है *hamẽ rīnā par bahut garv hai*

**prime minister** प्रधान मंत्री *pradhān mantrī*$^{M}$

**prince** राजकुमार *rājkumār*$^{M}$

**princess** राजकुमारी *rājkumārī*$^{F}$

**principal** मुख्य *mukhya*

**principle** सिद्धान्त *siddhānt*$^{M}$; in principle सिद्धान्त के तौर पर *siddhānt ke taur par*

**print, to** छापना *chāpnā*$^{N}$ — who will print this dictionary? यह शब्दकोश कौन छापेगा? *yah śabdkoś kaun chāpegā?*

**printed, to be** छपना *chapnā* — the new book will be printed next year नई किताब अगले साल छपेगी *naī kitāb agle sāl chapegī*

**private** (personal) निजी *nijī* — it's a private matter यह निजी मामला है *yah nijī māmlā hai*

**privilege** (good fortune) सौभाग्य *saubhāgya*$^{M}$ — this is a great privilege for me मेरे लिए यह बड़े सौभाग्य की बात है *mere lie yah baṛe saubhāgya kī bāt hai*

**prize** इनाम *inām*$^{M}$, पुरस्कार *puraskār*$^{M}$

**probably** (best expressed by the future tense, with or without शायद *śāyad*) — you will probably know आपको मालूम होगा *āpko mālūm hogā*; Trina probably understands त्रीना समझती होगी *trīnā samajhtī hogī*

**Insight**

Probably: statements expressing probability often feature a 'presumptive future', as in वह जानती होगी *vah jāntī hogī* 'she probably knows'.

**problem** समस्या *samasyā*<sup>F</sup>; (difficulty) मुश्किल *muśkil*<sup>F</sup>, कठिनाई *kaṭhināī*<sup>F</sup>; a problem to arise समस्या आना *samasyā ānā*, समस्या खड़ी होना *samasyā khaṛī honā* — some problems arose कुछ समस्याएँ आईं / खड़ी हुईं *kuch samasyāẽ āī̃ / khaṛī huī̃*; to face a problem समस्या का सामना करना *samasyā kā sāmnā karnā*<sup>N</sup> — we'll have to face many problems 💣 हमें कई समस्याओं का सामना करना होगा *hamẽ kaī samasyāõ kā sāmnā karnā hogā*

**procession** जुलूस *julūs*<sup>M</sup>; to lead a procession जुलूस निकालना *julūs nikālnā*<sup>N</sup> — they led a procession against the fundamentalists उन्होंने कट्टरवादियों के ख़िलाफ़ जुलूस निकाला *unhõne kaṭṭarvādiyõ ke khilāf julūs nikālā*

**produce** पैदावार *paidāvār*<sup>F</sup>

**produce, to** पैदा करना *paidā karnā*<sup>N</sup> (-*ā* in *paidā* invariable)

**profession** पेशा *peśā*<sup>M</sup>

**professional** पेशेवर *peśevar* — father was a professional writer पिताजी पेशेवर लेखक थे *pitājī peśevar lekhak the*

**profit** लाभ *lābh*<sup>M</sup>

**programme** प्रोग्राम *progrām*<sup>M</sup>, कार्यक्रम *kāryakram*<sup>M</sup>; (scheme, plan) योजना *yojnā*<sup>F</sup>

**progress** प्रगति *pragati*<sup>F</sup> — progress is being made प्रगति हो रही है *pragati ho rahī hai*

**progressive** प्रगतिशील *pragatiśīl*

**prohibit, to** मना करना *manā karnā*<sup>N</sup>; (see also 'prevent')

**prohibited** मना *manā*, वर्जित *varjit*

**promise** वादा *vādā*<sup>M</sup>; to promise (का) वादा करना *(kā) vādā karnā*<sup>N</sup> — Rishi promised to write a letter ऋषि ने पत्र लिखने का वादा किया *ṛṣi ne patra likhne kā vādā kiyā*

**promising** (having potential) होनहार *honhār* — a very promising boy बड़ा होनहार लड़का *baṛā honhār laṛkā*

**pronoun** सर्वनाम *sarvanām*$^{\text{M}}$

**pronunciation** उच्चारण *uccāraṇ*$^{\text{M}}$ — Sujata's pronunciation is very clear सुजाता का उच्चारण बहुत ही साफ़ है *sujātā kā uccāraṇ bahut hī sāf hai*

**proof** प्रमाण *pramāṇ*$^{\text{M}}$, सबूत *sabūt*$^{\text{M}}$

**proper** (suitable) उचित *ucit* — a proper suggestion उचित सुझाव *ucit sujhāv*; (correct) सही *sahī* — the proper address सही पता *sahī patā*; (thorough) बाक़ायदा *bāqāydā (-ā* invariable*)* — proper preparations बाक़ायदा तैयारियाँ *bāqāydā taiyāriyā̃*

**properly** ठीक से *ṭhīk se* — sit properly ठीक से बैठो *ṭhīk se baiṭho*

**property** (possessions) संपत्ति *sampatti*$^{\text{F}}$; (estate) जायदाद *jāydād*$^{\text{F}}$; (characteristic) गुण *guṇ*$^{\text{M}}$

**proprietor** मालिक *mālik*$^{\text{M}}$

**prose** गद्य *gadya*$^{\text{M}}$

**prostitute** वेश्या *veśyā*$^{\text{F}}$

**protect, to** (to defend) की रक्षा करना *kī rakṣā karnā*$^{\text{N}}$ — we must protect our rights हमें अपने अधिकारों की रक्षा करनी है *hamẽ apne adhikārõ kī rakṣā karnī hai*; (to save) बचाना *bacānā*$^{\text{N}}$ — you must protect the village from this danger आपको गाँव को इस ख़तरे से बचाना है *āpko gā̃v ko is* <u>*kh*</u>*atre se bacānā hai*

**proud** (conceited) घमंडी *ghamaṇḍī*; (feeling proper pride: see 'pride')

**prove, to** साबित करना *sābit karnā*$^{\text{N}}$, सिद्ध करना *siddh karnā*$^{\text{N}}$

**proverb** कहावत *kahāvat*$^{\text{F}}$ — there's an old proverb, he who holds the stick owns the buffalo पुरानी कहावत है, जिसकी लाठी उसकी भैंस *purānī kahāvat hai, jiskī lāṭhī uskī bhaĩs*

**public** (adj.) आम *ām* — public road आम सड़क *ām saṛak*; (noun, 'the people') जनता *jantā*$^{\text{F}}$ — the government should help the public सरकार को जनता की मदद करनी चाहिए *sarkār ko jantā kī madad karnī cāhie*

**publish, to** प्रकाशित करना *prakāśit karnā*$^{\text{N}}$

**publisher** प्रकाशक *prakāśak*$^{\text{M}}$

**pull, to** खींचना *khī̃cnā*[N]

**pulse** नाड़ी *nāṛī*[F]

**punish, to** दंड/सज़ा देना *daṇḍ/sazā denā*[N] — we'll be punished हमें सज़ा दी जाएगी *hamẽ sazā dī jāegī*

**punishment** दंड *daṇḍ*[M], सज़ा *sazā*[F]

**Punjab** पंजाब *panjāb*[M]

**Punjabi** (adj. & noun) पंजाबी *panjābī*[M]; the Punjabi language पंजाबी *panjābī*[F]

**puppet** कठपुतली *kaṭhputlī*[F]

**puppy** पिल्ला *pillā*[M]

**pure** शुद्ध *śuddh*

**purpose** मक़सद *maqsad*[M], उद्देश्य *uddeśya*[M]; on purpose जान-बूझकर *jān-būjhkar*

**push, to** (press, button etc.) दबाना *dabānā*[N]; (to shove) ढकेलना *ḍhakelnā*[N], धक्का देना *dhakkā denā*[N] — he/she pushed me उसने मुझे धक्का दिया *usne mujhe dhakkā diyā*

**put, to** रखना *rakhnā*[N] — put the box on the floor बक्से को फ़र्श पर रखो [रख दो] *bakse ko farś par rakho [rakh do]*; to put on (clothes) पहनना *pahannā*[N] I put on clean clothes मैंने साफ़ कपड़े पहने [पहन लिए] *maĩne sāf kapṛe pahane [pahan lie]*; to put on (a light) जलाना *jalānā*[N] — please put the light on बत्ती जलाइए *battī jalāie*; to put up with: see 'to tolerate'

# Q

**quarrel** झगड़ा *jhagṛā*[M]

**quarrel, to** झगड़ना *jhagaṛnā*, झगड़ा करना *jhagṛā karnā*[N]

**quarrelsome** झगड़ालू *jhagṛālū*

**quarter**[1] (fraction) चौथाई *cauthāī*[F] — a quarter of this इसकी एक चौथाई *iskī ek cauthāī*; a quarter of the people एक चौथाई लोग *ek cauthāī log*; minus a quarter, a quarter before पौने — a quarter to three पौने तीन बजे *paune tīn baje*; plus a quarter, a quarter after सवा *savā* — an hour and a quarter सवा घंटा *savā ghaṇṭā*; a quarter past three सवा तीन बजे *savā tīn baje*

**quarter**[2] (district of town) मुहल्ला *muhallā*[M]

**queen** रानी *rānī*[F]

**question** सवाल *savāl*[M], प्रश्न *praśn*[M]

**quickly** जल्दी *jaldī*

**quiet** (peaceful) शान्त *śānt* — a quiet place शान्त जगह *śānt jagah*;

(not speaking) चुप *cup*; to keep quiet चुप रहना *cup rahnā* — keep quiet! चुप रहो! *cup raho!*

**quietly** (stealthily) चुपके से *cupke se*, (gently) धीरे से *dhīre se*

**quilt** रज़ाई *razāī*[F]

**quite** (fairly) काफ़ी *kāfī* — quite good काफ़ी अच्छा *kāfī achhā*; (completely) बिलकुल *bilkul* — this is quite wrong यह बिलकुल ग़लत है *yah bilkul galat hai*

**quote, to** (to state price) दाम बताना *dām batānā*[N]; (to cite) उद्धृत करना *uddhṛt karnā*[N]

## R

**rabbit** ख़रगोश *khargoś*[M]

**race**[1] (ethnicity) नसल *nasal*[F]

**race**[2] (running contest) दौड़ *dauṛ*[F]

**racialism** नसलवाद *nasalvād*[M]

**racialist** (adj. & noun) नसलवादी *nasalvādī*[M]

**radio** रेडियो *reḍiyo*[M] — to play the radio loudly रेडियो ज़ोर से बजाना *reḍiyo zor se bajānā*[N]

**rag** चिथड़ा *cithṛā*[M]

**raid** छापा *chāpā*[M]; to raid छापा *chāpā mārnā*[N] — the police raided our office पुलिस ने हमारे कार्यालय पर छापा मारा *pulis ne hamāre kāryālay par chāpā mārā*

**rain** बारिश *bāriś*[F], वर्षा *varṣā*[F]

**rain, to** बारिश होना *bāriś honā*, पानी पड़ना *pānī paṛnā* — it's raining बारिश हो रही है *bāriś ho rahī hai,* पानी पड़ रहा है *pānī paṛ rahā hai*

**rains** (the rainy season) बरसात *barsāt*[F]

**raise, to** उठाना *uṭhānā*[N]

**rajah** राजा *rājā*[M] — three rajahs तीन राजा *tīn rājā*

**rape** बलात्कार *balātkār*[M]; to rape (का) बलात्कार करना *(kā) balātkār karnā*[N]

**rare** दुर्लभ *durlabh*

**rarely** बहुत कम *bahut kam*, कम ही *kam hī*

**rat** चूहा *cūhā*[M]

**rate** दर *dar*[F]

**rather** (somewhat) -सा *-sā* — rather big बड़ा-सा *baṛā-sā*; (but/or rather) बल्कि *balki* — not just in India but rather in the whole world केवल भारत में ही नहीं बल्कि सारी दुनिया में *keval bhārat mẽ hī nahī̃ balki sārī duniyā mẽ*

**raw** कच्चा *kaccā*

**reach, to** पहुँचना *pahũcnā* — we'll reach home in a little while हम थोड़ी देर में घर

पहुँचेंगे *ham thoṛī der mẽ ghar pahũcẽge*; (in train etc.) we've reached Delhi! दिल्ली आ गई! *dillī ā gaī!*

**read, to** पढ़ना *paṛhnā*$^N$; (to study a subject) की पढ़ाई करना *kī paṛhāī karnā*$^N$ — he's reading history वह इतिहास की पढ़ाई कर रहा है *vah itihās kī paṛhāī kar rahā hai*

**reading** (of poetry) (कविता-) पाठ *(kavitā-) pāṭh*$^M$ — there will be a poetry reading tonight आज रात को कविता-पाठ होगा *āj rāt ko kavitā-pāṭh hogā*

**ready** तैयार *taiyār*; to get (oneself) ready तैयार हो जाना *taiyār ho jānā* — get ready! तैयार हो जाओ! *taiyār ho jāo!*

**ready made** बना-बनाया — ready-made clothes बने-बनाए कपड़े *bane-banāe kapṛe*

**real** असली *aslī* — real life असली जीवन *aslī jīvan*; real ghee असली घी *aslī ghī*

**realistic** यथार्थवादी *yathārthvādī* — a realistic story एक यथार्थवादी कहानी *ek yathārthvādī kahānī*

**reality** यथार्थ *yathārth*$^M$

**realize, to** समझना *samajhnā*$^n$, समझ लेना *samajh lenā*$^N$; (to give real form to, to achieve) साकार करना *sākār karnā*$^N$ — I want to realize this dream मैं इस सपने को साकार करना चाहता हूँ *maĩ is sapne ko sākār karnā cāhtā hũ*

**really** सचमुच *sacmuc*

**rear** (of building) पिछवाड़ा *pichvāṛā*$^M$ — at the rear of the house घर के पिछवाड़े में *ghar ke pichvāṛe mẽ*

**reason** (cause) कारण *kāraṇ*$^M$, वजह *vajah*$^F$ — what's the reason for this? इसका कारण क्या है? *iskā kāraṇ kyā hai?*

**reasonable** वाजिबी *vājibī* — at a reasonable price वाजिबी दाम पर *vājibī dām par*; (amenable to reason) समझदार *samajhdār* — let's ask some reasonable person हम किसी समझदार व्यक्ति से पूछें *ham kisī samajhdār vyakti se pūchẽ*

**receipt** रसीद *rasīd*$^F$

**receive, to** पाना *pānā*$^N$; (or use the more colloquial मिलना *milnā* 'to be received') — I received your letter (मुझे) आपका पत्र मिला *(mujhe) āpkā patra milā*

**recent** हाल का *hāl kā* — in a recent meeting हाल

की एक मीटिंग में *hāl kī ek mīṭiṅg mẽ*

**recently** हाल में *hāl mẽ,* इधर *idhar*

**recite, to** सुनाना *sunānā*$^{N}$ — please recite some poem of yours अपनी कोई कविता सुनाइए *apnī koī kavitā sunāie*

**recognize** पहचानना *pahacānnā*$^{N}$

**red** लाल *lāl*

**red tape** (-ism) लालफ़ीताशाही *lālfītāśāhī*$^{F}$

**reduce, to** (intr.) कम होना *kam honā*; (tr.) कम करना *kam karnā*$^{N}$; to reduce weight, to slim वज़न कम करना *vazan kam karnā*$^{N}$

**reflection** (mirrored image) प्रतिबिंब *pratibimb*$^{M}$; (thought) चिन्तन *cintan*$^{M}$

**refusal** इनकार *inkār*$^{M}$

**refuse, to** (से) इनकार करना *(se) inkār karnā*$^{N}$ — he is refusing to work वह काम करने से इनकार कर रहा है *vah kām karne se inkār kar rahā hai*

**region** इलाक़ा *ilāqā*$^{M}$, क्षेत्र *kṣetra*$^{M}$

**regional** क्षेत्रीय *kṣetrīy*

**regret, to** (to be sorry) खेद होना *khed honā* — I regret that ... मुझे खेद है कि . . . *mujhe khed hai ki . . .*; (to feel remorse) पछताना *pachtānā*$^{N}$ — you'll regret it later! बाद में पछताओगे! *bād mẽ pachtāoge!*

**regular** नियमित *niyamit*

**regularly** नियमित रूप से *niyamit rūp se*; (often) अक्सर *aksar*

**reject, to** अस्वीकार करना *asvīkār karnā*$^{N}$; (to throw out) निकाल देना *nikāl denā*$^{N}$

**relation** (kinsman) रिश्तेदार *riśtedār*$^{M}$

**relationship** संबंध *sambandh*$^{M}$, रिश्ता *riśtā*$^{M}$ — we have no relationship with them उनसे हमारा कोई संबंध/रिश्ता नहीं है *unse hamārā koī sambandh/riśtā nahī̃ hai*

**release** (from custody) रिहाई *rihāī*$^{F}$; (launch of a book) विमोचन *vimocan*$^{M}$

**release, to** (from custody) रिहा करना *rihā karnā*$^{N}$ *(-ā* invariable in *rihā*); (to allow to go) जाने देना *jāne denā*$^{N}$

**religion** धर्म *dharm*$^{M}$

**religious** धार्मिक *dhārmik*

**rely, to** निर्भर होना *nirbhar honā*; (to put trust in) भरोसा रखना$^{N}$ — we'd relied on them

हमने उनपर भरोसा रखा था *hamne unpar bharosā rakhā thā*

**remain, to** रहना *rahnā*; (to be left over) बाक़ी रहना *bāqī rahnā*

**remaining** बाक़ी *bāqī*, शेष *śeṣ*

**remedy** इलाज *ilāj*[M]

**remember, to** याद होना *yād honā* — I don't remember मुझे याद नहीं *mujhe yād nahī̃*; (to commit to memory) याद करना *yād karnā*[N] — remember this, don't forget! इसे याद करना, भूलना मत! *ise yād karnā, bhūlnā mat!*; (to recall) की याद करना *kī yād karnā*[N] — remember your childhood *apne bacpan kī yād karo*; (to bear in mind) याद रखना *yād rakhnā*[N] — remember that we have to go out याद रखो कि हमें बाहर जाना है *yād rakho ki hamẽ bāhar jānā hai*

**remind, to** याद दिलाना *yād dilānā*[N] — please remind them उन्हें याद दिलाइए [दिला दीजिए] *unhẽ yād dilāie [dilā dījie]*

**remote** दूर का *dūr kā*, सुदूर *sudūr*

**remove, to** (to get rid of) दूर करना *dūr karnā*[N] — remove this defect इस ख़राबी को दूर करो *is kharābī ko dūr karo*; (to clear something out of the way) हटाना *haṭānā*[N] — remove these chairs इन कुरसियों को हटाओ [हटा दो] *in kursiyõ ko haṭāo [haṭā do]*; (to erase) मिटाना *miṭānā*[N] — remove these three words इन तीन शब्दों को मिटाओ [मिटा दो] *in tīn śabdõ ko miṭāo [miṭā do]*

**rent** (and fare) किराया *kirāyā*[M] — how much is the rent/fare? किराया कितना है? *kirāyā kitnā hai?*; to rent, hire किराये पर लेना/देना *kirāye par lenā*[N]/*denā*[N] — we've rented this house हमने यह घर किराये पर लिया है *hamne yah ghar kirāye par liyā hai*

**repair, to** की मरम्मत करना *kī marammat karnā*[N] — please repair my car मेरी कार की मरम्मत कीजिए *merī kār kī marammat kījie*

**repeat, to** दोहराना *dohrānā*[N] — please repeat these words इन शब्दों को दोहराइए *in śabdõ ko dohrāie*; (to say again) फिर से कहना *phir se kahnā*[N] — please repeat फिर से कहिए *phir se kahie*

**reply** जवाब *javāb*[M], उत्तर *uttar*[M]; to reply जवाब/उत्तर देना

*javāb/uttar denā*[N] — reply to his letter उसके पत्र का जवाब/ उत्तर दो *uske patra kā javāb/ uttar do*

**representative** प्रतिनिधि *pratinidhi*[M]

**request** निवेदन *nivedan*[M]; to request निवेदन करना *nivedan karnā*[N] — you are requested to return the money आपसे निवेदन है कि आप पैसा लौटाएँ [लौटा दें] *āpse nivedan hai ki āp paisā lauṭāẽ [lauṭā dẽ]*

**rescue, to** बचाना *bacānā*[N] — we rescued the cat from the fire हमने बिल्ली को आग से बचाया *hamne billī ko āg se bacāyā*

**research** शोध *śodh*[M], शोध-कार्य *śodh-kārya*[M] — I've come to India to do research in history मैं इतिहास में शोध-कार्य करने के लिए भारत आया हूँ *maĩ itihās mẽ śodh-kārya karne ke lie bhārat āyā hū̃*

**resemble, to** मिलना-जुलना *milnā-julnā* — she resembles you वह आपसे मिलती-जुलती है *vah āpse miltī-jultī hai*

**resident** रहनेवाला *rahnevālā*[M], निवासी *nivāsī*[M] — a resident of Delhi दिल्ली का निवासी/ रहनेवाला *dillī kā nivāsī/ rahnevālā*

**resign** पद/नौकरी त्याग देना *pad/naukrī tyāg denā*[N] — I resigned my job मैंने अपना पद त्याग दिया *maĩne apna pad tyāg diyā*

**respect** आदर *ādar*[M], सम्मान *sammān*[M]

**respect, to** आदर/सम्मान करना *ādar/sammān karnā*[N] — we should respect the elders हमें बड़ों का आदर करना चाहिए *hamẽ baṛõ kā ādar karnā cāhie*

**responsibility** ज़िम्मेदारी *zimmedārī*[F], उत्तरदायित्व *uttardāyitva*[M]

**rest**[1] (repose) आराम *ārām*[M]

**rest**[2] (the rest, remainder) बाक़ी *bāqī* — the rest of the money बाक़ी पैसा *bāqī paisā*

**rest, to** आराम करना *ārām karnā*[N] — you should rest आपको आराम करना चाहिए *āpko ārām karnā cāhie*

**restaurant** रेस्तराँ *restrā̃*[M], (modest, provincial) होटल *hoṭal*[M]; (roadside café) ढाबा *ḍhābā*[M]

**restless** (agitated) बेचैन *becain*

**restlessness** बेचैनी *becainī*[F]

**result** नतीजा *natījā*[M], परिणाम *pariṇām*[M]

**return, to** लौटना *lauṭnā*; (to come/go back) वापस आना/जाना *vāpas ānā/jānā*; (to give back) लौटाना *lauṭānā*$^{N}$, वापस करना *vāpas karnā*$^{N}$; in return for के बदले में *ke badle mẽ*

**revenge** बदला *badlā*$^{M}$; to take revenge (for) (का) बदला लेना *(kā) badlā lenā*$^{N}$

**revise, to**$^{1}$ (to amend) (का) संशोधन करना *(kā) sanśodhan karnā*$^{N}$ — please revise your article अपने लेख का संशोधन कीजिए *apne lekh kā sanśodhan kījie*; (to do revision for exam, etc.) पाठ को दोहराना *pāṭh ko dohrānā*$^{N}$

**revolution** (political) क्रांति *krānti*$^{F}$

**revolve, to** (intr.) घूमना *ghūmnā*

**reward** (prize) पुरस्कार *puraskār*$^{M}$; (fruits of actions) फल *phal*$^{M}$

**rib** पसली *paslī*$^{F}$

**rice** चावल *cāval*$^{M}$ (often used in plural) — I cooked rice मैंने चावल बनाए *maĩne cāval banāe*; (paddy, rice plant) धान *dhān*$^{M}$; (boiled rice) भात *bhāt*$^{M}$

**rich** अमीर *amīr*

**rickshaw** रिक्शा *rikśā*$^{M}$

**rickshaw wallah** रिक्शेवाला *rikśevālā*$^{M}$

**ride, to** (पर) सवार होना *(par) savār honā*; to ride a bicycle/horse साइकिल/घोड़े पर सवार होना *sāikil/ghoṛe par savār honā*

**ridiculous** हास्यास्पद *hāsyāspad*

**right**$^{1}$ (correct) ठीक *ṭhīk*, सही *sahī*; right here/there यहीं/वहीं *yahī̃/vahī̃*; right now अभी *abhī*

**right**$^{2}$ (right hand) दाहिना *dāhinā* — turn right दाहिने मुड़ना *dāhine muṛnā*

**right**$^{3}$ (authority) अधिकार *adhikār*$^{M}$ — you have a right to speak आपको बोलने का अधिकार है *āpko bolne kā adhikār hai*

**ring** (for finger) अँगूठी *ãgūṭhī*$^{F}$

**ring, to** (to sound) बजना *bajnā* — the bell is ringing घंटी बज रही है *ghaṇṭī baj rahī hai*; (to telephone) फ़ोन करना *fon karnā*$^{N}$ — we'll phone you tomorrow evening हम तुम्हें कल शाम को फ़ोन करेंगे *ham tumhẽ kal śām ko fon karẽge*

**riot** दंगा *daṅgā*$^{M}$, दंगा-फ़साद *daṅgā-fasād*$^{M}$

**ripe** पक्का *pakkā*; to ripen पकना *paknā*

**rise, to** उठना *uṭhnā*; (to increase) बढ़ना *baṛhnā* — prices are rising दाम बढ़ रहे हैं *dām baṛh rahe haĩ*

**rite** संस्कार *sanskār*ᴹ

**rival** प्रतिद्वंदी *pratidvandī*ᴹ

**rivalry** प्रतिस्पर्धा *pratispardhā*ᶠ

**river** नदी *nadī*ᶠ; riverbank नदी का किनारा *nadī kā kinārā*ᴹ, (steps to river) घाट *ghāṭ*ᴹ

**road** सड़क *saṛak*ᶠ, रास्ता *rāstā*ᴹ

**roam, to** घूमना *ghūmnā*

**roast, to** भूनना *bhūnnā*ᴺ

**robber** चोर *cor*ᴹ

**robbery** चोरी *corī*ᶠ

**role** भूमिका *bhūmikā*ᶠ

**roof** छत *chat*ᶠ

**room** कमरा *kamrā*ᴹ

**Insight**

Room: कमरा *kamrā* comes to Hindi via Portuguese *camara* from Latin *camera*. Cognates include the English word 'comrade', meaning originally 'room-mate'.

**rope** रस्सा *rassā*ᴹ, (lighter) रस्सी *rassī*ᶠ

**rose** गुलाब *gulāb*ᴹ; rose coloured, pink गुलाबी रंग का *gulābī raṅg kā*

**rough** (coarse, as cloth) मोटा *moṭā*; (uneven, as road) ऊबड़-खाबड़ *ūbaṛ-khābaṛ*; (dry, as food) रूखा-सूखा *rūkhā-sūkhā*; (violent, as behaviour) उग्र *ugra*; (unfinished, as work) कच्चा *kaccā*

**roughly** (approximately) तक़रीबन *taqrīban*, लगभग *lagbhag*

**round** (circular) गोल *gol*

**roundabout** (road) गोल-चक्कर *gol-cakkar*ᴹ

**route** रास्ता *rāstā*ᴹ

**row, to** (a boat) खेना *khenā*ᴺ

**row**[1] (line) पंक्ति *paṅkti*ᶠ — a row of shops दुकानों की पंक्ति *dukānõ kī paṅkti*

**row**[2] (argument) झगड़ा *jhagṛā*ᴹ — there was a row among the shopkeepers दुकानदारों में झगड़ा हुआ *dukāndārõ mẽ jhagṛā huā*

**rubbish** कूड़ा *kūṛā*ᴹ; (nonsense) बकवास *bakvās*ᶠ

**rude** (impolite) बदतमीज़ *badtamīz*, अशिष्ट *aśiṣṭ*

**rudeness** बदतमीज़ी *badtamīzī*ᶠ, अशिष्टता *aśiṣṭtā*ᶠ

**rug** (durrie) दरी *darī*[F] — to spread a rug दरी बिछाना *darī bichānā*[N]

**ruin, to** बरबाद करना *barbād karnā*[N] — you've ruined my work तुमने मेरे काम को बरबाद किया है [कर दिया है] *tumne mere kām ko barbād kiyā hai [kar diyā hai]*

**ruin, ruins** खंडहर *khaṇḍ'har*[M]

**ruined, to be** बरबाद होना *barbād honā* (see also 'to spoil')

**rule** (regulation) नियम *niyam*[M]

**rule, to** (to govern) शासन करना *śāsan karnā*[N] — these days the BJP (Bharatiya Janta Party) is governing इन दिनों भाजपा (भारतीय जनता पार्टी) शासन कर रही है *in dinõ bhājpā (bhārtīy jantā pārṭī) śāsan kar rahī hai*

**ruler** (potentate) शासक *śāsak*[M]

**rumour** अफ़वाह *afvāh*[F] — rumours spread अफ़वाहें फैलती हैं *afvāhẽ phailtī haĩ*

**run, to** दौड़ना *dauṛnā*; to run away, flee भागना *bhāgnā*; to run (a business) चलाना *calānā*

**rupee** रुपया *rupayā*[M]

**rust** ज़ंग *zaṅg*[M] — my car has a lot of rust मेरी गाड़ी में बहुत ज़ंग लगा हुआ है *merī gāṛī mẽ bahut zaṅg lagā huā hai*

**rustling** (sound) सरसराहट *sarsarāhaṭ*[F]

## S

**sack** बोरा *borā*[M] — two sacks of rice दो बोरे चावल *do bore cāval*

**sacred** पवित्र *pavitra,* पुण्य *puṇya*

**sacrifice** बलिदान *balidān*[M]

**sad** उदास *udās*; you're looking sad तुम उदास लग रहे हो *tum udās lag rahe ho*

**sadness** उदासी *udāsī*[F], ग़म *gam*[M]

**sadhu** साधु *sādhu*[M]

**safe** (made safe, secured) सुरक्षित *surakṣit*; (for 'not safe', use 'dangerous' ख़तरनाक *khatarnāk,* or an expression with 'danger' ख़तरा *khatrā*) — it wouldn't be safe to go there alone वहाँ अकेले जाना ख़तरनाक होगा, ख़तरे से ख़ाली नहीं होगा *vahā̃ akele jānā khatarnāk hogā, khatre se khālī nahī̃ hogā*

**safety** सुरक्षा *surakṣā*[F]

**salary** वेतन *vetan*[M]

**salt** नमक *namak*[M]

**salty** नमकीन *namkīn*

**same** (similar) समान *samān*, एक-जैसा *ek-jaisā*, वैसा ही *vaisā hī* — they're both the same दोनों समान / एक-जैसे / वैसे ही हैं *donõ samān / ek-jaise / vaise hī haĩ* — all policemen's faces look the same सब पुलिसवालों की सूरतें एक जैसी लगती हैं *sab pulisvālõ kī sūratẽ ek jaisī lagtī haĩ*; the same one, the identical एक ही *ek hī* — we both work in the same office हम दोनों एक ही दफ़्तर में काम करते हैं *ham donõ ek hī daftar mẽ kām karte haĩ*; the same one who... वही *vahī* — the same man who phoned yesterday वही आदमी जिसने कल फ़ोन किया *vahī ādmī jisne kal fon kiyā*; all the same, even so फिर भी *phir bhī*; at the same time एक ही समय *ek hī samay*, एक साथ *ek sāth*; the same as, similar to के समान *ke samān* — this room is the same as that one यह कमरा उस कमरे के समान है *yah kamrā us kamre ke samān hai*

**samosa** समोसा *samosā*ᴹ

**sample** नमूना *namūnā*ᴹ

**sand** बालू *bālū*ᴹ, रेत *ret*ᶠ

**sandal** चप्पल *cappal*ᶠ

**sandy** रेतीला *retīlā*

**Sanskrit** संस्कृत *sanskṛt*ᶠ; Sanskritized Hindi संस्कृतनिष्ठ हिन्दी *sanskṛtniṣṭh hindī*ᶠ

**sarcasm** व्यंग्य *vyaṅgya*ᴹ

**sarcastic** व्यंग्यात्मक *vyaṅgyātmak*

**sarcastically** व्यंग्य से *vyaṅgya se*

**sari** साड़ी *sāṛī*ᶠ

**satisfaction** संतोष *santoṣ*ᴹ

**satisfied** संतुष्ट *santuṣṭ* — the customers are not satisfied ग्राहक संतुष्ट नहीं हैं *grāhak santuṣṭ nahī̃ haĩ*

**satisfy, to** संतुष्ट करना *santuṣṭ karnā*ᴺ

**Saturday** शनिवार *śanivār*ᴹ

**saucer** तश्तरी *taśtarī*ᶠ

**save, to** बचाना *bacānā*ᴺ

**saved, to be** बचना *bacnā*

**savoury** नमकीन *namkīn*

**saw** (handsaw) आरी *ārī*ᶠ

**say, to** कहना *kahnā*ᴺ ('to', से *se*) — what was she saying to you? वह आपसे क्या कह रही थी? *vah āpse kyā kah rahī thī?*

**saying** (proverb) कहावत *kahāvat*ᶠ

**scarce** दुर्लभ *durlabh*

**scarcely** बहुत कम *bahut kam*

**scare, to** डराना *ḍarānā*[N] (see also 'to startle')

**scene** दृश्य *dṛśya*[M]

**schedule** प्रोग्राम *progrām*[M], कार्यक्रम *kāryakram*[F]

**scheme** योजना *yojnā*[F], परियोजना *pariyojnā*[F]

**scholar** पंडित *paṇḍit*[M]

**scholarship**[1] (grant) छात्रवृत्ति *chātravṛtti*[F]

**scholarship**[2] (erudition) विद्वत्ता *vidvattā*

**school** स्कूल *skūl*[M]

**science** विज्ञान *vijñān*[M] (pronounced 'vigyān')

**scientific** वैज्ञानिक *vaijñānik*

**scientist** विज्ञानी *vijñānī*[M]

**scissors** कैंची *kaĩcī*[F] (singular) — where are those scissors? वह कैंची कहाँ है? *vah kaĩcī kahā̃ hai?*

**scold, to** डाँटना *ḍā̃ṭnā*[N]

**scope** गुंजाइश *gunjāiś*[F] — there's a lot of scope for this इसके लिए बहुत गुंजाइश है *iske lie bahut gunjāiś hai*

**scrape, to** खुरचना *khuracnā*[N]

**scream, to** चीख़ना *cī<u>kh</u>nā* — he began screaming loudly वह ज़ोर से चीख़ने लगा *vah zor se cī<u>kh</u>ne lagā*

**screwdriver** पेंचकश *pẽckaś*[M]

**script** (alphabet) लिपि *lipi*[F]

**sculptor** मूर्तिकार *mūrtikār*[M]

**sculpture** (the art of) मूर्तिकला *mūrtikalā*[F]; (a work of) मूर्ति *mūrti*[F]

**sea** समुद्र *samudra*[M] — at the seaside समुद्र के किनारे *samudra ke kināre*

**search** तलाश *talāś*[F]

**search, to** तलाश करना *talāś karnā*[N] ('for', की *kī*), ढूँढ़ना *ḍhū̃ṛhnā*[N] — I was searching for you मैं आपकी तलाश कर रहा था *maĩ āpkī talāś kar rahā thā*, मैं आपको ढूँढ़ रहा था *maĩ āpko ḍhū̃ṛh rahā thā*

**season** ऋतु *ṛtu*[F]; मौसम *mausam*[M]

**seasonal** मौसमी *mausamī*

**seat** सीट *sīṭ*[F] — the back seat is free पीछेवाली सीट ख़ाली है *pīchevālī sīṭ <u>kh</u>ālī hai*

**seated** बैठा हुआ *baiṭhā huā*; she was seated on the ground वह ज़मीन पर बैठी हुई थी *vah zamīn par baiṭhī huī thī*

**second**[1] (other) दूसरा *dūsrā*

**second**[2] (60th of minute) सेकंड *sekaṇḍ*[M]; (moment) क्षण *kṣaṇ*[M]

**secret** (adj.: hidden, clandestine) गुप्त *gupt* — secret love गुप्त प्रेम *gupt prem*; (noun: a secret) भेद *bhed*[M]; (a mystery) रहस्य *rahasya*[M]

**secure** सुरक्षित *surakṣit*

**seize, to** पकड़ना *pakaṛnā*[N]

**Insight**

Secure: सुरक्षित *surakṣit* means literally 'secured'; the *-it* ending of the Sanskrit loanword equates to the '-ed' or '-en' endings of such words in English. Compare लिखित *likhit* 'written'.

**see, to** देखना *dekhnā*[N]; (to meet) मिलना *milnā* — some boy's come to see you कोई लड़का तुमसे मिलने आया है *koī laṛkā tumse milne āyā hai*; (to understand) समझना *samajhnā* — do you see what I mean? आप मेरी बात समझे? *āp merī bāt samjhe?*

**seed** बीज *bīj*[M]

**seem, to** लगना *lagnā*, जान पड़ना *jān paṛnā* — this work seems quite simple यह काम काफ़ी आसान लगता है *yah kām kāfī āsān lagtā hai*; it seems she doesn't even recognize me लगता है कि वह मुझे पहचानती भी नहीं *lagtā hai ki vah mujhe pahcāntī bhī nahī̃*

**seen, to be** (to come into view, be visible) दिखाई देना/पड़ना *dikhāī denā/paṛnā* (no ने *ne* construction) — two rickshaws were seen in the alley गली में दो रिक्शे दिखाई दिए *galī mẽ do rikśe dikhāī die*

**self-confidence** आत्मविश्वास *ātmaviśvās*[M]

**self-confident** आत्मविश्वासी *ātmaviśvāsī*

**selfish** स्वार्थी *svārthī*

**selfishness** स्वार्थ *svārth*[M]

**self-respect** आत्मसम्मान *ātmasammān*[M]

**sell, to** बेचना *becnā*[N]; (intr. sense: see 'to be sold')

**semester** सत्र *satra*[M]

**send, to** भेजना *bhejnā*[N]

**sense** (of hearing etc.) इंद्रिय *indriy*[M]; (consciousness) होश *hoś*[F] — come to your senses! होश में आओ! *hoś mẽ āo!*

**sensible** समझदार *samajhdār* — a sensible man समझदार आदमी *samajhdār ādmī*

**sentence** (gramm.) वाक्य *vākya*$^{M}$; (law) सज़ा *sazā*$^{F}$ — he/she will be given a jail sentence उसे जेल की सज़ा दी जाएगी *use jel kī sazā dī jāegī*

**separate** अलग *alag*

**separate, to** (intr., to become separate) अलग/जुदा होना *alag/judā honā* (*-ā* in *judā* invariable) — we separated two years ago हम दो साल पहले जुदा हुए [हो गए] *ham do sāl pahle judā hue [ho gae]*; (tr.) अलग करना *alag karnā*$^{N}$ — separate those two boys उन दो लड़कों को अलग करो [कर दो] *un do laṛkõ ko alag karo [kar do]*

**separation** (parting) जुदाई *judāī*$^{F}$

**September** सितंबर *sitambar*$^{M}$

**serial** (on television) धारावाहिक *dhārāvāhik*$^{M}$

**serious** गंभीर *gambhīr*; (solemn) संजीदा *sanjīdā*

**seriously** गंभीरता से *gambhīrtā se*

**seriousness** गंभीरता *gambhīrtā*$^{F}$

**servant** नौकर *naukar*$^{M}$ — we don't have a servant हमारे पास नौकर नहीं है *hamāre pās naukar nahī̃ hai*

**serve, to** सेवा करना *sevā karnā*$^{N}$ — he/she served in the army उसने सेना में सेवा की *usne senā mẽ sevā kī*; he serves his country वह अपने देश की सेवा करता है *vah apne deś kī sevā kartā hai*; to serve food खाना परोसना *khānā parosnā*$^{N}$ — the food was served at ten o'clock खाना दस बजे परोसा गया *khānā das baje parosā gayā*

**service** सेवा *sevā*$^{F}$

**set off, to** चल पड़ना *cal paṛnā* — we set off at two o'clock हम दो बजे चल पड़े *ham do baje cal paṛe*

**settle, to** (to settle a debt or bill) चुकाना *cukānā*$^{N}$; (to settle in a place) बसना *basnā*, बस जाना *bas jānā* — we settled in Delhi हम दिल्ली में बस गए *ham dillī mẽ bas gae*; (to subside) बैठ जाना *baiṭh jānā*

**seven** सात *sāt*

**seventeen** सत्रह *satrah*

**seventy** सत्तर *sattar*

**several** कई *kaī*, बहुत-से *bahut-se*

**sew, to** सीना *sīnā*$^{N}$

**sewing** सिलाई *silāī*$^{F}$

**sex** (general subject of) सेक्स *seks*$^{M}$; (gender) लिंग *liṅg*$^{M}$; (sexual intercourse) संभोग *sambhog*$^{M}$

**sexual** यौन *yaun*

**shade** साया *sāyā*[M], छाया *chāyā*[F] — to sit in the shade साये में बैठना *sāye mẽ baiṭhnā*

**shadow** परछाईं *parchāĩ*[F], छाया *chāyā*[F]

**shake, to** (intr.) (to move) हिलना *hilnā*; (to tremble) काँपना *kā̃pnā*; (tr., e.g. to shake a bottle) हिलाना *hilānā*[N]; to shake hands हाथ मिलाना *hāth milānā*[N]

**shallow** छिछला *chichlā*; (of person) ओछा *ochā*

**shame** शर्म *śarm*[F], लज्जा *lajjā*[F] — aren't you ashamed? तुम्हें शर्म/लज्जा नहीं आती? *tumhẽ śarm/lajjā nahī̃ ātī?*

**shape** आकार *ākār*[M]

**shape, to** (to mould, form) गढ़ना *gaṛhnā*[N]

**sharp** (of knife, eyes, mind, pain etc.) तेज़ *tez*

**shave, to** दाढ़ी बनाना *dāṛhī banānā*[N], शेव करना *śev karnā*[N]; (to shave the head) मुंडन करना *muṇḍan karnā*[N]

**shawl** शाल *śāl*[F]

**she** वह *vah*

**sheep** भेड़ *bheṛ*[F]

**sheet**[1] (bedsheet) चादर *cādar*[F]

**sheet**[2] (paper) काग़ज़ *kāgaz*[M]

**shell** (of egg) छिलका *chilkā*[M]; (of coconut) खोपड़ी *khopṛī*[F]

**shelter** शरण *śaraṇ*[M (F)]

**shine, to** चमकना *camaknā*

**shiny** चमकीला *camkīlā*

**ship** जहाज़ *jahāz*[M]

**shirt** क़मीज़ *qamīz*[F]

**shit, to** हगना *hagnā*

**shiver, to** काँपना *kā̃pnā* — my hands were shivering with cold मेरे हाथ ठंड से काँप रहे थे *mere hāth ṭhaṇḍ se kā̃p rahe the*

**shoe** जूता *jūtā*[M]

**shoot, to** गोली मारना *golī mārnā*[N]

**shop** दुकान *dukān*[F] — cloth shop कपड़े की दुकान *kapṛe kī dukān*; to go to the shops बाज़ार जाना *bāzār jānā*

**shopkeeper** दुकानदार *dukāndār*[M]

**shore** किनारा *kinārā*[M]

**short** छोटा *choṭā*; (in stature) छोटा *choṭā*, छोटे क़द का *choṭe qad kā* — a short man छोटे क़द का आदमी *choṭe qad kā ādmī*

**shortage** कमी *kamī*[F] — because of a shortage of money पैसे की कमी की वजह से *paise kī kamī kī vajah se*

**should** चाहिए *cāhie* (follows infinitive) — I should go मुझे जाना चाहिए *mujhe jānā cāhie*, they should learn Hindi उनको हिन्दी सीखनी चाहिए *unko hindī sīkhnī cāhie*

**shoulder** कंधा *kandhā*[M]

**shout, to** चिल्लाना *cillānā*

**shove, to** ढकेलना *ḍhakelnā*[N]

**show** (play) तमाशा *tamāśā*[M]; (ostentation) दिखावा *dikhāvā*[M]

**show, to** दिखाना *dikhānā*[N] — Vasu showed me some pictures वसु ने मुझे कुछ तस्वीरें दिखाईं *vasu ne mujhe kuch tasvīrẽ dikhāī̃*

**shower** (of rain) बौछाड़ *bauchāṛ*[F]

**shut** बंद *band*

**shut, to** बंद करना *band karnā*[N]

**shy** शर्मीला *śarmīlā*

**shyness** शर्म *śarm*[F], लज्जा *lajjā*[F]

**sick** (ill) बीमार *bīmār*

**sick, to be** (to vomit) उलटी करना *ulṭī karnā*[N]; to feel sick मितली आना *mitlī ānā* — I'm feeling sick (morning sickness etc.) मुझे मितली आ रही है *mujhe mitlī ā rahī hai*

**side** (of body, building etc.) बग़ल *bagal*[F] — on/at the side of की बग़ल में *kī bagal mẽ*; (in an argument) पक्ष *pakṣ*[M] — he'll take the government's side वह सरकार का पक्ष लेगा *vah sarkār kā pakṣ legā*; (of road, river) किनारा *kinārā*[M]; on the other side of, across के उस पार — on the other side of the river नदी के उस पार *nadī ke us pār*; (side of paper, cloth) तरफ़ *taraf*[F] — the other side of the paper काग़ज़ की उलटी/दूसरी तरफ़ *qāgaz kī ulṭī/dūsrī taraf*

**sigh** आह *āh*[F]

**sigh, to** आह भरना *āh bharnā*[N] — to heave a deep sigh ठंडी आह भरना *ṭhanḍī āh bharnā*[N]

**sight** (view) दृश्य *dṛśya*[M]; (spectacle) तमाशा *tamāśā*[M]; (faculty of seeing) दृष्टि *dṛṣṭi*[F]

**sign** (mark) निशान *niśān*[M]; (gesture) इशारा *iśārā*[M]; (indication) चिह्न *cihn*[M]; (symbol) प्रतीक *pratīk*[M]; (zodiac) राशि *rāśi*[F]

**sign, to** साइन करना *sāin karnā*[N], हस्ताक्षर करना *hastākṣar karnā*[N]

**signature** हस्ताक्षर *hastākṣar*[M] (usually used in plural) — your signature is needed on this form इस फ़ॉर्म पर आपके हस्ताक्षर चाहिए *is fārm par āpke hastākṣar cāhie*

**Sikh** (adj. & noun) सिख *sikh*ᴹ, सरदार *sardār*ᴹ (form of address: सरदारजी *sardārjī*)

**Sikhism** सिख धर्म *sikh dharm*ᴹ

**silence** ख़ामोशी *khāmośī*ᶠ; चुप्पी *cuppī*ᶠ; (stillness) सन्नाटा *sannāṭā*ᴹ; (absention from speech) मौन *maun*ᴹ

**silent** ख़ामोश *khāmoś*; (not speaking) चुप *cup* — she remained silent वह चुप रही *vah cup rahī*

**silk** रेशम *reśam*ᴹ

**silken** रेशमी *reśmī*

**silver** चाँदी *cā̃dī*ᶠ

**similar** समान *samān* — of similar kind समान ढंग का *samān ḍhaṅg kā*; they're all similar सभी एक समान हैं *sabhī ek samān haĩ*

**similarity** समानता *samāntā*ᶠ

**similarly** इसी तरह से *isī tarah se*, इसी प्रकार *isī prakār*

**simple** (easy) सरल *saral* — simple Hindi सरल हिन्दी *saral hindī*; (plain) सादा *sādā* — simple clothes सादे कपड़े *sāde kapṛe*

**sin** पाप *pāp*ᴹ

**sin, to** पाप करना *pāp karnā*ᴺ

**since** से *se* — since Monday सोमवार से *somvār se*; (since the time when) जब से *jab se* — since Sujata came जब से सुजाता आई *jab se sujātā āī*; (since then) तब से *tab se* — I haven't been home since then मैं तब से घर नहीं गया हूँ *maĩ tab se ghar nahī̃ gayā hū̃*; (because) क्योंकि *kyõki*; चूँकि *cū̃ki* (used when the reason precedes the consequence — since you have no money, you can't help me चूँकि आपके पास पैसा नहीं है, इसलिए आप मेरी मदद नहीं कर सकते *cū̃ki āpke pās paisā nahī̃ hai, islie āp merī madad nahī̃ kar sakte*)

**sincere** सच्चा *saccā*; (honest) ईमानदार *īmāndār*

**sincerely** सच्चाई से *saccāī se*; yours sincerely (in letter) भवदीय *bhavdīy*; (with female signatory) भवदीया *bhavdīyā*

**sinful** पापी *pāpī*

**sing, to** गाना *gānā*ᴺ; (of birds) चहकना *cahaknā*

**singing** गाना *gānā*ᴹ — I liked Erika's singing मुझे एरिका का गाना पसंद आया *mujhe erikā kā gānā pasand āyā*

**single** (sole) एकमात्र *ekmātra* (see also 'sole'); (unmarried) अविवाहित *avivāhit* — I'm single मैं अविवाहित हूँ, *maĩ avivāhit hũ*, मैं शादी-शुदा नहीं हूँ *maĩ śādī-śudā nahī̃ hũ*

**singular** (in grammar) एकवचन *ekvacan*

**sink, to** डूबना *ḍūbnā*

**sinner** पापी *pāpī*$^{M}$

**sip, to** घूंट लेना *ghũṭ lenā*$^{M}$

**sir** जी *jī*, सर *sar*

**sister** बहिन *bahin*$^{F}$; elder sister दीदी *dīdī*$^{F}$

**sister-in-law** (husband's sister) ननद *nanad*$^{F}$; (wife's sister) साली *sālī*$^{F}$

**sit, to** बैठना *baiṭhnā*; to sit down बैठ जाना *baiṭh jānā* — please sit down बैठ जाइए *baiṭh jāie*, (more formal) तशरीफ़ रखिए *taśrīf rakhie*; seated, sitting बैठा (हुआ) *baiṭhā (huā)* — she is sitting वह बैठी हुई है *vah baiṭhī huī hai*; to make someone sit किसी को बिठाना *kisī ko biṭhānā*$^{N}$

**sitar** सितार *sitār*$^{M}$

**site** स्थल *sthal*$^{M}$

**sitting room** बैठक *baiṭhak*$^{F}$

**situation** स्थिति *sthiti*$^{F}$ — the situation is becoming serious स्थिति गंभीर हो रही है *sthiti gambhīr ho rahī hai*

**six** छह *chah*

**sixteen** सोलह *solah*

**sixty** साठ *sāṭh*

**skilful** कुशल *kuśal*

**skill** कुशलता *kuśaltā*$^{F}$

**skin** (of person) चमड़ी *camṛī*$^{F}$; (of fruit) छिलका *chilkā*$^{M}$

**skinny** (thin) दुबला-पतला *dublā-patlā* — skinny boys दुबले-पतले लड़के *duble-patle laṛke*

**skull** खोपड़ी *khopṛī*$^{F}$

**sky** आकाश *ākāś*$^{M}$, आसमान *āsmān*$^{M}$

**slave** गुलाम *gulām*$^{M}$

**slavery** गुलामी *gulāmī*$^{F}$

**sleep** नींद *nī̃d*$^{F}$; to get to sleep नींद आना *nī̃d ānā* — I couldn't get to sleep all night मुझे रात भर नींद नहीं आई *mujhe rāt bhar nī̃d nahī̃ āī*

**sleep, to** सोना *sonā*; to go to sleep सो जाना *so jānā* — go to sleep! सो जाओ! *so jāo!*; to sleep comfortably आराम से सोना *ārām se sonā*, सुख की नींद सोना *sukh kī nī̃d sonā*

**slim** पतला *patlā*, छरहरा *charharā*

**slip, to** फिसलना *phisalnā*

**slip away, to** खिसकना *khisaknā*, खिसक जाना *khisak jānā* — I'll slip away quietly मैं चुपके से खिसक जाऊँगा *maĩ cupke se khisak jāũgā*

**slogan** नारा *nārā*$^{M}$ — to shout slogans नारे लगाना *nāre lagānā*$^{N}$

**slope** ढलान *ḍhalān*$^{F}$

**slow** धीमा *dhīmā*; (sluggish) सुस्त *sust*

**slowly** धीरे-धीरे *dhīre-dhīre*

**slum** बस्ती *bastī*$^{F}$

**small** छोटा *choṭā*

**smallpox** चेचक *cecak*$^{F}$

**smell** गंध *gandh*$^{F}$, बू *bū*$^{F}$ — there's a smell of smoke धुएँ की बू आ रही है *dhuẽ kī bū ā rahī hai*; pleasant smell ख़ुशबू *khuśbū*$^{F}$; unpleasant smell बदबू *badbū*$^{F}$

**smell, to** (intr., a smell to be emitted) बू आना *bū ānā*; (tr., to smell, sniff) सूँघना *sũghnā*$^{N}$

**smile** मुस्कराहट *muskarāhaṭ*$^{F}$

**smile, to** मुस्कराना *muskarānā*$^{N}$

**smoke** धुआँ *dhuā̃*$^{M}$ (oblique धुएँ *dhuẽ*)

**smoke, to** (to emit smoke, of fire) धुआँ देना *dhuā̃ denā*$^{N}$ — the fire is smoking आग धुआँ दे रही है *āg dhuā̃ de rahī hai*; (to smoke tobacco) पीना *pīnā*$^{N}$ — I don't smoke मैं सिग्रेट नहीं पीता *maĩ sigreṭ nahĩ pītā*

**smoking** (of tobacco: formal) धूम्रपान *dhūmrapān*$^{M}$ — smoking is prohibited धूम्रपान वर्जित है *dhūmrapān varjit hai*

**smooth** चिकना *ciknā*

**snake** साँप *sā̃p*$^{M}$

**snatch, to** छीनना *chīnnā*$^{N}$

**sneeze, to** छींकना *chĩknā*

**snow** बर्फ़ *barf*$^{F}$

**snow, to** बर्फ़ पड़ना *barf paṛnā*

**so** (therefore) तो *to*, इस लिए *is lie*, सो *so*; (thus) ऐसा *aisā* — you shouldn't speak so तुम्हें ऐसा नहीं बोलना चाहिए *tumhẽ aisā nahĩ bolnā cāhie*; so much/many इतना *itnā* — so many people इतने लोग *itne log*; so good इतना अच्छा *itnā acchā*; so what? तो क्या हुआ? *to kyā huā?*; so that ताकि *tāki*, जिससे कि *jisse ki* (+ subjunctive) — eat now, so that you don't get hungry later अभी खाना खाओ ताकि बाद में भूख न लगे *abhī khānā khāo tāki bād mẽ bhūkh na lage*

**soaked, to be** भीगना *bhīgnā*; to get soaked भीग जाना *bhīg* *jānā* — we got soaked in the rain हम बारिश में भीग गए *ham bāriś mẽ bhīg gae*

**soap** साबुन *sābun*^M

**sob** सिसकी siskī^F

**sob, to** सिसकना *sisaknā*

**so-called** तथाकथित *tathākathit*

**sociable** मिलनसार *milansār*

**social** सामाजिक *sāmājik*

**socialism** समाजवाद *samājvād*^M

**socialist** (adj. & noun) समाजवादी *samājvādī*^M

**society** समाज *samāj*^M

**sock** मोज़ा *mozā*^M

**sofa** सोफ़ा *sofā*^M

**soft** नरम *naram,* मुलायम *mulāyam*; (of sound) धीमा *dhīmā*

**soil** मिट्टी *miṭṭī*^F

**sold, to be** बिकना *biknā* — real ghee is sold in this shop इस दुकान में असली घी बिकता है *is dukān mẽ aslī ghī biktā hai*

**soldier** सैनिक *sainik*^M; (a private) जवान *javān*^M

**sole** (adj.) एकमात्र *ekmātra* — our sole support हमारा एकमात्र सहारा *hamārā ekmātra sahārā*; (of offspring) इकलौता *iklautā* — our sole son हमारा इकलौता बेटा *hamārā iklautā beṭā*

**solid** ठोस *ṭhos* (concrete & abstract senses) — he does solid work वह ठोस काम करता है *vah ṭhos kām kartā hai*

**solitude** अकेलापन *akelāpan*^M

**solution** समाधान *samādhān*^M — we're looking for a solution to the problem हम समस्या का समाधान ढूँढ़ रहे हैं *ham samasyā kā samādhān ḍhū̃ṛh rahe haĩ*

**solve, to** हल करना *hal karnā*^N — we'll solve your difficulty हम आपकी मुश्किल को हल करेंगे *ham āpkī muśkil ko hal karẽge*

**solved, to be** हल होना *hal honā* — the problem was solved समस्या हल हुई [हो गई] *samasyā hal huī [ho gaī]*

**some** कुछ *kuch* — some money कुछ पैसा *kuch paisā*; some books कुछ किताबें *kuch kitābẽ*; a certain one कोई *koī* — some man is standing outside कोई आदमी बाहर खड़ा है *koī ādmī bāhar khaṛā hai*

**somebody:** see 'someone'

**somehow** किसी तरह (से) *kisī tarah (se)*

**someone** कोई *koī* — someone's coming कोई आ रहा है *koī ā rahā hai*; someone or other कोई

न कोई *koī na koī*; someone's umbrella is lying on the floor किसी का छाता फ़र्श पर पड़ा है *kisī kā chātā farś par paṛā hai*

**sometime** कभी *kabhī*; sometime or other कभी न कभी *kabhī na kabhī*; sometimes कभी कभी *kabhī kabhī*

**somewhere** कहीं *kahī̃*; somewhere or other कहीं न कहीं *kahī̃ na kahī̃*; (a certain place) एक ऐसी जगह – we'll meet somewhere where nobody goes हम एक ऐसी जगह पर मिलेंगे जहाँ कोई नहीं जाता *ham ek aisī jagah par milẽge jahā̃ koī nahī̃ jātā*

**son** बेटा *beṭā*$^{M}$

**son-in-law** दामाद *dāmād*$^{M}$

**song** गाना *gānā*$^{M}$, गीत *gīt*$^{M}$

**soon** जल्दी *jaldī*, थोड़ी देर में *thoṛī der mẽ*; as soon as जैसे ही *jaise hī* — as soon as she arrives जैसे ही वह पहुँचती है *jaise hī vah pahũctī hai*, 💣 उसके पहुँचते ही *uske pahũcte hī*

**sorrow** दुःख *duḥkh*$^{M}$

**sorry:** I'm sorry (asking forgiveness) माफ़ कीजिए *māf kījie*; I'm sorry (regretful) 💣 मुझे खेद है *mujhe khed hai*

**soul** आत्मा *ātmā*$^{F}$

**soulful** भावपूर्ण *bhāvpūrṇ*

**sound** आवाज़ *āvāz*$^{F}$; a sound to be heard आवाज़ सुनाई देना/पड़ना *āvāz sunāī denā/paṛnā* (no ने *ne* construction) — the sound of the car was heard गाड़ी की आवाज़ सुनाई दी *gāṛī kī āvāz sunāī dī*; sound of someone coming, a footfall आहट *āhaṭ*$^{F}$

**sour** खट्टा *khaṭṭā*

**source** स्रोत *srot*$^{M}$

**south** दक्षिण *dakṣiṇ*$^{M}$ — south India दक्षिण भारत *dakṣiṇ bhārat*

**southern** दक्षिणी *dakṣiṇī*

**spade** फावड़ा *phāvṛā*$^{M}$

**spare time** फ़ुरसत$^{F}$ *fursat*, फ़ुरसत का समय$^{M}$ *fursat kā samay*, ख़ाली समय *khālī samay*$^{M}$

**spark** चिनगारी *cingārī*$^{M}$

**speak, to** बोलना *bolnā* — please speak slowly धीरे-धीरे बोलिए *dhīre-dhīre bolie*; -speaking -भाषी *-bhāṣī* — Hindi-speaking people हिन्दी-भाषी लोग *hindī-bhāṣī log*; 'speaking' on telephone — this is Kishor speaking 💣 मैं किशोर बोल रहा हूँ *maĩ kiśor bol rahā hū̃*

**speaker** वक्ता *vaktā*[M]

**special** ख़ास *khās,* विशेष *viśeṣ* — for some special reason किसी ख़ास वजह से *kisī khās vajah se,* किसी विशेष कारण से *kisī viśeṣ kāraṇ se*

**specialist** विशेषज्ञ *viśeṣajña*[M] (pronounced 'viśeṣagya')

**spectacles:** see 'glasses'

**speech** (lecture) भाषण *bhāṣaṇ*[M]; (language, way of speaking) बोली *bolī*[F] — the villagers' speech is very sweet गाँववालों की बोली बहुत मीठी है *gā̃vvālõ kī bolī bahut mīṭhī hai*

**speed** गति *gati*[F], रफ़्तार *raftār*[F] — the car was moving at high speed गाड़ी तेज़ रफ़्तार से चल रही थी *gāṛī tez raftār se cal rahī thī*

**spelling** हिज्जे *hijje*[M PL], वर्तनी *vartanī*[F]; to spell हिज्जे करना *hijje karnā*[N] — I can't spell 'bṛhaspativār' मुझे बृहस्पतिवार के हिज्जे करना नहीं आता *mujhe bṛhaspativār ke hijje karnā nahī̃ ātā*

**spend, to** (time) बिताना *bitānā*[N] — we spent two days there हमने वहाँ दो दिन बिताए *hamne vahā̃ do din bitāe*; (money) ख़र्च करना *kharc karnā*[N] — I spent 1000 rupees मैंने १००० रुपये ख़र्च किए *maĩne 1000 rupaye kharc kie*

**spice** मसाला *masālā*[M]

**spicy** मसालेदार *masāledār*

**spider** मकड़ी *makṛī*[F]

**spill, to** (intr.) छलकना *chalaknā*; (tr.) छलकाना *chalkānā*[N]

**spiritual** आध्यात्मिक *ādhyātmik*

**spite of, in** के बावजूद *ke bavjūd*

**split, to** (tr.) चीरना *cīrnā*[N]

**spoil, to** (tr.) ख़राब करना[N] *kharāb karnā* — you have spoilt my book तुमने मेरी किताब को ख़राब किया है [कर दिया है] *tumne merī kitāb ko kharāb kiyā hai [kar diyā hai]*

**spoilt, to be** बिगड़ना *bigarnā* — the atmosphere of the party was spoilt पार्टी का माहौल बिगड़ा [बिगड़ गया] *pārṭī kā māhaul bigaṛā [bigaṛ gayā]*; spoilt children बिगड़े हुए बच्चे *bigaṛe hue bacce*

**spoon** चम्मच *cammac*[M]

**sport(s)** खेल-कूद *khel-kūd*[M] — they're very fond of sports उन्हें खेल-कूद का बहुत शौक़ है *unhẽ khel-kūd kā bahut śauq hai*

**spot** (stain) धब्बा *dhabbā*[M]

**spread, to** (intr., to be spread) फैलना *phailnā*; (tr., to scatter, disperse) फैलाना *phailānā*[N]; (tr., to lay out, as bed sheet) बिछाना *bichānā*[N]

**spring** (season) बसंत *basant*[M]

**spy** जासूस *jāsūs*[M]

**spying** जासूसी *jāsūsī*[F]

**spy, to** जासूसी करना *jāsūsī karnā*[N]

**squander, to** उड़ाना *uṛānā*[N] — you shouldn't squander your money तुम्हें अपना पैसा नहीं उड़ाना चाहिए *tumhẽ apnā paisā nahī̃ uṛānā cāhie*

**square**[1] (in shape) चौकोर *caukor*

**square**[2] (urban space for market etc.) चौक *cauk*[M]

**squirrel** गिलहरी *gilahrī*[F]

**stage**[1] (platform) मंच *manc*[M]

**stage**[2] ('step' in a process) चरण *caraṇ*[M] — the final stage of the plan योजना का अंतिम चरण *yojnā kā antim caraṇ*

**stain** (on cloth) धब्बा *dhabbā*[M]; (on character) कलंक *kalaṅk*[M]

**stair, staircase** सीढ़ी *sīṛhī*[F] — to go up/down the stairs सीढ़ियाँ चढ़ना/उतरना *sīṛhiyā̃ caṛhnā/utarnā*

**stale** बासी *bāsī* — the smell of stale food बासी खाने की बू *bāsī khāne kī bū*

**stamp** (postage) टिकट *ṭikaṭ*[M (F)], डाक-टिकट *ḍāk-ṭikaṭ*[M (F)] — stick a stamp on the envelope लिफ़ाफ़े पर टिकट लगाओ [लगा दो] *lifāfe par ṭikaṭ lagāo [lagā do]*

**stand, to**[1] (to be standing) खड़ा होना *khaṛā honā;* (to stand up) उठ खड़ा होना *uṭh khaṛā honā* — she stood up वह उठ खड़ी हुई *vah uṭh khaṛī huī*

**stand, to**[2] (to tolerate) बरदाश्त करना *bardāśt karnā*[N] — I can't stand his arrogance मैं उसका घमंड बरदाश्त नहीं कर सकता *maĩ uskā ghamaṇḍ bardāśt nahī̃ kar saktā*

**standing** खड़ा *khaṛā* — your guests are standing outside आपके मेहमान बाहर खड़े हैं *āpke mehmān bāhar khaṛe haĩ*

**star** तारा *tārā*[M]; (filmstar) सितारा *sitārā*[M]

**start** (see 'to begin'); to set in motion चला देना *calā denā*[N] — start the fan पंखे को चला दो *paṅkhe ko calā do*; to start a car गाड़ी स्टार्ट करना *gāṛī sṭārṭ karnā*[N]

**startle, to** चौंकाना *caũkānā*[N] — the car startled me गाड़ी ने मुझे चौंकाया [चौंका दिया] *gāṛī ne mujhe caũkāyā [caũkā diyā]*

**starve, to** भूखों मरना *bhūkhõ marnā*

**state**[1] (condition) हालत *hālat*[F] — the state of the roads wasn't very good सड़कों की हालत बहुत अच्छी न थी *saṛkõ kī hālat bahut acchī na thī*; he was in a bad state वह बुरी हालत में था *vah burī hālat mẽ thā*

**state**[2] (province) प्रदेश *prades*[M]; (nation-state) राष्ट्र *rāṣṭra*[M]

**station** स्टेशन *sṭeśan*[M]; bus station बस अड्डा *bas aḍḍā*[M]; police station थाना *thānā*[M]

**statue** मूर्ति *mūrti*[F]

**stay, to** (to remain) रहना *rahnā*; (stay temporarily, stop) ठहरना *ṭhaharnā* — we're staying at the Taj हम ताज में ठहरे हुए हैं *ham tāj mẽ ṭhahre hue haĩ*; stay at our place हमारे यहाँ ठहरिए *hamāre yahā̃ ṭhaharie*

**steady** स्थिर *sthir*

**steal, to** (की) चोरी करना *(kī) corī karnā*[N] — he/she stole my watch उसने मेरी घड़ी चोरी की *usne merī ghaṛī corī kī*

**stealthily** चोरी-चोरी *corī-corī*

**steam** भाप *bhāp*[M]

**steel** इस्पात *ispāt*[M]

**step** (footstep; action) क़दम *qadam*[M]; (stair) सीढ़ी *sīṛhī*[F]

**step-** (in relationship) सौतेला *sautelā* — step-sister सौतेली बहिन *sautelī bahin*[F]

**stick** डंडा *ḍaṇḍā*[M]; (truncheon) लाठी *lāṭhī*[F]; twig, small branch लकडी *lākrī*[F]

**stick, to** (intr., to be fastened) चिपकना *cipaknā*; (tr., to fasten) चिपकाना *cipkānā*[N]

**stiff** (rigid) कठोर *kaṭhor*; (viscous) गाढ़ा *gāṛhā*

**still**[1] (even now) अभी भी *abhī bhī* — he's still working वह अभी भी काम कर रहा है *vah abhī bhī kām kar rahā hai*

**still**[2] (quiet) शान्त *śānt*; (not moving) निश्चल *niścal*

**sting, to** (as insect) डंक मारना *ḍaṅk mārnā*[N]

**stomach** पेट *peṭ*[M] — I have a stomache ache मेरे पेट में दर्द है *mere peṭ mẽ dard hai*; I have an upset stomach मेरा पेट ख़राब है *merā peṭ kharāb hai*

**stone** पत्थर *patthar*[M]; made of stone पत्थर का *patthar* *kā* — stone statues पत्थर की मूर्तियाँ *patthar kī mūrtiyā̃*; (pebble) कंकड़ *kaṅkaṛ*ᴹ; (pit in fruit) गुठली *guṭhlī*ᶠ

**stop, to** (intr.) रुकना *ruknā* — will the car stop? क्या गाड़ी रुकेगी ? *kyā gāṛī rukegī?*; (tr.) रोकना *roknā*ᴺ — will he stop the car? क्या वह गाड़ी को रोकेगा? *kyā vah gāṛī ko rokegā?*

**storey** (floor of building) मंज़िल *manzil*ᶠ — on the second storey दूसरी मंज़िल पर *dūsrī manzil par*; three-storey house तीन मंज़िल-वाला मकान *tīn manzil-vālā makān*

**storm** तूफ़ान *tūfān*ᴹ

**story** कहानी *kahānī*ᶠ — tell us a story हमें कोई कहानी सुनाओ *hamẽ koī kahānī sunāo*

**straight** सीधा *sīdhā* — give a straight answer सीधा जवाब दो *sīdhā javāb do*; (adverb) सीधे *sīdhe* — go straight सीधे जाइए *sīdhe jāie*

**straightforward** सीधा *sīdhā* — a fairly straightforward question सीधा-सा सवाल *sīdhā-sā savāl*; (straighforward in character) सीधा-सादा *sīdhā-sādā*

**strange** अजीब *ajīb*

**stranger** अजनबी *ajnabī*ᴹ

**strangle, to** गला घोंटना *galā ghõṭnā*ᴺ

**street** सड़क *saṛak*ᶠ

**strength** (in body etc.) बल *bal*ᴹ; (in drink, eyes etc.) तेज़ी *tezī*ᶠ; (durability) मज़बूती *mazbūtī*ᶠ

**stress** (tension) तनाव *tanāv*ᴹ — I began feeling stress 💣 मुझे तनाव महसूस होने लगा *mujhe tanāv mahsūs hone lagā*

**stress, to** ज़ोर देना *zor denā*ᴺ — we stressed the importance of studying हमने पढ़ने के महत्त्व पर ज़ोर दिया *hamne paṛhne ke mahattva par zor diyā*

**stretch, to** (intr. & tr.) तानना *tānnā*ᴺ

**strict** सख़्त *sakht*, कठोर *kaṭhor*

**strike** (withdrawal of labour) हड़ताल *haṛtāl*ᶠ

**strike, to**[1] (to withdraw labour) हड़ताल करना *haṛtāl karnā*ᴺ

**strike, to**[2] (to hit) मारना *mārnā*ᴺ

**string** रस्सी *rassī*ᶠ — tie the clothes with string कपड़ों को रस्सी से बाँधो *kapṛõ ko rassī se bā̃dho*

**strong** (of person etc.) बलवान *balvān*, (robust, healthy)

हृष्ट-पुष्ट *hṛṣṭ-puṣṭ*; (of drink, eyes etc.) तेज़ *tez*; (durable, of objects) मज़बूत *mazbūt*

**structure** (manner of construction) बनावट *banāvaṭ*F; (a building) इमारत *imārat*F

**struggle** संघर्ष *saṅgharṣ*M

**struggle, to** जूझना *jūjhnā* – we've been struggling with poverty for many years हम कई साल से ग़रीबी से जूझ रहे हैं *ham kaī sāl se ġarībī se jūjh rahe haĩ*

**stubborn** ज़िद्दी *ziddī*

**stubbornness** ज़िद *zid*F

**stuck, to be** फँसना *phãsnā* – I'm stuck in a long meeting मैं एक लंबी मीटिंग में फँसा हुआ हूँ *maĩ ek lambī mīṭiṅg mẽ phãsā huā hũ*

**student** विद्यार्थी *vidyārthī*M; छात्र *chātra*M, (female) छात्रा *chātrā*F

**study, studies** पढ़ाई *paṛhaī*F – my studies are going well मेरी पढ़ाई ठीक चल रही है *merī paṛhāī ṭhīk cal rahī hai*; (an analysis) अध्ययन *adhyayan*M – we are doing a study of the Ramayana हम रामायण का अध्ययन कर रहे हैं *ham rāmāyaṇ kā adhyayan kar rahe haĩ*

**study, to** पढ़ना *paṛhnā* (no ने *ne* construction in this sense) – Ravi studied in Banaras रवि बनारस में पढ़ा *ravi banāras mẽ paṛhā*

**stupid** (unintelligent) बुद्धू *buddhū*; (foolish) बेवक़ूफ़ *bevaqūf*

**stupidity** बेवक़ूफ़ी *bevaqūfī*F

**style** (in art etc.) शैली *śailī*F

**subject** (topic) विषय *viṣay*M – my favourite subject is history मेरा प्रिय विषय इतिहास है *merā priy viṣay itihās hai*

**submit, to** (to hand in) जमा करना *jamā karnā*N

**subtle** सूक्ष्म *sūkṣma*

**subtlety** सूक्ष्मता *sūkṣmatā*F

**subtract** घटाना *ghaṭānā*N

**succeed, to** सफल होना *saphal honā*

**success** सफलता *saphaltā*F

**successful** सफल *saphal*

**such** ऐसा *aisā* – such people ऐसे लोग *aise log*; (of this kind) इस तरह/प्रकार का *is tarah/prakār kā*; (such as, like) जैसा *jaisā* – a girl such as my daughter मेरी बेटी जैसी लड़की *merī beṭī jaisī laṛkī*; (so much) इतना *itnā* – such anger! इतना क्रोध! *itnā krodh!*

**suck, to** चूसना *cūsnā*$^{N}$

**suddenly** सहसा *sahsā*, अचानक *acānak*

**suffer, to** भोगना *bhognā*$^{N}$ – to suffer grief दुःख भोगना *duḥkh bhognā*$^{N}$

**suffering** दुःख *duḥkh*$^{M}$

**sufficient** काफ़ी *kāfī*, पर्याप्त *paryāpt*

**sugar** चीनी *cīnī*$^{F}$

**suggest, to** सुझाव देना *sujhāv denā*$^{N}$ – I suggested to them that they should stay मैंने उनको सुझाव दिया कि वे रहें *maĩne unko sujhāv diyā ki ve rahẽ*

**suggestion** सुझाव *sujhāv*$^{M}$

**suicide** आत्महत्या *ātmahatyā*$^{F}$; to commit suicide आत्महत्या करना *ātmahatyā karnā*$^{N}$

**suitability** योग्यता *yogyatā*$^{F}$

**suitable** (appropriate) उचित *ucit*; (worthy) योग्य *yogya*

**sulk, to** रूठना *rūṭhnā*

**summer** गरमी *garmī*$^{F}$, गरमियाँ *garmiyā̃*$^{F\ PL}$; in the summer गरमियों में *garmiyõ mẽ*; (note plural usage) summer holidays गरमी की छुट्टियाँ *garmī kī chuṭṭiyā̃*

**summit** शिखर *śikhar*$^{M}$

**sun** सूरज *sūraj*$^{M}$, सूर्य *sūrya*$^{M}$; (sunshine) धूप *dhūp*$^{F}$

**sunbathe, to** धूप खाना *dhūp khānā*$^{N}$

**sunshine** धूप *dhūp*$^{F}$

**Sunday** रविवार *ravivār*$^{M}$, इतवार *itvār*$^{M}$

**superstition** अंधविश्वास *andhviśvās*$^{M}$

**support** (help) सहारा *sahārā*$^{M}$

**support, to** सहारा देना *sahārā denā*$^{N}$

**suppress, to** दबाना *dabānā*$^{N}$

**sure** (confirmed) पक्का *pakkā*, तय *tay*; (to be sure of something) यक़ीन होना *yaqīn honā* – I'm sure (confident) that... मुझे यक़ीन है कि... *mujhe yaqīn hai ki . . .*

**surprise** आश्चर्य *āścarya*$^{M}$, ताज्जुब *tājjub*$^{M}$ – I was surprised मुझे आश्चर्य/ताज्जुब हुआ *mujhe āścarya/tājjub huā*

**surround, to** घेरना *ghernā*$^{N}$ – the children surrounded me बच्चों ने मुझे घेरा [घेर लिया] *baccõ ne mujhe gherā [gher liyā]*

**surrounded, to be** घिरना – the fort was surrounded on all sides

क़िला चारों तरफ़ से घिरा [घिर गया] *qilā cārõ taraf se ghirā [ghir gayā]*

**surveillance** निगरानी *nigrānī*[F]

**survive, to** बचना *bacnā* — all three men survived तीनों आदमी बचे [बच गए] *tīnõ ādmī bace [bac gae]*

**suspect, to** (पर) संदेह करना *(par) sandeh karnā*[N] — we began to suspect him हम उसपर संदेह करने लगे *ham uspar sandeh karne lage*

**swallow, to** निगलना *nigalnā*[N]

**sway, to** झूमना *jhūmnā*

**swear, to** (to abuse) गाली देना *gālī denā*[N] — he began swearing at me वह मुझे गालियाँ देने लगा *vah mujhe gāliyā̃ dene lagā*; (to promise: see 'promise')

**sweat** पसीना *pasīnā*[M]

**sweat, to** पसीना आना *pasīnā ānā* — I began sweating मुझे पसीना आने लगा *mujhe pasīnā āne lagā*

**sweep, to** बुहारना *buhārnā*[N], झाड़ू लगाना *jhāṛū lagānā*[N]

**sweet**[1] (adj.) मीठा *mīṭhā* — sweet talk मीठी बातें *mīṭhī bātẽ*; (dear) प्यारा *pyārā* — a very sweet boy बहुत प्यारा लड़का *bahut pyārā laṛkā*

**sweet**[2] (noun: sweetmeat) मिठाई *miṭhāī*[F]

**sweetness** मिठास *miṭhās*[F]

**swell, to** सूजना *sūjnā*

**swelling** सूजन *sūjan*[M]

**swim, to** तैरना *tairnā* — we're going swimming in the river हम नदी में तैरने जा रहे हैं *ham nadī mẽ tairne jā rahe haĩ*

**swing** झूला *jhūlā*[M]

**swing, to** (intr.) झूलना *jhūlnā*; (tr.) झुलाना *jhulānā*[N]

**sword** तलवार *talvār*[F]

**sycophancy** जी-हुज़ूरी *jī-huzūrī*[F]

**syllable** अक्षर *akṣar*[M]

**symbol** प्रतीक *pratīk*[M]

**sympathy** हमदर्दी *hamdardī*[F]; सहानुभूति *sahānubhūti*[F]; (compassion) दया[F] *dayā*

**system** तरीक़ा *tarīqā*[M], प्रणाली *praṇālī*[F]

## T

**tabla** तबला *tablā*[M]

**table** मेज़ *mez*[F]

**tablet** (pill) गोली *golī*[F]

**tail** पूँछ *pū̃ch*[F]

**tailor** दर्ज़ी *darzī*$^{M}$

**take, to** लेना *lenā*$^{N}$ — take this यह लो *yah lo*; (to convey, or take away) ले जाना *le jānā* — take Ram home राम को घर ले जाओ *rām ko ghar le jāo*, take this away इसे ले जाओ *ise le jāo*; (to take down/off) उतारना *utārnā*$^{N}$ — take off that hat वह टोपी उतारो *vah ṭopī utāro*; to take (time) लगना *lagnā* — it'll take five hours to reach Banaras बनारस पहुँचने में पाँच घंटे लगेंगे *banāras pahũcne mẽ pā̃c ghanṭe lagẽge*

**talk, to** बात करना *bāt karnā*$^{N}$ ('to', से *se*) — she wants to talk to me वह मुझसे बात करना चाहती है *vah mujhse bāt karnā cāhtī hai*; (for the sense 'speak', use बोलना *bolnā* — please talk/speak slowly धीरे धीरे बोलिए *dhīre dhīre bolie*)

**talkative** बातूनी *bātūnī*

**tall** (of people) लंबा *lambā*; (of buildings, trees) ऊँचा *ū̃cā*

**tame** (domesticated) पालतू *pāltū*

**tank** टंकी *ṭaṅkī*$^{F}$; (reservoir) हौज़ *hauz*$^{M}$; (pond) तालाब *tālāb*$^{M}$

**tap** टोंटी *ṭõṭī*$^{F}$, नल *nal*$^{M}$ (lit. 'pipe'); to turn tap on/off नल खोलना / बंद करना *nal kholnā*$^{N}$ / *band karnā*$^{N}$; tap water नल का पानी *nal kā pānī*

**taste** स्वाद *svād*$^{M}$ — the taste of honey शहद का स्वाद *śahad kā svād*

**taste, to** चखना *cakhnā*$^{N}$ — taste it and see! चखकर देखो! *cakhkar dekho!*

**tasty** लज़ीज़ *lazīz*, स्वादिष्ट *svādiṣṭ*

**tax** कर *kar*$^{M}$; to pay tax कर देना *kar denā*$^{N}$; to collect tax कर वसूल करना *kar vasūl karnā*$^{N}$

**taxi** टैक्सी *ṭaiksī*$^{F}$

**tea** चाय *cāy*$^{F}$

**teach, to** (a subject) पढ़ाना *paṛhānā*$^{N}$; (a skill) सिखाना *sikhānā*$^{N}$

**teacher** (male) अध्यापक *adhyāpak*$^{M}$; (female) अध्यापिका *adhyāpikā*$^{F}$

**tear**$^{1}$ (rip) चीर *cīr*$^{M}$

**tear**$^{2}$ (water in eye) आँसू *ā̃sū*$^{M}$; to shed tears आँसू बहाना *ā̃sū bahānā*$^{N}$

**tear, to** फाड़ना *phāṛnā*$^{N}$

**tease, to** चिढ़ाना *ciṛhānā*$^{N}$; (to harass) छेड़ना *cheṛnā*$^{N}$

**technical** तकनीकी *taknīkī*

**Insight**

Technical: with its dental consonant and its *-ī* ending, the Hindi word तकनीकी *taknīkī* shows an unusual degree of assimilation to Hindi patterns.

**technique** तरीक़ा *tarīqā*[M], विधि *vidhi*[F]

**telephone** फ़ोन *fon*[M]; to telephone फ़ोन करना *fon karnā*[N]; phone call फ़ोन *fon* – there's a call for you आपका फ़ोन है *āpkā fon hai*

**telescope** दूरबीन *dūrbīn*[F]

**television** टी० वी० *ṭī.vī.*[F] (the word दूरदर्शन *dūrdarśan* can be used in abstract senses ('I watch television'), but not in the sense 'a television set'; दूरदर्शन *dūrdarśan* doubles as the name of Indian state TV)

**tell, to** बताना *batānā*[N]; (to relate) सुनाना *sunānā*[N] – they told me their tale of woe उन्होंने मुझे अपनी राम-कहानी सुनाई *unhõne mujhe apnī rām-kahānī sunāī*

**temper** मिज़ाज *mizāj*[M]; (short temper) चिड़चिड़ापन *ciṛciṛāpan*[M]

**temperature** तापमान *tāpmān*[M] – the temperature falls and rises तापमान गिरता है और चढ़ता है *tāpmān girtā hai aur caṛhtā hai*; (fever) बुख़ार *bukhār*[M] – I have a temperature ☛ मुझे बुख़ार है *mujhe bukhār hai*

**temple**[1] (shrine) मंदिर *mandir*[M]

**temple**[2] (side of head) कनपटी *kanpaṭī*[F]

**temporary** अस्थायी *asthāyī*

**ten** दस *das*; tens of people दसों लोग *dasõ log*

**tenant** किरायेदार *kirāyedār*[M]

**tendency** प्रवृत्ति *pravṛtti*[F] – he/she had a tendency to over-eat ☛ उसमें ज़्यादा खाना खाने की प्रवृत्ति थी *usmẽ zyādā khānā khāne kī pravṛtti thī*

**tense**[1] (pulled tight) तना हुआ *tanā huā*; (ill at ease) बेचैन *becain*; (worried) परेशान *pareśān*

**tense**[2] (in grammar) काल *kāl*[M] – past tense भूतकाल *bhūtkāl*, present tense वर्तमान काल *vartmān kāl*, future tense भविष्यत् काल *bhaviṣyat kāl*

**tension** तनाव *tanāv*$^{M}$ — mental tension मानसिक तनाव *mānsik tanāv*; I have a lot of tension मुझे बहुत तनाव है *mujhe bahut tanāv hai*

**tent** तंबू *tambū*$^{M}$ — the tent could be pitched over there तंबू को उधर लगाया जाए *tambū ko udhar lagāyā jāe*

**term**$^{1}$ (condition) शर्त *śart*$^{F}$

**term**$^{2}$ (semester) सत्र *satra*$^{M}$

**term**$^{3}$ (specified duration) अवधि *avadhi*$^{F}$ — has the term of his employment been settled? क्या उसकी नौकरी की अवधि तय हुई? *kyā uskī naukarī kī avadhi tay huī?*

**terrible** भयानक *bhayānak*

**terror** आतंक *ātaṅk*$^{M}$

**terrorism** आतंकवाद *ātaṅkvād*$^{M}$

**terrorist** आतंकवादी *ātaṅkvādī*$^{M}$

**-th** (suffix for ordinal numbers) -वाँ *-vā̃* — tenth दसवाँ *dasvā̃*; the twelfth night बारहवीं रात *bārahvī̃ rāt* (some of the low numbers have special forms: first पहला *pahlā*, second दूसरा *dūsrā*, third तीसरा *tīsrā*, fourth चौथा *cauthā*, sixth छठाँ *chathā̃*, ninth नवाँ *navā̃*)

**than** से *se* — he is bigger than you वह तुमसे बड़ा है *vah tumse baṛā hai*

**thank, to** धन्यवाद देना *dhanyavād denā*$^{N}$

**thank you** धन्यवाद *dhanyavād*, शुक्रिया *śukriyā*; thank you, too! आपका भी धन्यवाद/शुक्रिया! *āpkā bhī dhanyavād/śukriyā!*

**that**$^{1}$ (pronoun) वह *vah* — who is that man? वह आदमी कौन है? *vah ādmī kaun hai?*; that is to say यानी *yānī*; that's why इसी लिए *isī lie*; that day, on that day उस दिन *us din*

**that**$^{2}$ (conjunction) कि *ki* — he says that he'll wait for us वह कहता है कि वह हमारा इंतज़ार करेगा *vah kahtā hai ki vah hamārā intazār karegā*

**the** (there is no definite article in Hindi — where is the key? चाबी कहाँ है? *cābī kahā̃ hai?*; a sense of 'the' is given to the object of a verb by adding को *ko* — I saw the cat मैंने बिल्ली को देखा *maĩne billī ko dekhā*)

**theft** चोरी *corī*$^{F}$

**their, theirs** उनका *unkā* — their sister उनकी बहिन *unkī bahin*

**then** तब *tab* — what happened then? तब क्या हुआ? *tab kyā* *huā?*; (as consequence) तो *to* — if he comes late, then what will we do? अगर वह देर से आएगा तो हम क्या करेंगे? *agar vah der se āegā to ham kyā karẽge?*

**there** वहाँ *vahā̃*; over there उधर *udhar*; there is है *hai*, there are हैं *haĩ* — there is a problem एक समस्या है *ek samasyā hai*

**therefore** इसलिए *islie,* अतः *ataḥ*

**these** ये *ye*; these people ये लोग *ye log*; these days इन दिनों *in dinõ*

**thesis** (dissertation) शोध प्रबंध *śodh prabandh*$^{M}$

**they** वे *ve*

**thick** मोटा *moṭā* — thick cloth मोटा कपड़ा *moṭā kapṛā*; (dense) घना *ghanā* — thick smoke घना धुआँ *ghanā dhuā̃*

**thief** चोर *cor*$^{M}$

**thieving** चोरी *corī*$^{F}$

**thigh** जांघ *jā̃gh*$^{F}$

**thin** पतला *patlā* — thin cloth पतला कपड़ा *patlā kapṛā*; (lean) दुबला-पतला *dublā-patlā* — three thin girls तीन दुबली-पतली लड़कियाँ *tīn dublī-patlī laṛkiyā̃*

**thing** चीज़ *cīz*$^{F}$, वस्तु *vastu*$^{F}$; (abstract) बात *bāt*$^{F}$ — think about these things इन बातों के बारे में सोचना *in bātõ ke bāre mẽ socnā*

**think, to** सोचना *socnā*$^{N}$ — what do you think? आप क्या सोचते हैं? *āp kyā socte haĩ?*; to think to oneself मन में सोचना *man mẽ socnā*$^{N}$

**thirst** प्यास *pyās*$^{F}$; to be thirsty प्यास लगना *pyās lagnā* — we're thirsty हमें प्यास लगी है *hamẽ pyās lagī hai*

**thirsty:** see 'thirst'

**thirteen** तेरह *terah*

**thirty** तीस *tīs*

**this** यह *yah*; this is Bhavani speaking (on phone) मैं भवानी बोल रही हूँ *maĩ bhavānī bol rahī hū̃*; this much इतना *itnā*

**thorn** काँटा *kā̃ṭā*$^{M}$

**those** वे *ve*; those people वे लोग *ve log*; those days उन दिनों *un dinõ*

**though** हालाँकि *hālā̃ki*; even though भले ही *bhale hī* (+ subjunctive) — even though he/she may be poor भले ही वह ग़रीब हो *bhale hī vah ġarīb ho*; as though जैसे *jaise* — as though he were rich जैसे वह अमीर हो *jaise vah amīr ho*

**thought** विचार *vicār*$^{M}$ — this thought saddened me 💣 इस विचार से मुझे दु:ख हुआ *is vicār se mujhe duḥkh huā*

**thousand** हज़ार hazār$^{M}$ — thousands of mosquitoes हज़ारों मच्छर *hazārõ macchar*

**thread** धागा *dhāgā*$^{M}$

**threat** धमकी *dhamkī*$^{F}$; (danger) ख़तरा *khatrā*$^{M}$

**threaten, to** धमकी देना *dhamkī dena*$^{N}$

**three** तीन *tīn*; three-quarters पौन, पौना *paun, paunā* — three-quarters of an hour पौन घंटा *paun ghaṇṭā*, three-quarters of a kilo पौना किलो *paunā kilo*

**throat** गला *galā*$^{M}$ — I have a sore throat 💣 मेरा गला ख़राब है *merā galā kharāb hai*

**throb, to** धड़कना *dharaknā*

**throne** गद्दी *gaddī*$^{F}$, सिंहासन *sĩhāsan*$^{M}$

**through** (by means of) के द्वारा *ke dvārā*; (American usage, as 'from…until': से लेकर…तक *se lekar…tak* — Monday through Thursday सोमवार से लेकर गुरुवार तक *somvār se lekar guruvār tak)*

**throw, to** फेंकना *phẽknā*$^{N}$; to throw upwards उछालना$^{N}$ *uchālnā*; to throw away फेंक देना *phẽk denā*$^{N}$ — throw away the old clothes पुराने कपड़ों को फेंको [फेंक दो] *purāne kapṛõ ko phẽko [phẽk do]*

**thumb** अँगूठा *ãgūṭhā*$^{M}$

**thunder** गरज *garaj*$^{F}$

**Thursday** गुरुवार *guruvār*$^{M}$, बृहस्पतिवार *bṛhaspativār*$^{M}$

**ticket** टिकट *ṭikaṭ*$^{M}$ (F)

**tie, to** बाँधना *bā̃dhnā*$^{N}$

**tiger** बाघ *bāgh*$^{M}$

**tight** (constricting) तंग *taṅg* — these trousers are very tight यह पैंट बहुत तंग है *yah paĩṭ bahut taṅg hai*; (taut) कसा हुआ *kasā huā* — is the rope tight? क्या रस्सी कसी हुई है? *kyā rassī kasī huī hai?*

**tighten, to** कसना *kasnā*$^{N}$

**time** समय *samay*$^{M}$ — at this/that time इस/उस समय *is/us samay*; I don't have time मेरे पास समय नहीं है *mere pās samay nahī̃ hai*; please make time for me मेरे लिए समय निकालिए *mere lie samay nikālie*; at the time of leaving चलते समय *calte samay*; (era) ज़माना

*zamānā*^M — in Grandfather's time दादाजी के ज़माने में *dādājī ke zamāne mẽ*; (occasion) बार *bār*^F — ten times दस बार *das bār*; for the first time पहली बार *pahlī bār* — I'm going to India for the first time मैं पहली बार भारत जा रहा हूँ *maĩ pahlī bār bhārat jā rahā hū̃*; Time काल *kāl*^M — Time is a great mystery काल एक बड़ा रहस्य है *kāl ek baṛā rahasya hai*; (time of day) बजा *bajā* — what's the time? कितने बजे हैं? *kitne baje haĩ?*

**times** (multiplied by) गुना *guna* — three times four is twelve तीन गुना चार बारह होते हैं *tīn gunā cār bārah hote haĩ*

**timetable** समय-सारणी *samay-sāraṇī*^F

**timid** भीरु *bhīru*

**timidity** भीरुता *bhīrutā*^F

**tiny** नन्हा *nanhā*

**tip** (point) नोक *nok*^F

**tired, to be** थकना *thaknā*; to become tired थक जाना — I became tired मैं थक गया *maĩ thak gayā*; she's tired वह थकी हुई है *vah thakī huī hai*; to be tired of (fed up with) तंग आना *taṅg ānā* — I'm tired of this noise मैं इस शोर से तंग आया हूँ [आ गया हूँ] *maĩ is śor se taṅg āyā hū̃ [ā gayā hū̃]*

**to** को *ko* — give this letter to Chotu यह पत्र छोटू को देना *yah patra choṭū ko denā*; 'to' a destination: the sense is carried by oblique case alone — we're going to the old city हम पुराने शहर जा रहे हैं *ham purāne śahar jā rahe haĩ*; ('to' as part of the infinitive verb is inherent in the Hindi *-nā* ending: 'to go' is जाना *jānā*)

**tobacco** तंबाकू *tambākū*^M

**today** आज *āj*

**toe** पैर की उँगली *pair kī ũglī*^F

**together** साथ-साथ *sāth-sāth* — let's go together हम साथ-साथ चलें *ham sāth-sāth calẽ*; (collected, in a group) इकट्ठा *ikaṭṭhā* (*-ā* is sometimes used as invariable) — they arrived together वे इकट्ठा/इकट्ठे पहुँचे *ve ikaṭṭhā/ikaṭṭhe pahũce*

**toilet** शौचालय *śaucālay*^M

**tolerant** सहनशील *sahanśīl*

**tolerate, to** सहना *sahnā*^N, बरदाश्त करना *bardāśt karnā*^N — how do you tolerate the London weather? आप लंदन

के मौसम को कैसे बरदाश्त करते हैं? *āp landan ke mausam ko kaise bardāśt karte haĩ?*

**tomato** टमाटर *ṭamāṭar*$^M$

**tomb** मक़बरा *maqbarā*$^M$, समाधि *samādhi*$^F$

**tomorrow** कल *kal* — tomorrow night कल रात *kal rāt*

**tongs** चिमटा *cimṭā*$^M$

**tongue** जीभ *jībh*$^M$; (language) भाषा *bhāṣā*$^F$, ज़बान *zabān*$^F$

**tonight** आज रात (को) *āj rāt (ko)* — I'll come tonight मैं आज रात को आऊँगा *maĩ āj rāt ko āũgā*

**too** (also) भी *bhī* (follows emphasized item) — I'll go too मैं भी जाऊँगा *maĩ bhī jāũgā*; too, too much बहुत ज़्यादा *bahut zyādā* — this picture is too expensive यह तस्वीर बहुत ज़्यादा महँगी है *yah tasvīr bahut zyādā mahãgī hai*

**tool** औज़ार *auzār*$^M$ — house-building tools घर बनाने के औज़ार *ghar banāne ke auzār*

**tooth** दाँत *dãt*$^M$ — my teeth are aching, I have toothache मेरे दाँत दर्द कर रहे हैं *mere dãt dard kar rahe haĩ*; my young son is teething मेरे छोटे बेटे के दाँत निकल रहे हैं *mere choṭe beṭe ke dãt nikal rahe haĩ*

**top** (lid) ढक्कन *ḍhakkan*$^M$; (peak) शिखर *śikhar*$^M$; on top of के ऊपर *ke ũpar*

**torch** (electric) टार्च *ṭārc*$^M$; (flaming) मशाल *maśāl*$^F$

**torn** फटा हुआ *phaṭā huā* — a torn sheet फटी हुई चादर *phaṭī huī cādar*

**totally** पूरी तरह से *pūrī tarah se*, पूर्ण रूप से *pūrṇ rūp se*

**touch, to** छूना *chūnā*$^N$; (to handle) हाथ लगाना *hāth lagānā*$^N$ — don't touch! हाथ मत लगाना! *hāth mat lagānā!*

**tourism** पर्यटन *paryaṭan*$^M$

**tourist** पर्यटक *paryaṭak*$^M$

**towards** की तरफ़/ओर *kī taraf/or* — towards me मेरी तरफ़/ओर *merī taraf/or*; (abstract sense, 'in respect of') के प्रति *ke prati* — he is very kind towards me वह मेरे प्रति बहुत दयालु है *vah mere prati bahut dayālu hai*

**towel** तौलिया *tauliyā*$^M$

**tower** मीनार *mīnār*$^{F\ (M)}$

**town** शहर *śahar*$^M$ — we're going to town today आज हम शहर जा रहे हैं *āj ham śahar jā rahe haĩ*

**toy** खिलौना *khilaunā*$^{M}$ — wooden toys लकड़ी के खिलौने *lakṛī ke khilaune*

**trade** व्यापार *vyāpār*$^{M}$

**trade, to** व्यापार करना *vyāpār karnā*$^{N}$

**tradition** परंपरा *paramparā*$^{F}$

**traditional** परंपरागत *paramparāgat*

**traditionalist** (adj. & noun) परंपरावादी *paramparāvādī*$^{M}$

**train** ट्रेन *ṭren*$^{F}$, रेलगाड़ी *relgāṛī*$^{F}$

**training** (artistic) तालीम *tālīm*$^{F}$; (technical) प्रशिक्षण *praśikṣaṇ*$^{M}$

**translate, to** (का) अनुवाद करना *(kā) anuvād karnā*$^{N}$ ('into', में *mẽ*) — translate this letter into Hindi इस पत्र का हिन्दी में अनुवाद करो *is patra kā hindī mẽ anuvād karo*

**translation** अनुवाद *anuvād*$^{M}$

**travel, to** सफ़र/यात्रा करना *safar/yātrā karnā*$^{N}$ — I'm fond of travelling मुझे सफ़र/यात्रा करने का शौक़ है *mujhe safar/yātrā karne kā śauq hai*

**traveller** मुसाफ़िर *musāfir*$^{M}$, यात्री *yātrī*$^{M}$

**tray** थाली *thālī*$^{F}$

**treat, to** (in health) (का) इलाज करना *(kā) ilāj karnā*$^{N}$ — we will treat your brother हम आपके भाई का इलाज करेंगे *ham āpke bhāī kā ilāj karẽge*; (in behaviour) व्यवहार करना *vyavahār karnā*$^{N}$ — he didn't treat me properly उसने मेरे साथ ठीक व्यवहार नहीं किया *usne mere sāth ṭhīk vyavahār nahī̃ kiyā*

**treatment** (behaviour) व्यवहार *vyavahār*$^{M}$

**tree** पेड़ *peṛ*$^{M}$

**tremble, to** काँपना *kā̃pnā*

**trick** (ruse) चाल *cāl*$^{F}$; to play a trick चाल चलना *cāl calnā*$^{N}$ (चलना *calnā*$^{N}$ is transitive here) — we'll play a trick too हम भी एक चाल चलेंगे *ham bhī ek cāl calẽge*; (deception) धोखा *dhokhā*$^{M}$ (see also 'deceit')

**trip** (journey) सफ़र *safar*$^{M}$ — a trip to New York न्यू यॉर्क का सफ़र *nyū yārk kā safar;* how was your trip? आपका सफ़र कैसा रहा? *āpkā safar kaisā rahā?*

**trouble** (inconvenience) तकलीफ़ *taklīf*$^{F}$, कष्ट *kaṣṭ*$^{M}$ — I'm troubling you मैं आपको तकलीफ़/कष्ट दे रहा हूँ *maĩ āpko taklīf/kaṣṭ de rahā hū̃*; please forgive the trouble

तकलीफ़ माफ़ कीजिए *taklīf māf kījie*; (difficulty) मुश्किल *muśkil*[F] — to get into difficulty मुश्किल में पड़ना *muśkil mẽ paṛnā*; (crisis) मुसीबत *musībat*[F] — to get involved in trouble मुसीबत में फँसना *musībat mẽ phãsnā*

**trouble, to** (to harass) परेशान करना *pareśān karnā*[N]

**troubled** परेशान *pareśān* – you're looking troubled आप परेशान लग रहे हैं *āp pareśān lag rahe haĩ*; (restless) बेचैन *becain*

**trousers** पैंट *paĩṭ*[M]

**true** सच *sac* – yes, this is true हाँ, यह सच है *hā̃, yah sac hai*; (loyal) सच्चा *saccā* – a true friend सच्चा दोस्त *saccā dost*

**truly:** see 'sincerely'

**trunk**[1] (suitcase) ट्रंक *ṭraṅk*[M], बक्सा *baksā*[M]

**trunk**[2] (part of body) धड़ *dhaṛ*[M]

**trunk**[3] (part of tree) तना *tanā*[M]

**trunk**[4] (part of elephant) सूँड़ *sū̃ṛ*[F]

**trust** विश्वास *viśvās*[M] – I don't trust what you say मुझे तुम्हारी बातों पर विश्वास नहीं है *mujhe tumhārī bātõ par viśvās nahī̃ hai*; (reliance) भरोसा *bharosā*[M]

**trust, to** भरोसा करना/रखना *bharosā karnā*[N]/*rakhnā*[N] — we can trust them, rely on them हम उनपर भरोसा कर सकते हैं *ham unpar bharosā kar sakte haĩ*

**truth** सच *sac*[M]

**truthfulness** सच्चाई *saccāī*[F]

**try, to** (की) कोशिश करना *(kī) kośiś karnā*[N] — try to understand समझने की कोशिश करो *samajhne kī kośiś karo*; I tried to read your letter मैंने आपका पत्र पढ़ने की कोशिश की *maĩne āpkā patra paṛhne kī kośiś kī*

**Tuesday** मंगलवार *maṅgalvār*[M]

**tune** धुन *dhun*[F]

**tune, to** (an instrument) सुर मिलाना *sur milānā*[N]

**turn** (in game) बारी *bārī*[F] — whose turn is it? किसकी बारी है? *kiskī bārī hai?*

**turn, to** (intr.) मुड़ना *muṛnā* — the car will turn left गाड़ी बायें मुड़ेगी *gāṛī bāyẽ muṛegī*; (tr.) मोड़ना *moṛnā*[N] — turn the car to the left गाड़ी को बायें मोड़ना *gāṛī ko bāyẽ moṛnā*

**turn over, to** (intr.) पलटना *palaṭnā*; (tr.) पलटाना *palṭānā*[N] — turn over that stone उस पत्थर को

पलटाओ [पलटा दो] *us patthar ko palṭāo [palṭā do]*; to turn over (change lying position) करवट बदलना *karvaṭ badalnā*[N]

**twelve** बारह *bārah*

**twenty** बीस *bīs*

**twice** (two times) दो बार *do bār*; (double) दुगुना *dugunā* – twice this much इसका दुगुना *iskā dugunā*

**twist** (in rope etc.) बल *bal*[M]

**twist, to** (intr.: to get twisted) बल खाना *bal khānā*[N]; (tr.) ऐंठना *aĩṭhnā*[N]

**two** दो *do*; two and a half ढाई *ḍhāī*

**type** तरह[F], प्रकार *prakār*[M] – what type of food do you like? आपको किस तरह/प्रकार का खाना पसंद है? *āpko kis tarah/prakār kā khānā pasand hai?*

## U

**ugly** बदसूरत *badsūrat*

**umbrella** छाता *chātā*[M] – put up the umbrella छाता लगाओ *chātā lagāo*

**uncertain** (of a matter) तय नहीं *tay nahī̃*, अनिश्चित *aniścit* – the programme is still uncertain कार्यक्रम अभी तय नहीं है *kāryakram abhī tay nahī̃ hai*; (of a person: use a noun such as विश्वास *viśvās*[M]) – I'm uncertain about (don't fully trust) their plan मुझे उनकी योजना पर पूरा विश्वास नहीं *mujhe unkī yojnā par pūrā viśvās nahī̃*

**uncertainty** अनिश्चय *aniścay*[M]; (doubt) संदेह *sandeh*[M]

**uncle** (father's elder brother) ताऊ *tāū*[M]; (father's younger brother) चाचा *cācā*[M]; (father's sister's husband) फूफा *phūphā*[M]; (mother's brother) मामा *māmā*[M]; (mother's sister's husband) मौसा *mausā*[M]

**unconscious** (in a faint) बेहोश *behoś*

**under** के नीचे *ke nīce* – under the sheet चादर के नीचे *cādar ke nīce*

**understand, to** समझना *samajhnā*[N]

**understanding**[1] (adj.) समझदार *samajhdār* – he's a very understanding man वह बहुत ही समझदार आदमी है *vah bahut hī samajhdār ādmī hai*

**understanding**[2] (noun) समझ *samajh*[F] – it's beyond my understanding यह मेरी समझ के बाहर है *yah merī samajh ke bāhar hai*

**undo, to:** see 'untie'

**unemployed** बेकार *bekār*, बेरोज़गार *berozgār*

**unemployment** बेकारी *bekārī*^F, बेरोज़गारी *berozgārī*^F

**unfair** (biased) पक्षपाती *pakṣpātī*; (unreasonable) बेजा *bejā*

**unfaithful** बेवफ़ा *bevafā*

**unfaithfulness** बेवफ़ाई *bavafāī*^F

**unhappiness** दुःख *dukh*^M, (gloominess) उदासी *udāsī*^F

**unhappy** दुखी *dukhī*; (glum) उदास *udās*

**uniform** वरदी *vardī*^F

**unintentionally** अनजाने में *anjāne mẽ*

**unity** एकता *ektā*^F

**unlike** असमान; (different) भिन्न *bhinn*, अलग *alag*

**unripe** कच्चा *kaccā*

**unsure:** see 'uncertain'

**untie, to** खोलना *kholnā*^N

**until** तक *tak* — until Thursday गुरुवार तक *guruvār tak*; (until the time when something happens) जब तक…न/नहीं *jab tak…na/nahī̃* — until I tell you जब तक मैं तुम्हें न बताऊँ *jab tak maĩ tumhẽ na batāū̃*; I stayed outside until he left मैं तब तक बाहर रहा जब तक वह नहीं गया *maĩ tab tak bāhar rahā jab tak vaha nahī̃ gayā*

**untrue** असत्य *asatya*

**Insight**

Until – जब तक न *jab tak na* indicates 'for as long as something doesn't happen' — i.e. *until* it does!

**universe** विश्व *viśva*^M

**university** विश्वविद्यालय *viśvavidyālay*^M, युनिवर्सिटी *yunivarsiṭī*^F

**unless** (say 'until') जब तक…नहीं *jab tak…nahī̃* — don't come unless he calls you जब तक वह तुम्हें न बुलाए तब तक मत आना *jab tak vah tumhẽ na bulāe tab tak mat ānā*

**untruth** असत्य *asatya*^M; (lie) झूठ *jhūṭh*^M

**up** ऊपर *ūpar* — look up ऊपर देखो *ūpar dekho*; up to तक *tak* — up to here यहाँ तक *yahā̃ tak*, up to now अभी तक *abhī tak*; it's up to you (your choice) आप की मर्ज़ी

*āpkī marzī*; upwards ऊपर की तरफ़/ओर *ūpar kī taraf/or*; to go up (ascend) चढ़ना *caṛhnā*; to go up (increase) बढ़ना *baṛhnā*

**upright** (standing, vertical) खड़ा *khaṛā*; (just, honest) ईमानदार *īmāndār*

**upset** (anxious) परेशान *pareśān*; (angry) नाराज़ *nārāz*

**upset, to** परेशान करना *pareśān karnā*ᴺ; घबड़ा कर देना *ghabṛā kar denā*ᴺ

**upstairs** (adverb) ऊपर *ūpar* — we live upstairs हम ऊपर रहते हैं *ham ūpar rahtẹ haĩ*; (adj.) ऊपरवाला *ūparvālā* — in the upstairs room ऊपरवाले कमरे में *ūparvāle kamre mẽ*

**upwards** ऊपर *ūpar*, ऊपर की तरफ़ *ūpar kī taraf*

**Urdu** उर्दू *urdū*ᶠ

**urgent** ज़रूरी *zarūrī* — an urgent letter ज़रूरी पत्र *zarūrī patra*

**urine** पेशाब *peśāb*ᴹ; to urinate पेशाब करना *peśāb karnā*ᴺ

**use** इस्तेमाल *istemāl*ᴹ; to be of use काम का होना *kām kā honā* — these things aren't of any use ये चीजें किसी काम की नहीं हैं *ye cīzẽ kisī kām kī nahĩ haĩ*

**use, to** (का) इस्तेमाल करना *(kā) istemāl karnā*ᴺ — you can use my computer तुम मेरे कम्प्यूटर का इस्तेमाल कर सकते हो *tum mere kampyūṭar kā istemāl kar sakte ho*

**used to** (past habits: use imperfective tense) — I used to live in a village मैं गाँव में रहता था *maĩ gā̃v mẽ rahtā thā*

**used to, to be** (to be accustomed to, in the habit of) (का) आदी होना *(kā) ādī honā* — we're not used to working hard हम मेहनत करने के आदी नहीं हैं *ham mehnat karne ke ādī nahĩ haĩ*

**useful** उपयोगी *upyogī*

**useless** बेकार *bekār* — it's useless saying anything to them उनसे कुछ कहना बेकार है *unse kuch kahnā bekār hai*

**usual** सामान्य *sāmānya*

**usually** आम तौर पर *ām taur par*; (frequently) अक्सर *aksar*

**utensil** बर्तन *bartan*ᴹ

**utter, to** मुँह से निकालना *mũh se nikālnā*ᴺ

**utterly** (completely) सरासर *sarāsar* — this is utterly wrong यह सरासर ग़लत है *yah sarāsar galat hai*

# V

**vacancy** ख़ाली जगह *khālī jagah*<sup>F</sup>

**vacant** ख़ाली *khālī*

**vacate, to** ख़ाली करना *khālī karnā*<sup>N</sup> — you'll have to vacate the house by March ☛ आपको मार्च तक मकान को ख़ाली करना पड़ेगा *āpko mārc tak makān ko khālī karnā paṛegā*

**vacation** छुट्टी *chuṭṭī*<sup>F</sup> — in the summer vacation गरमी की छुट्टियों में *garmī kī chuṭṭiyõ mẽ*

**vain** (conceited) गर्वीला *garvīlā;* (useless) बेकार *bekār;* (in vain) व्यर्थ *vyarth*

**valuable** क़ीमती *qīmatī*, मूल्यवान *mūlyavān*

**value** क़ीमत *qīmat*<sup>F</sup> — what would the value of this old table be? इस पुरानी मेज़ की क़ीमत क्या होगी? *is purānī mez kī qīmat kyā hogī?*

**vanish, to** ग़ायब हो जाना *gāyab ho jānā* — my things have vanished मेरा सामान ग़ायब हो गया है *merā sāmān gāyab ho gayā hai*

**various** विभिन्न *vibhinn;* various kinds of तरह-तरह का *tarah-tarah kā* — various kinds of

people तरह-तरह के लोग *tarah-tarah ke log*

**vegetable** सब्ज़ी *sabzī*<sup>F</sup>

**vegetarian** शाकाहारी *śākāhārī*<sup>M</sup> — I'm a vegetarian मैं शाकाहारी हूँ *maĩ śākāhārī hū̃*; we prefer vegetarian food ☛ हमें शाकाहारी खाना ज़्यादा पसंद है *hamẽ śākāhārī khānā zyādā pasand hai*

**vehicle** गाड़ी *gāṛī*<sup>F</sup>, वाहन *vāhan*<sup>M</sup>

**veil** घूँघट *ghū̃ghaṭ*<sup>M (F)</sup>; (including metaphorical senses) परदा *pardā*<sup>M</sup>

**veil, to wear** घूँघट करना *ghū̃ghaṭ karnā*<sup>N</sup> — some women wear the veil कुछ औरतें घूँघट करती हैं *kuch auratẽ ghū̃ghaṭ kartī haĩ*; to veil (पर) परदा डालना *(par) pardā ḍālnā*<sup>N</sup>

**venom** ज़हर *zahar*<sup>M</sup>, विष *viṣ*<sup>M</sup>

**venomous** ज़हरीला *zahrīlā*, विषैला *viṣailā*

**verb** क्रिया *kriyā*<sup>F</sup>

**very**<sup>1</sup> (extremely) बहुत *bahut*

**very**<sup>2</sup> (the same) वही *vahī* — the very man who came today वही आदमी जो आज आया था *vahī ādmī jo āj āyā thā*

**vest** बनियान *baniyān*<sup>F</sup>

**via** से होकर *se hokar* — to go to Delhi via Kanpur कानपुर से होकर दिल्ली जाना *kānpur se hokar dillī jānā*

**victim** शिकार *śikār*$^{M}$ — he fell victim to fraud वह धोखे का शिकार हुआ *vah dhokhe kā śikār huā*; ('distressed' as the victim of a natural disaster) पीड़ित *pīṛit* — to be a victim of flood/drought बाढ़/सूखे से पीड़ित होना *bāṛh/sūkhe se pīṛit honā*

**view** (scene) दृश्य *dṛśya*$^{M}$

**village** गाँव *gā̃v*$^{M}$; (in noun compounds) ग्राम *grām*$^{M}$ — village/rural development ग्राम-विकास *grām-vikās*$^{M}$

**villain** बदमाश *badmāś*$^{M}$; (in drama) खलनायक *khalnāyak*$^{M}$

**violence** हिंसा *hinsā*$^{F}$

**violent** हिंसात्मक *hinsātmak*; (fierce) उग्र *ugra*

**visa** विज़ा *vizā*$^{M}$; to apply for a visa विज़ा की अर्ज़ी देना *vizā kī arzī denā*$^{N}$

**visible, to be** दिखना *dikhnā* दीखना *dīkhnā* — the whole world is visible from here यहाँ से सारी दुनिया दीखती है *yahā̃ se sārī duniyā dīkhtī hai*; (to come into view) दिखाई देना/पड़ना *dikhāī denā/paṛnā* — the moon will be visible soon थोड़ी देर में चाँद दिखाई देगा *thoṛī der mẽ cā̃d dikhāī degā*

**visit, to** मिलना *milnā* — we'll come to visit you tomorrow हम कल आपसे मिलने आएँगे *ham kal āpse milne āẽge*

**vital** (essential) बहुत ज़रूरी *bahut zarūrī*

**voice** आवाज़ *āvāz*$^{F}$ — I could hear Uma's voice उमा की आवाज़ सुनाई दे रही थी *umā kī āvāz sunāī de rahī thī*; your voice is very sweet तुम्हारी आवाज़ बहुत मीठी है *tumhārī āvāz bahut mīṭhī hai*

**volcano** ज्वालामुखी *jvālāmukhī*$^{M}$

**Insight**

Volcano: ज्वालामुखी *jvālāmukhī*$^{M}$ 'flaming mouth' reflects the drama of an eruption.

**vomit, to:** see 'sick'

**vote** वोट *voṭ*$^{M}$

**vote, to** (को) वोट देना *(ko) voṭ denā*$^{N}$ — which candidate should I vote for? किस उम्मीदवार को वोट दूँ? *kis ummīdvār ko voṭ dū̃?*

**vow** (pious observance) व्रत *vrat*$^{M}$; to make/keep a vow व्रत लेना/रखना vrat *lenā*$^{N}$/*rakhnā*$^{N}$; (for non-ritual usages see 'promise')

**vulgar** अशिष्ट *aśiṣṭ*; (obscene) अश्लील *aślīl*

## W

**wage** वेतन *vetan*$^{M}$

**waist** कमर *kamar*$^{F}$

**wait, to** इंतज़ार करना *intazār karnā*$^{N}$ — we'll wait until five o'clock हम पाँच बजे तक इंतज़ार करेंगे *ham pā̃c baje tak intazār karẽge*; to wait for का इंतज़ार करना *kā intazār karnā*$^{N}$ — we'll wait for you हम आपका इंतज़ार करेंगे *ham āpkā intazār karẽge*

**wake up, to** (intr.) जागना *jāgnā* — I woke up early मैं जल्दी जागा [जाग गया] *maĩ jaldī jāgā [jāg gayā]*; (tr.) जगाना *jagānā*$^{N}$ — wake them up right now उन्हें अभी जगाओ [जगा दो] *unhẽ abhī jagāo [jagā do]*

**walk** (stroll) सैर *sair*$^{F}$; to go for a walk सैर करना *sair karnā*$^{N}$ — I go for a long walk in the evening मैं शाम को लंबी सैर करता हूँ *maĩ śām ko lambī sair kartā hū̃*

**walk, to** चलना *calnā*; (to go on foot) पैदल चलना *paidal calnā*

**wall** दीवार *dīvār*$^{F}$

**wallet** बटुआ *baṭuā*$^{M}$ — in my wallet मेरे बटुए में *mere baṭue mẽ*

**wander, to** (to ramble) घूमना *ghūmnā*; (to stray) भटकना *bhaṭaknā*

**want** (poverty) ग़रीबी *ġarībī*$^{F}$

**want, to** चाहना *cāhnā*$^{N}$ — I want to go मैं जाना चाहता हूँ *maĩ jānā cāhtā hū̃*; I want you to go मैं चाहता हूँ कि आप जाएँ *maĩ cāhtā hū̃ ki āp jāẽ*; what do you want? आप क्या चाहते हैं? *āp kyā cāhte haĩ?* (more commonly expressed with चाहिए *cāhie* 'wanted' — what do you want? आपको क्या चाहिए? *āpko kyā cāhie?*)

**war** युद्ध *yuddh*$^{M}$ — war could break out at any moment युद्ध कभी भी छिड़ सकता है *yuddh kabhī bhī chiṛ saktā hai*

**warm** गरम *garam*

**warm, to** गरम करना *garam karnā*$^{N}$, गरमाना *garmānā*$^{N}$

**warn, to** चेतावनी देना *cetāvnī denā*$^{N}$ – we tried to warn you हमने अपको चेतावनी देने की कोशिश की *hamne āpko cetāvnī dene kī kośiś kī*

**warning** चेतावनी *cetāvnī*$^{F}$

**wary** सावधान *sāvdhān*

**wash, to** धोना *dhonā*$^{N}$; to wash dishes बरतन माँजना *bartan mā̃jnā*$^{N}$; to bathe नहाना *nahānā*

**washed, to be** धुलना *dhulnā* – the clothes have been washed clean कपड़े साफ़ धुले हैं *kapṛe sāf dhule haĩ*

**washerman** धोबी *dhobī*$^{M}$

**waste, to** (time etc.) गँवाना *gā̃vānā*$^{N}$ (see also 'squander')

**watch** घड़ी *ghaṛī*$^{F}$, वॉच *vāc*$^{F}$ – my watch is fast/slow मेरी घड़ी आगे/पीछे है *merī ghaṛī āge/pīche hai*

**watch, to** देखना *dekhnā*$^{N}$; (to control, keep in check) संभालना *sambhālnā*$^{N}$ – watch your language! मुँह संभालकर बोलो! *mũh sambhālkar bolo!*

**watchman** चौकीदार *caukīdār*$^{M}$

**water** पानी *pānī*$^{M}$; (sacred or ritual) जल *jal*$^{M}$ – Ganges water गंगा जल *gaṅgā jal*

**water melon** तरबूज़ *tarbūz*$^{M}$

**wave** लहर *lahar*$^{F}$

**wave, to** (intr. & tr.) लहराना *laharānā*$^{N}$; (to wave hand) हाथ हिलाना *hāth hilānā*$^{N}$

**way** (method) तरीक़ा *tarīqā*$^{M}$; (road) रास्ता *rāstā*$^{M}$ – tell/show me the way to the station मुझे स्टेशन का रास्ता बताइए *mujhe sṭeśan kā rāstā batāie*; on the way रास्ते में *rāste mẽ*

**we** हम *ham*

**weak** कमज़ोर *kamzor*

**weakness** कमज़ोरी *kamzorī*$^{F}$

**wealth** धन *dhan*$^{M}$

**wealthy** अमीर *amīr*, धनी *dhanī*

**weapon** हथियार *hathiyār*$^{M}$; to wield a weapon हथियार चलाना *hathiyār calānā*$^{N}$

**wear, to** पहनना *pahannā*$^{N}$ – what should I wear? मैं क्या पहनूँ *maĩ kyā pahnū̃*?; he was wearing (= 'had put on') a white kurta उसने सफ़ेद कुरता पहना था *usne safed kurtā pahnā thā*, वह सफ़ेद कुरता पहने हुए था *vah safed kurtā pahne hue thā*; to wear glasses चश्मा लगाना *caśmā lagānā*$^{N}$

**weather** मौसम *mausam*$^{M}$

**web** जाल *jāl*$^{M}$

**wedding** शादी *śādī*[F]; to attend a wedding शादी में जाना *śādī mẽ jānā*

**Wednesday** बुधवार *budhvār*[M]

**week** हफ़्ता *haftā*[M], सप्ताह *saptāh*[M]; two weeks ago/later दो हफ़्ते पहले/के बाद *do hafte pahle/ke bād*

**weep, to** रोना *ronā*[n]; to weep and wail रोना-धोना *ronā-dhonā*

**weigh, to** तोलना *tolnā*[N]

**weight** वज़न *vazan*[M]; (measured weight) तौल *taul*[F]

**weird** अनोखा *anokhā*

**welcome** स्वागत *svāgat*[M] — welcome to India! भारत में आपका स्वागत है! *bhārat mẽ āpkā svāgat hai!*; to welcome का स्वागत करना *kā svāgat karnā*[N] — we will welcome our guests हम अपने मेहमानों का स्वागत करेंगे *ham apne mehmānõ kā svāgat karẽge*

**well** (for water) कुआँ *kuā̃*[M] — well water कुएँ का पानी *kuẽ kā pānī*

**well** (adj., healthy) ठीक *ṭhīk*, अच्छा *acchā*; (adverb) अच्छा *achhā* — she speaks well वह अच्छा बोलती है *vah acchā boltī hai*; (thoroughly) अच्छी तरह से *acchī tarah se*; well done! शाबाश! *śābāś!* (NB: this can sound patronizing if said to peers or seniors); (congratulations!) बधाई! *badhāī!*; well, anyway . . . (changing the subject) ख़ैर *khair*

**west** पश्चिम *paścim*[M]

**western** पश्चिमी *paścimī*

**wet** गीला *gīlā*; (soaked) भीगा हुआ *bhīgā huā*

**what** (interrogative) क्या *kyā* — what did you say? तुमने क्या कहा? *tumne kyā kahā?*; what kind of किस तरह/प्रकार का *kis tarah/prakār kā* — what kind of food do you like? आपको किस तरह का खाना पसंद है? *āpko kis tarah kā khānā pasand hai?*; (relative: 'that which') जो *jo* — what happened last night won't happen again कल रात जो हुआ वह दुबारा नहीं होगा *kal rāt jo huā vah dubārā nahī̃ hogā*

**whatever** जो भी *jo bhī* — whatever you like, जो भी तुम चाहो *jo bhī tum cāho*; whatever happens जो भी हो *jo bhī ho*

**wheat** गेहूँ *gehū̃*[M]

**wheel** पहिया *pahiyā*[M]; (disc) चक्र *cakra*[M]

**when** (interrogative) कब
*kab* — when will you go? आप
कब जाएँगे? *āp kab jāēge?*;
(relative) जब *jab* — when it
rains जब पानी पड़ता है *jab pānī
paṛtā hai*

**whenever** जब भी *jab bhī*

**where** (interrogative) कहाँ
*kahā̃* — where will you go?
आप कहाँ जाएँगे? *āp kahā̃
jāēge?*; (relative) जहाँ *jahā̃* —
where it rains जहाँ पानी पड़ता
है *jahā̃ pānī paṛtā hai*

**wherever** जहाँ भी *jahā̃ bhī*

**whether** चाहे *cāhe* — whether
I go or stay चाहे मैं जाऊँ या रहूँ
*cāhe maĩ jāū̃ yā rahū̃*; (or not)
कि… कि नहीं *ki… ki nahī̃* — I
don't know whether I should go
or not मैं नहीं जानता कि मैं जाऊँ
कि नहीं *maĩ nahī̃ jāntā ki maĩ
jāū̃ ki nahī̃*

**which** (interrogative) कौनसा
*kaunsā* — which car? कौनसी
गाड़ी? *kaunsī gāṛī?*; (relative:
the one which/that) जो *jo* — the
car which I saw जो गाड़ी मैंने
देखी *jo gāṛī maĩne dekhī*

**while** (during the time that)
जब *jab*, जिस समय *jis samay*;
(although) हालाँकि *hālā̃ki*; (while
on the other hand) जब कि *jab ki*

**whip** चाबुक *cābuk*$^M$, हंटर
*haṇṭar*$^M$

**whip, to** चाबुक लगाना *cābuk
lagānā*$^N$

**whisper, to** फुसफुसाना
*phusphusānā*

**whistle** सीटी *sīṭī*$^F$

**whistle, to** सीटी बजाना *sīṭī
bajānā*$^N$

**white** सफ़ेद *safed*; (of
complexion) गोरा *gorā*

**who** (interrogative) कौन
*kaun* — who will go? कौन
जाएगा? *kaun jāegā?*; (relative)
जो *jo* — the person who knows
जो जानता है *jo jāntā hai*; who
knows? (rhetorical) कौन जाने?
*kaun jāne?*

**whoever** जो भी *jo bhī*

**whole** पूरा *pūrā* — the whole
story is wrong पूरी कहानी ग़लत
है *pūrī kahānī galat hai*; (more
formal) संपूर्ण *sampūrṇ* —
the whole Ramayana संपूर्ण
रामायण *sampūrṇ rāmāyaṇ*;
the whole day दिन भर *din
bhar*; (unbroken, intact) साबुत
*sābut* — whole cumin seed
साबुत जीरा *sābut jīrā*

**whose** (interrogative) किसका
*kiskā* — whose shirt is this?
यह किसकी क़मीज़ है? *yah kiskī*

*qamīz hai?*; (relative) जिसका *jiskā* — the person whose shirt it is just left जिसकी क़मीज़ है वह अभी चला गया *jiskī qamīz hai vah abhī calā gayā*

**why** क्यों *kyõ* — why are you sad? तुम क्यों दुखी हो? *tum kyõ dukhī ho?*; I told her why I was sad मैंने उसे बताया कि मैं क्यों दुखी था *maĩne use batāyā ki maĩ kyõ dukhī thā*

**wicked** पापी *pāpī*

**wide** चौड़ा *caurā*

**widow** विधवा *vidhvā*^F

**widowhood** वैधव्य *vaidhavya*^M, विधवापन *vidhvāpan*^M

**wife** पत्नी *patnī*^F

**wild** (untamed) जंगली *jaṅglī* — wild animal जंगली जानवर *jaṅglī jānvar*

**will**¹ (testament) वसीयत *vasīyat*^F

**will**² (desire) इच्छा *icchā*^F

**willing** (to do something) तैयार *taiyār*; (agreeable) राज़ी *rāzī*; (keen) उत्सुक *utsuk*

**willingly** (with free will) अपनी इच्छा से *apnī icchā se*; (happily) ख़ुशी से *khuśī se*

**wind** हवा *havā*^F — a cold wind blows ठंडी हवा चलती है *ṭhanḍī havā caltī hai*

**window** खिड़की *khiṛkī*^F

**wing** (of bird) पंख *paṅkh*^M; (of party, organization) पक्ष *pakṣ*^M

**winter** सरदी *sardī*^F, जाड़ा *jāṛā*^M; in the winter सरदियों/जाड़ों में *sardiyõ/jāṛõ mẽ* (note plural usage)

**wipe, to** पोंछना *põchnā*^N

**wire** तार *tār*^M; electric wire बिजली का तार *bijlī kā tār*^M

**wise** बुद्धिमान *buddhimān*; (sensible) समझदार *samajhdār*

**wish** इच्छा *icchā*^F, कामना *kāmnā*; best wishes शुभ कामनाएँ *śubh kāmnāẽ*; with best wishes शुभ कामनाओं के साथ *śubh kāmnāõ ke sāth*

**wish, to** चाहना *cāhnā*^N; I wish that I could go too! काश कि मैं भी जा सकता! *kāś ki maĩ bhī jā saktā!*

**with** (in company of) के साथ *ke sāth* — he'll work with you वह आपके साथ काम करेगा *vah āpke sāth kām karegā*; (in a certain manner – 'with care', 'with patience' etc.) से *se* — he'll work with care, carefully वह सावधानी से काम करेगा *vah sāvdhānī se kām karegā;* he listens with attention, attentively वह ध्यान से सुनता है *vah dhyān se suntā hai*

**without** के बिना *ke binā* – without doing/saying/thinking/asking (use invariable *-e* participle) बिना किए/कहे/सोचे/पूछे *binā kie/kahe/soce/pūche*

**witness** गवाही *gavāhī*ᴹ, साक्षी *sākṣī*ᴹ

**woman** औरत *aurat*ᶠ, स्त्री *strī*ᶠ; (more genteel, 'lady') महिला *mahilā*ᶠ

**wood**[1] (timber, lumber) लकड़ी *lakṛī*ᶠ

**wood**[2] (forest) बन *ban*ᴹ, वन *van*ᴹ

**wool** ऊन *ūn*ᴹ

**woollen** ऊनी *ūnī* – woollen cloth ऊनी कपड़ा *ūnī kapṛā*

**word** शब्द *śabd*ᴹ; (promise) वादा *vādā*ᴹ – I gave you my word मैंने तुम्हें वादा दिया *maĩne tumhẽ vādā diyā*

**work** काम *kām*ᴹ karte haĩ?; this machine doesn't work यह मशीन काम नहीं करती *yah maśīn kām nahī̃ kartī*; (employment) नौकरी *naukrī*ᶠ; hard work, labour मेहनत *mehnat*ᶠ; work of art रचना *racnā*ᶠ, कृति *kṛti*ᶠ

**workman** (skilled artisan) मिस्तरी *mistrī*ᴹ, (labourer) मज़दूर *majdūr*ᴹ

**workmanship** कारीगरी *kārīgarī*ᶠ

**workshop** कारख़ाना *kārkhānā*ᴹ

**world** दुनिया *duniyā*ᶠ – third-world countries तीसरी दुनिया के देश *tīsrī duniyā ke deś*; in today's world आज की दुनिया में *āj kī duniya mẽ*; (universe) विश्व *viśva*ᴹ – world war विश्वयुद्ध *viśva-yuddh*ᴹ, world peace विश्व शान्ति *viśva śānti*ᶠ

**worry** परेशानी *pareśānī*ᶠ; (anxiety) चिन्ता *cintā*ᶠ

**Insight**

Work: the Hindi word काम *kām* derives from Sanskrit कर्म *karma*. The two words have separate meanings in Hindi and thus are 'doublets'.

**work, to** काम करना *kām karnā*ᴺ – where do you work? आप कहाँ काम करते हैं? *āp kahā̃ kām*

**worry, to** चिन्ता करना *cintā karnā*ᴺ – there's no need to worry चिन्ता करने की कोई

ज़रूरत नहीं है *cintā karne kī koī zarūrat nahī̃ hai*

**worse** बदतर *badtar* — worse than before पहले से बदतर *pahle se badtar*

**worship** पूजा *pūjā*[F]

**worship, to** (की) पूजा करना *(kī) pūjā karnā*[N] — we worship God हम ईश्वर की पूजा करते हैं *ham īśvar kī pūjā karte haī̃*

**worth** (के) लायक़ *(ke) lāyaq* — worth doing/seeing करने/देखने लायक़ *karne/dekhne lāyaq*; what's this picture worth? इस तस्वीर की क़ीमत क्या है? *is tasvīr kī qīmat kyā hai?*; it's not worth going there वहाँ जाने में कोई फ़ायदा नहीं है *vahā̃ jāne mẽ koī fāydā nahī̃ hai*

**worthy** योग्य *yogya,* लायक़ *lāyaq*

**would** (in reported speech use future tense) — he said he would come on time उसने कहा कि वह ठीक समय पर आएगा *usne kahā ki vah ṭhīk samay par āegā*; (for 'would have', use perfective participle + होता *hotā*) — if she had come I would have stayed here too अगर वह आई होती तो मैं भी यहाँ रहता *agar vah āī hotī to maĩ bhī yahā̃ rahtā*

**wound** घाव *ghāv*[M]

**wounded** घायल *ghāyal* — three men were wounded in the fighting लड़ाई में तीन आदमी घायल हुए *laṛāī mẽ tīn ādmī ghāyal hue*

**wrangle, to** झकझक करना *jhakjhak karnā*[N]

**wrap, to** (an object) लपेटना *lapeṭnā*[N]; (to put on clothing) ओढ़ना *oṛhnā*[N]

**wrist** कलाई *kalāī*[F]

**write, to** लिखना *likhnā*[N]

**writer** लेखक *lekhak*[M], (*female*) लेखिका *lekhikā*[F]

**writing** लेखन *lekhan*[M]; (hand writing) लिखावट *likhāvaṭ*[F]; in writing, in written form लिखित *likhit* — please give it in writing लिखित दीजिए *likhit dījie*

**wrong** ग़लत *galat*

**wrong, to go** ख़राब होना, हो जाना *k͟harāb honā, ho jānā* — my computer's gone wrong मेरा कम्प्यूटर ख़राब हो गया है *merā kampyūṭar k͟harāb ho gayā hai*

## Y

**yard**[1] (courtyard) आँगन *ā̃gan*ᴹ

**yard**[2] (measure) गज़ *gaz*ᶠ

**yawn** जँभाई *jā̃bhāī*ᶠ

**yawn, to** जँभाई लेना *jā̃bhāī lenā*ᴺ

**year** साल *sāl*ᴹ, वर्ष *varṣ*ᴹ, बरस *baras*ᴹ

**yearn, to:** see 'long'

**yellow** पीला *pīlā*

**yes** हाँ *hā̃*; (more polite) जी हाँ *jī hā̃*

**yesterday** कल *kal*; yesterday night कल रात *kal rāt*

**yet** अभी तक *abhī tak*; (but) लेकिन *lekin*

**yoga** योग *yog*ᴹ

**Insight**

Yoga: the long 'a' ending of the English pronunciation influences some Hindi speakers, who may pronounce this word as *yogā* in some circumstances.

**yoghurt** दही *dahī*ᴹ

**yoke** जुआ *juā*ᴹ

**you** तुम *tum*; (more formal) आप *āp*; (more intimate) तू *tū*

**young** जवान *javān*; younger (brother etc.) छोटा *choṭā* — my younger sister मेरी छोटी बहिन *merī choṭī bahin*; he's younger than me वह मुझसे छोटा है *vah mujhse choṭā hai*

**your, yours** तुम्हारा *tumhārā*; (more formal) आपका *āpkā*; (more intimate) तेरा *terā*; yours sincerely (in letter) भवदीय *bhavdīy* (from female signatory) भवदीया *bhavdīyā*

**youth** (young age) जवानी *javānī*ᶠ; (a young person) जवान *javān*ᴹ

## Z

**zeal** जोश *joś*ᴹ, उत्साह *utsāh*ᴹ

**zealot** कट्टरपंथी *kaṭṭarpanthī*ᴹ

**zero** शून्य *śūnya*ᴹ

**zone** क्षेत्र *kṣetra*ᴹ

**zoo** चिड़ियाघर *ciṛiyāghar*ᴹ

# Credits

**Front cover:** Oxford Illustrators Ltd
**Back cover:** © Jakub Semeniuk/iStockphoto.com, © Royalty-Free/Corbis, © agencyby/iStockphoto.com, © Andy Cook/iStockphoto.com, © Christopher Ewing/iStockphoto.com, © zebicho – Fotolia.com, © Geoffrey Holman/iStockphoto.com, © Photodisc/Getty Images, © James C. Pruitt/iStockphoto.com, © Mohamed Saber – Fotolia.com

# Notes

# Notes

# Notes

# Notes

# Notes

# Notes

# Notes